BARRON'S
THE TRUSTED NAME IN TEST PREP

AP®
English
Language and
Composition
PREMIUM

George Ehrenhaft, Ed.D.

Published by Kaplan North America, LLC d/b/a Barron's Educational Series
1515 West Cypress Creek Road
Fort Lauderdale, Florida 33309
www.barronseduc.com

ISBN: 978-1-5062-8773-7

10 9 8 7 6 5 4 3 2 1

Kaplan North America, LLC d/b/a Barron's Educational Series print books are available at special quantity discounts to use for sales promotions, employee premiums, or educational purposes. For more information or to purchase books, please call the Simon & Schuster special sales department at 866-506-1949.

About the Author

During his thirty-plus years as a high school English teacher, George Ehrenhaft introduced many hundreds of students to the riches of literature. He aimed to show how plot, character, and voice serve not only as a means to convey what authors and poets hope to say in their writings, but also, more important, to stimulate students to explore their own nature and discover thoughts and feelings residing within themselves. In short, he encouraged students not only to strive for 5's on AP exams but also to engage in a lifelong quest to learn what it means to be human.

In addition to AP books on literature and language, Ehrenhaft has written books on ACT and SAT preparation, on English grammar, on writing college application essays, and based on his personal experience—of all things—on the joys and frustrations of being a do-it-yourself home builder.

Table of Contents

How to Use This Book...vii

Barron's Essential 5 x

Acknowledgments xii

1 Getting Acquainted with the Test 1

Structure of the Exam 1

Multiple-Choice Questions...2

Reading Techniques 4

How to Increase Your Reading Power 6

Answering the Questions 19

Essay Questions from Previous AP Exams 20

Sample Synthesis Essay Question 24

Sample Analytical Question..34

Sample Argumentative Question 36

How Essays Are Read and Evaluated 37

Interpreting Essay Scores 38

How to Score the Essays 39

Scoring Your Own Essays 40

2 Diagnostic Test **43**

Introduction..43

Section I 47

Section II 66

Answer Key 75

Answer Explanations to Multiple-Choice Questions.....................................76

Answers to Essay Questions 80

How to Score the Essays 82

Essay Evaluation Worksheet..83

Test Score Worksheet 84

3 Mastering Multiple-Choice Questions **85**

Reading and Rhetoric 86

Writing Questions 95

Sample Passage and Writing Questions 96

4 Mastering Essay Questions..**101**

Steps for Writing the Perfect Essay 102

Writing the Synthesis Essay 103

How to Write a Synthesis Essay..107

Sample Synthesis Essay Question..117

Writing an Analytical Essay 128

Planning Your Analytical Essay 131

Writing an Argumentative Essay 133

Argumentative Essay Topics for Practice..135

Arranging Ideas 136

AP Essay Writing Style 137

Editing and Proofreading Essays 148

Sample Analytical Essays 187

Answer Key to Mini-Workouts 195

5   Practice Tests **201**

Practice Test 1 205

Section I 205

Section II 224

Answer Key 233

Answer Explanations to Multiple-Choice Questions 234

Answers to Essay Questions 237

How to Score the Essays 238

Essay Evaluation Worksheet 240

Test Score Worksheet 241

Practice Test 2 245

Section I 245

Section II 262

Answer Key 272

Answer Explanations to Multiple-Choice Questions 273

Answers to Essay Questions 276

How to Score the Essays 278

Essay Evaluation Worksheet 279

Test Score Worksheet 280

Practice Test 3 283

Section I 283

Section II 301

Answer Key 311

Answer Explanations to Multiple-Choice Questions 312

Answers to Essay Questions 315

How to Score the Essays 317

Essay Evaluation Worksheet 319

Test Score Worksheet 320

Practice Test 4 323

Section I 323

Section II 343

Answer Key 355

Answer Explanations to Multiple-Choice Questions 356

Answers to Essay Questions 359

How to Score the Essays 361

Essay Evaluation Worksheet 362

Test Score Worksheet 363

Appendix **365**

Glossary **369**

Index **379**

How to Use This Book

Welcome to the AP English Language and Composition exam. This book will take you on a virtual trip through every nook and cranny of the test. Its pages will acquaint you with the types of questions asked on the exam and show you how to write high-scoring essays.

Review and Practice

You'll find hundreds of sample questions and crucial test-taking tips. You'll also be introduced to principles of rhetoric and find a review of the grammar you need to know for the exam.

Diagnostic Test

You can first take the Diagnostic Test to gain an understanding of your strengths and weaknesses. You probably know that the AP English Language and Composition exam tests your understanding of how writers use language to convey meaning. It does this by asking you to respond to 45 **multiple-choice questions** about the text of five nonfiction prose passages written for different purposes and drawn from a range of historical periods.

The exam also contains three **essay questions**. The first essay, called the synthesis essay because in constructing your essay you must incorporate, or synthesize, material from at least three of five or more sources that comprise the question, or prompt, as it is commonly called.

To answer the second essay question, you must identify and analyze the rhetorical techniques used in a passage of nonfiction prose. A third question asks you to write an argument for or against a disputable idea expressed in a brief statement or passage.

The exam lasts three hours and 15 minutes and consists of two sections. The short-answer section takes one hour and counts for 45 percent of the total score. The essay section, lasting two-and-a-quarter hours, comprises 55 percent of your grade. As you take the Diagnostic Test, you can set a timer to create a similar setting.

SECTION I	SECTION II
45 multiple-choice questions based on five nonfiction prose passages (One hour) Two of the passages are followed by reading/rhetoric questions. The other three are followed by questions on writing.	**Question 1** ■ A synthesis essay that uses sources to support your position on a given issue **Question 2** ■ An essay that analyzes the style, rhetoric, and use of language in a selected prose passage **Question 3** ■ An essay in which you argue for or against an idea expressed in a given statement or brief prose passage (Two hours and 15 minutes)

Practice Tests

The final section of the book offers the opportunity to take four full-length practice tests that include all question types found on the actual exam. A comprehensive answer explanation is provided for each multiple-choice question, and a sample essay and rubric are provided for all writing. Take all of the practice tests, of course. They are meant to give you that extra edge that turns a good AP score into a better one.

Online Practice

There are three full-length online practice exams. You may take these exams in practice (untimed) mode or in timed mode. All questions include answer explanations.

For Students

Your score on the test is reported on a scale of 1–5. In general, scores are interpreted to mean that you are:

- **5** Extremely well qualified
- **4** Well qualifed
- **3** Qualified
- **2** Possibly qualified
- **1**   Not recommended for AP credit

A high score on the exam demonstrates a proficiency in English at least on a par with students who've passed an introductory college-level course in composition or rhetoric. Some colleges award academic credit or offer more advanced English courses to high-scoring students. Because each college or university makes its own policies regarding AP scores, be sure to check with the admissions office of the institution you hope to attend.

Keep in mind that preparation for the exam isn't instantaneous. For most students it's a gradual and often painstaking process of study, review, and more study. In other words, give yourself time. Take it slowly. If the exam is months away, set aside, say, 30 minutes a day to work your way through the pages of this book. Yes, 30 minutes takes a big bite out of a high school student's day, but to get ready for the AP exam, there's no substitute for the steady accumulation of knowledge over a long period of time. If time is short between now and the exam, cramming may help you earn a good score, especially if you familiarize yourself with the test instructions and the format of the exam—but, frankly, cramming is a less than perfect approach.

Regardless of how you go about preparing for the exam, I wish you luck. In May, when test day comes around, more than 500,000 students will be taking the exam. I wish every one of them lots of luck, but because you have used this book to prepare, I'll be rooting especially for you.

George Ehrenhaft

For AP English Teachers

For many AP teachers across the country, this book has been an invaluable resource. They've used questions and exercises from the book to stimulate thinking and inspire their students to write high-scoring essays. Some teachers have used the book as an instant syllabus for their classes because it contains so much of what a high-level course in language and composition might offer, including:

- Reading passages that range from easy to hard
- Numerous exam questions, discussed and analyzed
- Essential rhetorical terms
- Sample student essays (with comments by AP readers)
- Annotated passages
- An analysis of the synthesis essay question
- A full-length Diagnostic Test
- Four complete practice exams
- Three additional exams online
- Full explanations of all answers

As a veteran AP teacher, I know both the rewards you enjoy and the onerous hardships you face every day. Here's hoping that this book will lighten your load and help you provide your students with the best possible instruction as you prepare them for the AP exam.

BARRON'S ESSENTIAL 5

If you're aiming for a score of **5** on the AP English Language and Composition exam, this book can help. But to reach your goal, here are five things that you **MUST** do:

1 **Familiarize yourself with the language and effects of rhetoric.** Both the short-answer and essay questions require that you know how authors employ rhetorical strategies to create effects and convey meaning. Become conversant with the functions of tone, syntax, imagery, irony, point of view, and the other rhetorical techniques.

2 **Develop annotation skills.** Nothing will build your ability to analyze prose than a steady diet of annotation. Begin by reading nonfiction prose passages in this book and elsewhere. Make up your mind to figure out exactly what each author did to compose the passage. Identify rhetorical techniques and, more important, try to explain why the author chose each rhetorical component.

3 **Review elements of effective argumentation.** Familiarity with various forms of argumentation will help you in both the multiple-choice and the essay sections of the exam. Whenever you read nonfiction, pay attention to writers' claims about the subject. Examine the text for various kinds of evidence that the author used to justify claims: e.g., forceful language, kinds of reasoning (e.g., deductive and inductive), the testimony of experts, appeals to emotion, and much more.

Brush up on basic grammar skills. Don't bother memorizing terminology. Few, if any, multiple-choice questions require it. Concentrate on writing error-free essays because essay scores suffer when grammar rules are broken. Proofread all your practice essays. Look particularly for:

- sentence errors

- lack of agreement between subjects and verbs

- incorrect pronoun usage

- errors in verb choice

Plan and practice an essay-writing process. Develop a process for writing an essay in no more than forty minutes. Build in time to read the question, think of a main idea, and decide how to support it. Before you start writing, list your ideas and arrange them in sensible order. While composing your essay, be mindful of the need to:

- develop coherent paragraphs containing evidence that supports and develops the thesis

- vary sentences

- choose the best words to express ideas

- provide a brief conclusion

Set aside time for editing and proofreading.

Acknowledgments

Grateful acknowledgment is made to the following sources.

Page 12, Byron Williams, "Revolution Was Only the Start of the American Experiment," *Contra Costa Times*, December 17, 2015, p. A19.

Page 25, Alfie Kohn, "Homework: An Unnecessary Evil?" *www.psychologytoday.com*, November 24, 2012.

Page 26, Brian P. Gill and Steven L. Schlossman, "My Dog Ate My Argument," *Los Angeles Times*, December 11, 2003.

Page 27, Tom Loveless, "Do Students Have Too Much Homework?" Brown Center on Education Policy, Brookings Institution, October 1, 2003.

Page 28, "Average NAEP Reading Scale Scores of Students by Age and Amount of Assigned Daily Reading Homework," *Digest of Education Statistics*, National Center for Educational Statistics, 2012.

Page 29, Brian Haley, "What Is the Value of Homework?" July 6, 2006. *SearchWarp.com*.

Page 30, Gloria Chaika, "Help! Homework Is Wrecking My Home Life," *Education World*, August 8, 2000. © *EducationWorld.com*.

Page 31, Michael Hanson, "Analyzing 'the Homework Gap' Among High School Students," Brown Center on Education Policy, 2017.

Page 34, F. M. Esfandiary, "The Mystical West Puzzles the Practical East," *New York Times Magazine*, February 6, 1967. © F. M. Esfandiary.

Page 36, Clyde Kluckhorn, "An Anthropologist Looks at the United States," *Mirror for Man*, McGraw-Hill Book Co., NY, 1949.

Page 47, Richard Maxwell Brown, "Historical Patterns of Violence in America," *The History of Violence in America*, eds. Hugh Davis Graham and Ted Robert Gurr. National Commission on the Causes and Prevention of Violence. Task Force on Historical and Comparative Perspectives, U.S. Government Printing Office, Washington, D.C., 1969.

Page 67, Katherine Hansen, "What Good Is a College Education Anyway?" © Quintessential Careers, *www.quintcareers.com*.

Page 68, Lori Kurtzman, "Remedial Classes Teach Freshmen What They Should Already Know," *The Cincinnati Enquirer*, posted online July 30, 2006.

Page 71, Gregg Toppo and Anthony DeBarros, "Reality Weighs Down Dreams of College," *USA Today*, posted online February 2, 2005.

Page 72, Online blog, "Rob," Declining College Standards, "Say Anything," posted January 3, 2006.

Page 105, J. H. Pryor, K. Eagan, L. Palucki Blake, S. Hurtado, J. Berdan, and M. H. Case, "Trends of Reasons in Deciding to Go to College," *The American Freshman: National Norms Fall 2012*, Los Angeles, CA: Higher Education Research Institute, UCLA, 2012.

Page 118, Julie Hilden, "Does Celebrity Destroy Privacy?" *FindLaw* website, accessed June 28, 2006.

Page 119, "*jenblacksheep*," "Do Public Figures Have Privacy Rights?" *Hubpages.com*, 2018.

Page 120, Vincent M. de Grandpré, "Understanding the Market for Celebrity: An Economic Analysis of the Right of Publicity," Simpson, Thacher, and Bartlett, LLP, posted November 15, 2017, *www.stb.com*.

Page 121, "Entertainment to Environment Headlines of Prominent News Sources (Ratio of 5 to 1 or Greater)," Pew Research Center's Project for Excellence in Journalism, 2016.

Page 122, GNL, "For Today's Public Figures, Private Lives Really Matter," *www.Buzzle.com*, Buzzle.Com, Inc., Costa Mesa, CA, November 30, 2004.

Page 123, Jamie Nordhaus, "Celebrities' Rights to Privacy: How Far Should the Paparazzi Be Allowed to Go?" University of Texas School of Law, *Review of Litigation*, Volume 25, 2010.

Page 131, Laura Eirmann, DVM, "The Facts About Euthanasia," Cornell University Pet Loss Hotline, *vet.cornell.edu*, November 2004.

Page 205, Excerpt from *West with the Night* by Beryl Markham, © 1942, 1983 by Beryl Markham. Northpoint Press, a division of Farrar, Straus, and Giroux, LLC.

Page 225, "What Benefits Have Come from Medical Research Using Animals?" American Association for Laboratory Animal Science (AALAS), *www.foundation.aalas.org*.

Page 227, "Numbers of Animals Used in Research in the United Kingdom," Home Office (2004), *Statistics of Scientific Procedures on Living Animals*, Great Britain, 2003.

Page 228, Stuart Derbyshire, Ph.D., "Animal Experimentation," Speech at Edinburgh Book Festival, August 19, 2002.

Page 229, "The Ethics of Research Involving Animals: A Guide to the Report," Nuffield Council on Bioethics, May 25, 2005.

Page 230, Clare Haggarty, "Animals in Scientific Research: The Ethical Argument," National Anti-Vivisection Society, *www.navs.org*, 2005.

Page 231, Albert Einstein, *Out of My Later Years*, The Philosophical Library, Inc., 1950.

Page 263, "Stop Cyberbullying," *www.stopcyberbullying.com*, Wired Kids, accessed July 31, 2010.

Page 264, "The Legality of School Responses to Cyberbullying," Constitutional Rights Foundation, Chicago. Posted by *www.deliberating.org*, 2007.

Page 265, Victoria Kim, "Suit Blends Internet, Free Speech, School," *Los Angeles Times*, August 3, 2008.

Page 267, Nancy Willard, "School Response to Cyberbullying and Sexting," Center for Safe, Responsible Internet Use, August 2, 2010.

Page 268, Cindy Hsu, "N.J. School District Set to Battle Cyber Bullies," HD2, *wcbs.com*, August 1, 2008.

Page 269, "Cyberbullying Facts and Statistics, 2016–2018, Comparitech, *www.comparitech.com*.

Page 327, "Education Levels of Active Duty United States Armed Forces Personnel in 2019," www.statistics.com, 2019

Page 344, "Why Should We Go to Mars?" (information not available).

Page 345, Zahaan Barmal, "The Case Against Mars Colonization," *The Guardian,* August 29, 2018.

Page 346, Felix Baumgartner, "Mars Is a Waste of Money," *The Daily Telegraph,* 2012.

Page 347, Chris Carberry, "Six Essential Reasons Why We Need to Send Humans to Mars," Fox News Network, 2017.

Page 349, O. Glenn Smith and Paul D. Spudis, "Mars for Only $1.5 Trillion," *SpaceNews,* March 8. 2015.

Page 350, "Mars Generation: A Final Report for Mars Exploration," Poll Sponsored by the Boeing Company, 2013.

Page 351, Steven J. Dick, "Why We Explore: Societal Impact of the Space Age," NASA (undated report).

1
Getting Acquainted with the Test

Learning Objectives

→ A preview of the test
→ Types of short-answer questions
→ Four ways to read the passages
→ When to guess
→ A synthesis essay, an analytical essay, and an argumentative essay: how they differ
→ Using and citing sources
→ How essays are scored
→ What you can learn from past exams

Putting it simply, the AP exam tests your reading and writing skills. Understanding the words in five passages doesn't guarantee success, however. Rather, top scores are awarded to anyone who can do two additional things:

1. Correctly answer 23–25 questions related to the rhetoric used in the passages. You'll also be given 20–22 writing questions, which ask you to "read like a writer," meaning you'll be asked to decide which of several potential revisions of text in a passage is best.
2. Write three well-organized and insightful essays, each with a different purpose.

To succeed in both these tasks, you need to know something about rhetoric, such as how an author's choice of details contributes to the meaning of the passage or in what ways the structure of a passage relates to its content.

You'll also need to be well acquainted with such concepts as *theme, tone, diction, syntax, allusion, imagery, paradox, irony, satire,* and a variety of other rhetorical devices that you've probably studied in English classes.

Finally, you should know how to draw on your experience, reading, or observation to write an argument that supports, opposes, or falls somewhere in between an opinion expressed in a given statement.

Structure of the Exam

The exam lasts three hours and 15 minutes. For the first 60 minutes you'll read a handful of relatively short nonfiction passages and answer 45 multiple-choice questions about them. During the remaining time you'll write essays in response to three questions.

The prompt for the first essay question consists of a statement about an issue of concern in today's world. Accompanying the statement are several published documents—they are called **sources**—related to the issue, each less than a page long. One source will be an image—a photo, map, cartoon, or other visual presentation—also related to the issue. Another may be a graph, a chart, a table, or another image requiring a quantitative interpretation. Fifteen minutes are allotted to read the sources. Then you are expected to write an essay that takes a position on the issue and incorporates, or *synthesizes*, at least three of the sources into your discussion. In AP terminology, this essay goes by the name **synthesis essay**.

A second question consists of a prose passage about a page long and an assignment to write an **analysis essay** that discusses the rhetorical strategies used by the author of the passage.

The third question calls for a **written argument.** The prompt consists of a brief passage that expresses an opinion on a particular subject. Your essay must support, refute, or qualify the opinion stated by the author of the passage.

OUTLINE OF THE EXAM

Total time: Three hours and 15 minutes

Section I: One hour (45 percent of total score)

45 multiple-choice questions about several nonfiction prose passages. About half relate to reading and rhetoric, the other half to writing.

Section II: Two hours and 15 minutes

Three essays (55 percent of total score)

Essay 1: Take a position on an issue presented in a short passage. In your essay, synthesize or incorporate material from at least three of several given sources that comment on the issue.

Essay 2: Write a rhetorical analysis of a given passage.

Essay 3: Argue for or against an opinion expressed in a statement or short passage, or take a stand somewhere between the two extremes.

Multiple-Choice Questions

TIP

Ordinarily, it pays to answer each question as it comes, but if a question gives you trouble, skip it for the time being and return to it later.

The multiple-choice reading questions can be about virtually anything that the author of a passage has done to convey meaning or create an effect. For instance, you may be asked about why the passage has been structured in a certain way, the purpose of a particular word or phrase, the function of a certain paragraph, or how a specific idea contributes to the development of the passage as a whole.

To answer some questions, you need a sense of sentences, including how sentences function in a passage; how sentences of different lengths, structure, and type (simple, compound, complex, compound complex) relate to tone and meaning. To answer other questions you may need to understand why the author has structured the passage in a certain way. Another question may ask about individual sentences and their function in the passage. Other questions about sentences may offer five versions of a given sentence and ask you which one would be best in the context. You should be aware of the uses and effects of subordination, coordination, and parenthetical ideas. You may also be asked about word order, tone, diction (word choice), transitions, repetition, parallelism, and figurative language.

Questions that are related to writing focus on the best way to express ideas in a given context. For instance, you may be asked to decide which one of five different sentences would be best to introduce the topic of a given paragraph, or which version of a sentence might serve best as a transition between certain paragraphs of the passage. You may also encounter questions that ask you to rearrange the order of sentences in a paragraph, or which sentence would be most persuasive in refuting a particular idea, or what the author intended to accomplish by making a particular comparison or by arranging the sentences in a particular sequence.

As an AP student, you certainly know that you make many decisions while writing an essay—or writing anything else, for that matter. Well, when you take the AP exam, you'll be asked to analyze decisions made by authors and, when faced with multiple-choice questions, choose the best of five alternatives.

Two more facts you should know: (1) The order of multiple-choice questions usually coincides with the progress of each passage; and (2) neither the passages nor the questions are presented in order of difficulty.

Sample Reading Questions

1. Based on the fourth paragraph of the passage (lines 1–16), the writer introduces a hypothetical rhetorical situation in order to

   (A) illustrate the need for public support
   (B) inject a plea for adherence to the rule of law
   (C) contrast the modes of communication in two different wars
   (D) prepare the reader for the anecdote that follows in lines 17–21
   (E) support the claim made in lines 8–12 about using drones as weapons

2. Lines 22–30 could be used to support which of the following claims about the writer's tone?

   (A) His tone when discussing Bengston's art is mocking.
   (B) His tone when evaluating Ruscha's photos is respectful.
   (C) He adopts a sarcastic tone when commenting on art auctions.
   (D) He adopts a reverent tone when describing Renaissance paintings.
   (E) He adopts a self-righteous tone when recalling details of an art theft in 2014.

Sample Writing Questions

3. The writer wants to add the following sentence to the second paragraph of the passage to provide additional support to the essay's thesis:

   Researchers often study groups of children with different socioeconomic backgrounds.

   Where would the sentence best be placed?

   (A) Before sentence 3
   (B) After sentence 3
   (C) After sentence 4
   (D) After sentence 5
   (E) After sentence 6

4. Unhappy with the transitional phrase at the start of sentence 9, the writer plans to replace it with one that sets up a comparison with the idea in sentence 8.

   Which of the following best achieves that goal?

   (A) Furthermore,
   (B) To be sure,
   (C) For instance,
   (D) On the other hand,
   (E) In contrast,

The foregoing questions represent only a few of the many types of reading and writing questions on the exam. The following list will give you an idea of other kinds that have appeared on recent exams.

1. **IDENTIFY** the relationship of a sentence in the first paragraph to the passage as a whole.
2. **SELECT** the rhetorical strategy or device used in a particular section of the passage.
3. **IDENTIFY** the function of a sentence within a paragraph, or a paragraph within the whole.
4. **DISCERN** shifts in theme, tone, style, sentence structure, diction, syntax, effect, or rhetorical purpose between the two sections of the passage.
5. **DETERMINE** how unity (or point of view, emphasis, contrast, or other feature) is achieved in all or part of the passage.
6. **RECOGNIZE** the author's exigence in the passage.
   *One or more multiple-choice questions may ask about the author's "exigence," a word that refers to a problem or situation that needs attention. A **rhetorical exigence** is whatever has prompted the writing of the given passage.*
7. **INFER** the implied or stated purpose of particular words, images, figures of speech, sentence structure, or other rhetorical feature.

Many of the questions direct you to particular lines of the passage. To answer most of those questions you need to read the specified lines as though you are doing an annotation—i.e., a close textual analysis not only of what the words say but also why the writer may have chosen them (see especially pages 9–26). Some questions, however, require more than that. Some raise broad issues that can't be addressed unless you read at least the two or three lines that precede the lines designated by the question and the two or three lines that follow.

For multiple-choice questions, AP test writers ordinarily choose passages written between the 17th century and the present, although they might occasionally toss in a passage from ancient Greece or Rome. Passages are nonfiction and are composed by essayists, historians, journalists, diarists, autobiographers, political writers, philosophers, and critics. You won't find simple passages that leave little room for interpretation, nor will you find passages comprehensible only to those with sky-high IQs.

Authors and titles of the passages are not given, although the source of each passage may be briefly identified: "*a nineteenth-century memoir,*" "*a twentieth-century book,*" "*a contemporary journalist's diary,*" and so on. By and large, if you've taken an AP English class, you'll probably understand the passages and correctly answer the majority of questions. A robust reading background, both in school and on your own, as well as practice in close textual analysis will serve you well.

Reading Techniques

By this time in your school career you've probably taken numerous tests like the SATs or ACTs for which you have read passages like those on the AP English exam and answered multiple-choice questions. No doubt you've developed certain techniques of test taking and have observed that there is no technique that serves everyone equally. What works for others may not work for you, and vice versa.

Nevertheless, it's helpful to know which techniques help you do your best. Prepare for the exam by trying the alternatives described below. Experiment with each one as you make your way through the exercises and practice tests in this book. Gradually, you'll discover which technique, or combination of techniques, you can count on. Lean on them and ignore the others.

Technique 1: Read the Passage in Its Entirety

Keep in mind that the AP exam is not solely a test of reading comprehension. You need to know what the passages say, of course, but the questions pertain more to the *why*s and *how*s of the text than to its *what*s. For example, you may be asked to figure out *why* the author began a paragraph with a series of questions or with a particular quotation. Other questions may ask you *how* the author built an argument supporting, say, the value of social conformity. During your first reading of the passage, then, don't slow down to figure out nuances of meaning that in the end may be irrelevant to the questions. Rather, read for the big picture—an overall sense of the piece. Having an overview of the whole passage in mind when you start to answer the questions may ultimately be a time saver because you won't be starting from scratch. Familiarity with the passage, however slight or superficial, is apt to work in your favor.

All passages come with numbered lines. Because the questions invariably refer to those line numbers, use the questions as a kind of roadmap to identify the places in the text that you'll definitely need to read and analyze. Although you mustn't ignore the rest of the passage, concentrating on the question-related lines could serve you well.

The same applies to the writing passages, in which each sentence is numbered. As you proceed through each passage, circle the numbers of those that relate to questions. To answer many of the writing questions, you'll most likely have to consider the context in which a sentence appears, but not always. You may also find sections of the passage with no questions at all relating to them. A quick glance at them may be all that's necessary. Later, however, as you search for correct answers, knowing the details may become indispensable.

Technique 2: Skim the Passage

To get the general idea of the passage, read faster than you normally would. Try only to identify the general topic and the approach used by the author: Is the passage formal or informal? Personal or objective? Is it mainly a narrative? A description? An argument for or against some issue? The answers to these questions will be fairly apparent during a quick read-through. Make a mental note of any unusual words and phrases. Read intently enough to get an impression of the content and writing style of the passage, but don't dawdle. Then, as you answer the questions, refer to the passage.

Technique 3: Read Twice

Skim the passage for a general impression; then go back and read it more thoroughly, using your pencil to mark the passage and take notes. Two readings, one fast and one slow, allow you to pick out features of language and rhetoric that you might overlook during a single reading. Why? Because during the first reading you'll be discovering what the passage is about, and during the second you'll be able to focus on the features that contribute to its overall meaning and effect. After your second reading, proceed to the questions and then refer to the passage to check your answers.

Technique 4: Read Only the Questions

Do not look at the answer choices. Because it's virtually impossible to remember 8, 9, or more questions about material you haven't read, go through the questions quickly—only to become acquainted with the kinds of information you are expected to draw out of the passage. Label each

STRATEGY

Whatever you do, don't even think of answering the questions without thoroughly reading the passage from start to finish.

question with a notation: "MI" (main idea), "T" (tone), "POV" (point of view), "SS" (sentence structure), and so on. (Or you can devise your own system.) When you are tuned into the questions beforehand, you'll read the passage more purposefully.

Some students methodically read one question, then scour the passage in search of the answer before moving on to the next question. Before they know it, time has run out, and they are far from finishing. Moreover, such a fragmented approach reduces the likelihood of grasping the overall point of the passage.

How to Increase Your Reading Power

Strong readers often get that way by habitually analyzing what they read word by word, sentence by sentence, and paragraph by paragraph. They recognize that good authors carefully select every syllable they write, leaving nothing to chance—not the words, the sentences, the punctuation, the footnotes, the order and content of paragraphs, nor the overall structure of their work. Every bit of their prose has a point and purpose.

Your job on the AP exam is to read the passages and analyze how they were written and how they might be revised. The good news is that you can train yourself to make insightful analyses by dissecting whatever you read. Practice with a pencil in hand, and as you read almost any respectable piece of prose, jot down reasons why the author chose particular words and details. Examine sentence structure and the sequence of ideas. Identify how the author creates a tone and develops a main idea.

TIP

To become a first-rate annotator, get into the habit of dissecting passages line by line.

Like every other worthwhile skill, annotating a passage in this manner takes time, and to do it well takes even more time, especially at the start. It can be burdensome, frustrating, and even discouraging, but just a single reasonably astute insight can beget another and another after that. With regular practice, close reading can become almost addictive. Laying bare an author's creative process has whet the appetite of many students who now do it all the time. Even better, a heightened awareness of the reasons behind every choice that an author has made will lift your score on the AP exam. And perhaps even more important in the long run, it's likely to raise the level and maturity of your own writing. Considering all these potential rewards, how can you not try it?

How to get started as an annotator:

✔ Condense the main idea of whatever you read into a pithy sentence or two. (You might even jot down a brief summary.) If you can clearly and accurately identify the thesis, you've come a long way. Sometimes the thesis will be stated outright. In that case, underline or highlight it in some way. If the thesis is only implied by content, however, put it into your own words. Writing it down on paper or on a computer screen is a sure sign that you're serious about finding the essence of a passage.

✔ Look for clues to the author's attitude and intent. Is the passage meant largely to entertain? To inform? To provoke controversy? To inspire or to enlighten the reader? Does the author have a bias, an ax to grind, an ulterior motive? It's hard to conceive of a piece of writing in which the author's attitude is totally hidden. Take the paragraph you've just read. Can you tell what the author—me!—hoped to accomplish with his words? Well, if you're the least bit tempted to dissect a passage, then I've achieved my purpose—to convince you to give annotation a try.

✔ Analyze structure. Which ideas come first? Second? Third? Is there a reason for the sequence of ideas? How are ideas linked to each other? Does the end contain echoes of earlier ideas?

✔ Examine how the author creates an effect on the reader. Study word choice, sentence structure and length, the order of ideas, figures of speech, the use of rhythm and sound. How does the author keep you interested? Is the writing formal or informal? Is the author friendly or stand-offish, enthusiastic or cool?

✔ Think about the author's qualifications to write on a topic. Details usually reveal the authority of the writer. Authors who don't know what they are talking about often hide behind prose top-heavy with generalities. Study the footnotes, if any. Do they refer to sources that are reliable and up-to-date?

✔ Become an annotator. Mark up passages profusely, writing in margins and underlining noteworthy ideas and features.

What follows are three annotated passages. Although the notes are not exhaustive, they suggest what an alert reader might observe during a close reading of each passage.

Passage 2

This passage, written early in the twentieth century by Virginia Woolf, is an excerpt from an essay about the art of biographical writing. (Note: This passage is about one-quarter the length of passages typically used on the AP exam.)

❶ Thus the biographer must go ahead of the rest of us, ❷ like the miner's canary, detecting falsity, unreality, and the presence of obsolete
Line conventions. His ❸ sense of truth must be
(5) alive and on tiptoe. Then again, since we live in an age when a thousand cameras are pointed, by newspapers, letters, and diaries, at every character from every angle, he must be prepared to admit contradictory versions of the same
(10) face. Biography will enlarge its scope by hanging up looking glasses at odd corners. And yet from all this diversity it will bring out, ❹ not a riot of confusion, but a richer unity. And again since (so much is known that used to
(15) be unknown), the question now ❺ inevitably asks itself whether the lives of great men only should be recorded. ❻ Is not anyone who has lived a life and left a record of that life worthy of biography—the failures as well as the successes,
(20) the humble as well as the illustrious? And what is greatness? And what is smallness? ❼ We must revise our standards of merit and set up new heroes for our admiration.

—From *The Death of the Moth and Other Essays* by Virginia Woolf

1. "Thus" is a transitional word telling you that this paragraph is a continuation of a longer passage about writing biographies.

2. "like the miner's canary" is a simile admonishing biographers to be wary of information that appears to be the "truth," but isn't.

3. "sense of truth . . . alive and on tiptoe" is a personification. This figure of speech, along with the synecdoche "face" (line 10) and the metaphors, "a thousand cameras" (line 6) and "looking glasses" (line 11), indicates that figurative language is an important rhetorical feature of the passage.

4. Author uses sentences containing contrasts: "not . . . but" (lines 12–13) and "known . . . unknown" (lines 14–15) for emphasis.

5. The word "inevitably," along with the use of "must" as the main verb in several sentences (lines 1, 4, 8, and 22), adds assertiveness and confidence to the writer's tone.

6. Three rhetorical questions (lines 17–21) draw the reader into the discussion.

7. The concluding sentence articulates this passage's main idea and introduces the topic for the next paragraph—that biographers of the future may find a rich source of subjects (i.e., "heroes") not only among the rich and famous but also in the mass of ordinary people.

Annotation Summary

The passage consists entirely of Woolf's thoughts about the art of biographical writing. To strengthen her presentation, she adopts an earnest and self-confident tone. Almost half of the sentences in the passage use the verb "must," a sure sign that Woolf aims to instruct biographers in the requirements of their craft if they expect to tell the truth about their subjects.

Figurative language gives the passage its literary quality. The use of metaphor fits the topic because biography, after all, is not an objective, literal account of everything in a person's life. Rather, it is a figurative rendering of the subject, its details carefully chosen to create a certain image for the reader. Accordingly, since Woolf asserts that subjects for biography can be found among all types of people, her references to cameras and looking glasses—instruments that help us see things more clearly—are particularly apt.

A WORD FROM YOUR AUTHOR

If the Woolf passage has been your first brush with annotation, you may now find yourself muttering, "Are you kidding me?" or "No way, man!" or some even less delicate expressions of self-doubt.

Well, that's not an uncommon initial reaction. But, please, don't give up. Sure, annotating passages can be a challenge, especially at the start. But it's not all that difficult if you work at it. Here's a promise: The more annotating you do, the easier it gets. In fact, it is one of the purposes of this book to help you master this annotation stuff. Remember, too, that annotation is just a tool, a means to an end—the writing of a perceptive analytical AP essay. As you annotate passages, you'll gradually learn what to look for and begin to see the authors' rhetoric becoming more and more apparent. And as you grow accustomed to annotating passages, you'll also begin to find more and more rhetorical elements—maybe more than you ever expected. Then, as you plan your AP essay, you'll have some decisions to make—namely, which elements to write about, which of them to emphasize, and which to discuss first, second, third, and so on.

Passage 2

The following passage is by the renowned ornithologist John James Audubon. It is about half the length of passages typically used on the AP exam.

As soon as the pigeons discover a sufficiency of food to **❶** entice them to alight, they fly around in circles, reviewing the countryside
Line below. During these **❷** evolutions the dense
(5)   mass which they form presents a **❸** beautiful spectacle, as it changes direction; turning from a glistening sheet of azure, as the backs of the birds come simultaneously into view, to a suddenly presented rich, deep purple. After
(10) that they pass lower, over the woods, and for a moment are lost among the foliage. Again they emerge and glide aloft. They may now alight, but the next moment take to wing **❹** as if suddenly alarmed, the flapping of their wings
(15) producing a noise like the roar of distant thunder, as they sweep through the forests to see if danger is near.

❺ However, hunger soon brings them to the ground. On alighting they industriously throw
(20) aside the withered leaves in quest of the fallen mast.[1] The rear ranks continually rise, passing over the main body and alighting in front, and in such rapid succession that the whole flock seems still on the wing.

1. The verbs "discover" (line 1) and "reviewing" (line 3) attribute human qualities to a flock of pigeons, as though the author knows what goes on inside pigeons' heads. Likewise, "hunger" (line 18) brings the birds to the ground. In lines 28–29, the author ascribes frustration ("find his labor completely lost") to one of the birds. Note, too, the use of the personal pronoun "his" instead of "its."

2. The word "evolutions" suggests progressive change. As the passage continues, the writer portrays the birds in different stages: alighting, turning en masse, getting lost in the foliage, etc.

3. The "beautiful spectacle" of the birds in flight is captured by visual imagery and poetic language in lines 5–9. Sibilant sounds ("s," "sh," "z") suggest the swoosh of birds' wings. Sound imagery continues with a simile in lines 15–16 ("a noise like the roar of distant thunder . . .")

4. Writer continues to ascribe human qualities to the birds: "as if suddenly alarmed" (lines 13–14), "to see if danger is near" (lines 16–17).

5. A turning point in the passage: The pigeons are in flight during the entire first paragraph but on the ground in the second paragraph. The use of active verbs shows the birds in constant motion: e.g., "throw aside," "continually rise," "passing over," "alighting . . . in rapid succession" etc.

(25)   ❻ The quantity of ground swept in this way is ❼ astonishing. So completely has it been cleared that the gleaner who might follow in the rear of the flock would find his labor completely lost. While their feeding ❽ avid-
(30) ity is at times so great that in attempting to swallow a large acorn or nut, they may be seen to gasp for a long while as if in the agonies of suffocation.

—Excerpt from "Passenger Pigeon"
by John James Audubon (1813)

6. Allusion to the notion of evolution, introduced earlier. See note [2].
7. The writer reiterates astonishment over the birds' noteworthy behavior.
8. The word "avidity" applies to the flock's feeding behavior, but it also echoes the strength of the writer's own fondness for the birds.

---

[1] *nuts, acorns*

Annotation Summary

Using a tone of admiration and wonder, Audubon describes a flock of passenger pigeons. His language and imagery emphasize the birds' beauty as well as their human-like qualities, a rhetorical strategy that encourages readers to view the pigeons not as just another species but almost as ingenious, alert, and intelligent creatures. In two paragraphs, one devoted to detailing the movement of the airborne flock, the other, the birds' behavior on the ground, the writer creates a multi-dimensional portrait of the passenger pigeon.

Footnote: Audubon's contemporaries might well have understood why he alludes to the flock's "evolution." The passenger pigeon, once among the most numerous of North American birds, in 1913 was on the verge of extinction. The last one died in a Cincinnati zoo on September 1, 1914. Audubon may well have written the passage as a tribute to the dying species.

Passage 3

The passage below, a newspaper column, was published prior to the 2016 presidential election, a time when candidates spoke often of "American exceptionalism," the proposition that the United States, because of its unique stature in the world, has both extraordinary responsibilities and extraordinary rights.

Its length (608 words) is about the same as passages typically used on the AP exam.

The notion ❶ of American exceptionalism, first introduced by Alexis de Tocqueville[1] in his two-volume classic, *Democracy in America*, is
Line incongruent with the contemporary use of the
(5) term. ❷

Tocqueville wrote: "The position of the Americans is quite exceptional, and it may be believed that no democratic people will ever be placed in a similar one." ❸

(10) Void of context this statement is vague and ambiguous enough for us to fill in whatever blanks we want, even portraying America as the shining city of the hill where nirvana comfortably resides. But is this what de Tocqueville
(15) meant? ❹

In its full context the sentence reads: "The position of the Americans is therefore quite exceptional, and it may be believed that no democratic people will ever be placed in a simi-
(20) lar one. Their strictly Puritanical origin, their exclusively commercial habits, even the country they inhabit, have singularly concurred to fix the mind of the American upon purely practical objects. Their passions, their wants, their
(25) education, and everything about them seem to draw the native of the United States earthward; although his religion bids him turn, from time to time, a transient and distracted glance to heaven."

(30) What de Tocqueville wrote bears little resemblance to the manner that American exceptionalism is touted in contemporary discourse. ❺ In fact, an honest assessment of de Tocqueville's definition calls into question if he
(35) even meant the term as a compliment. ❻

---

[1] *A French political thinker and historian who toured the U.S. in 1831 and had his observations published in an acclaimed book,* Democracy in America.

1. The word "notion" indicates that "American exceptionalism" is not a fact but rather a theoretical construct or idea that's open to interpretation.
2. The opening sentence contains the thesis of the passage. All that follows is an argument meant to prove that de Tocqueville's notion has been misinterpreted.
3. A direct quote showing precisely where the notion of American exceptionalism originated.
4. This semi-rhetorical question implies that de Tocqueville's idea, when removed from its original context, invites faulty interpretations. The question also helps to unify the passage by serving as a transition to a word-for-word rendering of de Tocqueville's text, included in the next paragraph (lines 16–29) as evidence meant to convince readers that de Tocqueville's idea has been distorted.
5. The author again reminds readers of the passage's main point. The idea of exceptionalism has a deeper, more profound meaning than "America is different from other countries," as explained in lines 30–35.
6. The author questions de Tocqueville's intent, thereby prodding readers to reassess the meaning of the quotation.

In some circles, American exceptionalism has become the sophomoric ❼ litmus test to ascertain one's allegiance to the nation. The contemporary definition is nothing more
(40) than an anti-intellectual endeavor to rob the nation of one of its key elements, which is dissent. ❽ Dissent is the oxygen of any democratic society, and without it we risk choking on the fumes of our self-induced megalomania.[2]
(45) The lack of dissent prohibits a nation from self-reflection, which stagnates growth. It is to infuse the society with the toxins of arrogance and insularity. Rather than a foreign enemy, are not these weapons that topple superpowers? ❾

(50) America, in my view, ❿ is a unique nation, here is where its greatness is realized. It is unique because it was formed on an idea—an idea that was beyond the comprehension of the individuals who conceived it.

(55) "We hold these truths to be self-evident: that all men are created equal; that they are endowed by their Creator with certain unalienable rights; that among these are life, liberty, and the pursuit of happiness," ⓫ is not only
(60) the nation's mission statement but has been expanded upon, not without conflict, so that those words shine as bright today as they did when they were enshrined in the nation's ethos on July 4, 1776.

(65) At a time when the world was dominated by inequality, along comes a cabal of great men, pledging to one another their lives, fortunes and sacred honor for the unprecedented notion of equality. America need not rely on myth
(70) to support itself. Rather, it would be better served by embracing the words of Founding Father Benjamin Rush, who famously wrote: "The American war is over but this is far from being the case with the American Revolution.

---

[2]*Delusions of one's own greatness or grandeur.*

7. An allusion to "sophomoric" (i.e., ignorant, biased, closed-minded, etc.) politicians who use the idea as a means to measure people's patriotism.

8. The author not only abhors using the idea of American exceptionalism as a measure of patriotism, but also he claims that it destroys the right to dissent, one of America's basic values.

9. The author's choice of words with negative connotations ("megalomania," "stagnates," "toxins," "arrogance," "topple") adds emotional power to the argument.

10. Note the phrase "in my view." This shows the author's effort to reach out to the reader and acknowledge that he has a personal stake in what otherwise might be an academic argument. He strongly espouses American exceptionalism, calling the country a "unique nation," but for reasons far more noble than those cited by politicians.

11. Using profoundly evocative words from the Declaration of Independence and a reference to July 4, 1776, the author lifts the notion of America's exceptionalism above the fray of everyday politics. Inspiring figurative language ("words shine as bright today . . . enshrined in the nation's ethos") is meant to stir the reader's mind and heart.

(75) On the contrary, nothing but the first act of this great drama is closed." ⓬ While there is something about American exceptionalism that suggests our work is complete, Rush is offering a more arduous task. The revolution is the (80) ongoing narrative ⓭ for what is commonly referred to as the American experiment.

It was an experiment first articulated by Thomas Jefferson, put into practice by Washington, held together by Lincoln, sus- (85) tained by Roosevelt, and pushed to higher greatness by King. What other nation can lay claim to such a unique history? ⓮

—Adapted from Byron Williams, "Revolution Was Only the Start of the American Experiment," *Contra Costa Times*, December 17, 2015, p. A19.

12. Allusions to the Founding Fathers and to other inspiring figures from over two centuries of American history add still more substance and clarity to the notion of America's exceptionalism.
13. The term "ongoing narrative" reminds readers that the notion of American exceptionalism is both timeless and transcendent and must not be reduced to a simplistic political slogan.
14. The author leaves the reader with a rhetorical question that has only one possible answer.

Annotation Summary

The passage is an argument meant to persuade readers that the notion of American exceptionalism, originally articulated by de Tocqueville, has been distorted by politicians to mean a belief in American superiority. To prove his point, the author relies on a logical sequence of thought that includes the very words that de Tocqueville used to discuss the idea of America's exceptionalism. In its context the phrase refers to de Tocqueville's view that Americans differed from others because they are concerned with and devoted to mostly practical, everyday, down-to-earth matters.

Having shown that American exceptionalism is unrelated to patriotism, the author of the passage argues that the politicians' interpretation of the phrase undermines the very credo on which America was founded, especially the people's right to dissent. Quoting and paraphrasing evocative excerpts from the Declaration of Independence, he lauds the men who broke America's ties to England, fought the Revolution, and laid the foundation on which our democracy was built. To prove that America's spirit of revolt still survives, the author cites the contributions made to America's standing among nations by such legendary, almost mythic, figures as Lincoln, Roosevelt, and Martin Luther King.

Other annotators may have made different, yet equally valid, comments about each of the previous passages. What matters most is not that the details of the analyses differ from each other but that all of them more or less describe the essential anatomy of each passage.

Now try your hand at annotating a passage on your own. Read the passage that starts on the next page at least twice—first to see what it's about, and then, during the second reading, to jot down whatever you notice about its structure and composition. When you are done, write a summary of the main idea and state your perception of the author's tone. Finally, compare your notes to those provided by the author of this book. More than likely, you'll record ideas that he overlooked and vice versa.

Passage for Annotation

There are two deep-seated idiosyncrasies of human nature that bear on our acceptance or rejection of what is offered us. We have, in
Line the first place, an innate bias for the familiar.
(5) Whatever we're thoroughly unfamiliar with is apt to seem to us odd, or queer, or curious, or bizarre. For it is no mere trick of speech, but one of those appallingly veracious records of human nature and experience in which the history of
(10) words abounds, through which "outlandish" and "crude" attained their present meaning. For "outlandish" meant in the beginning only what doesn't belong to our own land, and "uncouth" was simply "unknown." The change in meaning
(15) registers a universal trait. Whatever is alien to our own ways—the costume, manners, modes of speech of another race or of other times—is strange; and "strange" itself, which started out by meaning merely "foreign," is only another
(20) record of the same idiosyncrasy. But there is still another trait that is no less broadly human. Whatever is too familiar wearies us. Incessant recurrence without variety breeds tedium; the overiterated becomes the monotonous, and the
(25) monotonous irks and bores. And there we are. Neither that which we do not know at all, nor that which we know too well, is to our taste. We are averse to shocks, and we go to sleep under narcotics.
(30)   Both the shock and the narcotic have, I grant, at times their fascination. But they are apt to be forward, not permanent, sweet, not lasting. The source of more or less abiding satisfaction for most normal human beings lies in a happy
(35) merging of the two—in the twofold delight in an old friend recognized as new, or a new friend recognized as old. The experience and the pleasure are universal. All the lovers who have ever lived have made experiment of it; a face that
(40) you have passed a hundred times, nor cared to see, remains the face you've always known, but becomes all at once the most beautiful and thrilling object in the world; the person you've

never known before, you find all at once you've
(45) known from all eternity. Now art, like love,
sends its roots deep into what we are. And our
most permanent aesthetic satisfaction arises as
a rule from things familiar enough to give the
pleasure of recognition, yet not so trite as to
(50) rob us of the other pleasure of surprise. We are
keen for the new, but we insist that it establish
some connection with what is friendly and our
own; we want the old, but we want it to seem
somehow new. Things may recur as often as
(55) they please, so long as they surprise us—like the
Ghost in *Hamlet*—each time they appear.

—From John Livingstone Lowes,
Convention and Revolt in Poetry, 1919

Your Annotation Summary

_____

_____

_____

_____

_____

_____

_____

Here is the same passage annotated by the author:

❶ There are two deep-seated idiosyncrasies of human nature that bear on our acceptance or rejection of what is offered us. We have, in *Line* the first place, ❷ an innate bias for the famil- (5) iar. ❸ Whatever we're thoroughly unfamiliar with is apt to seem to us odd, or queer, or curious, or bizarre. For it is no mere trick of speech, but one of those appallingly veracious records of human nature and experience in which the (10) history of words abounds, ❹ through which "outlandish" and "crude" attained their present meaning. For "outlandish" meant in the beginning only what doesn't belong to our own land, and "uncouth" was simply "unknown." (15) The change in meaning registers a universal trait. Whatever is alien to our own ways—the costume, manners, modes of speech of another race or of other times—is strange; and "strange" itself, which started out by meaning merely (20) "foreign," is only another record of the same idiosyncrasy. ❺ But there is still another trait that is no less broadly human. Whatever is too familiar wearies us. Incessant recurrence without variety breeds tedium; the overiterated (25) becomes the monotonous, and the monotonous irks and bores. ❻ And there we are. Neither that which we do not know at all, nor that which we know too well, is to our

1. The passage begins with its topic sentence. It promises a discussion of two idiosyncrasies of human nature.
2. The first trait is stated in lines 3–5.
3. For clarity, the author explains "bias for the familiar," not by defining the term but by citing examples of its opposite—i.e., our aversion to the unfamiliar. Four adjectives ("odd," "queer," etc.) show subtle gradations of meaning, suggesting both the richness and the complexity of the subject.
4. This may seem like a digression into word origins, but language is such an elemental part of what it means to be human that the author uses the history of words to show how deeply in our nature the rejection of the unfamiliar is embedded.

    A compilation of diverse examples (lines 10–21) helps the author to build a convincing case that we tend initially, at least, to be wary of the new.
5. The second trait is introduced and defined. Starting on line 25, the author plays with words by restating "monotonous" and using other redundant words and phrases—as though to give readers a taste of the very phenomenon being discussed.
6. A short four-word sentence interrupts the flow of ideas, giving the reader a chance to absorb the author's ideas. The recapitulation of the passage thus far also serves as a transition to the discussion that follows.

taste. **❼** We are averse to shocks, and we go to
(30) sleep under narcotics.

Both the shock and the narcotic have, I
grant, at times their fascination. **❽** But they
are apt to be forward, not permanent, sweet,
not lasting. The source of more or less abiding
(35) satisfaction for most normal human beings lies
in a happy merging of the two—in the twofold
delight in an old friend recognized as new, or
a new friend recognized as old. **❾** The experience and the pleasure are universal. All the
(40) lovers who have ever lived have made experiment of it; a face that you have passed a hundred times, nor cared to see, remains the face
you've always known, but becomes all at once
the most beautiful and thrilling object in the
(45) world; the person you've never known before,
you find all at once you've known from all
eternity. Now art, like love, sends its roots deep
into what we are. **❿** And our most permanent
aesthetic satisfaction arises as a rule from things
(50) familiar enough to give the pleasure of recognition, yet not so trite as to rob us of the other
pleasure of surprise. **⓫** We are keen for the
new, but we insist that it establish some connection with what is friendly and our own; we
(55) want the old, but we want it to seem somehow
new. Things may recur as often as they please,
so long as they surprise us—like the Ghost in
Hamlet—**⓬** each time they appear.

—From John Livingstone Lowes,
Convention and Revolt in Poetry, 1919

7. The author introduces another way to look at the issue.

8. Stylistically, the author is fond of using antith-eses—juxtaposing contrasting ideas, as in lines 26–29: "that which we do not know at all, nor that which we know too well." See also lines 32–34, 36–38, 45–47, et al. The technique not only provides a lilting rhythm to the prose but helps develop the author's point that satisfac-tion comes from "a happy merging of the two" (line 36).

9. A short, pithy sentence between two lengthy sentences adds variety and leaves an impact on the reader. The adjective "universal" is par-ticularly apt because the entire passage deals with a defining characteristic of humankind. The author alludes to two widely understood experiences, love and friendship, to heighten readers' understanding. In line 47, however, the author expands the discussion to include the abstract world of art.

10. The author reiterates the basic point of the discussion in terms of our emotional reactions to art.

11. The author once again rephrases and reiter-ates the main idea of the passage, perhaps to prepare readers for the literary reference at the end of the passage.

12. The allusion casts a new light on the ghost of Hamlet's father. We know beforehand that the ghost will show up, but its appearance never-theless gives us a start.

Annotation Summary

The opening sentence of the passage states the author's thesis—that there is a predictable pattern in humans' responses to stimuli that are familiar and to stimuli that are not. This idea is presented not as a hypothesis or a theory but as an indisputable fact.

With an authoritative, analytical voice, the author sets out to prove the validity of his thesis, first by citing a number of everyday words, all with unfavorable connotations and all pertaining to our suspicion or outright rejection of things that are new and unfamiliar. Unexpectedly, the author also claims that we humans don't necessarily adhere to the opposite—embracing the well-known and familiar. Rather, because we are apt to find overly-familiar matters equally undesirable, he draws the conclusion that "Neither that which we do not know at all, nor that which we know too well, is to our taste" (lines 27–29).

This juxtaposition of contrasting ideas is a stylistic motif evident throughout the passage. Several sentences contain antithetical constructs, as in: "But they are apt to be forward, not permanent, sweet, not lasting" (lines 32–34), and "the twofold delight in an old friend recognized as new, or a new friend recognized as old" (lines 36–38), and "we want the old, but we want it to seem somehow new" (lines 54–56).

Such a pattern of sentence structure not only echoes a crucial component of the passage, i.e., "two deep-seated idiosyncrasies." It also leads naturally to the allusion to Hamlet's father's ghost—an always expected but nevertheless surprising dramatic occurrence.

The clock won't permit lengthy annotations during the AP exam, but if you get into the habit of underlining salient ideas, words, and phrases, and generally scrawling your insights all over the things you read, it's likely that you'll be primed to sail through the passages on the exam. But proficiency in annotation, like a skill in any endeavor, diminishes with disuse. So, keep at it because it's easy to slip out of the groove if you stop for any length of time.

See Appendix (pages 365–368) for more practice in annotation.

Answering the Questions

Multiple-Choice Questions

Multiple-choice questions separate well-qualified students from those who are less qualified. To earn a "5" on the exam you must answer most of the questions correctly and write good essays. To earn a "3," you need to get about 50 or 60 percent of the short-answer questions right—provided that your essays are generally acceptable.

Each correct answer is worth one point. In scoring the test, each wrong answer and each answer left blank will be deducted from the total number of questions. If, for example, you were to leave two blanks and answer four questions incorrectly, a total of six points will be deducted from 45—the usual number of questions on the exam—making your short-answer score 39.

This scoring procedure means that it always pays to guess, even when a question stumps you completely. By guessing at random, you still have a one-in-five chance of getting it right, and by eliminating one or more choices, you dramatically increase the odds of picking the correct answer. In short, DON'T LEAVE BLANKS. ANSWER EVERY QUESTION.

When a question gives you trouble, and you can't decide among three choices, conventional wisdom says you should go with your first impulse. You may be right. Testing experts and psychologists agree there's a better than average chance of success if you trust your intuition. There are no guarantees, however. Because the human mind works in so many ways, relying on your initial choice may not always work.

Essay Questions

After an hour of answering multiple-choice questions, you'll have two hours to write three essays:

- A **synthesis essay** in which you use sources to argue your point of view on a given issue.
- An **analytical essay** that examines, interprets, and explains the meaning and structure of a prose passage.
- An **argumentative essay** that supports, refutes, or qualifies an opinion expressed in a statement or brief passage.

Before you're given the signal to begin writing your essays, you'll have 15 minutes to read the questions and the sources for the synthesis essay. However, you don't have to spend the whole time reading. During those 15 minutes you can plan your essay, underline noteworthy ideas, formulate a tentative thesis, or prepare a brief outline. You might even glance at the other essay questions. Essentially, the time is yours to fill as you wish but with one exception: you may not start writing your essay. That begins only after the proctor gives you the green light.

Write the essays in any order. The choice is yours. The suggested writing time for each essay is 40 minutes.

TIP

Questions are not arranged in order of difficulty as they are on some standardized tests. Usually, they follow the progress of the passage, but not always.

STRATEGY

Answer every question, even if you have to guess.

Essay Questions from Previous AP Exams

To give you an idea of the essays you are expected to write on the exam, here are essay topics that students were given during each of the last six years.

2014

1. In recent years college graduates in great numbers have failed to find jobs for which their education has prepared them. As a result, many people, including high school students and their parents, question whether a college degree is worth the expense required to attain one. Others, however, argue that a college education is not meant solely to prepare students for a job or career.

    After reading six sources related to this issue, write an essay that discusses whether a college education is worth the cost. Synthesize information from at least three of the sources into your essay.

2. In 1780, Abigail Adams wrote a letter of advice to her son John Quincy Adams, then traveling in Europe with his father, John Adams, the future second president of the United States. Read the letter carefully. Then, write an essay that analyzes the rhetorical strategies that Mrs. Adams uses to advise the young man.

3. Research by experts in education reveals that the creativity of children from kindergarten through sixth grade has suffered in recent years. A decline in creativity is alarming, especially when present and future world problems related to climate, economics, war and peace, and much more will require increasingly creative solutions.

    One proposal to reverse the decline in creativity is to actively teach creative thinking in school. Opinion is divided on whether this approach is worthwhile. State your view on this issue by writing to your school board. Explain what you mean by creativity and argue for or against starting a course in creativity.

2015

1. Many schools, colleges, and universities have instituted honor codes meant to discourage such practices as cheating, stealing, and plagiarizing. Students violating established codes are subject to a variety of punishments.

    After reading six sources related to the issue of honor codes, compose an essay that supports your position on whether your school should establish, maintain, revise, or eliminate an honor code or honor system. Your argument should incorporate ideas, quotations, paraphrases, or summaries found in at least three of the six sources that accompany this question.

2. To commemorate the tenth anniversary of Dr. Martin Luther King's assassination, labor union organizer and civil rights leader Cesar Chavez wrote an article that discusses non-violent resistance as a means to achieve certain social goals. After reading Chavez's words, write an essay that analyzes the rhetorical choices he uses to develop his argument.

3. Friendly phrases such as "How's it going?" and "Nice to meet you" are known as polite speech and are usually not taken literally. In an essay, develop your position on the value or function of polite speech in a culture or community with which you are familiar. To support your argument, use evidence drawn from your reading, experience, or observation.

2016

1. With the spread of globalization in recent decades, English has become the primary language for communicating in international finance, science, and politics. As the use of English has spread, foreign language learning in English-speaking countries has declined, making the use of only one language—English—the norm.

     Carefully read the six sources accompanying this question and then write an essay that takes a position on the claim that people who speak only English and no other language are at a disadvantage in today's world. In your discussion, synthesize appropriate quotations, ideas, paraphrases, or summaries found in at least three of the sources.

2. In 2004, upon the death of former president Ronald Reagan, the ex–prime minister of Great Britain, Margaret Thatcher, who had worked closely with Reagan, delivered a eulogy to the American people honoring her former colleague and friend. Read the eulogy carefully, and then write an essay that analyzes the rhetoric Thatcher used to convey her thoughts and feelings.

3. Back in the nineteenth century, the Irish author Oscar Wilde noted that "Disobedience, in the eyes of anyone who has read history, is man's original virtue. It is through disobedience that progress has been made, through disobedience and through rebellion." In an essay, argue your position on Wilde's claim that disobedience and rebellion promote progress. Support your views with evidence drawn from your reading, studies, experience, or observation.

2017

1. The growth of the Internet has, among other things, changed what and how people read and in so doing has generated controversy about the need for and future of traditional public libraries. Some observers question the relevance of today's libraries, while others see opportunities for libraries to grow and thrive in new ways. After reading six sources related to the future of libraries, write an essay that discusses your position on the future role, if any, of public libraries. As you develop your argument, be sure to incorporate, or synthesize, material from at least three of the sources that accompany this assignment. Whether you quote directly from a source or put its ideas into your own words, clearly identify each source you use either in the text of your essay or in a footnote.

2. At the beginning of a speech to the Women's National Press Club in 1960, the American journalist and politician Clare Booth Luce expressed her objections to a tendency of the press corps to give readers sensationalist stories rather than maintain journalistic integrity by writing serious, consequential news stories.

     After carefully reading her opening remarks, write an essay that analyzes the rhetorical strategies Luce used to prepare the audience for the disapproval that was central to the remainder of her speech.

3. In *Empire of Illusion*, the author Chris Hedges, referring to the world of politics and the consumer culture, argues that "the most essential skill . . . is artifice." That is, as Hedges explains, successful politicians "no longer need to be competent, sincere, or honest. They need only to appear to have these qualities." In other words, deception succeeds.

     After reading a short passage that develops Hedges's views, write an essay stating your opinion on the issue. Use appropriate, specific evidence to develop and illustrate your position.

2018

1. The power of a government to confiscate people's private property for public use is known as eminent domain. Although eminent domain is centuries old, it remains a contentious issue throughout the world.

    Read the six sources on the following pages. Then, using at least three of the sources, write a coherent essay that supports, opposes, or qualifies the principle that the governmental right of eminent domain is useful and productive. When quoting, paraphrasing, or summarizing material, be sure to identify each source in parentheses either with its letter (A, B, C, etc.) or with a description.

2. In 1997, U.S. Secretary of State Madeleine Albright delivered the commencement address at Mount Holyoke College, a women's college in Massachusetts. After reading a given excerpt from the speech, write a well-developed essay that identifies and analyzes the rhetorical choices Albright made to help convey her message to the audience.

3. In her book *Gift from the Sea*, the author and aviator Anne Morrow Lindbergh (1906–2001) reflects on how people make choices:

    "We tend not to choose the unknown which might be a shock or a disappointment or simply a little difficult to cope with. And yet it is the unknown with all its disappointments and surprises that is the most enriching."

    After carefully considering Lindbergh's position on choosing the unknown, write an essay that develops your own view on the value of exploring the unknown. Support your position with appropriate and specific evidence.

2019

1. Our society's increasing demand for energy has drawn attention of governments and consumers to large-scale wind power and away from traditional materials, such as coal, oil, and natural gas. Yet, the creation of large commercial wind farms has created controversy for a variety of reasons.

    Carefully read the following six sources, including the introduction to each one, and then write an essay that develops your position on the most important factors that an individual or agency should take into account when determining whether to establish a wind farm. As you develop your position, synthesize material from at least three of the sources.

2. In 1930 Mohandas "Mahatma" Gandhi led a nonviolent march in India protesting Britain's colonial monopoly on the taxation of salt. The Salt March, as it was called, triggered a civil disobedience movement that won India independence from Britain in 1947. Just prior to the march Gandhi had written to Viceroy Lord Irwin, who represented the British crown in India. The passage that follows is the conclusion of that letter. Read it carefully and then write an essay that analyzes the rhetorical choices Gandhi made to present his case to Lord Irwin.

3. The term "overrated" is commonly used to diminish concepts, geographic places, roles, books, movies, etc., that the speaker thinks fail to live up to their reputation. Choose something that in your judgment is overrated and then write a well-developed essay explaining your views. Use appropriate evidence from your reading, experience, or observation to support your argument.

2020

During the Covid-19 pandemic, Part 2 of the exam consisted of only one essay question—the rhetorical analysis. Below are three different versions of the question, which asked students to analyze the rhetorical choices made by the speaker:

1. In 1964, "Lady Bird" Johnson, who was at the time the First Lady of the United States, gave the following speech at the first anniversary luncheon of the Eleanor Roosevelt Memorial Foundation.
2. In 1985, President Ronald Reagan delivered a speech at a fundraising event held on behalf of the John F. Kennedy Presidential Library and Museum.
3. In August, 2009, President Barack Obama gave a eulogy at the funeral of Senator Edward Kennedy.

Instructions for each topic asked students to respond to the prompt with a thesis that analyzed the speaker's rhetorical choices:

- Respond to the prompt with a thesis that analyzes the speaker's rhetorical choices.
- Select and use evidence to support your line of reasoning.
- Explain how the evidence supports your line of reasoning.
- Demonstrate an understanding of the rhetorical situation.
- Use appropriate grammar and punctuation in communicating your argument.

2021

1. Handwriting instruction was virtually universal in schools throughout the nineteenth and through much of the twentieth century. Today, little if any time is devoted to such lessons. Some people argue that such instruction should still be offered today, while others maintain that digital technology has made such instruction obsolete.

   Carefully read the following six sources. Then write an essay that synthesizes material from at least three of them in order to develop your position on the place, if any, of handwriting instruction in today's schools.
2. In 2013, during his time in office, President Barack Obama made a speech in the National Statuary Hall of Fame of the United States Capitol building at the installation of a statue of Rosa Parks, the African-American woman who had been arrested in 1955 for refusing to give up her seat on a segregated bus in Montgomery, Alabama. After reading the passage carefully, write an essay that analyzes the rhetorical choices Obama makes to convey his message.
3. People of all ages devote considerable time and energy to achieve perfection in their professional or personal lives. At the same time, they often demand perfection in others, thereby creating expectations that may be challenging to achieve. Some people, however, believe that perfection is neither attainable or desirable.

   In your essay, argue your position on the value of striving for perfection.

Sample Synthesis Essay Question

SUGGESTED TIME:

15 MINUTES FOR READING THE QUESTION AND SOURCES

40 MINUTES FOR WRITING AN ESSAY

Homework has always been part of going to school. In recent years, efforts to improve education have included assigning more homework to students from kindergarten to twelfth grade. Many teachers, parents, and others applaud this increase. Critics, in contrast, claim that heavier loads of homework do more harm than good, not only to children but also to their families.

Carefully read the following six sources, including the material that introduces each source. Then, in an essay that synthesizes at least three of the sources, take a position on the claim that large amounts of homework have more negative consequences than positive ones.

Source A (Kohn)

Source B (Gill and Schlossman)

Source C (Loveless)

Source D (Chart)

Source E (Haley)

Source F (Chaika)

Source G (Hanson)

Instructions:

- Respond to the prompt with a thesis that may establish a line of reasoning.
- Provide evidence from at least three of the provided sources to support the thesis. Indicate clearly the sources used through direct quotation, paraphrase, or summary. Sources may be cited as Source A, Source B, etc., or by using the descriptions in parentheses.
- Explain the relationship between the evidence and the thesis.
- Demonstrate an understanding of the rhetorical situation.
- Use appropriate grammar and punctuation in communicating the argument.

Source A

Alfie Kohn, "Homework: An Unnecessary Evil?" *Psychology Today*, published online at *www.psychologytoday.com*, November 24, 2012.

The following passage is an excerpt from an article written by an author and specialist in behavior and education. His books include The Homework Myth *and* What Does It Mean to Be Well Educated?

At the high school level, the research supporting homework hasn't been particularly persuasive. There does seem to be a correlation between homework and standardized test scores, but (a) it isn't strong, meaning that homework doesn't explain much of the variance in scores, and (b) one prominent researcher, Timothy Keith, who did find a solid correlation, returned to the topic a decade later to enter more variables into the equation simultaneously, only to discover that the improved study showed that homework had no effect after all.

. . . When homework is related to test scores, the connection tends to be strongest—or, actually, least tenuous—with math. If homework turns out to be unnecessary for students to succeed in that subject, it's probably unnecessary everywhere.

Along comes a new study, then, that focuses on the neighborhood where you'd be most likely to find a positive effect if one was there to be found: the effect of math and science homework on grades in high school . . . .

This result clearly caught the researchers off-guard. Frankly, it surprised me, too. When you measure "achievement" in terms of grades, you expect to see a positive result—not because homework is academically beneficial but because the same teacher who gives the assignments evaluates the students who complete them, and the final grade is often based at least partly on whether, and to what extent, students did the homework.

It's important to remember that some people object to homework for reasons that aren't related to the dispute about whether research might show that homework provides academic benefits. They argue that (a) six hours a day of academics are enough, and kids should have the chance after school to explore other interests and develop in other ways—or be able simply to relax in the same way that most adults like to relax after work; and (b) the decision about what kids do during family time should be made by families, not schools.

Source B

Brian P. Gill and Steven L. Schlossman, "My Dog Ate My Argument," Op/Ed page of the *Los Angeles Times*, December 11, 2003.

The following passage is an excerpt from an opinion article written by a social scientist at the RAND Corporation and a history professor at Carnegie Mellon University.

In our view, homework is the prime window into the school for parents to see, understand and connect with the academic mission of the teachers. It is the primary arena in which children, parents and schools interact on a daily basis. Yet it gets less systematic thought and attention than any other key component of education. Other than the admonition that kids should do more of it, we pay almost no attention to how to improve its design and content. Nor do we do much to prepare teachers to use and evaluate homework, to hold administrators accountable for monitoring the homework load or to cultivate parents' collaboration. Homework remains an orphan child of the educational excellence movement.

. . . After half a century of failure to increase student buy-in, it's time to rethink how to make homework a more valued part of the pedagogic process. In addition to promoting academic achievement, homework can inculcate habits of self-discipline and independent study and can help inform parents about the educational agenda of their school. We must find ways to make homework an interesting and challenging educational experience for students, instead of the uniform, seat-bound, memorization-focused solo exercise it has been. Otherwise, all our talk about high standards and improving student achievement will run up against the same roadblock that has stymied the pursuit of educational excellence in the past.

Source C

Tom Loveless, "Do Students Have Too Much Homework?" A report for the Brown Center on Education Policy at the Brookings Institution, Washington, D.C., 2003.

The following passage is excerpted from a report on American education.

The most reliable data support the following conclusions: 1) the typical student, even in high school, does not spend more than an hour per day on homework, 2) the homework load has not changed much since the 1980s, 3) the students whose homework has increased in the past decade are those who previously had no homework and now have a small amount, 4) most parents feel the homework load is about right and, of those who would like to change it, more parents would rather see homework increased than decreased.

. . . Research shows that the relationship of homework with student achievement is positive for both middle and high school students and neutral for elementary school students. The research does not prove causality, an ever-present difficulty with research on many educational practices. High-achieving students in high school, for example, may do more homework because they enjoy studying. They take tough classes that require a lot of work. That does not necessarily mean that homework is boosting their achievement. Low-achieving students in elementary school, on the other hand, may do more homework because they are struggling to catch up. The homework is not causing their learning problems.

Source D

"Average NAEP Reading Scale Scores of Students by Age and Amount of Assigned Daily Reading Homework," *Digest of Education Statistics*, National Center for Educational Statistics, 2012.

The table below has been adapted from research conducted by the National Association of Educational Progress, the nation's largest testing agency responsible for assessing what America's K–12 students know and can do in various subjects.

Average NAEP Reading Scale Scores of Students by Age and Number of Pages of Assigned Daily Reading Homework, 2012

Age	5 or fewer	6–10	11–15	10–20	21 or more
17	274	283	289	297	301
13	251	261	266	268	271
9	207	219	225	226	227

Source E

Brian Haley, "What Is the Value of Homework?" July 6, 2006. *SearchWarp.com.* Accessed August 2, 2006, *http://www.searchwarp.com*

The passage that follows is adapted from an article published by a website that promotes the writing of authors in many disciplines, including education.

Assigning homework serves various educational needs. It serves as an intellectual discipline, establishes study habits, eases time constraints on the amount of curricular material that can be covered in class, and supplements and reinforces work done in school. In addition, it fosters student initiative, independence, and responsibility, and brings home and school closer together.

. . . Like mowing the lawn or taking out the garbage, homework seems to be a fact of life. . . . But the value of homework extends beyond school. We know that good assignments, completed successfully, can help children develop wholesome habits and attitudes. . . . It can teach children to work independently, encourage self-discipline and responsibility (assignments provide some youngsters with their first chance to manage time and meet deadlines), and encourage a love of learning. . . . Homework can help parents learn about their children's education and communicate both with their children and the schools.

Research in the last decade has begun to focus on the relationship between homework and student achievement and has greatly strengthened the case for homework. Although there are mixed findings about whether homework actually increases students' academic achievement, many teachers and parents agree that homework develops students' initiative and responsibility and fulfills the expectations of students, parents, and the public. Studies generally have found homework assignments to be most helpful if they are carefully planned by the teachers and have direct meaning to students.

Source F

Gloria Chaika, "Help! Homework Is Wrecking My Home Life," *Education World,* August 8, 2000.

The following passage is from an article for school administrators published in an online educational journal.

"Teachers should devote energy to creating homework that is stimulating and provocative rather than banal," says Howard Gardner of the Harvard Graduate School of Education. "And parents or mentors should go shoulder-to-shoulder with youngsters, helping to motivate them, thinking of ways in which to help them without giving the answer, and being aware of the child's special gifts and weaknesses."

It sounds great, "but you need parent input for kids to perform, and with the increase in single-parent families, there's no one at home to help," veteran fifth-grade teacher Loretta Highfield told *Education World.*

"It isn't that the kids don't want to do homework; the majority of my students don't have the skills to go home and do it independently," added Highfield, a teacher at Florida Avenue Elementary in Slidell, Louisiana. "Even young students are not getting the help at home that they used to."

The same seems to hold true for older children. "I have students who have been thrown out of the house or have a financial situation brought on by an ill parent," Northshore High School (Slidell, Louisiana) teacher Kathleen Modenbach told *Education World.* "There are others whose after-school jobs pay for car insurance and clothes or whose involvement in extra-curricular activities, private lessons, or sports leaves little time for homework."

"For some students, a lot of homework can seem irrelevant," Modenbach added. "High school students become expert at evaluating the validity of assignments and assigning priorities to them. Kids who wouldn't dream of cheating on a test or copying a research paper think nothing of copying homework. I find students will do homework when it must be done to pass the class. Anything else is a waste of time and feeds into the vicious circle of beating the homework system."

Therefore, as kids deal with assigned homework in their own ways—or grow increasingly frazzled—their too-busy parents are uncertain what to do. Some, wanting their children to be academically competitive, demand extra homework, while others wonder just how much is too much.

Source G

Michael Hanson, "Analyzing 'the Homework Gap' Among High School Students," Brown Center on Education Policy, 2017.

Researchers have struggled for decades to identify a causal, or even a correctional, relationship between time spent in school and improved learning outcomes for students. Some studies have focused on the length of the school year while others have focused on hours in a day or week, and others on hours spent on homework.

Measuring the relationship between homework and outcomes like test scores can be difficult. Researchers are primarily confounded by an inability to determine what compels students to choose homework during their time off over other activities. Are those who spend more time on homework just extra motivated? Or are they struggling students who need to work harder to keep up? What role do social expectations from parents and peers play?

Previous studies have examined the impact of this outside time use on educational outcomes for students. A recent study from Berea College in Kentucky identified a causal relationship between hours spent studying and a student's academic performance through an interesting measure. The researchers took advantage of randomly assigned college roommates, paying attention to those who came to campus with smart phones packed with video games. They hypothesized students randomly assigned to a roommate without much interest in video games would study more, since all other factors remained equal. That hypothesis held up, and that group also received higher grades, demonstrating a causal relationship.

Other research has relied on data collected through the American Time Use Survey, a study of how Americans spend their time, and [has] shown the existence of a gender gap and a parental-education gap in homework time. Other studies have looked at the relationship between holding a job and students' time use in discretionary activities, like sleep, media consumption, and time spent on homework.

Answering the Synthesis Question

Homework. Now, there's a topic that you must know something about. Being a seasoned doer of homework, you're probably bursting with ideas on the pros and cons of the stuff and could probably argue brilliantly for or against homework, or come down somewhere between the two poles. Regardless of where you stand, you're not apt to find yourself short of ideas on the issue. In fact, you may be overloaded and find yourself sifting out only the best arguments among many to include in an essay on the subject.

But beware. This essay assignment is not intended simply to give you a chance to vent about homework. Although your biases will no doubt shape your argument, you mustn't rely solely on your personal experience and observations. This, after all, is what the AP people call a "**synthesis essay**," a label that you've got to take seriously.

What it means is that your essay must be based not solely on your personal opinion but to some extent on your interpretation of **at least three** of the sources. You can use the sources as evidence to support your point of view, or you can comment on them in other ways. For example, you can criticize them for inaccuracies or reject them as dead-wrong observations of the homework scene. You can quote from them directly, use indirect quotations, paraphrase ideas, or put ideas into your own words. But remember this: However you incorporate the sources, you must say where the material came from. That is, you must give credit to each source you use, as though you are writing a term paper for a class.

Cite Sources

Stylistically, it may serve you well to use phrases like *"According to Source C, . . ."* or *"In Loveless's opinion . . .",* or *"A study of students' reading scores (Source D) shows that . . . ,"* etc. Or you can simply cite your sources with parenthetical references—(*Source A, Source B*)—in your text. Another approach is to name the author or even the title of the sources, but writing out lengthy titles uses up precious time. AP essay readers will look for citations and will penalize essays that contain fewer than three. At the same time, however, you won't earn extra credit for citing more than three.

Whether or not you agree with the premise that "large amounts of homework have more negative effects than positive ones," your task is to write an argument that defends your point of view. Because a researched argument is meant to sway readers whose views may be contrary to yours, you need to gather compelling evidence in support of your position.

Let's say that you think homework is generally good for you and the more you get, the better. Right off the bat, then, you have a main idea, or thesis, for your essay. But even if you know immediately where you stand on the issue, take the time to read all the sources carefully, underscoring or circling those ideas you might consider mentioning in your essay. It's good to read the material with which you don't agree, too, because in making your case, you can bolster your argument by refuting and revealing the weaknesses in what you'd expect your opponent to say.

TIP

Cite three sources; there's no extra credit for more.

TIP

Be sure to read all the sources carefully.

Support Your Position

In building a convincing case, it often pays to gather at least three compelling reasons to support your position. Although AP students ought not be constrained by the familiar "five-paragraph" essay, you won't go wrong following its structure: an introduction, three paragraphs of development, and a conclusion. Why *three* paragraphs of development? Mainly because *three* is a number that works. If you can come up with three different arguments, you appear to speak with the voice of authority. One paragraph is too simple. Two is better but still shallow. Three is thoughtful. It suggests depth and insight. Psychologically, three also creates a sense of wholeness for the reader, like the beginning, middle, and end of a story. (Incidentally, it's no accident that the number three recurs in all literature, from *Goldilocks and the Three Bears* to the Bible.)

Use the sources to bolster your arguments for or against large amounts of homework. But you needn't depend totally on the sources. In fact, AP readers are likely to look kindly on your own original ideas, provided they are relevant to the issue, clearly expressed, and well-developed. On the positive side, you might pick out such ideas as:

- Homework permits parents to participate with teachers in the education of their children. (Source B)
- "[T]he relationship between the amount of reading homework and performance on reading tests is especially positive for high school students." (Source D)
- Homework fosters the development of individual initiative and effective study habits. (Source B)
- Homework provides opportunities for low-achieving students to catch up. (Source C)
- Homework leads to a lifelong love of learning. (Source F)
- Homework generally contributes to higher grades, and higher grades can lead to admission to higher-quality colleges. (Source G)

Or, if you have an unfavorable view of homework, the following ideas can be used to support your argument:

- Years of educational research have found only a weak correlation between homework and student achievement. (Source A)
- Large amounts of homework can keep a student from pursuing worthwhile personal interests. (Source C)
- Homework assigned during vacations is counterproductive; it turns kids away from the joys of learning and deprives them of reading for pleasure. (Source E)
- More homework does not necessarily lead to better grades. (Source E)

The given sources either support or decry homework. A middle-of-the-road position may be difficult to defend unless you build a case by refuting arguments presented on both sides of the issue. Source F, which argues against homework, for example, quotes an apparently frustrated teacher: "It isn't that kids don't want to do homework; the majority of my students don't have the skills to go home and do it independently."

Because the word "majority" can mean *almost all or just over half*, the teacher appears to have overlooked the fact that some students can be counted on to work on their own. By generalizing about all students, the teacher in effect deprives some of her kids the opportunity to learn at home. An essay that argues neither for nor against homework might emphasize that universal policies regarding homework don't work. In other words, when it comes to education, one size cannot fit all.

Determine Order

Once you've collected your ideas for or against the issue, stop for a moment to figure out which idea to put first, which to put second, and so on. Order is important. The best order is the clearest order, the arrangement that readers can follow with the least effort. No plan is superior to another, provided you have a valid reason for using it. The plan least likely to succeed is the aimless one, the one in which you state and develop ideas in random order as they happened to come to mind. It's better by far to rank your ideas in order of importance by deciding which provides the strongest support for your thesis. Although your best argument may be listed first in your notes, save it for last on the essay. Giving it away at the start is self-defeating because everything that follows will be anticlimactic. An excellent way to arrange your ideas is to lead with your second best, save your best for the end, and sandwich the others in between. This structure recognizes that the end and the beginning of an essay are its most critical parts. A good opening draws the reader in and creates an all-important first impression, but a memorable ending, coming last, is what readers have fresh in their minds when they assign you a grade. But, as always, don't just follow these guidelines slavishly. If you can justify another organization, by all means use it.

AP exam readers won't judge your essay based on the opinion you express. Even if they disagree with you, they are obliged to ignore their own biases and grade you according to the criteria of good writing. They may think that your view is off the wall, but a cogent, forceful essay that smoothly integrates the sources and demonstrates mastery of argumentation will merit a high score.

TIP

Work *toward* your best point, not away from it.

No matter how skillfully written, your essay will be penalized for faulty reasoning and misinformation.

Sample Analytical Question

SUGGESTED TIME: 40 MINUTES

Read the following passage published back in 1967 by *The New York Times*. Then write an essay in which you analyze how the structure of the passage and the use of language help convey the writer's views.

Instructions:
- Respond to the prompt with a thesis that may establish a line of reasoning.
- Select and use evidence to develop and support the line of reasoning.
- Explain the relationship between the evidence and the thesis.
- Demonstrate an understanding of the rhetorical situation.
- Use appropriate grammar and punctuation in communicating the argument.

*Note: Remember that the author's views reflect the values of the time when the essay was written, decades ago: Your job is not to judge the validity of those views but rather to discuss the rhetorical techniques the author used.

Americans and Western Europeans, in their sensitivity to lingering problems around them, tend to make science and progress their scapegoats. There is a belief that progress has precipitated widespread unhappiness, anxieties, and other social and emotional problems.
Line Science is viewed as a cold mechanical discipline having nothing to do with human warmth
(5) and the human spirit.

But to many of us from the nonscientific East, science does not have such repugnant associations. We are not afraid of it, nor are we disappointed by it. We know all too painfully that our social and emotional problems festered long before the age of technology. To us, science is warm and reassuring. It promises hope. It is helping us at long last gain some

(10) control over our persecutory environments, alleviating age-old problems—not only physical but also, and especially, problems of the spirit.

Shiraz, for example, a city in southern Iran, has long been renowned for its rose gardens
and nightingales; its poets, Sadi and Hafiz; and its mystical, ascetic philosophy, Sufism.
Much poetry has been written in glorification of the spiritual attributes of this oasis city.
(15) And to be sure, Shiraz is a green, picturesque town, with a quaint bazaar and refreshing gardens. But in this "romantic" city thousands of emotionally disturbed and mentally retarded
men, women, and children were, until recently, kept in chains in stifling prison cells and
lunatic asylums.

Every now and again, some were dragged, screaming and pleading, to a courtyard and
(20) flogged for not behaving "normally." But for the most part, they were made to sit against
damp walls, their hands and feet locked in chains, and thus immobilized, without even
a modicum of affection from their helpless families and friends, they sat for weeks and
months and years—often all their lives. Pictures of these wretched men, women, and children can still be seen in this "city of poetry," this "city with a spiritual way of life."

(25) It was only recently that a wealthy young Shirazi who, against the admonitions of his
family, had studied psychology at the University of Teheran and foreign universities,
returned to Shiraz and after considerable struggle with city officials succeeded in opening a
psychiatric clinic, the first in those regions. After still more struggle, he arranged to have the
emotionally disturbed and the mentally retarded transferred from prison to their homes, to
(30) hospitals, and to his clinic, where he and his staff now attend them.

They are fortunate. All over Asia and other backward areas, emotionally disturbed men
and women are still incarcerated in these medieval dungeons called lunatic asylums. The
cruel rejection and punishment are intended to teach them a lesson or help exorcise evil
spirits.

(35) The West, still bogged down in its ridiculous romanticism, would like to believe that
emotional disturbances, dope addiction, delinquency are all modern problems brought
on by technological progress, and that backward societies are too spiritual and beautiful to
need the ministrations of science. But while the West can perhaps afford to think this way,
the people of backward lands cannot. . . .

(40) . . .The obstacles are awesome, the inertia too entrenched, the people's suffering too
anguished, their impatience too eruptive. Moreover, the total cultural reorganizations such
as Asia and Africa are undergoing inevitably engender their own temporary dislocations
and confusions. But their goals, the direction, remain constant. We are on the move, however awkwardly at first, to a saner, better world.

How to Answer This Question

Go back to the original question, which asks you to analyze two features of the passage: (1) its
structure, or organization, and (2) its language. The first aspect is fairly specific. As you read
the passage, you need to observe what the author discusses first, second, third, and so on. Your
essay should explain not only the order of ideas but also the reasons the author may have chosen
that order.

The second part of the question is more general. It invites you to analyze the use of language,
which may include the author's choice of words (diction), syntax (word order), figures of speech,
use of evidence (such as statistics or logical reasoning), sentence structure, rhythm, sound, tone,
or just about any other characteristics of style and rhetoric you choose.

Although the question directs you to write about two different aspects of the passage, your essay itself should be unified. That is, a good essay should not consist of, say, two disparate paragraphs, one exclusively devoted to structure and another to language. Rather, the essay should include material that shows the interrelationship of structure and language in the passage and how those elements contribute to the meaning and effect of the passage. This might be covered in a separate paragraph, or it could be woven into the overall fabric of the essay.

Before you begin to write, read the passage at least *twice:* once for an overview and once as you write your analysis. You may notice early on that the opening paragraph contains generalizations about Westerners' concepts of science and progress. Then the author contrasts the Western view of science and progress with the Eastern view. Immediately, you see that the author, by using the first-person pronoun (as in "many of us") is speaking from the perspective of an Easterner. Consequently, his discussion of Eastern views is apt to come across as more well-informed, more authoritative, perhaps more personal.

To support his position, the author gives an extended example—the city of Shiraz—to illustrate just how different the East is from the West. The description and vivid images of Shiraz memorably convey the idea that the "spiritual way of life" has a side to it that many Westerners don't know about. This is the heart of the passage. The use of quotation marks around "romantic" and "city of poetry" is meant to point out the discrepancy between the idealized and real versions of Shiraz.

Nearing the end, the author reiterates his initial contrast between West and East, with emphasis on the East. The last paragraph offers a generalized statement about conditions in Asia and Africa, reminding the reader of the contrast made at the very beginning of the passage. Tying the end to the beginning of the passage creates a sense of unity—a desirable feature in any piece of writing.

Sample Argumentative Question

SUGGESTED TIME: 40 MINUTES

> The following paragraph is adapted from *Mirror for Man*, a book written by anthropologist Clyde Kluckhorn in the middle of the twentieth century. Read the passage carefully. Then, write an essay that examines the extent to which the author's characterization of the United States holds true today. Use appropriate evidence to support your argument.
>
> **Instructions:**
> - Respond to the prompt with a thesis that may establish a line of reasoning.
> - Select and use evidence to develop and support the line of reasoning.
> - Explain the relationship between the evidence and the thesis.
> - Demonstrate an understanding of the rhetorical situation.
> - Use appropriate grammar and punctuation in communicating the argument.

Technology is valued as the very basis of the capitalistic system. Possession of gadgets is esteemed as a mark of success to the extent that persons are judged not by the integrity of their characters or by the originality of their minds but by what they seem to be—so far as can be measured by their wealth or by the variety and material goods which they display. "Success" is measured by their investments, homes, and lifestyles—not by their number of mistresses as in some cultures.

TIP

Read the passage at least twice— once for an overview and again as you write your analysis.

How to Answer This Question

Whether you agree, disagree, or have mixed views on the content of the passage, your job is to write a convincing argument that expresses your opinion. Initially, the word *argument* may suggest conflict or confrontation. But rest assured that your essay need not be combative. Rather, make it a calmly-reasoned explanation of your opinion on a debatable subject. Your goal is to persuade the reader that your opinion, supported by examples, facts, and other appropriate evidence, is correct.

If you have strong feelings about the topic, of course you should state them in your essay. But express them in calm, rational language. Be mindful that the essay should be well-reasoned, not be an emotional rant for or against the issue.

Consider first whether you agree with Kluckhorn's definition of "success." Is it, as Kluckhorn asserts, measured by income and material possessions? Or do you think that a more accurate standard of success in today's America should be determined by less tangible criteria—things such as happiness or self-respect? Or do you stand somewhere in between those two extremes?

The actual position you take on the issue is less crucial than your ability to support it fully by drawing from your knowledge, background, experience, or observation. Regardless of your position, be sure to include more than one example. An argument that relies on a single example, however compelling, will fall flat.

In the prompt, Kluckhorn's notion of success seems to refer broadly to American society. Resist responding in kind. That is, a short essay shouldn't focus on the whole of society but only on an identifiable segment—perhaps college-educated professionals or urban, blue-collar Americans. The point is that a narrowly focused essay on a limited topic will always turn out better than one that tries to cover too much ground in just a few paragraphs.

> **TIP**
>
> An argumentative essay should not be an emotional rant for or against an issue.

How Essays Are Read and Evaluated

When it comes time to make judgments about writing, the word *effectively* comes up repeatedly. It's a popular word because it's easy to use. But it's also hard to define. It means so much, and yet so little. You probably know effective writing when you see it, but what the AP folks have in mind is the thoughtful organization of ideas, appropriate word choice, proper syntax, varied sentence structure, a mature style of writing, sensible paragraphing, coherent development, and correct mechanics (grammar, spelling, and punctuation).

AP readers don't sit there with a checklist to see whether your essay meets all these criteria, however. Rather, they read it *holistically*, meaning that they read it quickly for an overall impression of your writing and then assign your essay a grade from 1 (low) to 5 (high). Readers are trained to look for clearly organized, well-developed, and forceful responses that reveal a depth of understanding and insight.

Frankly, the 40 minutes suggested for each essay is not a great deal of time to read the question, plan what you will say, write a few hundred words, edit and proofread your draft, and submit a finished piece of work. In effect, you must condense into a short time what would normally take far longer. A saving grace, however, is that the AP test readers don't expect three polished pieces of immortal prose, just three competently written essays.

Each year in early June, thousands of college and high school teachers get together to read and evaluate the essays written by students like you from across the country and overseas. Readers are chosen for their ability to make sound judgments about student writing and are trained to use a common set of scoring standards.

> AP readers don't expect three polished pieces of immortal prose, just three good essays.

A WORD ABOUT WORD COUNT

Are 250 words enough? Yes, but the number of words in your essays is up to you. To AP essay readers, length takes a back seat to answering the question and covering the subject. A single paragraph most likely won't allow you to fully develop ideas. Multiparagraph essays allow you to be expansive, to use a variety of details to support your main idea, and to show that you have what it takes to cover a complex subject clearly and logically. Keep in mind that the number of words is less crucial than what the words say.

Each essay is read by a different reader—an experienced English teacher who doesn't know your name, your school, your gender, or anything else about you. Nor do readers know the score you earned on other essays or on the multiple-choice questions. They rate essays according to standards that customarily apply to those written in college-level English courses. A score of 1–6 is assigned to each essay.

Essay Score	Rating	College Grade Equivalent
6	Extremely well qualified	A+, A
5	Well qualified	A−, B+
4	Qualified	B, B−, C+
3	Possibly qualified	C, C−
2	Unqualified	D
1	No recommendation	n/a

As part of their training, AP essay readers are given guidelines to ensure that all essays are evaluated as fairly and uniformly as possible. Readers are instructed:

- To read an essay only once
- To read it quickly
- To read primarily for what the writer has done well in terms of organization, word choice, clarity, purpose, mechanics of writing, and so on
- To assign a grade promptly
- To ignore poor handwriting as much as possible
- Not to penalize a well-developed but unfinished essay
- Not to penalize the writer for supporting or rejecting a particular point of view on an issue
- Not to consider length as a criterion of evaluation
- To keep in mind that even a marginal response to the question should be judged according to the logic of the argument developed by the writer
- To remember that each essay is a first draft written under pressure in about 40 minutes by a seventeen- or eighteen-year-old.

Interpreting Essay Scores

What do AP essay scores tell you about your writing? You'll find some answers below, and you'll also see what AP essay readers think about while on the job.

How to Score the Essays

The following essay-scoring guidelines apply to all three essays on the exam. The maximum score on an essay is 6; the minimum, 0.

Points are awarded in three categories:

1. Thesis (0–1 point)
2. Evidence and Commentary (0–4 points)
3. Sophistication (0–1 point)

THESIS (0–1 POINT)

No credit is given for an absent, erroneous, or incoherent thesis or one that merely restates or paraphrases the essay prompt.

One point is awarded for a thesis that states or strongly implies a reasonable interpretation of the issue raised by the prompt for Essay #1, the synthesis essay. Similarly, for Essay #2 one point is given for a reasonable thesis related to rhetoric in the given passage. For Essay #3 add a point for a thesis that clearly articulates a position on the issue raised by the prompt.

EVIDENCE AND COMMENTARY (0–4 POINTS)

No points are given for restating the thesis in different words or for material irrelevant to the prompt.

One point is earned for evidence that tends to help develop the thesis.

Two points are given for evidence that clearly supports the thesis but may not add significantly to the writer's line of reasoning.*

Three points are awarded in Essay #1 for evidence that supports the thesis and also begins to show how source material supports your point of view. Give three points for evidence in Essay #2 that identifies and offers some analysis of rhetoric in the passage. Likewise, in Essay #3, give three points for specific evidence that helps to develop an argument for or against the main idea expressed by the prompt.

Four points indicate that you have consistently and effectively included compelling evidence to support all claims in a line of reasoning and also have clearly employed at least three sources to strengthen your position on the given issue (Essay #1), identified ample relevant evidence of rhetoric in the given passage (Essay #2), and cited compelling evidence to support your argument in favor of or against the given issue (Essay #3).

SOPHISTICATION (0–1 POINT)

No credit is given for ideas, however discerning, that you mention but don't develop.

One point is awarded for the development of ideas that broaden an interpretation of the issue (Essay #1), cite and explain significant rhetorical features of the passage (Essay #2), and discuss the opinions expressed in the given passage (Essay #3) by one or more of the following:

(a) Identifying and discussing complexities or tensions in the text.
(b) Illuminating an interpretation of the work by situating it within a broader context.
(c) Suggesting alternative interpretations of the work.
(d) Employing a consistently vivid and persuasive writing style.

Use of Standard English: No specific credit is given for the use of standard English. Readers are bound to be favorably impressed, however, by well-expressed, economical, virtually error-free prose.

---

*The term **"line of reasoning"** refers to the means by which an idea or thesis is supported. For instance, an essay may focus on the writer's choice of words, use of logic, sequence of ideas, or even the essay's title in order to validate the thesis. A poor line of reasoning exists when there is a gap between the thesis and the evidence presented.

Scoring Your Own Essays

Get psyched to spend plenty of time on each of your essays— maybe more time than it took to write.

After you take the Diagnostic Test (pp. 47–84) or any of the Practice Tests (pp. 205–363), your essays need to be scored. Evaluating your own essays takes objectivity that can't be acquired overnight. In effect, you've got to disown your own work—that is, view it through the eyes of a stranger—and then judge it as though you have no stake in the outcome. A word of caution: Don't expect to breeze through the evaluations. Set aside plenty of time. Many English teachers vividly recall their snail-like progress as novice essay readers—sometimes spending hours on grading a single essay and rereading it again and again. In short, scoring essays can be challenging, and it takes practice.

If you accept the challenge, begin by reading the following essay-writing instructions (printed in boldface). On the exam, these instructions are included as part of the prompt for each essay. In effect, they are your essays' ingredients. Because AP readers will look for evidence that you have followed these instructions as they score your essays, it's important for you to understand what each one tells you to do.

1. Respond to the prompt with a thesis that may establish a line of reasoning.

Each of your essays must have a thesis, or main idea. It may be placed anywhere in your essay, and can be built in as a separate sentence, a part of a sentence, or even as pieces of two or more sentences. Sometimes the thesis need not be stated at all if the contents of the essay make the main idea so obvious that it would be redundant to spell it out.

However you construct the thesis, it must in some way reflect the purpose of the assignment—a different one for each of the essays: (1) to use at least published sources to support your position on an issue; (2) to analyze the rhetoric in a given passage; and (3) to write a convincing argument backed up by evidence drawn from your reservoir of knowledge and experience. Ideally, the thesis of your essay should be visible to the reader from the start, or at least soon thereafter.

The thesis may also "establish a line of reasoning." That is, it may explain how you intend to support your essay's main idea. For instance, in the synthesis essay, you may plan to discuss the issue by citing ideas drawn from two of the textual sources and by statistics found in a chart or graph. Or, the thesis of your argument essay may state or imply your intention to build a case using evidence based on your reading or perhaps on your observations or personal experience.

2A. *(The following instruction applies only to Essay 1, the Synthesis Essay. See 2B for the instruction that applies only to Essays 2 and 3.)*

Provide evidence from at least three of the provided sources to support the thesis. Indicate clearly the sources used through direct quotation, paraphrase, or summary. Sources may be cited as Source A, Source B, etc., or by using the descriptions in parentheses.

Although your thesis may be based on your personal opinion on the issue, build your argument with references to the sources. You needn't depend solely on the sources with which you agree. By refuting those opposed to your views, you might strengthen your own argument.

2B. *(The following instruction applies only to Essays 2 and 3, the Rhetorical Analysis and the Argument. See 2A [above] for the instruction that applies to Essay 1.)*

Select and use evidence to develop and support your line of reasoning.

This instruction reminds you to formulate a claim and support it with convincing and relevant evidence drawn from your studies, reading, observation, and personal experience. You have abundant choices: facts, anecdotes, statistics, analogies, theories, examples, testimonies, expert opinions, your own values and recollections, and more—whatever will bolster your main idea. Each piece of evidence need not be presented as a separate statement. That is, consider blending the evidence gradually into the development of your entire essay.

3. Explain the relationship between the evidence and the thesis.

Whatever evidence you choose, be sure to explain its pertinence to your thesis. Although the connection may be obvious to you, there is no guarantee that a reader will see it as you do. Connections might be pointed out with stand-alone statements or pronouncements or, less blatantly, by artfully weaving them into the development of the entire essay.

This part of assessing your own essay requires a degree of objectivity that is unnatural for many people. After all, you have devoted considerable time—but, even more important, intellectual and emotional energy—to produce a piece of work that represents your very best efforts. You will earn still greater rewards, however, with an essay that demonstrates what the AP people call "sophistication," which means that you have expanded your essay's reach beyond the basics by identifying and discerning subtle complexities and tensions. For example, you might propose alternative interpretations of the text or discuss a situation from a viewpoint different from your own. In order to allow a degree of perspective to take shape, let the essay cool for a while (days, if possible), but even then you may need considerable self-discipline and willpower to detach yourself from the essay in order to read it through the eyes of a stranger. As you reread the essay, you may find unexpected rewards—thought-provoking connections between the evidence and your thesis that you would have forgotten or overlooked before. Perhaps they'll appear not as separate pronouncements but as assertions gradually and gracefully built into your text. Give yourself credit for those, but beware of deluding yourself by praising features that don't exist.

4. Demonstrate an understanding of the rhetorical situation.

Each of the three essays has a distinct "rhetorical situation," or purpose. Rather than stating it outright, you might demonstrate your grasp of the rhetorical purpose by implication—that is, simply by fulfilling the assignment. By writing an essay that takes a stand on a particular issue and citing material from three of the given sources, you will have shown comprehension of the synthesis essay's rhetorical situation. Likewise, following the stated instructions for each of the other essays is evidence enough that you've understood the rhetorical situation.

5. Use appropriate grammar and punctuation in communicating your argument.

Use the conventions of standard written English. Unless you need them for effect, avoid street talk, emojis, acronyms, and the abbreviations so common in e-communications.

2

Diagnostic Test

Learning Objectives

→ Taking a full-length AP exam
→ Finding the *best* answers
→ Checking your answers
→ How to score your own essays
→ What the numbers tell you
→ Calculating your AP test score

Introduction

This self-assessment test is similar in length and format to the AP exam. Use it to determine your readiness to take the actual exam, administered in May of each year.

Take the test as though it were the real thing. Set aside three hours and 15 minutes. Be sure you are wide awake and your mind is fresh. Remove all distractions, sharpen your pencil,* read the directions, and go to work.

Allow yourself one hour to answer the multiple-choice questions. Use the answer sheet provided. At the end of the hour take a five-minute break and then tackle the essay questions. Write your essays on standard 8½″ × 11″ composition paper, the approximate size of an official AP essay response sheet. For the first essay, the synthesis essay, allot 15 minutes to read the sources and 40 minutes to write the essay. Then, allow 40 minutes each for Essays 2 and 3.

When you have finished, check your answers with the Answer Key on page 75. Then read the Answer Explanations. Spend some time analyzing your wrong answers. Try to identify the reason you missed each question: Did you misinterpret the question? Was your choice too specific or too general? Did you misread the passage? Did you base your answer on the wrong material in the passage? Did you jump to a conclusion that led you astray? Knowing why you stumbled can help you avoid similar errors on future tests.

At the same time, don't ignore the questions you got right. Check all the answer explanations. Do they coincide with your reasons for making the correct choices? If so, give yourself a pat on the back for nailing the reasoning techniques you're expected to employ while answering these questions. If your rationale for choosing the answer differs from the given explanation, however, don't fret. On the contrary, rejoice, because, unless your choice was only a stab in the dark, you may have devised a functional new tactic for answering multiple-choice questions that even the professionals who wrote the test hadn't considered.

Although it is hard to evaluate your own essays, don't shy away from trying. Let the essays cool off for a while—maybe even for a day or two—and then, insofar as possible, reread them with an open mind and a fresh pair of eyes. Rate your essays using the Essay Self-Scoring Guide on pages 82–83.

Finally, using data from the Answer Key and the Essay Self-Scoring Guide, calculate the grade you earned on this test.

---

*Some observers say that a dull pencil point shortens the time it takes to fill in the spaces on multiple-choice answer sheets. No one has actually proved it, but why not give it a go? A dull pencil might reward you with a few minutes to check or rethink your answers.

ANSWER SHEET
Diagnostic Test

Multiple-Choice Questions

Time—1 hour

1. Ⓐ Ⓑ Ⓒ Ⓓ Ⓔ   13. Ⓐ Ⓑ Ⓒ Ⓓ Ⓔ   25. Ⓐ Ⓑ Ⓒ Ⓓ Ⓔ   37. Ⓐ Ⓑ Ⓒ Ⓓ Ⓔ

2. Ⓐ Ⓑ Ⓒ Ⓓ Ⓔ   14. Ⓐ Ⓑ Ⓒ Ⓓ Ⓔ   26. Ⓐ Ⓑ Ⓒ Ⓓ Ⓔ   38. Ⓐ Ⓑ Ⓒ Ⓓ Ⓔ

3. Ⓐ Ⓑ Ⓒ Ⓓ Ⓔ   15. Ⓐ Ⓑ Ⓒ Ⓓ Ⓔ   27. Ⓐ Ⓑ Ⓒ Ⓓ Ⓔ   39. Ⓐ Ⓑ Ⓒ Ⓓ Ⓔ

4. Ⓐ Ⓑ Ⓒ Ⓓ Ⓔ   16. Ⓐ Ⓑ Ⓒ Ⓓ Ⓔ   28. Ⓐ Ⓑ Ⓒ Ⓓ Ⓔ   40. Ⓐ Ⓑ Ⓒ Ⓓ Ⓔ

5. Ⓐ Ⓑ Ⓒ Ⓓ Ⓔ   17. Ⓐ Ⓑ Ⓒ Ⓓ Ⓔ   29. Ⓐ Ⓑ Ⓒ Ⓓ Ⓔ   41. Ⓐ Ⓑ Ⓒ Ⓓ Ⓔ

6. Ⓐ Ⓑ Ⓒ Ⓓ Ⓔ   18. Ⓐ Ⓑ Ⓒ Ⓓ Ⓔ   30. Ⓐ Ⓑ Ⓒ Ⓓ Ⓔ   42. Ⓐ Ⓑ Ⓒ Ⓓ Ⓔ

7. Ⓐ Ⓑ Ⓒ Ⓓ Ⓔ   19. Ⓐ Ⓑ Ⓒ Ⓓ Ⓔ   31. Ⓐ Ⓑ Ⓒ Ⓓ Ⓔ   43. Ⓐ Ⓑ Ⓒ Ⓓ Ⓔ

8. Ⓐ Ⓑ Ⓒ Ⓓ Ⓔ   20. Ⓐ Ⓑ Ⓒ Ⓓ Ⓔ   32. Ⓐ Ⓑ Ⓒ Ⓓ Ⓔ   44. Ⓐ Ⓑ Ⓒ Ⓓ Ⓔ

9. Ⓐ Ⓑ Ⓒ Ⓓ Ⓔ   21. Ⓐ Ⓑ Ⓒ Ⓓ Ⓔ   33. Ⓐ Ⓑ Ⓒ Ⓓ Ⓔ   45. Ⓐ Ⓑ Ⓒ Ⓓ Ⓔ

10. Ⓐ Ⓑ Ⓒ Ⓓ Ⓔ   22. Ⓐ Ⓑ Ⓒ Ⓓ Ⓔ   34. Ⓐ Ⓑ Ⓒ Ⓓ Ⓔ

11. Ⓐ Ⓑ Ⓒ Ⓓ Ⓔ   23. Ⓐ Ⓑ Ⓒ Ⓓ Ⓔ   35. Ⓐ Ⓑ Ⓒ Ⓓ Ⓔ

12. Ⓐ Ⓑ Ⓒ Ⓓ Ⓔ   24. Ⓐ Ⓑ Ⓒ Ⓓ Ⓔ   36. Ⓐ Ⓑ Ⓒ Ⓓ Ⓔ

Section I

TIME: 1 HOUR

DIRECTIONS: *Questions 1–12.* Carefully read the following passage and answer the accompanying questions.

The passage below is an excerpt from an essay on violence in America, written by a contemporary historian.

Passage 1

On September 26, 1872, three mounted men rode up to the gate of the Kansas City Fair, which was enjoying a huge crowd of perhaps 10,000 people. The bandits shot at the ticket seller, hit a small girl in the leg, and made off for the woods with something less than a
Line thousand dollars. It was highhanded, and it endangered the lives of a whole host of holiday-
(5) minded people for comparatively little reward.

What makes the robbery and the violence notable is not the crime itself but the way it was reported in the Kansas City *Times* by one John N. Edwards. In his front-page story he branded the robbery "so diabolically daring and so utterly in contempt of fear that we are bound to admire it and revere its perpetrators."

(10) Two days later the outlaws were being compared by the *Times* with knights of King Arthur's Round Table:

"It was as though three bandits had come to us from storied Odenwald, with the halo of medieval chivalry upon their garments and shown us how the things were done that poets sing of. Nowhere else in the United States or in the civilized world, probably, could this
(15) thing have been done."

Quite likely this deed was perpetrated by the James brothers: Jesse and Frank, and a confederate. The details really do not matter. What pertains is the attitude of the innocent toward the uncertainly identified guilty. The act had been perpetrated by violent, lawless men. If the *Times* is any indication, a respectable section of people approved of their action.
(20) No one, of course, thought to ask the little girl with the shattered leg how she felt about such courage. Nearly 17 months later, Edwards was quoted in the St. Louis *Dispatch* as preferring the Western highwayman to the Eastern, for "he has more qualities that attract admiration and win respect . . . . This comes from locality . . . which breeds strong, hardy men—men who risk much, who have friends in high places, and who go riding over the land, tak-
(25) ing all chances that come in the way." The purpose here is not to belabor one reasonably anonymous newspaperman of nearly a century ago, but merely to point up a fact—and a problem—of the American frontier.

The frontier placed a premium on independent action and individual reliance. The whole history of the American frontier is a narrative of taking what was there to be taken.
(30) The timid never gathered riches, the polite nearly never. The men who first carved the wilderness into land claims and town lots were the men who moved in the face of dangers, gathering as they progressed. The emphasis naturally came to be placed on gathering and not on procedures. Great tales of gigantic attainments abound in this frontier story; equally adventurous tales of creative plundering mark the march from Jamestown to the Pacific. It
(35) was a period peopled by giants, towers of audacity with insatiable appetites. The heroes are

not the men of moderate attitudes, not the town planners and commercial builders, not the farmers nor the ministers nor the teachers. The heroes of the period, handed along to us with all the luster of a golden baton, are the mighty runners from Mt. Olympus who ran without looking back, without concern about social values or anywhere they might be going
(40) except onward.

We revere these heroes because they were men of vast imagination and daring. We have also inherited their blindness and their excesses.

1. In the opening paragraph of the passage (lines 1–5), the author tells the story of robbery primarily to

    (A) portray the character of life in Kansas City.
    (B) suggest that lawlessness was common back in the 1870s.
    (C) juxtapose the action against the response to it.
    (D) create suspense as to the identity of the outlaws.
    (E) contrast the crowd's enjoyment with the violence taking place in their midst.

2. In lines 6–15, which of the following best describes the writer's main purpose?

    (A) To condemn the opinions and writing style of a particular journalist
    (B) To convey disapproval over the newspaper coverage of the incident at the fair
    (C) To express shock about the public's reaction to the crime
    (D) To stress the uniqueness of America's social and cultural history
    (E) To imply that values and customs from the medieval world are still alive and well

3. The rhetorical effect of the sentence in lines 6–7 ("What makes . . . Edwards.") is heightened by the strategy of

    (A) using "What" as the first word, suggesting that a question will follow.
    (B) emphasizing harsh words such as "crime" and "violence."
    (C) placing it immediately after the story of the robbery.
    (D) asserting why the event was not noteworthy before saying why it was.
    (E) following it up with a vividly written description of the robbery.

4. In context, the statement that "a respectable section of people approved of their action" (line 19) could be used to support which of these descriptions of the writer's opinions about the events in Kansas City?

    (A) He excuses the outlaws' behavior because as Midwesterners they suffered hardships.
    (B) He is more sympathetic toward Westerners than toward Easterners.
    (C) He adopts a semi-admiring tone of the outlaws.
    (D) He is outraged by the outlaws' insensitivity.
    (E) He is troubled by the public's response to the episode.

5. The phrase "such courage" (lines 20–21) can best be interpreted as an example of

    (A) a subtle use of irony.
    (B) a metaphorical allusion.
    (C) a witty aphorism.
    (D) a paradox.
    (E) an oxymoron.

6. The quotation from the St. Louis newspaper (lines 22–25) serves the author's purpose in which of the following ways?

    (A) It makes a pitch for more accuracy in news reporting.
    (B) It makes clear the author's intention to destroy Edwards's reputation as a journalist.
    (C) It further illustrates the thinking of many Americans.
    (D) It reinforces the author's view expressed earlier that the bandits were "violent" and "lawless."
    (E) It provides a generalization on which the author will comment in the next paragraph.

7. In the sixth paragraph (lines 28–40), the writer introduces an extended analogy in order to

    (A) heap praise on the spirit of the people who once populated America's frontier.
    (B) compare the Kansas City outlaws to men of the Old West.
    (C) suggest that the values of frontier people still exist in America.
    (D) excuse the behavior of the Kansas City outlaws.
    (E) explain why the Kansas City newspaper failed to condemn the outlaws.

8. In the context of the passage, all of the following phrases refer to the same qualities EXCEPT

    (A) "contempt of fear" (line 8).
    (B) "attract admiration and win respect" (lines 22–23).
    (C) "taking all chances" (lines 24–25).
    (D) "independent action" (line 28).
    (E) "without concern for social values" (line 39).

9. Which of the following quotations from the passage best supports the author's claim that frontier men valued "independent action and individual reliance" (line 28)?

    (A) "the James brothers" (line 16)
    (B) "a problem—of the American frontier" (lines 26–27)
    (C) "The timid never gathered riches" (line 30)
    (D) "creative plundering" (line 34)
    (E) "march from Jamestown to the Pacific" (line 34)

10. Toward the end of the passage (lines 35–37), the writer includes a series of phrases, each beginning with "not . . ." etc. The writer uses this construction in order to

    (A) undermine the position of the Kansas City newspaper vis-à-vis the crime.
    (B) break down readers' stereotypical conceptions of frontier settlers.
    (C) reinforce a theory stated earlier about the alleged robbers.
    (D) reiterate the main point of the passage.
    (E) emphasize the unique stature of the Old West's heroes.

11. The writer ends the passage with two sentences meant to suggest that Americans' attitude toward the frontier and its heroes

    (A) needs to be updated.
    (B) has long been distorted.
    (C) suffers from sentimentality.
    (D) will never be revised.
    (E) helps make America great.

12. Which of the following best describes the writer's exigence in the passage?

    (A) Some people's insensitivity toward others
    (B) Americans' distorted legacy of the Old West
    (C) Consequences of the decline of law and order
    (D) The erosion of old-fashioned values in America
    (E) The harm that comes from an uninformed citizenry

DIRECTIONS: *Questions 13–23.* Carefully read the following passage and answer the accompanying questions.

This passage is a speech delivered in 1873 by the renowned social reformer and advocate for women's suffrage, Susan B. Anthony.

Passage 2

Friends and fellow citizens:

I stand before you tonight under indictment for the alleged crime of having voted in the last presidential election, without having a lawful right to vote. It shall be my work this
Line evening to prove to you that in thus voting, I not only committed no crime, but, instead,
(5) simply exercised my *citizen's rights*, guaranteed to me and all United States citizens by the National Constitution, beyond the power of any State to deny . . . . The preamble of the Federal Constitution says:

"We, the people of the United States, in order to form a more perfect union, establish justice, insure *domestic* tranquillity, provide for the common defense, promote the general

(10) welfare, and secure the blessings of liberty to ourselves and our posterity, do ordain and establish this Constitution for the United States of America."

It was we, the people; not we, the white male citizens; nor yet we, the male citizens; but we, the whole people, who formed the Union. And we formed it, not to give the blessings of liberty, but to secure them; not the half of ourselves and the half of our posterity, but to *(15)* the whole people—women as well as men. And it is downright mockery to talk to women of their enjoyment of the blessings of liberty while they are denied the use of the only means of securing them provided by this democratic-republican government—the ballot.

For any state to make sex a qualification that must ever result in the disenfranchise-ment of one entire half of the people is to pass a bill of attainder,[1] or an *ex post facto* law,[2] *(20)* and is therefore a violation of the supreme law of the land. By it the blessings of liberty are forever withheld from women and their female posterity. To them this government has no just powers derived from the consent of the governed. To them this government is not a democracy. It is not a republic. It is an odious aristocracy; a hateful oligarchy[3] of sex; the most hateful aristocracy ever established on the face of the globe; an oligarchy of wealth, *(25)* where the rich govern the poor. An oligarchy of learning, where the educated govern the ignorant, or even an oligarchy of race, where the Saxon rules the African, might be endured; but this oligarchy of sex, which makes father, brothers, husbands, sons, the oligarchs over the mother and sisters, the wife and daughters of every household—which ordains all men sovereign, all women subjects, carries dissension, discord and rebellion into every home of *(30)* the nation.

Webster, Worcester and Bouvier all define a citizen to be a person in the United States, entitled to vote and to hold office. The only question left to be settled now is: Are women persons? And I hardly believe any of our opponents will have the hardihood to say they are not. Being persons, then, women are citizens; and no State has a right to make any law, or to *(35)* enforce an old law, that shall abridge their privileges or immunities. Hence, every discrimi-nation against women in the constitutions and laws of the several States is today null and void, precisely as in every one against negroes.

_____

[1] *An act that takes away one's civil rights.*
[2] *A law that imposes punishment for an act not punishable when it was committed.*
[3] *The exercise of power in the hands of a privileged few.*

13. In the opening paragraph (lines 1–7), in which the speaker asserts she is "under indictment for the alleged crime of having voted in the last presidential election. . . . ," her primary inten-tion is to

(A) shock the crowd into paying attention.
(B) win the sympathy and support of her audience.
(C) introduce members of the crowd to the major theme in her speech.
(D) establish an emotional connection to the women in the audience.
(E) trick the audience into thinking she would tell a story about her indictment.

14. The speaker's rhetorical reason for quoting the Preamble to the Constitution (lines 8–11) is to

    (A) support her position that the United States is a nation of laws, not men.
    (B) underscore the principle that "We the people . . ." refers to all people, not just to males.
    (C) remind the audience of where the "blessings of liberty" originated.
    (D) make an emotional appeal meant to stir up feelings of patriotism.
    (E) contrast "domestic tranquility" with her perception that American homes are plagued by "dissension, discord and rebellion" (line 29).

15. All of the following claims about the speaker's tone in lines 12–17 are valid EXCEPT

    (A) her tone is self-righteous.
    (B) her tone when discussing the extent to which women enjoy the "blessings of liberty" is resentful.
    (C) she adopts a passionate tone throughout.
    (D) she adopts an irreverent tone in dealing with voting rights.
    (E) she adopts a critical tone when discussing the ballot.

16. Throughout the second paragraph (lines 12–17), the speaker's rhetorical strategy most in evidence is

    (A) antithesis.
    (B) abstract allusion.
    (C) sentimentality.
    (D) euphemism.
    (E) extended metaphor.

17. The rhetorical effect that the speaker hopes to achieve by alluding to "a bill of attainder" and an "*ex post facto* law" in line 19 is

    (A) heightened interest in her point of view triggered by a new dimension of her argument.
    (B) support for her cause from an audience that most likely appreciates freedom and deplores tyranny.
    (C) anger that such abuses still exist in a democracy.
    (D) feelings of relief that such abuses of power are illegal.
    (E) to incite protest, violently—in the streets, if necessary.

18. Starting in line 22 the speaker's diction begins to include repetition of certain words and phrases, such as "*not* a democracy" and "*not* a republic," etc. Which of the following best describes the rhetorical effect of such a repetition in the remainder of the paragraph?

    (A) It conveys directly to the audience a sense of the speaker's moral outrage.
    (B) It heightens the passion the speaker brings to the issue.
    (C) It enables the audience to understand more fully why men and women have different rights.
    (D) It helps listeners grasp the consequences of the injustice being forced on disenfranchised women.
    (E) It reflects the double-sided, divisive situation that has inspired the speech.

19. Which of the following best interprets the substance of the third paragraph of the speech (lines 18–30)?

    (A) History shows that voting rights for women is long overdue.
    (B) Without the right to vote, women lack all the customary privileges of citizenship.
    (C) The United States is a democracy in name but not in reality.
    (D) The vast majority of people across the country want women to have the vote.
    (E) The pursuit of happiness is a fundamental principle in a democratic society.

20. The speaker's dominant tone can best be characterized as

    (A) proud and idealistic.
    (B) stubborn and inflexible.
    (C) pompous, yet generally cautious.
    (D) embarrassed and self-righteous.
    (E) angry and resentful.

21. In the context of the passage, all of the following phrases refer to the same idea EXCEPT

    (A) "a lawful right to vote" (line 3).
    (B) "*citizen's rights*" (line 5).
    (C) "*domestic* tranquility" (line 9).
    (D) "the blessings of liberty" (line 10).
    (E) "oligarchy of sex" (line 26).

22. The word "Hence," used at the beginning of the last sentence of the passage (line 35), is meant to indicate that the speaker's conclusion

    (A) is based on deductive reasoning.
    (B) must be assumed to be true.
    (C) cannot be refuted.
    (D) is a universally accepted theory.
    (E) adheres to everyday common sense.

23. Which of the following best characterizes a change in the speaker's main rhetorical strategy in the last paragraph (lines 31–37)?

    (A) She invokes voices of authority to settle the issue.
    (B) She softens her approach with an emotional appeal.
    (C) She relies on logical thinking.
    (D) She tries to enlist the audience's sense of morality.
    (E) She beseeches the audience to use common sense.

> **DIRECTIONS:** *Questions 24–31.* Carefully read the following passage and answer the accompanying questions.

The passage below is a draft of a case study being prepared for a college psychology class.

Passage 3

(1) Basically, Reuben was emotionally flat, completely unresponsive to any and all shows of feeling. (2) While he could speak brilliantly of science and art, when it came to his feelings—even for Amara—he fell silent. (3) Try as Amara might to elicit some passion from
Line him, Reuben was impassive, oblivious. (4) "I don't naturally express my feelings," Reuben
(5) told the therapist he saw at her insistence. (5) When it came to emotional life, he added, "I don't know what to talk about; I have no strong feelings, either positive or negative." (6) Amara was not alone in being frustrated by Reuben's aloofness. (7) As he confided to his therapist, he was unable to speak openly about his feelings with anyone in his life. (8) The reason: He did not know what he felt in the first place. (9) So far as he could tell he had no
(10) anger, no sadness, no joys, colorless.

(10) As his own therapist observes, this emotional blankness makes Reuben and others like him colorless, bland. (11) "They bore everybody. (12) That's why their wives send them into treatment." (13) Reuben's emotional flatness exemplifies what psychiatrists call alexithymia, from the Greek "lack," *lexis* for "word," and *thymos* for "emotion." (14) Such people
(15) lack words for their feelings. (15) Indeed, they seem to lack feelings altogether, although this may actually be because they are verbally challenged rather than from absence of emotion altogether. (16) Such people were first noticed by psychoanalysts puzzled by a class of patients who were untreatable by that method because they reported no feelings, no fantasies, and colorless dreams—in short, no inner emotional life to talk about at all. (17) The
(20) clinical features that mark alexithymics include having difficulty describing feelings—their own or anyone else's—and a sharply limited emotional vocabulary. (18) What's more, they have trouble discriminating among emotions as well as between emotions and bodily sensation, so that they might tell of having butterflies in the stomach, palpitations, sweating, and dizziness—but they would not know they are feeling anxious.

(25) (19) "They give the impression of being different, alien beings, having come from an entirely different world, living in the midst of a society which is dominated by feelings," is the description given by Dr. Godfrey Sullivan, an ex-Harvard psychiatrist who four decades ago coined the term *alexithymia*. (20) Alexithymics rarely cry, for example, but if they do their tears are copious. (21) Still, they are bewildered if asked what their tears are all
(30) about. (22) One patient with alexithymia was so upset after seeing a movie about a woman with eight children who was dying of cancer that she cried herself to sleep. (23) When her therapist suggested that perhaps she was upset because the movie reminded her of her own mother, who was actually dying of cancer, the woman sat motionless, bewildered, and silent. (24) When her therapist then asked her how she felt at the moment, she said she felt
(35) "awful," but couldn't clarify her feelings beyond that. (25) And, she added, from time to time she found herself crying, but never knew exactly what she was crying about.

24. Which of the following explains the rhetorical function of the passage's first sentence?

    (A) It introduces a conflict to be resolved by the end of the passage.
    (B) It defines the limits of the discussion that follows.
    (C) It establishes the author as an expert on the subject of the passage.
    (D) It makes a claim that the writer will try to prove in the remainder of the passage.
    (E) It describes a situation that illustrates the central concern of the passage.

25. Which of the following sentences, if placed before sentence 1, would both capture readers' interest and provide the most effective introduction to the topic of the paragraph?

    (A) A man named Reuben was engaged to be married to a woman named Amara.
    (B) An engaged couple, Reuben and Amara, visited art galleries and museums on Saturday afternoons three or four times a year.
    (C) Reuben infuriated his fiancée, Amara, even though he was intelligent, thoughtful, and successful.
    (D) Amara and Reuben decided to become engaged approximately six months after they met.
    (E) Through an online dating service, Reuben and Amara were brought together.

26. In sentence 15 (reproduced below) which of the following versions of the underscored text best conveys the writer's understanding of the malady?

    Indeed, they seem to lack feelings altogether, although this may actually be because they are verbally challenged rather than from absence of emotion altogether.

    (A) of their resemblance to folks that claim they don't have a knack for foreign languages
    (B) of their inability to express emotion
    (C) they lack the adequacy to reveal their thoughts
    (D) they fear being criticized or laughed at by others
    (E) they are like stutterers who physically can't utter the words

27. In order to highlight the two sides of Reuben's personality discussed in sentence (2), the writer plans to change the beginning of the sentence. Which of the following revisions would be most effective?

    (A) Replace "While" with "Regardless,"
    (B) Replace "While" with "In spite of the fact that . . ."
    (C) Delete "While"
    (D) Replace "While" with "Considering that . . ."
    (E) Replace "While" with "Even though . . ."

28. The writer plans to add the following sentence to the second paragraph (sentences 10–13) in order to provide a more complete portrait of people like Reuben:

    They don't give off vibes that attract friendships, isolating them even more.

    Where would the sentence best fit?

    (A) Before sentence 10
    (B) After sentence 10
    (C) After sentence 11
    (D) After sentence 12
    (E) After sentence 13

29. Which of the following rhetorical strategies employed by the writer of the passage most effectively informs readers about the sociological symptoms of alexithymia?

    (A) The introduction to Reuben and Amara (sentences 1–6)
    (B) Amara's frustrations expressed in sentences 7–9
    (C) The lexicological roots of the word "alexithymia" (sentences 13–15)
    (D) the therapist's description of Reuben's symptoms (sentences 10–18)
    (E) The testimony of Dr. Godfrey Sullivan (sentence 19)

30. Based on the content of sentences 19–25, which sentence or combination of sentences functions as the topic sentence of the third paragraph?

    (A) Sentence 19
    (B) Sentences 20 and 21
    (C) Sentence 24
    (D) Sentences 24 and 25
    (E) None; topic implied by entire paragraph

31. The speaker's central rhetorical method throughout the passage can best be described as

    (A) introducing a series of generalizations that will subsequently be supported.
    (B) citing specific examples to illustrate general concepts.
    (C) a combination of choices (A) and (B).
    (D) making inferences based on logical thinking.
    (E) supporting hypotheses with plausible explanations.

DIRECTIONS: *Questions 32–37.* Carefully read the following passage and answer the accompanying questions.

This passage is adapted from a publication of the National Committee for the Prevention of Child Abuse.

Passage 4

(1) Surveys show that not all children find someone to greet them when they arrive home from school. (2) Do they feel proud, trusted, responsible, independent, and grown up? (3) Or doesn't it matter very much one way or the other?

Line
(5)
(4) One of the most revealing portraits, albeit unscientific, came about as an accidental outcome of a survey by Sprint, a language arts magazine published for fourth- to sixth-grade children by Scholastic, Inc. (5) Readers were invited to respond in writing to this theme: "Think of a situation that is scary to you. (6) How do you handle your fear?" (7) The editors got an overwhelming response—probably more than seven thousand e-mails and text messages, more than 70 percent of them dealing with the fear of being home alone, especially

(10) after school while parents were working. (8) According to the U.S. Bureau of Labor Statistics, 69 percent of two-parent families and 71 percent of single parents report that their work schedule leaves their children in need of supervision after school. (9) In addition, other studies, also, carefully and cautiously carried out, constructed with the greatest quality in mind and fastidious, detailed attention to assure the validity of Sprint's findings.

(15) (10) There are other studies, too, carefully constructed, that bear out the findings suggested in the responses to Sprint. (11) Sociologists Long and Long report that many children in self-care fear attack from intruders and from other children, particularly siblings. (12) Zill's national survey of children is consistent with these findings. (13) Some 32% of the males and 41 percent of the females reported that they worried when they had to stay home

(20) without an adult; 20% of both boys and girls admitted to being afraid to go outside and play. (14) Rodman and his colleagues, however, report no significant difference between children in self-care and children under the care of adults. (15) Rodman's two-year-long studies were done in a medium-size midwestern city with a mixed race population and a number of immigrant families from various places around the world. (16) Rodman contends that stud-

(25) ies reporting more fear among children in self-care lack appropriate comparison groups. (17) Not only that, but researchers are subject to interviewer bias. (18) In other words, they read the studies in ways that twist words in ways that favor their own biases and opinions, and thereby getting the results they wanted to get in the first place. (19) Long and Long claim that their studies have probed more deeply, and that they have done a better job of

(30) establishing a relationship with children in which they can express their fear. (20) Another explanation for the discrepancies is that the level of fear for children in self-care varies from setting to setting, being the greatest for children in urban apartments (the locus of the Longs' research) and least for children whose homes are in safer small towns, rural areas, or close-knit neighborhoods.

(35) (21) Steinberg studied 865 children in grades five, six, and eight in a medium-sized city in Massachusetts. (22) He classified their after-school experience on a continuum from "home with parent, other adult, or older sibling" to "unsupervised hanging out." (23) He found that the less directly supervised the children, the more likely they were to be susceptible to peer pressure—*i.e.*, to conform to peer influence rather than make decisions for themselves.

(40) (24) What is more, children whose parents use an "authoritative" manner rather than an "authoritarian" or "permissive" one are less susceptible to peer influence. (25) *Authoritative* here means parents who ask children for their opinions but maintain ultimate control.

    (26) Analysis of the calls made by children in self-care to telephone support services provide additional clues to their experience. (27) In State College, Pennsylvania, *(45)* "PhoneFriend" provides a case in point. (28) Of the 1,370 calls received during the first year of operation, 60% were classified as "just want to talk" or "bored," while 19% were classified as "lonely" and 15% as "scared," "worried" or "sad or crying." (29) Relatively few dealt with practical emergencies such as cuts and scrapes (4%) or home maintenance problems (3%). (30) Who did the calling? (31) Children seven or younger made up 33% of the calls; another *(50)* 33% were from eight- to nine-year-olds, 17% from ten- to eleven-year-olds and 17% from children twelve and older.

32. If it replaced sentence 1 of the passage, which of the following sentences would both evoke reader interest and provide an effective introduction to the topic of the essay?

    (A) Every weekday afternoon, any number of schoolchildren go home to empty houses and apartments.

    (B) From Monday to Friday, empty houses and apartments await many school kids' arrival home.

    (C) How do children feel when they come home from school to an empty house or apartment?

    (D) On every school day afternoon, untold amounts of young return to homes and apartments where nobody is home to greet them.

    (E) After a day at school, many youngsters go home and spend the rest of the afternoon looking after themselves.

33. For the sake of clarity, the writer wants to revise the underlined portion of sentence 4 (reproduced below). Which version best achieves that goal?

    One of the most revealing portraits, albeit unscientific, <u>came about as an accidental outcome of a survey by Sprint</u>, a language arts magazine published for fourth- to sixth-grade children by Scholastic, Inc.

    (A) (leave as it is)

    (B) by chance happened accidentally as an outcome of Sprint's survey

    (C) was accidentally painted after a survey by Sprint

    (D) occurred by accident after a survey by Sprint

    (E) was accidentally disclosed from a survey by Sprint

34. The writer is considering whether to keep or to delete sentence 8 (reproduced below).

    According to the U.S. Bureau of Labor statistics, 69 percent of two-parent families and 71 percent of single parents report that their work schedule leaves their children in need of supervision after school.

    Which of the following is the best way to proceed?

    (A) Keep because it provides data for the writer to show that Scholastic's survey reveals the existence of a critical nationwide problem.
    (B) Delete because nationwide statistics are irrelevant to readers in the localities where self-care studies were conducted.
    (C) Keep because the information helps the writer to confirm the validity of Scholastic's survey.
    (D) Delete because it diverts attention from the discussion of children's fears and behavior.
    (E) Keep because such important facts are apt to inspire readers to help alleviate the problems being described.

35. Which of the following versions of sentence 9 (reproduced below) most effectively and correctly expresses its meaning?

    In addition, other studies, also, carefully and cautiously carried out, constructed with the greatest quality in mind and fastidious, detailed attention to assure the validity of Sprint's findings.

    (A) Additional studies, carried out with careful, fastidious attention to detail.
    (B) In addition, high quality, carefully constructed, and detailed attention, such studies also confirm Sprint's findings.
    (C) Other studies, constructed fastidiously to assure high quality. They confirm Sprint's findings because they paid great and fastidious attention to details.
    (D) Other studies, constructed fastidiously to assure high quality, confirm the validity of Sprint's findings.
    (E) Sprint's findings, assured by additional studies that are of high validity and were fastidiously and carefully made in order to be sure that they are valid.

36. The writer is thinking about reducing the word count of the passage by editing the underlined section of sentences 16–18, reproduced below.

> *Rodman contends that studies reporting more fear among children in self-care lack appropriate comparison groups. Not only that, but researchers are subject to interviewer bias. In other words, they read the studies in ways that twist words in ways that favor their own biases and opinions, and thereby getting the results they wanted to get in the first place.*

Which version best achieves this goal without significantly altering meaning or ignoring standard written English?

(A) studies, in addition, interviewers, in order to assure their desired outcomes, are subject to purposely maintaining their pre-conceived biases

(B) groups. Not only that, but researchers, known to have been subject to interviewer bias, conducted studies that twisted words in their favor and thereby had gotten the results they desire in the first place

(C) groups, needed to avoid interviewer bias and to prevent researchers from reaching pre-conceived conclusions

(D) groups. What's more, researchers subject to interview bias—in other words, reading studies in ways that twist words favorable to their opinions, enabling them to achieve their desired results

(E) groups that are essential for the purpose of making sure that researchers, who are often influenced by their own pre-conceived biases and opinions, don't skew the results in their own favor in a biased way

37. In order to provide additional information, the writer wants to add the following sentence to the paragraph that begins with sentence 26.

> *Some callers asked for help with math or other homework.*

Where would this sentence best be added?

(A) Before sentence 27

(B) After sentence 27

(C) After sentence 28

(D) After sentence 29

(E) After sentence 30

DIRECTIONS: *Questions 38–45.* Carefully read the following passage and answer the accompanying questions.

What follows is an excerpt from a draft of a book review to be published in a journal for personnel of the CIA in 2002.

Passage 5

(1) In a robust democracy like the United States, public channels of information such as newspapers and television are more or less exempt from government restrictions. (2) But during wartime, controlling the public's access to information becomes a difficult and con-
Line troversial proposition, much more than a simple constitutional or legal issue. (3) Domestic
(5) morale and support for wartime policies depend heavily on an informed public. (4) If citizens are denied access to reasonable amounts of information, or, worse, if they are deceived about policies and events, all hell will break loose. (5) During wartime guarding classified information sought by our adversaries, networks of enemy spies tirelessly hack top-secret information. (6) The current war on terrorism is no different. (7) Information once consid-
(10) ered innocuous—such as structural data for stadiums, bridges, and public works—is now considered to have intelligence value for terrorists. (8) But how can such information be controlled? (9) Who manages public information? (10) What kinds of information need to be protected? (11) Who enforces restrictions? (12) What is the relationship between censorship, intelligence, security, and propaganda?
(15)   (13) During World War II, President Roosevelt had the power to control information given to the media. (14) Legislation had been passed in 1938 that forbade unauthorized photographs, sketches, or maps of military bases. (15) It also gave the President the authority to define which types of military information needed security protection. (16) The President was reluctant to exercise these authorities. (17) He recalled the overzealous
(20) application of espionage laws during World War I. (18) He recalled many hundreds of people were jailed. (19) He recalled they were socialists and pacifists that criticized President Wilson for war profiteering, and anti-German violence. (20) Believing that it was critical for Americans to receive news about the war, he set two conditions for the media: their stories must be accurate and they could not help the enemy.
(25)   (21) To oversee the nation's censorship activity, Roosevelt set up an Office of Censorship and asked Byron Price, head of the Associated Press, to head it. (22) The supervision staff was responsible for overseeing censorship, however less concerned with the amount of cases of censorship than whether they were done right. Price put the onus for censorship directly on the journalists. (23) His methods were to nudge and talk them into compliance
(30) under his motto: "Least said, soonest mended." (24) He also delegated release of information to "appropriate authorities," meaning that those directly involved—from combat commanders to government department heads—decided what information about their activities could be made public. (25) This kept Price's office out of numerous controversies. (26) A case in point was the famous episode in which Gen. George Patton slapped a soldier
(35) suffering from battle fatigue. (27) Newsmen filed requests to print the story. (28) General Dwight Eisenhower, the Supreme Allied Commander, gave his approval.
(29) Price worked hard to keep the system voluntary and to solve the problem of finding a proper balance between wartime secrecy and the public's right to know. (30) In general, the system worked. (31) Self-censorship created a supportive culture among reporters

(40)   and editors. (32) Price beat off an attempt by the Military Intelligence Division of the War Department to enforce stronger censorship of information about the military. (33) A rumor at the *Chicago Tribune* alleged that America had broken the Japanese war code. (34) The Navy jumped to the conclusion that certain information in a news article came from classified documents. (35) In fact, a *Tribune* reporter had seen a copy of a message from Admiral

(45)   Nimitz [the American fleet's commander] carelessly listing the Japanese ships that were part of the task force set to attack Midway Island in the Pacific.

(36) Price convinced the newspaper editors to squelch the story in order to keep the Japanese from discovering that we had broken their secret code. (37) Censors also restricted photographs of the President and information about his whereabouts. (38) During the 1944

(50)   election campaign, these restrictions allowed him to hide the fact that he had polio and was confined to a wheelchair. (39) Censorship also allowed him to cover up his affair with an old friend Lucy Rutherford. (40) But if there was any mistake by the censorship authorities, it probably came near the end of the war. (41) Military intelligence, with initial agreement from the Office of Censorship, refused to release information to the public about Japanese

(55)   balloon-born bombs that were carried over the American northwest by prevailing winds. (42) The intention was to keep Tokyo in the dark about the effectiveness of the balloon "attacks." (43) Price subsequently asked for at least a partial release of information on the potential danger of the balloon bombs. (44) However, the Navy refused. (45) The news clampdown, a rare shortsighted blunder, may have contributed to some of the few casual-

(60)   ties that the bombs caused.

38.   In sentence 4 (reproduced below) the writer wants to substitute text that will serve as an effective transition between sentences and will preserve the tone of sentences 1–3.

> *If citizens are denied access to reasonable amounts of information, or, worse, if they are deceived about policies and events,* <u>*all hell will break loose*</u>*.*

Which of the following versions of the underlined text best achieves this goal?

(A) (keep it as it is)

(B) they will file a million lawsuits screaming for new elections

(C) their support can turn to opposition

(D) there is an insistence likely to shut down the government

(E) (delete the underlined text)

39. The writer is thinking about revising the underlined section of sentence 5 (reproduced below) for clarity and correctness.

    > During war time, guarding classified information _sought by our adversaries, networks of_
    > _enemy spies tirelessly hack top-secret information._

    In which version of sentence 5 is that goal most evident?

    (A) networks of enemy spies tirelessly hacking top-secret information.
    (B) sought by a network of enemy spies must be a priority of the homeland security personnel.
    (C) sought by our adversaries through a network of enemy spies that must become a priority of homeland security personnel.
    (D) being sought by our adversaries, must become a priority of homeland security personnel.
    (E) to keep it from our enemy spy adversaries, is a necessary priority of homeland security personnel.

40. In sentences 8–12, the writer asks several questions for all the following reasons EXCEPT

    (A) to name issues of importance to the intelligence wing of the government.
    (B) to provide a preview of what is likely to be covered in the remainder of the passage.
    (C) to assert that previous wars are not far different from the war on terror.
    (D) to urge readers to ask questions of government officials.
    (E) to promote the need for government control of information.

41. For the sake of coherence, the writer wants to add an appropriate link between sentences 15 and 16, reproduced below.

    > _(15) It also gave the President the authority to define which types of military information_
    > _needed security protection. (16) The President was reluctant to exercise these authorities._

    In which version is that goal achieved most effectively?

    (A) (15) It also gave the President the authority to define which types of military information needed security protection. (16) The President, as a matter of fact, was reluctant to exercise these authorities.
    (B) Although it also gave the President the authority to define which types of military information needed security protection, protection that the President was reluctant to exercise.
    (C) (15) It also gave the President the authority to define which types of military information needed security protection. (16) The President was reluctant, on the other hand, to exercise these authorities.
    (D) (15) It also gave the President the authority to define which types of military information needed security protection. (16) The President, however, was reluctant to exercise these authorities.
    (E) It also gave the President the authority to define which types of military information needed security protection; however he was reluctant to exercise these authorities.

42. The writer wants to revise sentence 22 (reproduced below) in order to state its idea in standard English without changing the meaning.

    The supervision staff was responsible for overseeing censorship, however less concerned with the amount of cases of censorship than whether they were done right.

    Which version best accomplishes this goal?

    (A) Less concerned with the amount of cases of censorship than whether they were done right, the supervision staff was responsible for overseeing censorship.
    (B) The supervision staff, responsible for overseeing censorship, were less concerned with the amount of cases than whether they did them correctly.
    (C) The supervisory staff responsible for overseeing censorship were less concerned about the amount of cases of censorship than if they were done right.
    (D) The supervisory staff was responsible for overseeing censorship but less concerned with the number of cases than whether they had been done right.
    (E) The members of supervision staff responsible for overseeing censorship were less concerned with the amount of cases of censorship than if they were flawlessly corrected.

43. While proofreading this draft of the passage, the writer decided to reduce wordiness and repetition in sentences 17–19 (reproduced below).

    (17) He recalled the overzealous application of espionage laws during World War I. (18) He recalled many hundreds of people were jailed. (19) He recalled they were socialists and pacifists that criticized President Wilson for war profiteering, and anti-German violence.

    Which revision of the text best accomplishes this goal?

    (A) He recalled the overzealous application of espionage laws during World War I, which led to the jailing of hundreds of socialists and pacifists for criticizing President Wilson's war profiteering and anti-German violence.
    (B) He recalled the overzealous application of espionage laws during World War I, and he remembers the many hundreds of socialists and pacifists who were jailed. In his remembrance they've been criticizing President Wilson, accusing him of war profiteering, and anti-German violence.
    (C) He recalled the overzealously executed espionage laws passed during World War I, the results of which sent many hundreds of people to jail, mostly socialists and pacifists, and imprisoned because they were critical of President Wilson for both war profiteering and anti-German violence.
    (D) He recalled anti-espionage laws that were passed during World War I against many hundreds of socialists and pacifists. They were overzealously applied and resulted in a large amount of people having been sent to jail. Those people were found guilty, based on their criticizing President Wilson for war profiteering, and anti-German violence.
    (E) He recalled World War I's overzealous and excessive enforcement of espionage laws being applied to many hundreds of socialists and pacifists who having been found guilty and sent to jail because of criticizing President Wilson for war profiteering, and anti-German violence.

44. The writer is thinking about relocating sentence 30 (reproduced below) to a place where it would best contribute to the coherence of the passage.

    In general, the system worked.

    Where would the sentence best be placed?

    (A) (keep it where it is)
    (B) After sentence 31
    (C) After sentence 32
    (D) After sentence 34
    (E) After sentence 36

45. In sentence 45 (reproduced below) which of the following versions of the underlined text best establishes the writer's position on the main argument of the passage?

    The news clampdown, <u>a rare, shortsighted blunder</u>, may have contributed to some of the few casualties that the bombs caused.

    (A) (as it is now)
    (B) an egregious violation of freedom of the press
    (C) which fomented considerable controversy during the war
    (D) one of the most heinous abuses of government power
    (E) a policy embraced by the American people

Section II

Three Essay Questions

TIME: 2 HOURS AND 15 MINUTES

Write your essays on standard 8½″ × 11″ composition paper. At the exam you will be given a bound booklet containing 12 lined pages.

Essay Question 1

SUGGESTED TIME:

15 MINUTES FOR READING THE QUESTION AND SOURCES

40 MINUTES FOR WRITING AN ESSAY

Because an educated population generally enjoys levels of prosperity, culture, and well-being unavailable to many individuals who don't continue their education after high school, some people argue that all students, regardless of their ability to pay, should go to college—or at least be pushed hard in that direction.

Carefully read the following six sources, including the material that introduces each source. Then, in an essay that synthesizes at least three of the sources, take a position on the claim that all students should attend college.

Source A (Hansen)

Source B (Kurtzman)

Source C (Banya)

Source D (Herbig)

Source E (Toppo and DeBarros)

Source F (Rob)

Instructions:
- Respond to the prompt with a thesis that may establish a line of reasoning.
- Provide evidence from at least three of the provided sources to support the thesis. Indicate clearly the sources used through direct quotation, paraphrase, or summary. Sources may be cited as Source A, Source B, etc., or by using the descriptions in parentheses.
- Explain the relationship between the evidence and the thesis.
- Demonstrate an understanding of the rhetorical situation.
- Use appropriate grammar and punctuation in communicating the argument.

Source A

Katherine Hansen, "What Good Is a College Education Anyway?" Quintessential Careers, *www. quintcareers.com*. Accessed August 7, 2006.

The following passage is excerpted from an online article describing the value of a college education, and was written by an authority on career management.

Research shows that children of college-educated parents are healthier, perform better academically, and are more likely to attend college themselves than children of those with lower educational attainment.

Your education builds a foundation for your children—for our nation's children, and for the children of our global community—which leads to the last point: Education is the cornerstone of public progress.

Education is the essence of the democratic ideals that have elevated the United States from a backward land of rebellious colonists to the greatest, most spirited, powerful and successful nation in the world.

. . . And the relationship between a college education and success will become more and more significant in our information-driven global economy. Higher education will be increasingly important for landing high-paying jobs. Technology and the information age are not the only reasons to be well educated; the trend is toward multiple jobs and even multiple careers, and higher education prepares you to make the transition to new fields.

So what more could you ask of your investment in higher education than prosperity, quality of life, the knowledge that bolsters social change, a legacy for your children, and the means to ensure the continuing success of the American dream?

Source B

Lori Kurtzman, "Remedial Classes Teach Freshmen What They Should Already Know," *The Cincinnati Enquirer*, July 30, 2006.

Of the thousands of freshmen entering Ohio colleges and universities this fall, it's a safe bet that more than one-third won't be completely ready for the next level of their education. Recent figures show that 41 percent of newly minted Ohio high school graduates who went to Ohio public colleges enrolled in remedial math or reading courses during their freshman year . . . .

. . . So why be concerned over some students playing a little bit of catch-up? Education experts say this isn't just about a student taking a few extra classes. Remediation, which often affects minorities from poor families in low-income public districts, has an impact that stretches from families to schools to taxpayers.

Remedial needs strain the student, who might pay hundreds or thousands of dollars for classes that don't count toward a degree.

. . . They strain colleges, too, which devote instructors, classrooms and supplies to classes that ideally wouldn't be necessary.

And they strain the state—in essence, taxpayers—to the tune of about $30 million a year in remedial costs . . . .

But perhaps the greatest problem is what so often happens to students who require remediation: They struggle. They fail. They drop out. They lose the earning power of a college degree. The state tracked a group of students for six years and found that among the remedial students, only 15 percent earned a bachelor's degree in that time; nearly three times as many nonremedial students received their degrees . . . .

Source C

The following excerpt comes from "College Education Provides Intangibles to Student, Society," by Dr. Kingsley Banya, Chair of Department of Teacher Education at Misericordia University, *Education News*, September 2011.

Why is a college education important?

At face value, that appears to be a simple question to answer. More opportunities, better job security and advanced critical-thinking skills are just a few of the advantages college graduates enjoy. One of the major benefits of the college experience is the intangible impact college-educated individuals have in our society. Cultural enrichment that occurs from interacting with individuals from all over the world is immeasurable. In today's multicultural and complex world, understanding the cultures of other nations and individuals is invaluable. Many of society's prejudices and stereotypes come from the lack of understanding of other cultures and how that impacts behavior at global, national, and individual levels.

The appreciation of a work of art, a painting and, yes, a piece of music is a byproduct of culture. College endeavors to teach students to appreciate these cultural artifacts in addition to whatever field of study a student may be interested in studying. Higher education also imbues students with a sense of service to others. Indeed, many academic classes have service-learning components to them. Graduates often say that their introduction to new cultures was the highlight of their college experience and has prepared them to contribute to society in a myriad of positive ways. One cannot put a price tag on such learning.

Many such people, having left college as cultured individuals, will eventually work for non-governmental organizations and community agencies because they take pride in helping others less fortunate in society. They are more likely to vote and participate in civic society, and for many of them, the environment will become a major concern.

Another aspect of the intangible impact of a college education is the camaraderie among students that is promoted through sports, club activities, and other related outlets. Many residential colleges have athletic complexes and special activities for students that teach the value of teamwork, healthy living, and leadership. These opportunities contribute to making society more productive, help to reduce health care costs, and also produce more well-rounded individuals.

The concept of lifelong learning that society is promoting is best exemplified in a collegiate setting. The chances are that a good number of college graduates will continue to want to learn during their lifetime. Having been exposed to the joy and beauty of learning and the possibilities that follow, college graduates will not be content with their current knowledge and skill set. More and more people are returning to college—not necessarily to get a degree—but to learn new skills and improve on their hobbies or interests, be it painting or their appreciation of music. These are byproducts of a college education that cannot be easily quantified financially.

Source D

The graph below appeared in *The Quick and the Ed*, an online publication of the Education Sector of the American Institute for Research, August 2011.

Survey conducted by Shawn Herbig, IQS Research, among residents of Louisville, Kentucky, 2010.

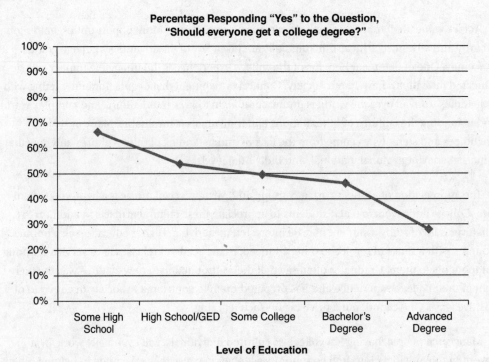

Percentage Responding "Yes" to the Question, "Should everyone get a college degree?"

Level of Education

Source: *Community Perceptions of Higher Education: How Does Greater Louisville Perceive the Value of Higher Education?* (Louisville, KY: IQS Research, 2010).

Source E

Gregg Toppo and Anthony DeBarros, "Reality Weighs Down Dreams of College," *USA Today*, posted online February 2, 2005.

What follows is part of a newspaper article that describes the trend toward increased college enrollment.

New research reveals a huge gap between aspirations and reality, especially for poor and minority students. For them, high school dropout rates remain high and college graduation rates low.

. . . Recent studies also show that many low-income and minority students who aspire to college are poorly served by their schools and their families, arriving at college unprepared and forcing colleges and universities to spend an estimated $1 billion a year on remediation.

"There is a real gap between the aspirations teenagers have and the realities of what happens to them," says Christopher Swanson of the Urban Institute, a think tank in Washington, D.C. "Teenagers grow up hearing these 'college for all' expectations, and they internalize this. While rhetorically it makes sense, in reality all students are not going to go to college."

". . . We're not being honest with a lot of kids today," says Thomas Toch, author of *High Schools on a Human Scale*. "We're telling kids that they can do it, when we're not giving them the academic tools to be successful. We're not giving them an education that will truly prepare them to be successful in college."

Nudged by economic trends showing manufacturing, farming and other blue-collar jobs disappearing or being shipped overseas, public schools are telling students—even low-income and underperforming students—that they need college degrees.

Source F

"Rob," Declining College Standards, "Say Anything," an online blog, posted January 3, 2006.

In the following passage, a blogger identified as "Rob" makes observations about what it means to go to college.

I can't speak for other places in this country, but my experience in my community during my post high-school days (which weren't just a few years ago) was one where college was "just something you do" after high school. Kids who didn't plan to go to college were considered "lazy" or "unambitious," while those who did go to college usually didn't even know what they wanted to do with their careers. I often wondered if a lot of the kids who decided to hold off on college weren't making the wiser decision. After all, drifting through a couple of years of classes with no real career direction was a good way to waste many thousands of dollars.

But not a lot of kids do this, mostly because I think kids go off to college seeking the "college experience" rather than a real education for a specific career. They go off looking for the frat parties, sporting events, campus life and activism, all of which is commonly associated with higher education. What many of them don't understand is that while all that stuff has its place it doesn't exactly translate into a lot of intellectual capital for the business market. I don't know how many acquaintances of mine have graduated from college with a "business" or "criminal justice" degree and absolutely no idea how to get a job with it. Most of them end up starting on the bottom rung of some company, about where they would have started without a degree, only now with a degree and thousands of dollars of debt.

Essay Question 2

SUGGESTED TIME: 40 MINUTES

(This question counts as one-third of the total score for Section II.)

The passage below, adapted from an essay written in 1920 by A. A. Milne, is a mock-serious reflection on the passing of summer. Read it carefully. Then, in a well-written essay, analyze how the rhetorical strategies that Milne uses reveal the speaker's personality and values.

Instructions:
- Respond to the prompt with a thesis that may establish a line of reasoning.
- Select and use evidence to develop and support the line of reasoning.
- Explain the relationship between the evidence and the thesis.
- Demonstrate an understanding of the rhetorical situation.
- Use appropriate grammar and punctuation in communicating the argument.

Last night the waiter put the celery on with the cheese, and I knew that summer was indeed dead. Other signs of autumn there may be—the reddening of the leaf, the chill in the early-morning air, the misty evenings—but none of these comes home to me so truly. There

Line may be cool mornings in July; in a year of drought the leaves may change before their time;
(5) it is only with the first celery that summer is over. . . .

There is a crispness about celery that is the essence of October. It is as fresh and clean as a rainy day after a spell of heat. It crackles pleasantly in the mouth. Moreover, it is excellent, I am told, for the complexion. One is always hearing of things which are good for the complexion, but there is no doubt that celery stands high on the list. After the burns and

(10) freckles of summer one is in need of something. How good that celery should be there at one's elbow. . . .

"Season of mists and mellow fruitfulness," said Keats, not actually picking out celery in so many words, but plainly including it in the general blessings of autumn. Yet, what an opportunity he missed by not concentrating on that precious root. Apples, grapes, and nuts

(15) he mentions specially—how poor a selection! For apples and grapes are not typical of any month, so ubiquitous are they, while as for nuts, have we not a national song which asserts distinctly, "Here we go gathering nuts in May"? Season of mists and mellow celery, then let it be. A pat of butter underneath the bough, a wedge of cheese, a loaf of bread and—Thou.

How delicate are the tender shoots that unfold layer by layer. Of what a whiteness is the

(20) last baby one of all, of what a sweetness his flavor. It is well that this should be the last rite of the meal so that we may go straight on to the business of the pipe. Celery demands a pipe rather than a cigar, and it can be eaten better in an inn or a London tavern than in the home.

Yes, and it should be eaten alone, for it is the only food which one really wants to hear oneself eat. Besides, in company one may have to consider the wants of others. Celery is

(25) not a thing to share with any man. Alone in your country inn you may call for celery; but if you are wise you will see that no other traveler wanders into the room. Take warning from one who has learnt a lesson. One day I lunched alone at an inn, finishing with cheese and celery. Another traveler came in and lunched too. We did not speak—I was busy with my celery. From the other end of the table he reached across for the cheese. That was all right!

(30) It was the public cheese. But he also reached across for the celery—my private celery for which I owed. Foolishly—you know how one does—I had left the sweetest and crispest shoots till the last, tantalizing myself pleasantly with the thought of them. Horror! To see them snatched from me by a stranger. He realized later what he had done and apologized, but of what good is an apology under such circumstances? Yet at least the tragedy was not

(35) without its value. Now one remembers to lock the door.

I can face the winter with calm. I suppose I had forgotten what it was really like. I had been thinking of the winter as a horrid, wet, dreary time fit only for professional football. Now I can see other things—crisp and sparkling days, long pleasant evenings, cheery fires. Good work shall be done this winter. Life shall be lived well. The end of the summer is not

(40) the end of the world. Here's to October—and, waiter, some more celery.

Essay Question 3

SUGGESTED TIME: 40 MINUTES

(This question counts as one-third of the total score for Section II.)

> The paragraph below comments on the issue of second chances. After reading it, write a well-organized essay that develops your position on the phenomenon of giving people second chances. Use appropriate evidence from your reading, experience, or observations to support your argument.
>
> **Instructions:**
> - Respond to the prompt with a thesis that may establish a line of reasoning.
> - Select and use evidence to develop and support the line of reasoning.
> - Explain the relationship between the evidence and the thesis.
> - Demonstrate an understanding of the rhetorical situation.
> - Use appropriate grammar and punctuation in communicating the argument.

At one time or other, we all do or say things that we regret and would like to do over or take back. Most of the time we must live with our mistakes, but sometimes, we get a second chance. Some people take a dim view of second chances, claiming that second chances

Line   not only foster irresponsible behavior but also weaken our character. Others see value in

(5) second chances. They say that second chances help us learn and permit us to take intellectual, creative, and other kinds of risks instead of always playing it safe. In your opinion, are second chances desirable, or not?

ANSWER KEY
Diagnostic Test

Answers to Multiple-Choice Questions

1.	C	13.	C	25.	C	37.	D
2.	B	14.	B	26.	B	38.	C
3.	D	15.	D	27.	A	39.	B
4.	E	16.	A	28.	B	40.	D
5.	A	17.	B	29.	E	41.	D
6.	C	18.	E	30.	A	42.	D
7.	E	19.	C	31.	C	43.	A
8.	B	20.	E	32.	C	44.	A
9.	D	21.	E	33.	A	45.	A
10.	E	22.	A	34.	D		
11.	B	23.	C	35.	D		
12.	B	24.	E	36.	C		

Summary of Answers in Section I (Multiple-Choice)

Number of correct answers _____

Use this information when you calculate your score for this exam. See page 84.

Answer Explanations to Multiple-Choice Questions

Passage 1—An excerpt from Richard Maxwell Brown, "Historical Patterns of Violence in America"

1. **(C)** To answer the question, you must read at least through the second paragraph, which asserts that the robbery was notable for the reaction it produced in the local newspaper.

2. **(B)** Other choices, such as (C) and (E), are mentioned further on, but they don't qualify as the main purpose.

3. **(D)** All the choices contribute something to the rhetorical impact of the sentence, but structuring a sentence by juxtaposing a negative against a positive is a popular and effective rhetorical device.

4. **(E)** The word "respectable" has a double meaning: proper in the sense of behavior as well as sizable in terms of the number of people. Although both definitions seem to apply, the author is most troubled by the first definition. When respectable people compare the bandits to courageous knights, the author is troubled.

5. **(A)** The phrase refers to the shooting of a little girl, an action that can hardly be called courageous.

6. **(C)** The quotation exemplifies a mentality prevalent in parts of America—a way of thinking that, as the author goes on to explain, originated on the frontier. (A) is irrelevant in the context. (B) is not accurate, because the author specifically denies in lines 25–26 that he is out to "belabor one reasonably anonymous newspaper man"—i.e., Edwards. (D) doesn't apply in the context. (E) has some merit because the author discusses frontier mentality in the next paragraph, but in the context (E) does not accurately describe the author's purpose.

7. **(E)** The author reflects on the values and spirit of the frontier to explain why the press had not excoriated the bandits. The reason: Although their actions were heinous, they still represented the frontier, which at the time of the incident (1872) still existed in some form or another.

8. **(B)** All the other choices are traits suggesting mindless derring-do and recklessness.

9. **(D)** The phrase "creative plundering" describes an action that most clearly exemplifies "independent action and self-reliance." (A) names two infamous outlaws who did not represent frontier values. (B) and (C) represent values contrary to "independent action," etc. (E) describes the frontier's movement, not a characteristic of frontier life.

10. **(E)** The writer's intent is to stress that frontier people were heroes of legendary "imagination and daring" (line 41).

11. **(B)** Courage, adventure, and enduring hardship dominate memories of the frontier. Such a view fails to take into account an alternate truth—that the frontier teemed with violence.

12. **(B)** The writer, devoting much of the passage to analyzing the robbery's aftermath, assigns responsibility for the public's response to an overly romantic fascination with the life and people of the frontier.

Passage 2—A speech by Susan B. Anthony

13. **(C)** In one way or another, all the choices have some validity. The speaker's fighting spirit and the issues she raises indicate, however, that she had no purpose other than to convince the audience that women have the right to vote. Getting right to the point enabled her to quickly build an increasingly compelling case.

14. **(B)** All the other choices may be implied by the passage, but (B) is supported by the sentence that follows (line 12): "It was we, the people, not we, the white male citizens . . . , etc." In short, the speaker points out the disconnect between the inspiring, idealistic words of the Constitution and reality.

15. **(D)** Voting rights are a sacred be-all and end-all for the speaker.

16. **(A)** An antithesis sets up an opposition or contrast of ideas. This paragraph is dominated by contrasts between conditions as they exist and conditions as they should be, according to the Constitution. (B) is a tempting answer because the paragraph alludes to the language of the Constitution, but by no means are the allusions abstract. (C) does not apply. If anything, the language in the paragraph is direct and down-to-earth. (D) is not in the speaker's repertoire—just the opposite, in fact, because she describes the unjust treatment of women in vivid terms. (E) is not a good answer, because the speaker's words should be taken literally.

17. **(B)** Both are legal terms likely to be anathema to freedom-loving people. Almost certainly, they would trigger an emotional response in the audience.

18. **(E)** The repetitive words and phrases heighten the passion that the speaker brings to the issue. The major conceit throughout the passage is a contrast and comparison of the voting rights of women and men.

19. **(C)** The passage is full of strong language that reflects the speaker's bitterness about women's being deprived of their rights. Without these rights, the government is a "hateful oligarchy" that sows discord throughout the land.

20. **(E)** The speech from start to finish reveals Susan B. Anthony's indignation about women's disenfranchisement.

21. **(E)** Only (E) refers to an undesirable characteristic—i.e., total control in the hands of one gender over all others.

22. **(A)** "Hence" is often used as a synonym for "therefore," suggesting that a conclusion has been determined by logical thinking, in this case deductive reasoning—i.e., basing a conclusion on one or more pieces of evidence.

23. **(C)** In general, the speech is a passionate position statement. For effect, at the end the speaker turns to logic. Therefore, the entire paragraph is structured as a syllogism to prove that women should have the right to vote; i.e., a citizen is a person who has the right to vote; a woman is a person; therefore, she has the right to vote. Case closed!

Passage 3—Adapted from Daniel Goleman, *Emotional Intelligence.* © 1996

24. **(E)** The opening sentence introduces a person with a problem: the inability to express emotion. That is the main concern of the passage. (A) introduces a transitional word that doesn't

fit the context. (B), (C), and (D) name functions often performed by introductory sentences, but they don't apply here.

25. **(C)** All the other choices are innocuous statements about an engaged couple. But (C) is different because its verb, *infuriated*, is unusual in the context and is apt to raise a reader's curiosity about the couple's relationship. Even more to the point, it serves as an appropriate prelude to the main subject of the passage, namely Reuben's affliction.

26. **(B)** Choice (A) refers to a kind of learning problem rather than an emotional barrier. In addition, the use of "folks" is not in keeping with the tone of the passage. (C) relates to thinking rather than feeling. (D) raises an issue beyond the scope of the passage, and (E) pertains to a physical handicap rather than an emotional one.

27. **(A)** is the best choice. (B) doesn't change the meaning but is wordy. (C) creates a run-on sentence. (D) converts a grammatical sentence into nonsense. (E) is repetitious; see sentence 1 of the passage.

28. **(B)** The given sentence both amplifies the description and supports the notion of a "colorless" and "bland" personality. (C) is a reasonable choice, but it would weaken the connection of ideas between sentences 12 and 13.

29. **(E)** Dr. Sullivan's take on alexithymia is that, because its potency increases in a society "dominated by feelings," victims suffer isolation more acutely.

30. **(A)** The quotation presents the paragraph's main idea. The remaining sentences support Dr. Sullivan's observation.

31. **(C)** The passage begins with an account of Amara and Reuben, whose story leads to a clinical explanation of alexithymia. Afterward, the speaker reverses presentation by describing a specific individual who manifests the symptoms of the condition.

Passage 4—Adapted from Peter Coolsen, "When School's Out and Nobody's Home"

32. **(C)** This is the best answer, first, because it asks a provocative question for readers to ponder, and also because the next two sentences ask related questions that presumably will be discussed in the passage.

33. **(A)** Not the perfect answer, because in standard English portraits usually don't "come about," (A) is nevertheless the best choice. (B) contains a redundancy: "by chance" and "accidentally." (C) eliminates the verb, thereby turning the locution into a sentence fragment. (D) In standard English, portraits don't "occur." (E) In standard English usage, the preposition "by" should replace "from."

34. **(D)** Unless the writer adds some unifying transitional ideas or phrases, the sentence weakens the overall coherence of the passage. The other choices may have validity, but they do little to improve the passage.

35. **(D)** Choice (D) avoids all the defects found in the other sentences: incomplete construction in (A), (C), (E); redundancies in (A), (B), (C), (E); repetition in (C), (E); mixed sentence construction in (B); pronoun reference problems in (C); and others.

36. **(C)** Choice (A) is more economical than the original. It distorts the meaning, however, by claiming that researchers "purposely" participate in interviewer bias. It also contains a comma splice. (B) captures the basic meaning of the original, but the sentence is marred by an incorrect shift in verb tense. (D) contains a sentence fragment, and (E) has more words than it needs to express the idea.

37. **(D)** Sentence 29 introduces a "problems" category into which math homework fits comfortably for many pre-teens.

Passage 5—Adapted from Robert J. Hanyok, "Study of Intelligence," *Journal of American Intelligence Professional*

38. **(C)** Choice (A) fails to maintain the restrained tone of the passage. (B) contains faulty modification. (D) contains awkward usage that interferes with meaning. (E) leaves behind an incomplete sentence.

39. **(B)** Choice (A) contains a dangling participle. The construction that begins with *guarding classified information* must modify a noun that performs the action. (C), which lacks a grammatical verb, is a sentence fragment. (D) contains faulty punctuation that obscures the intended meaning. (E) contains redundancies.

40. **(D)** A list of questions such as this could have multiple purposes. Considering the content of the passage thus far, (D) is incongruent with the thrust of the passage.

41. **(D)** In the context, the phrases inserted in both (A) and (C) are inappropriate. In (B), a choice that conveys the gist of the original sentences, the grammatical subject *It* lacks a verb. (E) ignores standard punctuation.

42. **(D)** In choice (A), by moving the grammatical subject, the writer has changed the emphasis—and, therefore, the meaning—of the sentence. (B) and (C) incorrectly use "amount" instead of "number"—a diction error. Choice (C), like (E), needlessly repeats the word "censorship."

43. **(A)** Although some repetition has been reduced or eliminated, other problems appear—(B): awkwardness of expression, inconsistent verb tense; (C): redundancy; (D): diction error ("amount" instead of "number"), shift in verb tense; (E): incomplete sentence.

44. **(A)** In its present location sentence 30 supports the previous sentences and also introduces several other examples of the system's success.

45. **(A)** As stated, it provides an honest appraisal of the program: mistakes were made, but overall it helped the American war efforts. None of the other choices accurately describes the clampdown.

Answers to Essay Questions

For an overview of how essays are graded, turn to "How Essays Are Read and Evaluated," page 37.

Although answers to the essay questions will vary greatly, the following descriptions suggest a possible approach to each question and contain ideas that could be used in a response to the question. Perhaps your essay contains many of the same ideas. If not, don't be alarmed. Your ideas may be at least as insightful, or even more so, as those below.

Essay Question 1, Based on the Topic: "College for All"

As an AP student on the verge of college, you're likely to hold some strong views on the issue of college for all. Your opinions can serve as the core of your essay, but the sources offer a number of ideas on both sides of the question that you may not have considered before.

Arguments in favor of college for all may include:

- Education is the key to progress and prosperity. (Source A)
- Education is the essence of democracy; it gives everyone an equal chance to succeed. (Source A)
- Investment in education has long-lasting personal and financial benefits. (Source A)
- Graduates' understanding of other cultures helps them to contribute to society in countless ways. (Source C)
- People lacking a college degree know how hard it is to find good jobs. (Source D)
  Note: This is one interpretation of the graph in Source D. See below for another view.
- A college degree is necessary for jobs that formerly required less education. (Source E)

Arguments against college for all may include:

- Many students are not academically prepared for college work. (Source B)
- The cost of remedial work for unprepared students strains resources. (Source B)
- The drop-out rate for remedial students is very high. (Source B)
- Many people with college and graduate degrees doubt the true value of a degree in an uncertain economy. (Source D)
  Note: This is one interpretation of the graph in Source D. See above for another view.
- Many graduates find themselves working in jobs that don't require a college degree. (Source F)
- Students with unreal aspirations are doomed to be disappointed and disillusioned by the reality of college. (Source E)

Essay Question 2, Based on "A Word for Autumn" by A. A. Milne

Most readers are likely to find Milne's mock-serious essay witty, lighthearted, and urbane—not to be taken seriously. Some, however, may legitimately see a solemn purpose behind Milne's musings on celery. Both responses are valid, provided that readers can support their views with evidence from the passage.

Those in the first group might immediately point out that assigning significance of any kind to something as inconsequential as celery is just plain silly. Yes, silly it is, and that is just the point. Milne is out to entertain his readers by playing with a ridiculous idea, exaggerating the importance of celery beyond all reason: Celery marks the change of seasons, it enhances the complexion, it is an excellent end to a meal, and it is a prelude to smoking a pipe rather than a cigar.

What sort of person would actually put such ideas on paper? Well, the sort that is the speaker in the passage. Presumably, he is a man of independent means who dines out a lot and takes himself to be a gentleman. He is cultured enough to quote Keats, but he seems to take no interest in the affairs of the world. His main concerns are being comfortable, feeling good, enjoying the benefits of his station in life, and enjoying "crisp and sparkling days, long pleasant evenings, cheery fires." Then he adds, toward the end of the passage, "Life shall be lived well."

Other readers, searching between the lines, may find the essay as a piece of social criticism. A case can be made that the speaker represents an egocentric, hedonistic, empty-headed class of people, whose existence serves no useful purpose. Milne uses celery as a symbol to represent the trivialities that dominate the speaker's life. Not only is the man out of touch with the real world, he contributes nothing to it. That Milne chose celery as the speaker's concern merely emphasizes the speaker's shallowness. The anecdote about lunch at the inn reinforces the point. "Horror!" says the speaker about having his celery snatched, an event he also terms a "tragedy," as though the stranger had done something truly horrendous. Although Milne chose celery as the subject, anything of equal insignificance could have served his purpose.

Essay Question 3, Based on the Issue of "Second Chances"

Theoretically, an argument that either supports or is dead set against the principle of second chances in every imaginable circumstance might be made, but a moderate stance—one that leans in one direction or the other—is likely to be far more rational and convincing.

Once you've pondered the issue, you could begin your essay by describing a real or imagined scenario in which someone has erred. After revealing the circumstances surrounding the misstep, discuss why the perpetrator should or should not be granted a second chance.

In developing your essay, you might take into account the nature of the mistake, the offender's age and position in life, the time and place of the offense, and what occurred as a consequence of the transgression. Consider such matters as whether the perpetrator should have known better or whether there were mitigating conditions beyond his or her control. You might also question whether the action was self-motivated or whether the individual may have been influenced by others. Was the action impulsive or had it been thought out beforehand? What, if any, significant harm was done, and especially what might be gained or lost as a result of offering a second chance? In effect, your essay would explore relevant variables used to determine whether people ought to be held accountable for certain actions.

Another way to approach this topic is to base your decision mainly on the seriousness of the offense. Did it ignore standards that govern day-to-day social behavior, such as being unkind to others, telling lies, making threats, deceiving others, disturbing the peace, and so forth? Or did the mistake literally violate laws against, say, theft, underage drinking, texting while driving, physically damaging property, injuring people, and many, many others? Because not every offense is equally serious, weigh the appropriateness of granting second chances in a variety of circumstances.

A third approach might be to analyze a specific experience in which a second chance should have been granted but wasn't, or a time when granting a second chance backfired in some way. Rather than simply write a narrative of what happened, analyze the reasons why the decision was faulty and what conclusions might be drawn from the results.

In a way, this essay topic obliges you to confront and explain aspects of who you are and what you value. By addressing the topic thoughtfully, you'll not only inform AP readers about your ability to write a perceptive analytical essay, you could also learn something important about yourself.

How to Score the Essays

The following essay-scoring guidelines apply to all three essays on the exam. The maximum score on an essay is 6; the minimum, 0.

Points are awarded in three categories:

1. Thesis (0–1 point)
2. Evidence and Commentary (0–4 points)
3. Sophistication (0–1 point)

THESIS (0–1 POINT)

No credit is given for an absent, erroneous, or incoherent thesis or one that merely restates or paraphrases the essay prompt.

One point is awarded for a thesis that states or strongly implies a reasonable interpretation of the issue raised by the prompt for Essay #1, the synthesis essay. Similarly, for Essay #2 one point is given for a reasonable thesis related to rhetoric in the given passage. For Essay #3 add a point for a thesis that clearly articulates a position on the issue raised by the prompt.

EVIDENCE AND COMMENTARY (0–4 POINTS)

No points are given for restating the thesis in different words or for material irrelevant to the prompt.

One point is earned for evidence that tends to help develop the thesis.

Two points are given for evidence that clearly supports the thesis but may not add significantly to the writer's line of reasoning.*

Three points are awarded in Essay #1 for evidence that supports the thesis and also begins to show how source material supports your point of view. Give three points for evidence in Essay #2 that identifies and offers some analysis of rhetoric in the passage. Likewise, in Essay #3, give three points for specific evidence that helps to develop an argument for or against the main idea expressed by the prompt.

Four points indicate that you have consistently and effectively included compelling evidence to support all claims in a line of reasoning and also have clearly employed at least three sources to strengthen your position on the given issue (Essay #1), identified ample relevant evidence of rhetoric in the given passage (Essay #2), and cited compelling evidence to support your argument in favor of or against the given issue (Essay #3).

SOPHISTICATION (0–1 POINT)

No credit is given for ideas, however discerning, that you mention but don't develop.

One point is awarded for the development of ideas that broaden an interpretation of the issue (Essay #1), cite and explain significant rhetorical features of the passage (Essay #2), and discuss the opinions expressed in the given passage (Essay #3) by one or more of the following:

(a) Identifying and discussing complexities or tensions in the text.
(b) Illuminating an interpretation of the work by situating it within a broader context.
(c) Suggesting alternative interpretations of the work.
(d) Employing a consistently vivid and persuasive writing style.

Use of Standard English: No specific credit is given for the use of standard English. Readers are bound to be favorably impressed, however, by well-expressed, economical, virtually error-free prose.

---

*The term **"line of reasoning"** refers to the means by which an idea or thesis is supported. For instance, an essay may focus on the writer's choice of words, use of logic, sequence of ideas, or even the essay's title in order to validate the thesis. A poor line of reasoning exists when there is a gap between the thesis and the evidence presented.

Essay Evaluation Worksheet

In the spaces below enter the number of credits earned in each category. See pages 82 for detailed scoring guidelines.

	Essay 1 Synthesis Essay	Essay 2 Analytical Essay	Essay 3 Argumentative Essay
Category			
Thesis (0–1)			
Evidence and Commentary (0–4)			
Sophistication (0–1)			
TOTAL SCORE ON EACH ESSAY (0–6)			

Enter each essay score on the Test Score Worksheet.

Test Score Worksheet

Use this page to calculate your score on the AP English Language Diagnostic Test
(as well as Practice Tests 1, 2, 3, and 4).

SECTION 1. Multiple-Choice Questions

STEP A   Enter the number of correct answers (out of 45) _____

SECTION 2. Essay Questions

STEP B   Transfer your essay scores (0–6) from your Essay Evaluation Worksheet.

Essay 1 (Synthesis) _____   Essay 2 (Analysis) _____   Essay 3 (Argumentative) _____

Add the three essay scores   _____   (This is your Essay Raw Score.)

STEP C   Multiply Essay Raw Score by 3.055 _____

For your Final Essay Score, round to the nearest whole number. _____

SECTION 3. Composite Score

To determine your Composite Score, add the figures from STEP A and STEP C.

STEP A _____   +   STEP C _____   =   Composite Score _____

SECTION 4. Convert Composite Score to AP Test Score

Composite Score	AP Grade
90–100	5
68–89	4
36–67	3
13–35	2
1–12	1

NOTE: *Your score only approximates what you might earn on the actual exam. Exact figures vary from test to test. Therefore, your score on this test as well as on other tests in this book may differ from your score on an actual AP exam.*

3
Mastering Multiple-Choice Questions

Learning Objectives

Two types of questions

→ Rhetoric/reading questions
- Main purpose
- Tone
- Diction
- Sentences

→ Writing questions
- Organization
- Developing a thesis
- Use of evidence
- Sequence of ideas
- Figurative language

The Diagnostic Test has given you a taste of the types of questions that are coming your way on the AP exam. Whether you breezed through the Diagnostic Test or struggled with every question, it's worth your while to look at the following tried-and-true techniques for answering multiple-choice questions.

Untold numbers of students have relied on the following rules of thumb. You should, too.

FIVE RULES OF THUMB

1. Read each question carefully. To be sure you understand what a question asks, put it into your own words. Then reread the question to be sure you haven't misread it.

2. Read the five choices. Remember that you must select the *best* choice, which could mean that one or more of the incorrect choices may be partially valid. With a stroke of your pencil or an "X" in the margin, eliminate all the choices that are obviously wrong. Then concentrate on the others. Examine each remaining choice for irrelevancies and for meanings that merely approximate what the passage says. If a question refers you to a specific line or lines in the passage, reread not only those lines but also the two or three lines that come both before and after the designated lines. Knowing the context in which the lines appear can lead you to the correct answer.

3. After you've made your choice, scan the passage for evidence to support your decision. Just before filling the space on your answer sheet, be sure the question number is correct, and reread the question to check whether you've interpreted every word correctly.

4. If you're stumped by a question, make a tentative guess and put a "?" in the margin. Come back to it later, if you can. A return visit can provide a new perspective that helps you find the best answer. Also mark any questions about which you have any doubts.

5. If time remains after you've filled in all the blanks, review your answers, especially those, if any, that gave you trouble. Oh, yes, one more thing: Ridiculous as it may sound, make sure you've put your answers in the right places. Don't blacken a space for question 12 in a space for question 11, etc. (Please don't snicker; it's been done, and not just once.)

TIP

Before choosing your answer, eliminate the other choices.

While taking the practice tests in this book, practice these five guidelines. At first, they may seem cumbersome, even nitpicky. But as you grow accustomed to using them, your pace will pick up, and you'll answer questions more quickly and efficiently. That's a promise.

But remember, mastery of test-taking techniques can take you only so far toward earning a top score on the AP exam. What will take you the rest of the way is your knowledge of language and rhetoric.

Reading and Rhetoric

All the question-answering techniques in the world won't do you much good without knowledge of the subject matter covered by the exam. Moreover, a book like this can't tell you everything you need to know or should have remembered from years of English classes. But it can hit some of the highlights. That is, it can call your attention to matters regularly included in past AP exams. That's what the following pages aim to do.

Rhetoric and Reading Questions

You'll answer between 23 and 25 multiple-choice reading and rhetoric questions on the exam. Typically, the questions will ask how a certain feature—such as, say, a particular phrase, a certain sentence structure, the diction used as the writer expresses an opinion, or even the opinion itself—contributes to the meaning or effect of the passage.

Here's a typical example:

Which of the following best describes the rhetorical function of the last sentence of the first paragraph (lines 10–17)?

(A) It changes the tone of the passage from objective to personal.
(B) It contrasts the personalities of the two doctors.
(C) It explains the general significance of the details about the pandemic.
(D) It describes the impact of poverty in the country.
(E) It hints at a dilemma that will become important in the events that follow.

Another type of rhetorical question, such as the one that follows, is based on a whole paragraph by the American author Washington Irving. It asks you to analyze the way in which it is written rather than to consider only what it says:

In the second paragraph (reproduced below) the writer uses which of the following rhetorical techniques to convey his impression of the country:

> Her mighty lakes, like oceans of liquid silver; her mountains, with their bright aerial tints; her valleys, teeming with wild fertility; her tremendous cataracts, thundering in their solitudes; her boundless plains, waving with spontaneous verdure; her broad deep rivers, rolling in the solemn silence to the ocean; her trackless forests, where vegetation puts forth all its magnificence; her skies, kindling with the magic of summer clouds and glorious sunshine;—no, never need an American look beyond his own country for the sublime and beautiful of natural scenery.

(A) providing factual information
(B) visual imagery
(C) a progression of evocative details
(D) cataloguing unusual features of the landscape
(E) appealing to the five senses

Notice that the paragraph—except for the clause after the dash—consists of a single sentence composed of a series of nouns and modifiers, most followed by a participle phrase. The effect of this pattern is cumulative. It creates an image of the vastness of America, an idea aided not only by the piling up of visual images but also by the repeated use of adjectives such as "tremendous," "boundless," and "broad."

Therefore, (C) is the best answer.

Questions about rhetoric also test your understanding of such concepts as tone, diction, syntax, imagery, irony, figures of speech, theme, point of view, and many others. Also, you'll most certainly have a chance to demonstrate your awareness of how certain kinds of sentences reveal an author's intent and convey meaning.

Rhetoric is a broad term. Having come this far in your education, you are already acquainted with many of its varieties. Everything you have ever written or read—from a movie review to a college application—is subject to analysis in rhetorical terms.

In fact, virtually all writing has a rhetorical purpose. If authors aim to describe a place, person, or object, they try to recreate the look, the sound, the smell, the taste, and the feel of things. If their purpose is to tell a story, they narrate an event or a sequence of events by selecting and arranging particulars, usually in the order they occurred. An author with a point to make may take a position and offer reasons to support it. Whatever the mode, the author's choice of words, syntax (order of words and phrases), sentence sound and structure, the sequence of ideas, the selection of details—all these elements and more are meant to serve the purpose of the whole.

The purpose is often more complex than simply conveying an experience or telling a story. Authors may, for example, want to stimulate certain responses in their readers, who may react to a vivid recreation of an experience as though they themselves had the experience: they may laugh out loud, become tense or frightened, weep, grow angry. A biographer may want to communicate the facts of his subject's life. A. Scott Berg, for instance, wrote a prize-winning biography of Charles Lindbergh. In doing so, Berg established a tone that revealed his own thoughts about Lindbergh. In laying out the facts about the individual, he also meant to convince the reader that Lindbergh was both an admirable and a reprehensible figure. He wants us to admire and despise the man at the same time, just as he, the biographer, does. Notice how the rhetoric used by a reviewer of Berg's book highlights both sides of Lindbergh, the man:

> Charles Lindbergh's one-man flight from New York to Paris in 1927 made him the most admired man on earth, and the kidnapping and death of his firstborn son won him the world's sympathy in 1932. But after Pearl Harbor, memories of his obdurate opposition to American intervention in the war against Hitler caused millions to see him as a Nazi sympathizer, a defeatist, perhaps even a traitor. "Imagine," his sister-in-law wrote, "in just 15 years he had gone from Jesus to Judas."

Of course, a writer's attitude toward the subject is not necessarily identical with the response of the reader. An advertising copywriter for Nike may be totally indifferent to the shoes he crows about, but since his job is to make readers feel a certain way, he purposefully uses words to produce a particular response—namely, to turn readers into consumers of Nike products.

Tone

In the multiple-choice section of the exam, you will certainly need to deal with tone. One of the most common questions asks you to identify the tone of a passage, a sentence, or even a single word or phrase. To answer the question you will need a sense of the narrator's or speaker's attitude toward the subject of the passage. This may differ from the author's attitude, of course. An author may portray a scoundrel in a favorable way, but that doesn't necessarily mean the author has a soft spot in his heart for scoundrels.

Everything you've ever written can be analyzed in rhetorical terms.

Language molds the reader's attitude toward the subject discussed. And tone determines precisely what that attitude will be.

Because an author's tone may be complex or may shift part way through a passage, it can be described in innumerable ways, often by one or more adjectives. For example,

Negative

bitter	facetious	patronizing	scornful
condescending	flippant	pedantic	teasing
contemptuous	indignant	petty	threatening
disdainful	irreverent	sarcastic	
disgusted	mocking	satiric	

Positive

benevolent	ecstatic	enthusiastic	learned
compassionate	effusive	hopeful	supportive
determined	elegiac	laudatory	sympathetic

Neutral

bantering	detached	informal	scholarly
colloquial	didactic	objective	
confident	factual	restrained	

Words themselves and the manner in which they are expressed work together to establish the tone. Consider the simple question, "Who are you?" Depending on the tone in which the words are expressed, the question may be funny, sassy, inquisitive, challenging. Because the inflection of the speaker's voice is not available to writers, they must rely more on diction—the writer's choice of words, including figures of speech—to establish a tone. The differences between "Shut your mouth," "Please keep still," and "Would you be kind enough not to talk now?" are apparent. In a general sense the three sentences mean the same thing. The tone in each, however, could hardly differ more, because the words chosen to convey the meaning evoke very different feelings.

While the form of sentences significantly influences tone, other rhetorical elements also play a major part, especially diction, metaphors, and other figures of speech, such as symbols and allusions. One way an author reveals tone is by the form of sentences.

In essence, tone is the psychological quality of the words.

Exclamatory Sentences

An exclamatory sentence expresses a wish, a desire, a command—and is often, but not always, indicated with an exclamation point:

Heads up!

May the Force be with you!

Have a nice day!

Such sentences can express various gradations of begging, beseeching, praying, imploring, apologizing, requesting, advising, commanding, persuading, and so on. "Let the word go forth," intoned John F. Kennedy in his inauguration address, "that the torch has been passed to a new generation . . . ." Kennedy's inspirational tone is initiated by the use of the imperative verb *let*. The highsounding verb *go forth* and the metaphorical use of *torch* also contribute a sense of mission to the mood of the occasion.

Interrogative Sentences

An *interrogative* sentence also offers a writer a variety of tones. Questions are usually asked in order to obtain information: "When is the next train to Mount Kisco?" But the tone of a question can also be:

> **A CHALLENGE:** Who are you calling a nerd, Mac?
>
> **A DENIAL:** Do you actually think that I'm capable of such a thing?
>
> **DISBELIEF:** Can you believe the nerve of that driver?
>
> **HESITATION:** Do you really think I should step off the edge of the cliff?

and so on.

On the AP exam, you're also likely to be asked about rhetorical questions—questions whose answers are implied by the questions themselves. Used in an argument, a rhetorical question calls attention to an obvious proposition—or it can be used to make an argument more dramatic and convincing. The author of the following uses a series of questions and answers, structured somewhat like a dialogue:

> When our ancestors condemned a woman for one crime, they considered that by this single judgment she was convicted of many transgressions. How so? Judged unchaste, she was also deemed guilty of poisoning. Why? Because, having sold her body to the basest passion, she had to live in fear of many persons. Who are these? Her husband, her parents, and the others . . . .

Declarative Sentences

A *declarative* sentence, the most common form of sentence, makes a factual statement. Unlike exclamatory and interrogative sentences, the declarative sentence does not blatantly reveal its tone. Much of the time, the tone of a declarative sentence is neutral. It merely states information in a matter-of-fact way:

> In 1897, Columbia University moved from 49th Street and Madison Avenue, where it had stood for 40 years, to its present location on Morningside Heights at 116th Street and Broadway.

While this matter-of-fact tone is prevalent in scientific and other informational prose, declarative sentences can also be highly charged with emotion:

> People who knew the American novelist Thomas Wolfe recall that he habitually roamed down the long aisles of the library stacks, grabbing one book after the other from the shelves and devouring its contents as if he were a starving man suddenly let loose in an immense storehouse of food. He wrote with abandon, turning out incredible quantities of manuscript, filling whole packing cases with the product of his frenzied pen.

TIP

Although these pages pertain to "rhetoric" questions on the exam, they are equally relevant to the "writing" questions.

On the surface, this may seem like a factual description of Thomas Wolfe. The writer is informing us that Wolfe read many books and wrote prodigiously. But the words create a portrait of an awe-inspiring, larger-than-life figure. The simile, "as if he were a starving man suddenly let loose in an immense storehouse of food," while possibly overstating Wolfe's behavior in the library, does not exaggerate the passion Wolfe evidently felt for reading books.

Sentence Length

Sentences can vary in length between one word ("Walk!") and hundreds, even thousands, of words. Usually, the complexity of an idea determines sentence length, but not always. Profound ideas can also be expressed in very few words: "I think, therefore I am."

On the AP exam you could be asked why an author may have chosen to write very long sentences or why the author put a short sentence in a particular place or wrote a whole string of very short sentences. In general, long sentences allow authors to differentiate important ideas from less important ideas. Material in subordinate clauses, appositives, or any other secondary sentence element receives less emphasis than an idea expressed in the main clause. On the other hand, when an author uses several brief sentences in a row, no one sentence stands out. All are equally emphatic, and a thoughtful author most likely has a rhetorical reason for structuring a passage that way.

Short sentences are easier to grasp. A short sentence makes its point quickly and often with considerable force, as in this sample passage about authors and critics:

> **A person who pries into the private lives of others, with no other motive but to discover their faults and tell the world about them, deserves a name that can't be published here, just like a reviewer who reads books with an eye toward destroying the reputation of the author. Both are odious vermin.**

The blunt closing sentence produces a mild jolt, especially because it sits next to a windy 50-word sentence. The effect is intentional.

Sentence Structure

Experienced writers know how sentence parts should be arranged to convey meaning and affect a reader's response to the sentence. Of the three main sections of a sentence—the beginning, the middle, and the end—the end is the best place for emphasizing an idea. Why? Because the reader comes to a very brief stop at the end of a sentence—brief, but still long enough for the last idea to sink in.

This principle underlies the use of so-called *periodic* sentences—sentences that save the most important idea for the end. Compare these two sentences:

1. **A harmful economic system develops when a worker cannot get a job that pays enough to support a family.**
2. **When a worker cannot get a job that pays enough to support a family, a harmful economic system develops.**

Both sentences state their point clearly, but if the writer wanted to stress that certain conditions lead to a destructive economic system, the second sentence does it more emphatically. In sentence 1, the main point is stated first but is then pushed into the background by the example of the underpaid worker.

What distinguishes a periodic sentence from its opposite, the *loose* sentence, is that its thought is not completed until the end. In a way, the reader is held in suspense. The loose sentence, in contrast, gives away its "secret" at the start. It follows the most common structure of English sentences: subject-verb, as in *Geraldo texted*, or subject-verb-object: *Geraldo used his new iPhone*.

As you probably know, every sentence has a main clause consisting of at least a subject and a verb. That's all a *simple* sentence needs to be complete—a subject and a verb. Even if many modifiers and objects are added, it still remains a *simple* sentence.

For example, both of the following sentences, despite the disparity in their length, are *simple* sentences:

Berkeley admitted Freda.

Situated on the eastern side of San Francisco Bay, Berkeley, the University of California's flagship institution, admitted Freda as a freshman in the class of 2026, to the delight not only of Freda herself but to the satisfaction of her family, teachers, and friends.

Leaving aside the wordiness and wisdom of including so much miscellaneous information in the second sentence, you still find a simple declarative sentence—*Berkeley admitted Freda*—lurking within its jumble of modifiers, participles, prepositional phrases, and appositives.

To turn a *simple* sentence into a *compound* sentence, add a conjunction, a word like *and* or *but,* as in

Berkeley admitted Freda, and she was delighted.

You can infer from this example that a *compound* sentence is made up of at least two simple sentences joined by a conjunction. What is rhetorically noteworthy about a compound sentence is that the author gives more or less equal emphasis to the information in each of the clauses. Clauses of equal rank and structure are called *coordinate clauses* and are joined by *coordinating conjunctions* (*and, but, or, nor, yet, so*) and sometimes by a semicolon with connective words like *however, moreover, nevertheless, otherwise, therefore, consequently,* and others. In this case, whether logical or not, Freda's acceptance has been given equal importance to her reaction to the news.

If the author's intent, however, is to emphasize Freda's state of mind, the sentence might best be turned into a *complex* sentence—that is, a sentence that contains both a subordinate and a main clause:

Because Berkeley admitted her, Freda was delighted. (Subordinate clause italicized)

Here, the cause-and-effect relationship between the two ideas is made clearer. The addition of a subordinating conjunction *because* gives prominence to the information in the main, or independent, clause. (Other widely used subordinating conjunctions include *although, before, even though, while, unless, if,* and *when.*)

Diction

Diction, or word choice, is one of the elements of style that gives each person's writing a quality that is uniquely his or her own. Diction determines whether an author has succeeded in communicating a particular message to a particular audience. In the following passage, from an article titled "Fenimore Cooper's Literary Offenses," Mark Twain comments on the diction of a well-regarded American writer.

An author's diction, or word choice, is crucial. It determines tone, creates effects, and ultimately conveys meaning for the reader.

Cooper's word sense was singularly dull. When a person has a poor ear for music, he will flat and sharp right along without knowing it. He keeps near the tune, but it is not the tune. When a person has a poor ear for words, the result is a literary flatting and sharping; you perceive what he is intending to say, but you also perceive that he doesn't say it. This is Cooper. He was not a word musician. His ear was satisfied with the approximate word. I will furnish some circumstantial evidence in support of this charge. My instances are gathered from half a dozen pages of the tale called Deerslayer. He used "verbal" for "oral"; "precision" for "facility";

"phenomena" for "marvels"; "necessary" for "predetermined"; "unsophisticated" for "primitive"; "preparation" for "expectancy"; "rebuked" for "subdued"; "dependent on" for "resulting from"; "fact" for "condition"; . . . "brevity" for "celerity"; "distrusted" for "suspicious"; "mental imbecility" for "imbecility"; "eyes" for "sight"; "counteracting" for "opposing"; . . . . There have been daring people in the world who claimed that Cooper could write English, but they're all dead now.

Apparently, Cooper's diction left much to be desired. In Twain's view, Cooper was insensitive to the connotation of many, many words. "The difference between the right word and the approximate word," wrote Twain, "is the difference between 'lightning' and 'lightning bug.'" Presumably, Cooper's prose is full of bugs. He may well have known the definitions of words, but he had a so-called tin ear when it came to understanding the words in context. He seems deaf to the feelings that words represent, and, therefore, chose his words badly.

Authors usually can select from several possibilities words that are best suited to their purposes. For instance:

insult/slur, spit/expectorate, complain/gripe, excellent/superior, eat/stuff one's face

The words in each pair mean more or less the same thing, but none is a perfect synonym for another. Some are plain, others are fancy. Some are clinical, euphemistic, or slang; each has a distinct connotation.

Connotation

Words derive their connotation from two sources: people's common experience and an individual's personal experience. Words represent not only ideas, events, and objects, but also the feelings we attach to ideas, events, and objects. Thus, the word *rat* represents a certain kind of rodent—among other things. That is its *denotative* meaning. But a rat also evokes in us feelings of fear and disgust—its *connotation*. What is true of *rat* is also true of countless other words: *mother, home, candy, money, grease, America, dog,* and so on. They all evoke feelings and ideas.

Connotations may change over time, and our personal experience often adds connotative value to words that may at first mean nothing beyond their definition. Scientific words that at one time merely named physical phenomena or technical achievements—*cloning, abortion, www.com*—have since acquired rich connotative meanings.

Really good descriptive writing often gets its power from the author's choice of connotative words. The more closely you read a passage, the more you may enjoy it. Notice how the following passage employs connotation to create a graphic impression of a very agreeable place:

There couldn't be a more idyllic spot in May than Albion, on the Mendocino coast. The land, strung between redwood groves and sea, is lush with flowers. Summer crowds are weeks away, and it's still possible to find a quiet beach or stroll the cliffs above the ocean without seeing another soul. Four miles from the coastal highway, the road narrows, loses its paving, and curves into the woods. A graveled driveway winds to a graceful country house close to a pond and surrounded by park-like grounds. A trellis of interlocking timbers draped with vines leads to the front door of the house. A Chinese lantern hangs overhead. From high on a post a clay mask stares at passersby. Pieces of driftwood lie on a wooden bench weathered to a silver-grey. Attention has been paid to make visitors feel welcome.

In familiar but carefully chosen words the author of the passage has conveyed the pleasure of visiting Albion—a feeling he wants his readers to share. References to things that most people enjoy and value—redwood groves, flowers, a quiet beach, a country house—create a sense of peace and contentment.

Metaphorical Language

Because figures of speech often reveal an author's tone, be prepared to deal with questions that refer to the most common figures of speech found in nonfiction prose:

- ✔ Metaphor
- ✔ Simile
- ✔ Allusion
- ✔ Analogy
- ✔ Metonymy
- ✔ Synecdoche

As a group, these figures of speech constitute what might be called generally *metaphorical language*.

When an author can't find the exact words to describe a feeling or to capture experiences that seem almost inexpressible, a metaphor may come to the rescue: "She has a voice of gold," says the music critic, using a metaphor to express not only the beauty of her voice but also its value. Indeed, in a particular context the metaphor could mean that the singer makes big money with her voice. Figures of speech are economical. They condense a lot of thought and feeling into a few words. Ernie Pyle, a famous World War II war correspondent, reported his stories as though they were being told by the average GI lying in a foxhole. He said, "I write from a worm's eye point of view." The idea gives a fresh slant to an old expression and cogently fixes Pyle's position on the battlefield.

Because metaphorical language evokes mental images, it has a good deal to do with the emotional content of a piece of writing. An author relying on trite, second-hand expressions to convey an idea, using such metaphors as *walking on air* or *life in the fast lane,* apparently has nothing new or surprising to say. On the other hand, an author who fills a passage with fresh metaphorical language may give readers rich new insights and understandings.

Allusion

An allusion—an implied or direct reference to something in history or culture—is, like a richly connotative word, a means to suggest far more than it says. An allusion of a single word or phrase can expand the reader's understanding more completely than could a long, discursive comparison. Take, for example, Robert Frost's poem "Out, Out . . .," a narrative poem that recounts a farmyard accident that kills a young boy. A theme of the poem, the uncertainty and unpredictability of life, is alluded to in the title, which you may know comes from Macbeth's soliloquy upon hearing of his wife's death: "Out, out, brief candle./Life's but a walking shadow, . . ." Macbeth's speech is a reflection on both the tragedy of a premature death and the impermanence of life. While readers unfamiliar with *Macbeth* might read "Out, Out . . ." with insight and empathy, understanding the allusion to Shakespeare's play enriches the experience.

Literature isn't the only source of allusions. History, religion, politics, sports—almost every human endeavor can spawn allusions. Think of the origin and implications of such metaphorical allusions as a football team that "sinks like the *Titanic,*" your "hitting a homerun" on a math test, a scandal termed "Irangate," and nicknaming a malevolent and tyrannical school principal "Lord Voltemart."

Such metaphors are potent when used well, but metaphorical language that seems inappropriate to the general tone and purpose of the passage will grate on readers and weaken the overall effect that the author has in mind. It also suggests that the author lacks a clear sense of purpose or

Metaphorical language functions as a means of making comparisons.

Figures of speech have the power to make something clearer or more vivid, or to turn a vague impression into something concrete.

 TIP

Good writers choose metaphors carefully.

just doesn't know how to achieve a particular purpose. Take, for example, this attempt to describe how memories of childhood fade with the passing of time:

> **As you grow older, your memory of childhood is obliterated like a bus blown to bits by a terrorist.**

Isn't it obvious that the author missed the point? After all, memories fade slowly, not cataclysmically. Whatever tone the author may have intended is lost in the incongruity of the simile. A more appropriate way to capture the idea that memories erode gradually might be:

> **As you grow older, memories of childhood vanish like sand dunes at the edge of the sea.**

Of course, there may be another possibility. Perhaps the author wrote an incongruous metaphor for a particular purpose. To heighten interest, authors often try to surprise their readers. They introduce an inappropriate or contradictory metaphor, for instance, for the sake of contrast. They invent a figure of speech with a connotation that is off kilter in order to create a kind of tension or to make an ironic or amusing comment.

During the Spanish Civil War, Ernest Hemingway, writing a dispatch from the front lines, said of the enemy planes, "If their orders are to strafe the road on their way home, you will get it [be wounded or killed]. Otherwise, when they are finished with their jobs on a particular objective, they go off like bank clerks, flying home." The comparison of deadly fighters and bank clerks may seem frivolous, but it does make the point effectively. Both are eager to scurry away from their jobs as quickly as possible. Moreover, by contrasting bank clerks—generally harmless, well-meaning functionaries—with ruthless fighters, Hemingway heightens the viciousness of the enemy aircraft strafing the people on the road.

Analogy

Another form of comparison is the *analogy,* usually defined in words like these: *A comparison of two objects or situations that have several common characteristics.* An extended analogy, showing parallels between two unlike things, can simplify a complicated idea and leave a powerful impression on a reader. Consider the tone established in the following excerpt from a speech by President Woodrow Wilson:

> **I had a couple of friends who were in the habit of losing their tempers, and when they lost their tempers they were in the habit of using very unparliamentary language. Some of their friends induced them to make a promise that they never would swear inside the town limits. When the impulse next came upon them, they took a street car to go out of town to swear, and by the time they got out of town they did not want to swear . . . . Now, illustrating the great by the small, that is true of the passions of nations.**

Wilson used this analogy in support of his position that a country must not jump into a war in the heat of passion. By using colloquial words (e.g., "a couple of friends") and telling a personal anecdote, Wilson established a folksy tone. The analogy, which would be accessible to every listener, draws on everyday experience, and makes good common sense. Wilson, in effect, has taken on the persona of one of the guys. Neither moralistic nor panicky, he creates the image of a fellow whose judgment the country can trust in a crisis.

Metonymy

An author's use of metonymy and synecdoche also contributes to the establishment of tone. Unlike metaphors, which make comparisons, these two figures of speech make substitutions— usually something abstract for something concrete (or vice versa), a container for the thing contained (or vice versa), a part for the whole, a cause for the effect, and so on.

In the statement, "Gilberto has a good head," the word *head* has been substituted for *brain* (the container for the thing contained). But *head* also means "IQ" or "intelligence"—both abstract concepts that are made more tangible by the use of *head*. To some degree, metonymy can simplify an idea—unlike a metaphor, which tends to complicate a thought—particularly when a concrete substitution is made for an abstraction, as in "Your hands made you rich," in which the word *hands* means occupation, trade, or line of work.

TIP

In general, metonymy tends to bring a kind of vitality to a phrase or idea.

Synecdoche

Synecdoche is a type of metonymy, in which a part is substituted for the whole, or vice versa. Any time you use the word *sail* for ship ("A fleet of a hundred sails"), or call a truck an *eighteen-wheeler,* you are using synecdoche. When Hamlet is about to remove the body of Polonius from Gertrude's bedchamber, he says, "I'll lug the guts into the neighbor room." His synecdoche *guts* clearly stands for corpse, but its connotation also suggests the disdain that Hamlet felt for Polonius. Indeed, both metonymy and synecdoche can be rich with implied meaning.

As you consider the metaphorical language in passages on the AP exam, keep in mind the passages' purpose and tone. Ask yourself whether each figure of speech is appropriate and how it contributes to or detracts from the reader's response.

Writing Questions

As someone who's probably written hundreds of essays, papers, book reports, stories, homework assignments, and text messages over the years, you must be well acquainted with the principle behind the AP exam's writing questions—namely, that the work of a nonfiction writer involves more than just slapping words on a page. Rather, anyone who takes writing seriously must carefully select the best words and arrange them in the best order.

To do that successfully, writers make countless decisions about which words to use and how to put them into sentences, which must then be grouped coherently into paragraphs that themselves must be sequenced in a way that helps readers understand and appreciate the writer's overall purpose.

For those reasons, the AP exam includes 20–22 multiple-choice questions on writing. They are based on three separate nonfiction prose passages, with six to eight questions on each. All the passages are "drafts," i.e., works in progress that need improvement. They may contain parts that are poorly phrased, inappropriate, wordy, ambiguous, ungrammatical, irrelevant, illogical, or incoherent, or that are in some other way defective. Your job is to think like an editor—in other words, choose the alternatives that best eliminate writing problems. Not all the questions pertain to flaws, however. You may also be asked to rearrange the order of sentences or add an appropriate transition between ideas, or to decide which of several sentences might be inserted into a certain place in the text to help develop the writer's thesis.

Correct answers demonstrate, among other things, that you understand the rhetorical situation of the passage: its purpose, audience, the author's claims, use of evidence, line of reasoning, tone—basically, the whole panoply of the ingredients that generally constitute a readable passage.

Sample Passage and Writing Questions

This passage, an excerpt from the draft of a book written late in the 20th century, discusses Paul Brown, the head coach of the Cleveland Browns, a professional football team.

(1) Back in Massillon High School, Ohio, the coach's rules had served as a sort of Ten Commandments of social welfare, teaching the boys to develop self-control and discipline. (2) Years later in Cleveland, his role-modeling continued as he imposed dress codes on
Line his players and insisted on curfews and a strict study regimen with playbooks, constant
(5) lectures, and testing. (3) Systematizing the team's procedures and requirements served a new postwar ethic: it enhanced an image, the image of a well-run organization.

(4) "We want you to reflect a special image in pro football," Brown told his players in a speech at the opening of each season. (5) They were not to smoke or drink in public. (6) They were to wear jackets and ties, slacks and polished shoes in public. (7) They were to
(10) display proper "decorum" and not curse in public. (8) If they so much as lounged on the ground during a game, they were fined. (9) They were never to behave in a manner that would make the team look "low class"—in other words, that would remind anybody of the league's origins in the mills and mines.

(10) "Class always shows," Brown maintained, and what he wanted his men to show
(15) was the face of a new, white-collar bourgeoisie. (11) "I didn't want them to look like the stereotype of the old-time pros," Brown said. (12) "College players had a good reputation, but the public perception of the professional football player back then was of a big, dumb guy with a potbelly and a cheap cigar. (13) That kind of person disgusted me, and I never wanted anyone associating our players with that image." (14) What Brown wanted was a
(20) managerial look: polished and uniform, college-educated but not effetely so, aspiring but conformist. (15) What he wanted was a team represented by organization men who lived up to the expectations of the team's owners and fans. (16) With his contained demeanor, trim frame, and bland corporate suits, he looked like the archetypal suburban husband about to board the commuter train to his desk job in the city.

1. Which of the following sentences, if placed before sentence 1 (reproduced below), would both capture the audience's interest and provide the most effective introduction to the topic of the passage?

Back in Massillon High School, Ohio, the coach's rules had served as a sort of Ten Commandments of social welfare, teaching the boys to develop self-control and discipline.

(A) (No change)
(B) For years, football coach Paul Brown's list of rules shaped the lives of his players.
(C) Players called their head football coach a fearsome dictator.
(D) En route to fame and fortune in Cleveland, Paul Brown coached both high school and college football teams.
(E) The Cleveland Browns were named after their longtime coach.

Explanation

A question about a passage's introductory sentence has particular importance. Not only is it probably the first question, but also it's likely to offer clues to the subject of the entire passage while introducing the text, establishing the tone, and perhaps setting the passage's limits—all potentially useful information to have as you deal with this and subsequent questions.

To answer this question, you must of course read sentence 1 and then decide how or whether it is related in meaning to the proposed additional sentence. In short, determine whether sentence 1 is developed or clarified by the new sentence. If not, choose (A) as the answer. To make sure, however, read sentence 2, which, in fact, turns out to be related to sentence 1. You may have noticed that the two sentences together have begun to shape the theme of the passage.

Choices (C) and (D) also relate to sentence 1, but their connections are far weaker than that of choice (B), which serves both of the purposes stated in the original question: it introduces the topic of the passage and to some extent stimulates readers' curiosity about how the coach shaped players' lives. (C), while both interesting and true, fits more comfortably late in the passage—say, after the writer has detailed what the coach demanded of his players. (D) relates to the coach, of course, but has no place in the passage—not yet, at any rate. And (E), a piece of trivia—albeit interesting—has no apparent relevance at the moment.

2. In sentence 3 (reproduced below) which of the following versions of the underlined text best develops the writer's position on the main point of the passage?

Systematizing the team's procedures and requirements served a new postwar <u>ethic: it enhanced an image, the image of a well-run organization.</u>

   (A) (as it is now)
   (B) ethic, however, different in time and spirit from the wartime stress and worry on the home front.
   (C) ethic; which should have been familiar to the huge population of WW II veterans.
   (D) ethic: but not altogether different; the objective was still to win!
   (E) ethic—a system promoting the perfectibility of human character, action, and ends.

Explanation

Although the focus of the question is on the underlined section of the text, be sure to read the whole sentence. In fact, it would have been useful to have read or skimmed the whole passage beforehand, because some choices may refer directly to ideas stated later in the text. (See "Reading Techniques," page 4.) If a choice refers to something nowhere to be found in the passage, by default it is incorrect. For that reason, therefore, eliminate choices (B) and (C). Although Choice (D) has potential, it is a stretch to equate winning a world war to winning a football game. (E), too, has possibilities, but the passage tells of Brown's efforts only to shave rough edges off his team of unpolished young toughs, not to turn them into icons of decorum and sophistication. That leaves (A) as the best choice, an answer that is supported by sentences 10–12.

An altogether different reason for choosing (A) is its punctuation. Look closely: (A) is the only properly punctuated choice. The word *ethic* is followed by a colon, which introduces a complete sentence that defines the nature of the ethic. (B) tosses in the adverb *however*, which is surrounded by a pair of pointless commas. In (C) the semicolon should be followed by a grammatically complete sentence, but isn't. (D) includes a colon that should be followed by a clear statement of the "ethic," but isn't. And (E) uses a dash—an appropriate mark of punctuation in the context, but in this case what follows is an elegant statement devoid of relevance in the context.

3. In sentences 4–8 the writer lists some of Coach Brown's rules for his players. At the start of sentence 9 (reproduced below), the writer wants to add a phrase to suggest the relative importance of that rule in comparison to the previous ones.

They were never to behave in a manner that would make the team look "low class"—in other words, that would remind anybody of the league's origins in the mills and mines.

Adjusting capitalization and punctuation as needed, which of the following best accomplishes that goal?

(A) Of uppermost degree,

(B) And when all is said and done—

(C) Last but not least:

(D) But priority-wise,

(E) Foremost, however,

Explanation

To answer this question, study each choice for tone, style, punctuation, and meaning. (E) is the best choice because it uses the superlative adjective *foremost* to make a legitimate comparison. (A) sounds good but is not stated in idiomatic English. Both (B) and (C) are clichés that serious writers (like you) ordinarily eschew. Equally unacceptable is jargon-laden choice (D).

4. In sentence 17 (reproduced below), which of the following versions of the underlined text best establishes the writer's position on the main idea of the passage?

What he wanted was a team represented by organization men, <u>who lived up to the expectations of the team's owners and fans</u>.

(A) committed heart and soul to the Cleveland team

(B) who flew first-class and stayed in five-star hotels

(C) middle-class men without tattoos and who said "Pardon me" when they belched

(D) who could be counted on to work as hard at football as businessmen did in the office

(E) with the sort of look he himself exemplified

Explanation

(E) is the best answer because it is the culmination of an idea expressed piecemeal throughout the passage, starting with sentence 2, which discusses Brown's efforts to create a favorable image of his players, by implication the image he himself projected: "the face of a new, white-collar bourgeoisie," (sentence 10); the old image of football players "disgusted" him (sentence 13). "Class always shows" (sentence 10), he claimed, adding that he wanted a "managerial look" (sentence 14) with "a contained demeanor," like the "archetypal . . . suburban commuter" (sentence 17).

5. In the third paragraph, the writer wants to add the following sentences to provide additional information about Brown's standards for his players.

Or worse, were the occasional players who got arrested for breaking the law. Brown observed that they were those whose actions on the field earned the most penalties, although he couldn't say for sure that one caused the other. In any case, guilty or not, those players were immediately suspended from the team.

Where would the sentence best be placed?

(A) Before sentence 10 but in the previous paragraph

(B) After sentence 10

(C) After sentence 11

(D) After sentence 12

(E) After sentence 13

Explanation

To find the best location, read each of the sentences listed. Chances are that the correct place can be located by keeping in mind the opening phrase, "Or worse," which necessarily follows a reference to a bad situation, but one not as awful as the "worse" one about to be described. A review of the five choices shows that sentence 12 is filled with a list of the public's stereotypical views of professional football players, all of them disparaging. To intensify the claim, the writer wants to add still more defamatory details, by starting the next sentence with "Or worse . . ."

4
Mastering Essay Questions

Learning Objectives

→ Reaching your goal: three essays in 135 minutes
→ Two analytical essays: what AP readers look for
→ Choosing and narrowing a topic
→ Arranging ideas purposefully
→ A writing style that works
→ Polishing your essays for a top score
→ Sample questions and student responses

Just as you don't learn to play the piano, twirl a baton, or break-dance by reading books on music, baton-twirling, or break-dancing, you're not likely to become a better writer of essays by reading about essay writing. The best this book can do is to lay out some basic principles of essay writing for you to contemplate and incorporate into the writing you do every day. The more experience you have, the more control you'll have, and the better you'll perform not only on the AP exam, but also in future college courses and whatever work you do afterward.

Our language contains many adjectives that describe good writing: *eloquent, well-written, lively, stylish, polished, descriptive, honed, vivid, engaging*, and countless others. On the AP exam you're instructed to write "well-organized" or "carefully reasoned" or "effective" essays—directions that mean, in effect, that your writing should be:

1. **CLEAR**, or easy to follow, because your ideas need to be clear to you before you can make them clear to others.
2. **INTERESTING**, or expressed in economical, entertaining language, because readers are put off by dull and lifeless prose.
3. **CORRECT**, because you and your work will inevitably be judged according to how well you demonstrate the conventions of writing.

If your ideas are expressed clearly, interestingly, and correctly, there is no reason that you can't expect to write three winning essays on the exam.

Steps for Writing the Perfect Essay

You won't have time to invent an essay-writing process during the exam. So, it pays to have a process in mind ahead of time, one that helps you to work rapidly and efficiently. Try to map out in advance the steps to take during each stage of the writing process. The plan that follows is a place to start. Use it while writing a few practice essays, but alter it in any way that helps you produce the best essays you can.

FIRST STAGE PREWRITING

Prewriting consists of the planning that needs to be done before you actually start writing an essay:

- ✓ Reading and analyzing the question, or prompt
- ✓ Choosing a main idea, or thesis, for your essay
- ✓ Gathering and arranging supporting ideas

SECOND STAGE COMPOSING

- ✓ Introducing the thesis
- ✓ Developing paragraphs
- ✓ Choosing the best words for expressing your ideas
- ✓ Structuring sentences for variety and coherence
- ✓ Writing a conclusion

THIRD STAGE EDITING and PROOFREADING

- ✓ Editing for clarity and coherence
- ✓ Editing to create interest
- ✓ Checking for standard usage and mechanical errors, including spelling, punctuation, and capitalization

How Long Does Each Stage Last?

The truth is that the three stages overlap and blend. Writers compose, revise, and proofread simultaneously. They jot down sentences during prewriting, and even late in the process may weave new ideas into their text. In fact, no stage really ends until the final period of the last sentence is put in place—or until the AP proctor calls "Time!"

No book can tell you how to divide up the 40 minutes recommended for each essay. What works for you may be different from what works for others. But most students get good results by devoting between 25 and 30 minutes to composing and roughly 5–10 minutes each to prewriting and editing/proofreading.

How to Prepare

During the weeks before the exam, or even sooner, write an essay a day for several days in a row, until you get the feel of 40 minutes' writing time. Pace yourself and keep track of how much time you spend thinking about the topic, how many minutes you devote to composing the essay, and how long it takes you to proofread and edit.

To make every second count, don't waste time inventing titles for your essays (no titles are needed on the exam). Don't count words, and don't expect to re-copy your first drafts. Because AP readers understand that the essays are first drafts, feel free to cross out, insert words using carets (^), and move blocks of text with neatly drawn arrows. If necessary, number the sentences to make their sequence clear. You won't be penalized for sloppy-looking essays. Just be sure they're legible.

Once you've developed a pattern that works, stick to it, and practice, practice, practice until it becomes second nature.

Don't waste time inventing titles; you don't need them.

Writing the Synthesis Essay

- ✓ Using sources to your advantage
- ✓ Developing a persuasive argument
- ✓ Pitfalls to avoid
- ✓ Integrating sources into your essay
- ✓ Sample question and student responses

The first essay question on the exam calls for a synthesis essay—an essay that argues your point of view on a given issue. Along with a prompt that describes the issue, you are given several sources related to the issue. One of the sources is an image, such as a photo, chart, graph, or cartoon. From at least three of the sources you are to draw facts, ideas, information—any relevant evidence you can use to bolster your argument.

A 15-minute reading period is built into the test before you start writing. How you fill the time is up to you, but you'll make the most productive use of those 15 minutes by first focusing on the prompt. Read it carefully, with pencil in hand. Underline the words that tell you exactly what you must do. Then, think hard about the issue and jot down a tentative thesis for your essay. With a main idea in mind, search the sources for ideas to incorporate into your essay and prepare a working outline. In other words, use the time to get ready to write.

> **A Message from the Author**
>
> The following pages are full of pointers for writing the synthesis essay. But many of the guidelines also apply to writing the other two essays on the exam.

A Typical Prompt for the Synthesis Essay

In many high schools students are threatened with suspension or worse for wearing T-shirts or other clothing printed with obscenities, inflammatory language, X-rated content, and messages that may be offensive to ethnic, racial, LGBTQ, religious, or other groups. School officials have implemented this policy because, among other reasons, offensive messages undermine the learning environment necessary for an educational institution to do its job effectively. Free-speech advocates and civil-liberties organizations disagree, claiming that a ban on controversial clothing violates students' constitutional rights and is inconsistent with the mission of schools to teach and to show by example the values of a free society.

Carefully read the following six sources, including the material that introduces each source. Then, in an essay that synthesizes at least three of the sources, take a position on the claim that schools should not allow students to wear clothing that may be objectionable to some members of the school population.

Be sure to focus the essay on your point of view and use the sources to support and illustrate your position. Don't simply summarize the sources. You may paraphrase, adapt, and quote material directly and indirectly from the sources. In your essay be sure to indicate which sources you use. Refer to them as Source A, Source B, and so on, or by the key words in the parentheses below.

The prompt contains the topic for the synthesis essay. Be sure you understand it before you begin to write your essay.

The first paragraph of the prompt does little more than introduce the topic. It may stir up your thinking, but it doesn't tell you how to proceed. The next two paragraphs do that by spelling out the instructions: *read the sources and write an essay*—not just any essay but one that *takes a position* that agrees or disagrees with the assertion that schools should prohibit students from wearing clothing that may be objectionable to some members of the school population. Remember that you're not required to wholeheartedly defend or oppose the assertion. Instead, you can take a position that falls somewhere in between.

What It's About

A synthesis essay is basically an **argumentative** essay. At the heart of the essay lies a claim, or statement of opinion. Call it a *main idea* or a *thesis statement*. The main idea spells out the overall purpose of the essay. Once you've made clear where you stand on the issue, the rest of the essay should back up your claim using a variety of supporting evidence.

The evidence you choose is likely to make or break your argument. Solid evidence consists of facts, observations, statistics, the opinions of experts, relevant anecdotes, and more. But you'll get the most mileage from a series of logically presented ideas. No doubt you've had experience trying to convince someone to agree with you—to see an issue your way. Maybe you've tried to talk a teacher into raising a grade. Or how about the time you wanted to drive with your friends to a rap concert 200 miles away, and you had to persuade your parents to let you go? You probably cited reasons why you thought it was a good idea, gave examples of your maturity, reminded them of past instances when you acted responsibly, cited the fact that Scott's and Chris's parents have already given their consent, and so on. In short, you chose and shaped the most convincing evidence you could think of to fit the audience—your parents.

When you write the synthesis essay, you are faced with a similar task. Your audience, of course, will be AP essay readers, and your task is to convince them first, that you understand the essay assignment and second, that you can apply both your own ideas and other ideas you've found in the sources to build a persuasive argument.

Before you begin to write, however, you must read the sources.

Reading the Sources

Some students are blessed with lightning-quick minds that can instantly analyze an issue and articulate a thoughtful position on it. If you happen to be one of them, you're light-years ahead of the pack. Enjoy your head start and plunge right into the sources to look for the evidence with which to build your case.

The rest of us, unless we happen to have thought about the issue in the past, will start from scratch. We'll begin reading sources with relatively open minds and will weigh all the evidence we can find before making up our minds.

The sources will offer a variety of interpretations and points of view for you to consider. Don't be satisfied that you know what any individual source is all about until you've analyzed it thoroughly and can say clearly what it contributes to the discussion of the issue. If you think it's okay to read only some of the sources in order to find enough ideas for your essay, please think again. In other words, read every source from start to finish before you start to write. After all, the most irresistible idea could pop up in the final paragraph of the last source.

As you read the sources, keep in mind the following purposes:

- **READ TO UNDERSTAND WHAT THE SOURCE HAS TO SAY.** Quickly underline or circle striking ideas, topic sentences, and other key words and phrases. Use your pencil sparingly, though, or you may end up with most of each passage marked up. A note or two scribbled in the margin can serve later as shorthand reminders of what the passage says.
- **READ TO ANALYZE THE AUTHOR'S POSITION ON THE ISSUE.** Read each source to determine where the author stands on the issue. Where the author presents evidence in favor of the claim, put a check in the margin. Where the evidence opposes it, write an X. Later, when you've decided on your own position, these notations will lead you quickly to ideas you may wish to include in your essay.

- **READ FOR EVIDENCE AND DATA THAT HELP DEFINE YOUR POSITION ON THE ISSUE.**
The position you take should be the one about which you have the most compelling things to say. The sources will offer a variety of perspectives. Read them in search of evidence that makes the most sense to you. The sooner you know where you stand, the better. If you've read the sources and still can't decide what position to take, make two lists, one for arguments in favor of the issue, one for those opposed. With any luck, the arguments on one side will speak to you more forcefully than those on the other.

    You won't be penalized for taking an unpopular or politically incorrect stance, but you'll get little credit for promoting an unrealistic or illogical position. If you wish, you can straddle the fence on the issue with the "it-all-depends" argument. That approach is safe but not too exciting. But if your judgment tells you that the question warrants a middle-of-the-road response, don't hesitate to write one. In the end, readers will be less impressed by your position than by the potency of your presentation.

- **INTERPRET THE VISUAL SOURCE.** The visual source won't require much reading, but it still must be analyzed for what it communicates. Your job is to interpret the graph, the chart, the image, the cartoon, or whatever, and determine its relationship to the other sources. Ask yourself what relevant information it contributes to the discussion of the issue. Once you understand its point, you can use it as evidence in your essay.

    Because visual sources often convey a large amount of information, they can be interpreted in various ways. It all depends on your perspective. Take, for example, the following line graph that comes from a recent census:

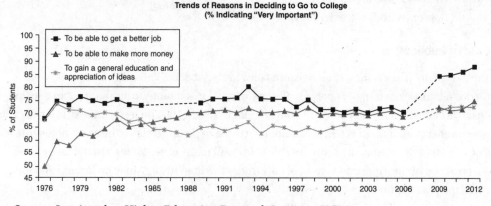

Source: Los Angeles: Higher Education Research Institute, UCLA.

Analyze what the graph tells you about why American students decided to attend college. In the spaces below, write three different conclusions that can be drawn from the graph.

1. _____

2. _____

3. _____

One of the more obvious conclusions shown by the graph is that students persist in putting a premium on job-related reasons to go to college. The graph also tells you that between 2006 and 2012, getting a better job jumped significantly higher than the other reasons for attending college.

If you were writing an essay on an issue related to, say, how the state of the economy affects choices made by college-bound students, you might focus on long-term trends, especially on students' relative indifference toward making money in 1976 compared with their eagerness in 2012 to attend college mainly to boost their future income.

Based on one interpretation of the graph, you might conclude:

American students are becoming increasingly materialistic and money hungry.

Another writer, taking a different point of view, might say:

Knowing that a college education is the key to financial security, students are likely to work harder and take their studies more seriously.

In other words, what you make of a visual source while writing your synthesis essay depends greatly on the topic and your point of view on the issue.

Assessing the Validity of Sources

Because not all sources are equally reliable, it pays to think about their validity before tapping them for evidence to include in your essay. For each source, determine insofar as possible:

- [✓] When it was published
- [✓] Where it came from
- [✓] Who its readers were likely to be
- [✓] What its purpose was
- [✓] How objectively it was written

Date of Publication

TIP

A passage from a blogger's website can't be completely trusted.

The date of the piece is important because facts, ideas, what we know, how we think, what we do—almost everything—is perpetually changing. Consequently, information can become obsolete almost before we know it. A source written, say, in 1990 on a scientific subject, such as climate change or human genetics, cannot be trusted to be up-to-date. The same holds true for discussions of the media, the economy, lifestyles, and many other topics. On the other hand, observations of the American system of government written in 1837 may be just as valid today as when they were written.

Some sources will seem more reliable than others. But always be cautious. Don't believe everything you read, and don't depend too heavily on any single source in your essay.

Place of Publication

A passage that comes from, say, a blogger's website, a supermarket tabloid, or the pen of a politician with an ax to grind can't be completely trusted. On the other hand, a passage taken from a scholarly journal, a report published by a foundation, a government document, a popular mass magazine, or a book written by a reputable author is likely to be more reliable. But, frankly, there are no guarantees.

The Intended Audience

Authors almost always slant their writing to appeal to certain audiences. An article on children's health meant for a mass audience, for example, will be different from an article directed toward subscribers of a pediatrics journal. Likewise, an author writing for an audience of nursing home residents will include certain material that would be inappropriate in a publication read mostly by college students. Knowing the intended audience, then, can help you weigh the validity of any source.

Author's Purpose

An essay you write for school will be different from an email you write to a friend, mainly because the reason for writing is different. Every piece of writing has one or more purposes. Think of all the possibilities: to inform, to entertain, to anger, to provoke, to inspire, to move, to convince, to calm down, to compliment, to declare love, and on and on. Knowing why an author has written a particular passage helps you figure out how trustworthy it is.

Tone and Language

Check the source for objectivity. If the author expresses a view in rational terms and supports the idea with sound evidence—even if you don't agree with it—you can pretty well count on the reliability of the material. A source full of excessively passionate and inflammatory language, on the other hand, should not be accepted at face value.

For example, which of the following reports of a fire is a more reliable source of information?

#1: At 3:30 P.M. on September 21, the Bedford Fire Department received a call that a residence at 330 Holly Road was on fire. Ten minutes later, the first fire truck arrived at the site and found a conflagration on an unfinished porch. Firemen promptly extinguished the fire. Damage was limited to the wood frame of the unfinished structure. The cause of the fire is yet to be determined.

#2: Charlotte Robbins, a 36-year-old widow and mother of four young children, wept profusely as she surveyed the charred ruins of the unfinished porch outside her Bedford home last weekend.

"Poor Fred, he would have been devastated," she sobbed, referring to her husband, a disabled mechanic, dead only three weeks, whose dream had long been to build a porch for his loving family. "Why, oh, why did this happen to me?" Charlotte asked, but no one could answer. The cause of the fire remains a mystery, but the misery and heartbreak it caused for Fred's survivors is readily apparent.

The contrast between these two passages is easy to detect. The first account states just the facts; the second gushes with emotion. Sources used for the synthesis essay won't often be as extreme as these sample passages. But you can be sure that analyzing the tone and language of the sources will help you determine their validity.

How to Write a Synthesis Essay

Don't be misled by the title of this section. It promises more than it can deliver. The reason is that no one learns to master essay writing by reading about how to do it. You learn to write masterful essays by writing essays, by messing around with ideas and words, by experimenting, practicing, and doing. Many of the essays you've written in English, social studies, and other classes have probably been good practice for writing a synthesis essay. And if you've ever written a research paper containing a thesis you had to prove, you've already done it.

In a sense, this AP essay is a mini-research paper. You are given a topic and sources to study. You must devise a thesis and bring in evidence to support it. The AP guidelines require that in one way or another you refer to **at least three** of the sources. In addition, you may use your own knowledge, observations, and experience to support your point of view. In fact, you shouldn't rely solely on the sources. An essay derived partly from your own thinking about the issue stands a

TIP

Refer to at least three sources in your essay. You may also use your knowledge, observations, and experience to support your point of view.

greater chance for a top score because your own ideas can add depth that would be absent from an essay based only on the sources.

Making a Case

To make a case in support of your position, follow the same steps recommended for writing the perfect essay: prewriting, composing, editing, and proofreading—all discussed on page 102. But take note: The process may be similar, but writing a position paper also imposes a unique set of demands, because you are making a claim that you want your readers to accept. And they're more likely to accept it if you take steps to prove its validity.

The odds of writing a convincing position paper grow exponentially with a good, solid statement or claim. When composing your statement, beware of hyperbole. That is, avoid overemphasizing the truth of your claim. Dogmatism has its place, but absolute statements can often be discredited. Therefore, don't hesitate to qualify your claim with words such as *often, usually, most*, and *sometimes*. As a case in point, which of the following claims has greater validity?

1. Video games turn children violent.
2. Excessive use of video games often turns children violent.

It's obvious, isn't it, that sentence 1 exaggerates the effect of video games, and sentence 2 makes a claim that is beyond dispute?

A position paper requires evidence, or grounds, on which to base your claim, and nothing is more persuasive than a body of factual information and data. Expert testimony drawn from several of the sources that accompany the essay question also adds credence to your argument. Emotion appeals to many readers, too. Use it freely to support your point of view, but don't overdo it. To legitimize your claim, balance emotion with rational evidence.

Finally, an effective argument may not be complete without a rebuttal of some kind. Regardless of how thoroughly you've built your argument, a counterclaim may still be possible. Your job as an essayist is to anticipate the counterclaim and preempt it by pointing out its flaws.

Keeping in mind these basic principles of constructing a persuasive essay, use the following pages as a step-by-step guide through the composition of a first-rate synthesis essay.

Introducing Your Position

TIP

State your position with precise, unambiguous words.

Avoid writing a fuzzy, overly complicated position statement. Make your position crystal clear with precise, unambiguous language. No rule says that a position statement is limited to a single sentence, although that's not a bad idea. A concise declarative sentence that focuses the reader on the issue may do the trick.

For example, let's assume that a synthesis essay topic deals with the effects of gambling. The issue is whether positive aspects of gambling outweigh its harmful effects, or whether the reverse is true—that gambling causes more harm than good. After weighing the evidence, a student claims:

Gambling is an activity that affects the lives of millions of Americans.

Well . . . the problems with that statement nearly jump off the page. Just count its flaws:

1. It's too broad.
2. It fails to state a position or express the writer's opinion.
3. It's not arguable (no reasonable person would disagree with it).
4. It ignores the issue raised by the question.

In short, its weaknesses disqualify it as a viable claim.

Now, look at another position statement on the same topic:

The economic effects of gambling are generally positive.

This position statement works. Why?

1. It's specific enough to be the topic of a short paper.
2. It expresses the writer's opinion.
3. It's controversial—worthy of an argument.
4. It addresses the issue raised by the question.

Where to Put Your Thesis

Ordinarily, an essay's thesis or main idea is stated early in the essay. How early? It can be the first sentence, or part of the first sentence, although creating a context for the thesis is often a desirable thing to do. That is, before stating your thesis, search through the sources for interesting ideas that you can adapt for an opening that will draw readers into your essay. Then, consider any of the following introductory techniques. Or use one that you've invented.

> ### Use of Qualifying Words
>
> Notice the word *generally* in the position statement, "The economic effects of gambling are generally positive."
>
> *Generally* is a qualifying term that makes the statement less dogmatic. Without the word, the statement implies that gambling *always* has a positive effect on the economy, a claim that is hard to defend and nearly impossible to prove. Just a single exception would destroy its credibility. When you write a position statement, therefore, consider making the claim more difficult to challenge by including an appropriate qualifier, such as *almost, frequently, generally, in most cases, likely, often, might, maybe, probably, sometimes, customarily,* and so forth.

1. Begin with a brief incident or anecdote related to the point you plan to make in your essay:

    Until Harrah's introduced casino gambling, Joliet, an Illinois steel town 40 miles from Chicago, was a depressed place, with high unemployment, low wages, and slum conditions. With the coming of the casino, the city enjoyed a remarkable economic rebirth. Jobs were created, opportunities for businesses multiplied, and the place became a magnet for investment in new housing, businesses, restaurants, and motels. While gambling is known to harm millions of Americans, the revitalization of Joliet demonstrates that <u>its overall effect on a community can nevertheless be positive.</u> (Thesis statement is underlined.)

2. State a provocative idea in an ordinary way or an ordinary idea worded in a provocative way:

    Gambling casinos pay higher wages to their employees than almost any other businesses except salmon fisheries in Alaska. <u>In spite of its potential for positive economic effects, however, the gambling industry harms American society more than it helps.</u> (Thesis statement is underlined.)

3. Use a quotation from the prompt, from one of the sources, or from your reading, your experience, your grandmother:

    "All you need is a dollar and a dream." These catchy words have enticed millions of gullible New Yorkers into throwing their money away with the hope that they'll win the state lottery. <u>Because low-income people play the Lottery more often than well-off people, the lure of gambling harms them more than it does others.</u> (Thesis statement is underlined.)

4. Knock down a commonly held assumption, or define a word in a startling new way:

Last February, when Sophie Whittaker, a waitress in St. Louis, Missouri, eagerly boarded a Mississippi River boat for an evening of playing slot machines, she had no idea that winning really meant losing. She won five hundred dollars that night and came back the next weekend to win some more. But the gambling gods had other ideas. Sophie lost, and lost big. To make up for losing nearly a thousand dollars, she returned a few nights later. Two days later she went back once more, and then again and again, sometimes calling in sick to her boss in order to spend the evening hoping for a jackpot. She won a few dollars now and then but slid ever deeper into debt, pulled down by her new-found addiction. Sophie's experience is not unique. Hers is but one of countless similar stories about Americans who have surrendered to the gambling habit, an unquestionable plague on American society. (Thesis statement is underlined.)

5. Ask an interesting question or two that you'll answer in the essay:

Why have Native Americans fought so hard in Washington for the right to run casinos on their tribal lands? The answer is simple. Casinos make their owners rich. In addition, gambling profits can pay the bills for schools, hospitals, roads, and other needs. In effect, in the right circumstances gambling does more good than harm. (Thesis statement is underlined.)

An introduction invites your readers into the essay. It enriches the essay and adds a layer of depth, suggesting that your essay hasn't been written merely to fulfill the assignment, but that it has been prepared with care and thought.

But if none of these techniques for writing introductions works for you, or you don't have the time to devise another, just state your position up front. Don't phrase your position like an announcement, however, as in, "In this essay, I am going to prove that gambling does greater harm than good." State your point, as in "Gambling does greater harm than good," and go from there.

QUESTION: How important is the introduction?

ANSWER (from a veteran AP reader): "I can't overemphasize the importance of a strong lead-in and thesis statement to grab my attention. I read 500+ papers a day during a long week of reading. Therefore, the lead-in and first paragraph speak volumes to alert me to a student's artistry."

—Suzanne Skipper, Lake Howell High School (FL)

Supporting Your Position with Appropriate Evidence

Each paragraph in your essay should contribute to the development of the main idea. It should contain facts, data, examples—reasons of all kinds to corroborate the thesis and to convince readers to agree with you. If you reread what you've written and find that the evidence fails to support the thesis, cross it out or revise it. Be ruthless! Even though you may admire your own words, give them the boot if they don't help to strengthen your case.

How Much Evidence to Include

A rule of thumb is that three distinct and relevant reasons will usually suffice to prove a point. But essay writing is far from an exact science. Three or more is usually better than one or two, but which works best depends largely on the issue, the potency of the reasons, and the skill and grace with which the essay is written.

Regardless of how many ideas you present, each one may not require the same amount of emphasis. You might dispose of the weakest ideas in just a few sentences, while the others require at least a paragraph or more. But whatever you emphasize, be sure that each idea is separate and distinct. Don't mislead your readers by rehashing an earlier idea in different words. Remember also that whatever the number of reasons, the argument will be weak if the reasons themselves are weak.

Here's an outline written by a student under the impression that each reason supports the thesis that *the effects of gambling on the economy are generally positive:*

Reason 1: Gambling occurs in many places, including the Internet.
Reason 2: If you can't afford to lose money, you shouldn't gamble.
Reason 3: The money you lose goes into someone else's pocket.

The outline consists of three reasons, each one trite and largely irrelevant to the writer's position, although reason 3 vaguely refers to the economic consequences of gambling. Evidence of this caliber would certainly fail to make a sufficient case.

In contrast, check these reasons:

Reason 1: Gambling casinos create jobs, especially in rural areas.
Reason 2: Taxed at a high rate, casinos serve as a rich source of revenue for the states in which they operate.
Reason 3: Casinos attract tourists who spend money for food, lodging, and services.

Using these distinct and relevant reasons, a writer could construct a solid argument, especially if the reasons are sensibly arranged.

The arrangement of ideas recommended for an analytical essay (*see page 34*) applies equally to the synthesis essay: sort through your reasons, pick the best ones, and put them in order of importance. Then decide which reason provides the strongest evidence. That reason may be listed first in your outline, but save it for last in your essay. Giving it away too soon diminishes the

TIP

Find at least three separate and distinct ideas to support your thesis.

TIP

Save your best idea for last.

impact of the less important reasons. In other words, it will help you work toward your best point, not away from it. By no means is this the only way to structure an argument, but it's one that usually works.

Refuting Opposing Viewpoints

Another decision you must make in writing a synthesis essay is whether to include a counterargument, or refutation—a paragraph or more that points out weaknesses in the evidence likely to be used by someone who disagrees with you. In order to write a counterargument, you must, of course, anticipate the arguments that a prospective opponent might use. A counterargument isn't essential, but it's highly desirable because it weakens your opponent's position while strengthening yours. In fact, it can add potency to an essay that can't be achieved in any other way.

To see how an argument can be refuted, consider the claim that the negative economic effects of gambling outweigh its positive effects. Here are three reasons that could be used to support that point of view:

Reason 1: Gamblers squander money that has better uses, such as education, housing, family life, donations to charity, etc.

Reason 2: Compulsive gambling is a disease that requires costly treatment to cure.

Reason 3: Gambling drains community resources, such as the extra amount spent for law enforcement.

> **TIP**
>
> A counterargument adds punch to your argument.

All three reasons sound valid enough, so how can they be refuted? Well, if you focus on Reason 3, you might begin by saying that it makes a good point, but it's not foolproof. You could argue that casinos generate considerable tax revenue that pays for additional law enforcement, or point out that gambling facilities tend to increase the price of nearby housing, thereby raising the standard of living in a community. Since wealthier people usually pay higher property taxes, the community should have no trouble raising money to pay for a larger police force. While refuting claims made by your opposition, it's important to resist the temptation of tearing to shreds every one of their arguments. Your essay will seem far more rational and circumspect if you concede the possibility that one or two of the reasons offered by the opposition may at least be somewhat valid.

Where to Put a Counterargument

There's no formula for where in your essay to put counterarguments. Sometimes it fits best near the end of an essay, just before the conclusion. At other times it should be stated early in the essay. A counterargument can also be discussed briefly in each paragraph. As you develop your case, anticipate opposing arguments and refute them then and there. In the end, the location of your counterargument is less important than the message it delivers: that the evidence you offer is superior to that of your adversary.

Avoiding Faulty Reasoning

Evidence must logically support your essay's main idea. As a case in point, let's consider a synthesis essay question on the issue of tracking, or ability grouping, a longtime controversy in high school education. Some educators argue that students make greater educational gains when they are grouped according to ability. Others claim that ability grouping does more harm than good.

To judge the quality of evidence, let's examine an argument that comes from an essay written in favor of ability grouping. The topic sentence of one of its paragraphs reads:

Intelligent and capable students are often bored in mixed classes.

What would you expect the writer of this statement to say next? From the following list, choose the sentence that provides the most logical and appropriate evidence in support of the topic sentence:

☐ **1.** The quality of education improves when students are homogeneously grouped.
☐ **2.** Bright students in mixed classes are often left waiting for slow students to catch up.
☐ **3.** Pity the poor teachers tearing their hair out while trying to teach those godawful mixed classes.
☐ **4.** No one with his head on straight supports mixed classes.
☐ **5.** Homogeneous classes usually offer more intellectual stimulation for intelligent and capable students.

All five sentences more or less relate to the subject of the essay. But not all of them offer a logical follow-up to the claim that mixed classes bore smart students.

1. In Sentence 1, the broad generalization raises issues far beyond the topic sentence.
2. Sentence 2 works well; it provides a relevant detail that supports the writer's view.
3. Sentence 3 is an emotional outburst that has no place in a rational discussion of the topic.
4. Sentence 4 contains inappropriate language that diverts the discussion away from the topic.
5. Sentence 5 provides a point that follows logically from the topic sentence.

Sentences 1, 3, and 4 illustrate three types of faulty reasoning that inevitably weaken an essay: overgeneralization, emotionalism, and distracting language. In your thinking and writing, try to avoid such pitfalls as well as these other types of faulty reasoning:

TIP

Beware of over-generalizations, emotionalism, and inappropriate language.

1. IRRELEVANT TESTIMONY:

The Golden State Warriors superstar Steph Curry says, "I hated mixed classes in high school."

Is it logical to cite the classroom experience of a professional basketball player (or any other celebrity) in a serious educational argument?

2. SNOB APPEAL:

The best AP English students everywhere agree that ability grouping is the way to go.

There's nothing logical about this statement. It is a crude appeal to readers who think they are or wish to be part of an elite group. It adds nothing to a discussion of the pros or cons of ability grouping.

3. CIRCULAR REASONING:

I favor ability grouping because it separates students with different skills and interests.

The fallacy here is that the writer has tried to justified a bias toward ability grouping simply by defining the term. Precisely why the writer prefers ability grouping remains unclear.

4. ABSENCE OF PROOF:

Grouping has been studied time and again, but I have never seen proof that mixed grouping is educationally superior to ability grouping.

A writer's admitted lack of knowledge can never be logically used as evidence to support a claim.

5. **OVERSIMPLIFICATION:**

> When you get right down to it, ability grouping is like life; people prefer to be with others like themselves.

It's neither logical nor helpful to reduce a controversial and complex issue to a simple platitude.

6. **TELLING ONLY HALF THE STORY:**

> Ability grouping is better because it serves the educational needs of both the smartest and the slowest students.

The writer has ignored the mass of students in the middle.

7. **GOING TO EXTREMES:**

> If ability grouping were abolished, the system of American education as we know it would no longer exist.

This sort of thinking suggests desperation. By offering only the most extreme position, the writer ignores all other possibilities.

Incorporating Sources

Instructions for the synthesis essay tell you to incorporate **at least three** sources into your essay. You won't earn extra credit for citing more than three, but neither will it hurt to refer to four or more if the additional citations bolster your position on the issue.

The simplest and most obvious way to use a source in your essay is to state your position and back it up with evidence pulled from the source. Suppose, for instance, that the essay question relates to the effects of digital media on young people. You plan to make the point that it's virtually impossible to escape from the influence of electronic communication.

One of the sources—let's call it *Source A*—discusses the pervasiveness of digital technology in 21st-century America and contains this paragraph:

> The most important and most multidimensional of the forces shaping youth culture is electronic communication. Smartphones, iPads, texting, Twitter, e-books, and especially the all-consuming substitute environment, the Internet, have enveloped today's youth in a cocoon of sensory information. I think it is doubtful that anyone who grew up before the turn of the last century can appreciate how much the senses of the young are being bombarded, even tyrannized, by electronic communication. Indeed, the digital media—in the broadest sense of the word—are not only influencing a whole environment. To those coming of age at the present time, they are the environment.

Ideas from this paragraph can be woven into an essay using any of the following techniques:

- Direct Quotes
- Indirect Quotes
- Paraphrasing
- Commentary

TIP

Learn to use both direct and indirect quotes.

Direct Quotes

Direct quotes are word-for-word reproductions of material found in a source. Everything—grammar, spelling, capitalization—must duplicate the original exactly, and the words must be enclosed in quotation marks:

> For most young people, the digital media have permanently altered the environment. In fact, according to the author of Source A, "To those coming of age at the present time, they are the environment."

If you wish to omit words from the original for grammatical or other reasons, use an ellipsis (. . .) consisting of three periods to mark the place where material has been deleted.

> The author of Source A writes, "I think it is doubtful that anyone who grew up before the turn of the last century can appreciate how much the senses of the young are being bombarded . . . by electronic communication."

If you find it necessary to add words for clarity or any other reason, enclose the words in brackets [like this]. Brackets inform readers that the bracketed words are not part of the original quotation.

> Source A sums up the situation by saying, "To those coming of age at the present time, they [the media] *are* the environment."

Indirect Quotes

An indirect quote reports an idea without quoting it word-for-word. No quotation marks are needed.

> Most young people accept digital communication as a fundamental part of their environment. In fact, Source A claims that it virtually *is* the environment to those coming of age at the present time.

A WORD OF CAUTION

In your essay, use direct and indirect quotations sparingly and only as illustrative material. Use them to support ideas that you have first stated in your own words. Although you may be tempted to use lots of quoted material to make your case, don't do it. Don't let quotes dominate your essay. After all, the AP exam is a test of your writing ability, not of your ability to quote others.

Notice how the author of the following paragraph relied too heavily on quotations:

Even though most young people accept almost without question the use of electronic communication, it profoundly influences their environment. *"Smartphones, iPads, texting, Twitter, e-books, and especially the all-consuming substitute environment, the Internet, have enveloped today's youth in a cocoon of sensory information."* It is clear that for anyone *"coming of age at the present time,"* the digital media *"are the environment."*

Paraphrasing

Paraphrasing is restating someone else's idea in your own words. A paraphrase contains the same information and should be roughly the same length as the original.

> Today's teens are creatures of the digital age. Most of them are inured to how completely surrounded they are by electronic communications. *In fact, the author of Source A says that digital media actually have become the environment for young people coming of age now or in the near future.*

Commentary

The sources provided on the exam are meant to give you information and to stimulate your thinking about the issue. They also give you ideas to discuss in your essay. With a little practice, you can learn to pick material from a source, transfer it verbatim to your essay, adapt it, or shape it any way you want to build your main idea. But to write a more distinctive essay, one that reveals your ability to interpret and analyze source material, try not only to draw from the sources but also to comment on them. Think of the sources as a one-sided conversation with the authors. Once the authors have their say, it's your turn to respond by commenting on their ideas, their reasoning, their points of view.

Thus, it would be perfectly appropriate to incorporate sources with such comments as:

> "The author of Source B offers a short-sighted view of . . ."

> "To a point I agree with the author of Source B, although he doesn't carry the argument far enough. To strengthen his case, he should have included . . ."

> "In Source B, the author says that . . . , an assertion that supports my own views. I would add, however, that . . ."

> "Clearly, the author of Source B has a bias against . . . , a failing that weakens her argument."

TIP

Comment on some of the material in the sources.

Notice that you need not comment only on sources with which you agree. Feel free to quarrel with authors whose ideas differ from yours. Show that they are all wet, out to lunch, or have loose screws—but please use more refined language than that. Avoid name-calling (*moron, airhead, ignoramus*, etc.) and exclamations such as, "That's the dumbest idea I've ever heard!" Refuting the opinions of others can bolster an argument, but treat even wrongheaded opinions with respect.

Citing Sources

In your essay, you must acknowledge the source of all direct and indirect quotations. Custom also requires you to give credit to any source from which you borrow, paraphrase, or adapt ideas.

Don't bother to cite the source of everyday factual material that's known by most literate, reasonably alert people. No citation is needed, for example, if you draw from the sources the information that the United States is a republic, that Thanksgiving falls on the fourth Thursday in November, or that most kids like to stay up late at night.

Many different formats exist for acknowledging sources, but on the AP exam you need no more than a brief parenthetical reference within the text of your essay, as in:

> According to a school psychologist, "Some children may be better off if they escape their parents' grip, healthier if they grow up wild and free and sort things out on their own" (Source A).

Instead of writing *Source A* inside the parentheses, you may insert the last name of the author, as in:

> One panel member summed up the conflict by saying, "Young people want a larger share in the decision-making about their lives" (Collins).

(Note that the end punctuation comes after the close of the parentheses and outside the quotation marks.)

Another technique for naming sources is to integrate the information more fully into the text, as in

> Dean Marcy Denby argues that "the basic purpose of a university education has always been . . . etc."

Which method you use to cite sources on the AP exam is up to you. It's probably better to choose one method and stick to it. Using a variety can make you appear indecisive, maybe even confused.

THE PROBLEM OF PLAGIARISM

The one basic rule about plagiarism is this: **Don't do it!**

Why? For one thing, it's dishonest, it's immoral, and it can get you into a whole mess of trouble. Intentional or not, plagiarism is theft. Stealing someone else's words or ideas and passing them off as your own is, to put it bluntly, a stupid thing to do.

To avoid even the slightest hint of plagiarism on the AP exam, give credit to your sources. It's simple: Whenever you take words or ideas from a source, identify their origin inside a pair of parentheses: (*Source B*), (*Jones*), or ("*Title*"). If you forget, your essay score will suffer. Even a brilliant essay that might otherwise earn an 8 or 9 may receive a score of 2 or 3 if you fail to document sources. When in doubt about the need to document a particular idea in your essay, play it safe and smart. Err on the side of inclusion, not exclusion.

Sample Synthesis Essay Question

What follows is a sample synthesis essay question. It is followed by the essays of three students. The essays were handwritten under AP testing conditions: 15 minutes to read the sources and 40 minutes to write the essay, with no access to a computer, a dictionary, or any other book. By reading the essays you'll see what it takes to earn a high score. Read the comments, too. They'll alert you to some pitfalls to avoid when you write a synthesis essay of your own.

SUGGESTED TIME:

15 MINUTES FOR READING THE QUESTION AND SOURCES

40 MINUTES FOR WRITING AN ESSAY

The U.S. Constitution makes no explicit mention of the right to privacy. The courts, however, have recognized that privacy is a fundamental right in a free society. Yet, public figures—from politicians to athletes to entertainers—often have their private lives revealed by the media. Is this fair? Shouldn't celebrities enjoy as much privacy as ordinary citizens? Or should they expect to pay a price for fame by having details of their private lives made public? Is the public's right to know stronger than the right of celebrities to maintain their privacy?

Carefully read the following six sources, including the material that introduces each source. Then, in an essay that synthesizes at least three of the sources, take a position on the claim that celebrities have the same right to privacy enjoyed by other citizens.

Source A (Hilden)
Source B (jenblacksheep)
Source C (DeGrandpré)
Source D (Graph)
Source E (GNL)
Source F (Nordhaus)

Instructions:
- Respond to the prompt with a thesis that may establish a line of reasoning.
- Provide evidence from at least three of the provided sources to support the thesis. Indicate clearly the sources used through direct quotation, paraphrase, or summary. Sources may be cited as Source A, Source B, etc., or by using the descriptions in parentheses.
- Explain the relationship between the evidence and the thesis.
- Demonstrate an understanding of the rhetorical situation.
- Use appropriate grammar and punctuation in communicating the argument.

Source A

Julie Hilden, "Does Celebrity Destroy Privacy?" published by *FindLaw*, an online legal news and commentary site for lawyers, businesses, students, and consumers.

The passage below is an excerpt from an article entitled "Is Disclosure of Private Facts About Celebrities Justified?" written by Julie Hilden, an attorney and columnist.

Often, it is the intensely private aspects of a celebrity's life—involving drugs, sex, or sexual orientation, marital discord, issues with children or other family members, or similar topics—that the public and the media deem newsworthy. (Illegality only ratchets up the stakes, and increases interest in the story.) But is the public entitled to know such private details about a celebrity, just because that person is a public figure?

Two basic theories are used to justify the exposure of celebrity privacy. One is the "waiver theory," which holds that celebrities have given up their privacy by choosing to appear in the public eye. Those who believe in this theory see celebrities as having made a sort of Faustian bargain: lifelong fame in exchange for the lifelong loss of privacy.

Another widely cited argument for celebrities having forfeited their privacy is what I will call the "hypocrisy theory." It holds that celebrities who, in their statements to the public, have lied about or deceptively omitted a private fact about themselves cannot then complain when the truth becomes known.

Neither of these theories is entirely valid, but the "waiver" theory is by far the weaker of the two. It seems somewhat unfair to say that because a person's gift lies in acting, basketball, or singing, rather than, for example, engineering, architecture, or computer science, that he or she has somehow "chosen" to give up all of his or her privacy.

Source B

"jenblacksheep," "Do Public Figures Have Privacy Rights?" *Hubpages.com,* 2018

The passage below is an excerpt from an article posted on a British website that publishes opinion pieces related to issues of politics, social conditions, and human rights.

The definition of privacy (according to the Oxford English Dictionary) states that people should be "free from public attention, as a matter of choice or right." In my opinion, taking a position of power takes away from this area of privacy.

It seems obvious that there are areas of one's life that someone would wish to keep private but would be in the public's interest to disclose. There are some cases of media invasion that are completely justified. The public needs to know if a politician is abusing his position, accepting bribes, or has a hidden agenda that could lead him to act in his own interests rather than the national interest.

In 2015, it was reported that the then Prime Minister of England, David Cameron, had taken drugs at school. He refused to comment until after he left office, when he admitted to it, but defended himself saying, "I didn't spend the early years of my life thinking: "I better not do anything because one day I might be a politician." It is my opinion that events occurring in someone's past should remain there, as they are not a realistic reflection of what that person is now.

. . . Although public figures have no legal rights to privacy from the media, there are an increasing number of cases where it seems justified for privacy to be overridden. The most obvious of these is when a person of responsibility is abusing a position of power. The thought here is that in fact they don't really have the right to privacy in this area, even if they wish a deed to remain private. If a public figure has a personal problem that is affecting his or her ability to do the job, then it seems that it is in the public's interest to divulge this.

Source C

Vincent M. de Grandpré, "Understanding the Market for Celebrity: An Economic Analysis of the Right of Publicity," published online by Simpson, Thacher, & Bartlett, LLP, November 15, 2017.

The following passage is an excerpt from a monograph prepared by a New York law firm.

. . . What explains the public's interest in celebrities?

In his provocative work *Life: The Movie*, Neal Gabler argues that entertainment, and the movies in particular, have become so important to our individual existence that American public life itself has evolved to resemble the movies. Gabler argues that this trend has reshaped every sphere of human activity from politics to religion to the arts, all because of the need for these activities to rival readily available entertainment in keeping public attention. Not only have moving pictures become the central metaphor for understanding American public life, they have changed our epistemology, the very understanding of the world in which we live. According to Gabler, we now live in the "lifies." This "lifies" metaphor not only captures the reality that Americans use a significant portion of their income to be entertained; it conveys the idea that we have populated our lives with celebrities, those lead actors whose stories we eagerly watch and weave into our lives.

Our urge to know and associate with celebrities is not only motivated by our desire to be entertained, however. As one author notes, "celebrities have become, in recent decades, the chief agents of moral change in the United States." They have come to embody abstract issues of points of view, and are shorthand forms for ideals or expertise. Theorists have also argued that celebrities attract us because we see them as individuals who stand out in our anonymous, mass society. We seek them because they make us feel in-the-know or on the inside; in our mass society, they humanize our lives. "Stars" attract us because they seem to be free, on-the-go and liberated from the constraints of daily life.

Source D

"Entertainment to Environment Headlines of Prominent News Sources (Ratio of 5 to 1 or Greater),"
from Pew Research Center's Project for Excellence in Journalism, 2016

---

*The graph below shows the frequency of reporting on celebrities or entertainment-related topics
compared to reporting on environmental issues.*

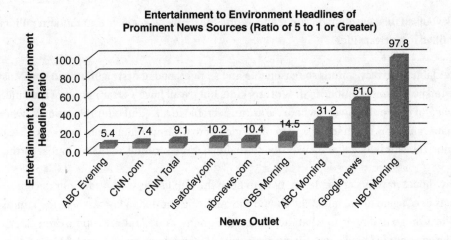

Source E

GNL, "For Today's Public Figures, Private Lives Really Matter," *Buzzle.com, Intelligent Life on the Web*, November 30, 2004.

The passage below is adapted from an article published in an online British periodical, of general interest to contemporary readers.

Ask yourself this question: do you really—and I mean really—believe that modern politicians are entitled to a private life?

The claim to privacy sounds so reasonable and so right, and at first sight indeed it is. Most of us are not politicians or public figures of any kind, but we all have a clear notion of the difference between our own public lives—where we are answerable to all—and our private ones—where we are answerable only to ourselves and to those closest to us. How much more necessary, we reason, must it be for public figures, exposed to so much more scrutiny, to maintain that distinction?

Why should partners and children have to be in the public eye, we wonder, our decent instincts once again to the fore. Why should the public be entitled to know where the famous go on holiday, or go to dinner, or what they spend their money on? And why, some even assert, do we have any right to know about their private mistakes and their sexual secrets? Nobody denies that such things are often interesting, but surely that is not the point. Would we not all be happier people living in a better society if we drew the line?

Source F

Jamie Nordhaus, "Celebrities' Rights to Privacy: How Far Should the Paparazzi Be Allowed to Go?" University of Texas School of Law, *Review of Litigation*, Volume 25, 2010.

The excerpt below comes from an article written in a journal read by law school students, practicing attorneys, judges, and others interested in matters pertaining to the individual rights of citizens.

Celebrities are entitled to the same general right of privacy that extends to all individuals. However, the degree to which that right is protected is much narrower for public figures. . . . As a result, a broad spectrum of information concerning celebrities is transferred from the protective shield of privacy into the realm of the public interest.

Various rationales exist for affording a smaller degree of protection to the private lives of public figures than to private figures . . . . The first rationale is that most public figures seek and consent to publicity. Actors and actresses strive to be stars who are known and recognized worldwide. The same holds true for politicians striving to attain higher positions, as well as other individuals who relish their moments in the spotlight.

. . . Second, the personalities and affairs of celebrities are viewed as inherently "public." In this sense, the public nature of celebrities' occupations is construed as waiving their rights to privacy. This waiver should be regarded, however, as a limited waiver, restricting the press to examining and exposing only that information that has some bearing on the individual's position in society.

. . . Finally, the press has a right to inform the public about matters of public interest. As celebrities cultivate their positions in the public spotlight, they generate continued interest in their activities. The public begins to feel as if they "know" the individual and are thus entitled to be privy to their private lives.

Sample Student Responses

Whitney's Response

(Printed as it was written)

In dentists' waiting rooms, on Facebook and U-Tube, and on magazine racks all over the country, the public likes to read, see, and hear about the Kardashians, Britany Spears, Shawn Mendes and countless other celebrities. They enjoy photos, videos, and stories about famous people. They are curious about who is going out with whom, who is getting divorced or having children. They enjoy photos of TV and movie stars shopping at Target, eating a pizza, or just walking down the street or washing dishes. That helps them identify with headline-making stars engaged in everyday activities. It makes them think that being famous is not that big of a deal because even celebrities have to take out the garbage once in a while. In addition, when we think of celebrities as just plain folks like us, we feel "in the-know or on the inside" (Source C). In a way, imagining that we really "know" famous people, the writer of Source C says, in our mass society, celebrities "humanize" our lives" by making us feel important.

Problems arise when a famous person wants to maintain privacy, however. He or she has that right, of course, but the public also has the right to try to find out as much as they can about celebrities. The case of Ray Rice is a good example. Rice was a member of the Baltimore Ravens football team and was caught on camera punching his girlfriend late one night in an Atlantic City hotel elevator. A security guard sold the video to TMZ, the notorious website that is all gossip all the time. The video went viral and afterwards, the National Football League suspended Rice indefinitely from his football career. If Rice had been just an ordinary person, the incident would probably have been ignored or forgotten. But it wasn't, and Rice paid a huge price for being famous.

Once a person such as Rice and other public personalities start to make headlines, in effect, they give up their right of privacy. Julie Helden, the author of Source A, calls this the "waiver theory," which says that when someone makes the choice to become a public figure, they trade privacy for fame. Although Helden doesn't agree that it is right, it is inevitable.

Well-known people who crave privacy must take steps to get it. J.D. Salinger, the author of *Catcher in the Rye* is an example. For much of his life, he escaped to the mountains of Vermont because he wanted no part of public life. He gave no interviews and refused to show his face in public.

Politicians are a different story. They may want to keep their lives private, but the actions of such people in powerful positions, as Source B, says, "will necessarily be of public attention," and they have no legal rights to privacy. This often happens when politicians behave badly or when their past contains evidence of outrageous racial, sexual, religious, or other kinds of prejudice. A controversial is Roy Moore, who hoped for a seat in the US Senate representing Alabama a few years ago. During the campaign word got out that he had sexually abused teenage girls. Some people voted for him nevertheless, but most voters, disgusted by his history, refused to support him. The author of Source E sums up the situation very well: "The way people live their private lives does tell is things that can help to make judgments about them as public people."

It's less important to know intimate details about singers, actors, and other stars. Yet, many such entertainers seek to be photographed and also encourage reporters to write and broadcast stories about them. They even hire publicists whose job is to make them famous. When Beyoncé goes to the grocery store, her agent alerts the press. Many ordinary people long for a few minutes of fame. Some put themselves through degrading experiences on reality television in order to be noticed or considered to be out of the ordinary.

Some people argue that trying to be different or nonconforming is part of human nature. However, once they make a name for themselves, they often discover that fame is not everything. Since nobody forces them to make this "Faustian bargain" (Source A), they have to accept the that the eyes of the people will be on them from then on, and they have no right to complain.

Your impressions: _____

_____

_____

_____

Comment to Whitney from an AP Reader

You engage your reader immediately by showing that the issue of your essay is current and widespread. By explaining both the desire and the rewards of knowing about famous people, you provide a context for your thesis statement at the beginning of the second paragraph. To support your point of view, you cite examples not only from the sources but from your own fund of knowledge, and set up a particularly apt contrast between the behavior of J.D. Salinger and Roy Moore. In various ways throughout your essay, you emphasize the psychological need of the public to know details about the lives of famous figures. That emphasis leaves unaddressed the issue of the public's right to know, although you imply that a *need* to know is tantamount to the *right* to know.

Let me commend you for making the most of your references. You not only cite three sources as you develop your ideas, but you enter into a kind of dialogue with the authors. For example, you embrace the "waiver theory" espoused by Source A. By integrating it into your essay, you permit the author to participate in the development of your essay's main idea.

Another strength of your essay is that it discusses issues surrounding the pursuit of fame, including some people's extraordinary efforts to achieve it. The examples you chose—such as those about Ray Rice and Beyoncé—are quite startling and lead seamlessly and convincingly to your conclusion that those who have sought fame have no right to complain when their privacy is violated.

The essay demonstrates your maturity as a thinker. Awkwardness in your use of language and some minor missteps in sentence construction weaken its overall effect, but these flaws are relatively minor, not serious enough to keep the essay from earning a top score.

SCORE: 6

Sonya's Response
(Printed as it was written)

One of the rights all Americans enjoy is the right to privacy. However, not everyone can enjoy it because of who they are. As Source F says, "Various rationales exist for affording a smaller degree of protection to the private lives as public figures." This is very true. Some people have become successful personalities who have become household names through television, movies, sports, and other areas. Because their faces are well known, they are often recognized wherever they go. People don't leave them alone, taking selfies with them or asking for their autographs. It's hard to imagine never being left alone to go on a walk with the dog, ride a bike, go out to eat, stop at the pharmacy or supermarket. Every time you leave your home, your face is recognized, and people therefore think they can point to you and speak to you, as though you are not entitled to be anonymous.

But the thing is that they have a choice. In the Source B makes the point that a wish to have complete privacy requires a decision not to become famous. It's different if someone becomes a public person by accident, through no fault of their own. They might win the lottery jackpot, for example, and suddenly their story is broadcast online and everywhere else. Since it's not their fault, they deserve to stay in the background as a private citizen. These people have a right to complain if their privacy is violated.

In contrast to them, the author of Source B points out the "Waiver Theory." This means that a celebrity or a candidate running for a government office automatically gives up their right to privacy "by choosing to appear in public.," which is called a "Faustian bargain."

They should be aware that their privacy will be put in danger before they decide to seek an office, and if they think that they can avoid being noticed on the street or having their background revealed by media, they are extremely naïve. They don't really deserve to be elected by the public. Their judgment is really not very strong.

Source C describes the situation that I agree with the most. We, the public, don't really "have the right to know about their private mistakes and their sexual secrets." Such facts are interesting, but that's "not the point," as the author says. I agree with the conclusion that we'd be a happier and better society "if we drew the line." Basically, it is easy for ordinary people to look at a famous person and feel envious of their money and their lifestyle. But the next time you are tempted to do that, imagine walking in their shoes and you will see that privacy is too valuable to give up.

Your impressions: _____

_____

_____

_____

Comment to Sonya from an AP Reader

By stating your thesis early and often, you leave no doubt about where you stand on the issue of privacy for celebrities. Your essay's unity, therefore, is one of its obvious strengths, and perhaps a weakness, too. Each paragraph restates the notion that lack of privacy leads to lack of freedom, unquestionably a thoughtful idea. But by limiting yourself to that single notion, you oversimplify the whole right-to-privacy issue and miss a chance to discuss it in depth.

The sources you cite are closely linked to your thesis, but they shape your argument. By leaning on them too heavily, you have abandoned control of the discussion. It would have been preferable to state your positions and then integrate source material as supporting evidence instead of relying on sources for the topic and the starting point of each paragraph.

Your essay follows the popular five-paragraph structure. For that you cannot be faulted, although it turns what could be a fresh and scintillating essay into something more conventional. As it should, the final paragraph brings closure to the essay, but at the same time it raises a new issue—that privacy is too precious to give up for the trappings of celebrity. This is an observation worth pondering, but is only tangentially related to your essay's main concern, the right to privacy.

SCORE: 4

Ricky's Response

(Printed as it was written)

People like Justin Timberlake, Beyoncé and the Kardashians are celebrities always on TV and in the newspaper. But who cares about their drug habit, sex life, marriage problems, issues with children or other family members, or similar topics? I know I don't. If I asked my friends they would not care either.

When Cameron the former prime minister of England was a young man he took drugs. He defended himself by saying that everybody did it in those days. It does not matter whether he did it or not. It is none of anybody's business but his own, and who really cares?

Brad Pitt's romance with ---- (I forgot her first name) Jolie is also no one else's business and Brad Pitt is less important than England's prime minister. If people cared about Cameron's drug use they did not have to vote for him.

The question I ask is what explains the public's interest celebrities? The author Neal Galber says that movies are so important that our lives resemble movies, so naturally we are interested in celebrities. We see them as outstanding individuals and so we want to know how they got that way. One author said, they humanize our lives, which means they make us more human. Even so their privacy is not our business so we should stay away from them. When they want to become more popular, some do outrageous things and want their photographs in the paper. Sometimes they put their home addresses on the web. Most of the time they are just regluar people trying to get along, so we should leave them alone.

Your impressions: _____

_____

_____

_____

Comment to Ricky from an AP Reader

Your essay deserves a low score mainly because it lacks unity and fails to synthesize any of the sources. To be sure, you clearly make the point that the private lives of celebrities don't matter to you. Yet, you explain that we are curious about celebrities because they are outstanding in some way. At the end you contradict yourself again by declaring that celebrities are "just regular people." Despite the overall incoherence of these and other ideas, the essay contains occasional insights—your discussion of Neal Gabler's theory, for example. But they remain under-developed and get lost in the confusion.

Your failure to synthesize sources is a particular shortcoming. Synthesis requires documentation of the sources cited. Although some of your ideas are drawn from the sources, you give them no credit. Using others' ideas without acknowledgment is unacceptable in an AP essay.

Score: 1

Writing an Analytical Essay

An analytical essay examines the purpose, content, structure, and rhetoric of a passage.

☑ Picking "rhetorical strategies" to write about
☑ Reading the passage with eyes wide open
☑ Arranging ideas pragmatically
☑ Using a down-to-earth writing style
☑ The nuts and bolts of polishing an essay
☑ Sample questions and student responses

For the analytical essay, you must read a passage and **analyze** it. (A question sometimes contains two short passages to be analyzed and compared.) To start you off in the right direction, you're often given the author, date, and context of the passage.

The prompt usually instructs you to write about the author's use of "rhetorical strategies." In other words, you are expected to analyze how the passage conveys its meaning, achieves its purpose, or creates an effect. Your job is to break the passage into its component parts in order to explain how the author put it together.

Reading and Analyzing the Topic

At the risk of stating the obvious, read the question, or prompt, very, very carefully. Read it two or three times, if necessary, underlining important ideas and words until you know exactly what you are being asked to write about.

> Here is a recent AP analytical essay question. As you read it, underline the words that tell you precisely what to do:
>
> *Read carefully the following autobiographical narrative by Gary Soto. Then, in a well-written essay, analyze some of the ways in which Soto recreates the experience of being six years old and feeling guilty about something he did. You might consider such devices as contrast, repetition, pacing, diction, and imagery.*

You're on the right track if you underlined <u>analyze</u>, the key word in the instructions. It means that your job is to disassemble the passage, looking at how the author recreated the experience of his childhood guilt.

The instructions say that you "might consider such devices as contrast, repetition, pacing, diction, and imagery." Hold on now, and stop for a second! Have you noticed that the AP test writers have just given you a gift? The phrase "might consider" has just turned a requirement into a suggestion, a suggestion that you may accept or reject. Since the choice is yours, consider ignoring the suggestion. Why? Because AP essay readers, who read scores of similar essays a day, often look kindly on essays that break the mold, that show a spark of originality.

After reading, say, a hundred essays that discuss contrast, repetition, pacing, and the rest, they might relish knowing what you have to say, for example, about tone or sequence of thought or sentence structure or figurative language or any other rhetorical feature that helps the author achieve his purpose.

Practice in Reading and Analyzing Questions

Read the following pair of AP questions carefully. Underline the key words that define the task to be performed. Then, write your interpretation of the task in the blank spaces provided.

Question A   Carefully read the following excerpt from an essay by the columnist Charles Donahue entitled "People With Noses in the Air." Then write an essay in which you define Donahue's attitude toward snobs and analyze the rhetorical strategies the writer uses to communicate that attitude.

Required task: _____

_____

_____

Explanation

Question A—about snobs—doesn't include the word tone but instead refers to the author's attitude toward his subject, which amounts to pretty much the same thing. (Incidentally, in AP lingo, the term *rhetorical stance* is sometimes used in place of *tone*.) In this instance, Donahue may employ a sarcastic tone to ridicule snobbish behavior, or he may convey resentment or envy or disbelief or any number of other feelings about snobs.

An essay responding to the question must contain at least two things: (1) a definition of Donahue's attitude toward snobs, and (2) a discussion of how Donahue communicated that attitude—that is, what rhetorical methods he used to achieve his goal.

The essay might deal with (1) and (2) separately, or it might discuss both issues simultaneously. However the material is organized, though, it must address both concerns.

TIP

Don't get bogged down in every rhetorical detail. Focus only on those that help shape the author's point and purpose.

Question B   Carefully read the following passage from _____(Title)_____ written by _____(Author)_____. Then write an essay on the given passage analyzing the rhetorical strategies the author used to achieve her purpose.

Required task: _____

_____

_____

Explanation

This question gives you the chance to write about virtually any rhetorical technique that you can find in the passage. You may think that's easy because the choice is completely yours. But be careful. It may be a challenge to locate rhetorical techniques that help shape the author's purpose. Because you happen to find a metaphor or an example of personification doesn't necessarily make figurative language significant to the passage. To be important, figures of speech must seriously contribute to the overall impact that the passage leaves on its readers. In other words, this open-ended question forces you to scrutinize the passage with great care in order to locate rhetorical devices that have helped the author to achieve her goal.

Reading the Passage

Reading a passage to analyze it in an essay differs little from reading a passage in order to answer multiple-choice questions. If anything, the approach is somewhat simpler because you need not zero in on every tiny detail but only on the rhetorical strategies specified by the question.

If the prompt instructs you to discuss figurative language, search the passage for metaphors, symbols, analogies, samples of irony and imagery, and so forth. If you're told to analyze diction, look for words and phrases that serve as clues to the author's background, personality, and especially the author's tone and purpose.

TIP

Depend on the prompt to tell you what to search for while reading the passage.

Read the passage at least twice—first for an overview of its point and purpose and then to track down examples of rhetorical devices. Mark up the page with underscoring, asterisks, circles, and arrows, highlighting only those features of the passage you might use in your essay. Scribble notes in the margin. Jot down thoughts and ideas that occur to you as you read. Your notes may well serve as an outline of an essay.

Regardless of the question, an understanding of the content of the passage is crucial. That means reading *every word*, not just enough of it to give you a vague sense of the passage's main idea. By the time you've finished reading you ought to be able to complete the following statement in ten or fewer well-chosen words:

This passage is about _____.

Everything you discuss in your essay must be tied to your understanding of the passage's content. It won't be enough simply to identify examples of highly charged words or figures of speech, or to say the tone is nostalgic or the writing style is sophisticated. What counts is your analysis of the author's rhetorical choices—or how the purpose of the passage was achieved.

Planning Your Analytical Essay

Preparing an Outline

Spend a few minutes outlining your essay before writing your opening sentence. You don't need a formal outline, but just a list of ideas arranged in the order that you'll use them in your essay. It speaks well of you as a writer when you present ideas in a well-thought-out sequence instead of spilling them onto the page in the order they happened to pop into your head. Since time is short on the AP exam, your outline may consist of no more than scrawled words or phrases that tell you what each paragraph will be about.

> **STRATEGY**
>
> In general, an essay outlined in advance is likely to be clearer and more coherent than one thrown together willy-nilly.

After reading the following passage, Bridget B, a high school senior, prepared an outline for an essay that analyzed the author's use of rhetorical devices.

This passage by Laura Eirmann appeared on the website of the Cornell University Pet Loss Hotline.

Passage

When an owner and veterinarian decide that a pet is suffering or unlikely to make a recovery, euthanasia offers a way to end a pet's pain. The decision is difficult for both the owner and the veterinarian, but we should recognize that sometimes this is the kindest
Line thing we can do in the final stage of a pet's life.
(5) Understanding how the procedure is performed may help an owner in this decision. It may also help an owner decide whether they wish to be present during the euthanasia. Initially, a pet is made as comfortable as possible. Some veterinarians will perform the procedure in a pet's home. If the animal is brought to the hospital, veterinarians often choose a quiet room where the pet will feel at ease. Sometimes a mild sedative or tranquilizer is first given if the
(10) animal appears anxious or painful. Frequently an indwelling catheter is placed in the pet's vein to ensure that the euthanasia solution is delivered quickly. The euthanasia solution is usually a barbiturate—the same class of drugs used for general anesthesia. At a much higher dose, this solution provides not only the same effects as general anesthesia (loss of consciousness, loss of pain sensation), but suppresses the cardiovascular and respiratory
(15) systems. As the solution is injected, the animal loses consciousness and within minutes the heart and lungs stop functioning. Since the pet is not conscious, they do not feel anything. Most times, the animal passes away so smoothly, that it is difficult to tell until the veterinarian listens for absence of a heartbeat. The eyes remain open in most cases. Sometimes, the last few breaths are what's termed "agonal," meaning involuntary muscle contractions,
(20) but again, the pet is not aware at this point. After the animal dies, there is complete muscle relaxation, often accompanied by urination and defecation. This is completely normal and is something an owner should expect. In addition, after death, chemicals normally stored in nerve endings are released causing occasional muscle twitching in the early post-mortem period. Many owners who choose to stay with their pets are surprised how quickly and eas-
(25) ily the pet is put to rest.

The decision to stay or not stay with a pet is a very personal one. Some owners feel they could comfort their pet in its final minutes. Others feel their emotional upset would only upset their pet. Those who choose not to stay may wish to view the pet's body after the procedure is complete. Euthanasia is emotional for veterinarians as well. Sometimes, the vet-
(30) erinarian has known the pet for a long time or has tried very hard to make the animal well again. James Herriot stated the view of most veterinarians in *All Things Wise and Wonderful:* "Like all vets I hated doing this, painless though it was, but to me there has always been a comfort in the knowledge that the last thing these helpless animals knew was the sound of a friendly voice and the touch of a gentle hand."

After reading the passage carefully, Bridget jotted down her impressions of the passage and its author:

1. The author of the passage is a veterinarian.
2. The passage was written for an audience of pet owners.
3. The passage reflects the writer's concern for the well-being of animals.
4. The writer is trying to help pet owners make decisions about taking the life of their terminally ill pets.
5. The writer describes the process of pet euthanasia unemotionally.

Using these thoughts as a springboard, Bridget prepared an outline for an essay on the author's rhetorical strategies.

(For the record, Bridget's outline below is far more detailed than an outline hurriedly written during an AP test.)

Point of passage: to help pet owners deal with euthanasia

Main idea: Author's tone, point of view and diction comfort pet owners, put them at ease about making a difficult decision.

1. Tone: Uses compassionate tone

   Avoids harsh words—e.g., kill, destroy, put to death, deathly ill.
   Uses euphemisms and soft words: "euthanasia," (line 2) "end a pet's pain," (2) "put to rest," (25) "final stage of . . . life" (4)

2. Point of view: Author identifies with pet owner, maybe to help relieve owner's guilt about killing a pet.

   (Implication: We're in this together, so don't blame yourself.)
   – – difficult decision for both owner and vet (2–3)
   – – emotional for vets (29–31)
   – – – quote by J. Herriot (32–34)

3. Dicton (word choice)

   Plenty of repetition of words with connotations that stress painlessness, ease, and speed of the euthanasia "procedure"
   Painless: "Pet is made . . . comfortable" (7)
       Quiet room where pet feels "at ease" (8–9)
       "sedative," "tranquillizer," "same as general anesthesia," "loss of pain," etc.
   Ease of process: "animal passes away so smoothly" (17)
   Speed of process: "solution delivered quickly" (11)
       Owner's surprise at "how quickly and easily the pet is put to rest" (24–25)

Possible conclusion: Author covers process thoroughly from start to finish; thoroughness shows respect for pet owner, causing pet owner to feel confident in the vet.

As you prepare for the AP exam, get into the habit of writing outlines. If you're not accustomed to outlining before you write, it may take a while to get into the groove. But once in, the rewards may astound you.

Choosing a Main Idea

The purpose, or point, of any essay is its **main idea**, also called its **thesis**. Essays may be written with beautiful words, contain profound thoughts, and make readers laugh or weep. But without a main idea, an essay remains just words in search of a meaning, causing readers to scratch their heads and ask, "Huh? What's the point?"

Open-ended essay questions on general topics invite you to range far and wide in search of a main idea. Not on the AP exam, however. Because the analytical essay question asks you to perform a specific writing task, devising a main idea is reasonably simple: just identify the relationship between the rhetorical strategies used in a passage and the point or purpose of the passage. In fact, a main idea may include the actual words or a paraphrase of the question itself. For example:

> Laura Eirmann, the author of the passage, makes use of such rhetorical devices as a sympathetic tone, a friendly point of view, and a soothing choice of words to achieve her purpose.

This opening sentence won't win a prize for originality, but it gets the job done. It shows that the writer understands the question and suggests that the essay to follow will contain a three-part analysis of Eirmann's writing style.

It's not essential, nor is it particularly desirable, to state the main idea at the essay's outset. In fact, it's often preferable to lead up to your main idea with a general discussion of the context in which the passage was written. For instance,

> Pet owners, experiencing great anxiety when their pets develop incurable illnesses, often face the terrible decision of whether to let their pets suffer until they die or to "put them to sleep." Knowing that pet owners agonize over what to do, Laura Eirmann carefully constructed an essay intended to help pet owners make an informed, guilt-free decision about euthanizing their pets. *To make readers feel comfortable, Eirmann uses a sympathetic tone, a friendly point of view, and a soothing choice of words.*

Still another approach is to save the thesis statement for your conclusion. Instead of giving away your main idea at the start, let it emerge naturally and inevitably from evidence presented in all the prior paragraphs.

The guidelines for placing main ideas in analytical essays are no different from those for persuasive essays, although it may often be advantageous to make clear your position early on in a persuasive essay. By stating your opinion at the outset, you can build a strong argument step-by-step through the remainder of the essay. On the other hand, an essay that makes its main point less overtly, or one that uses suspense to frame an argument leading to an incisive conclusion, may engage a reader more fully—always a desirable outcome on an AP essay.

Writing an Argumentative Essay

The third essay on the exam requires you to respond to an idea contained in a short statement or paragraph. Your response must be written as an argument that either supports or refutes a writer's views on a particular subject. Or, if you prefer not to take an either/or position, you can adopt a stance somewhere in between the two.

Writing a persuasive essay involves more than simply expressing your opinion on an issue. The validity of your position must be based on sound evidence. Passion alone won't do it. You need to corral evidence from your experience, reading, studies, and observation in order to prove that your opinion has merit.

To argue in behalf of your position, find at least two (three is even better) distinct arguments to support it. It helps, too, to develop a counterargument—an argument most likely to be used by someone who opposes your views—that you can refute in order to persuade readers that you are right and your opponent is not.

Because topics for AP persuasive essays are unpredictable, it makes sense to arm yourself with a ready-to-use essay-writing strategy—one that, regardless of the topic, lays out the steps to take during the approximately forty minutes it takes to complete the essay. Chances are that you've written reams of essays during your school career. Over the years, you may have developed a method for writing blue-ribbon essays. But in case you haven't, here is a list of steps you can count on. Follow them while you write essays for practice. Then, based on the results you get, amend the list in ways that enable you to write the best essays you can.

TIP

Back up your opinion with solid evidence.

- ✓ Read and analyze the prompt.
- ✓ Jot down ideas that might be used to argue both sides of the issue.
- ✓ Review the ideas and choose a position on the issue.
- ✓ Articulate a main idea, or thesis, for your essay.
- ✓ Arrange supporting ideas purposefully—not simply in the order they occurred to you.
- ✓ Introduce the main idea of your essay.
- ✓ Develop unified paragraphs in support of your main idea.
- ✓ Devote at least part of your essay to refute an argument likely to be used by someone whose opinion differs from yours.
- ✓ Choose words and structure sentences that concisely convey your thoughts.
- ✓ Write a memorable conclusion but not a brief summary of your essay.
- ✓ Edit your essay for clarity, interest, and correctness.

Writing an essay in 40 minutes
- **5–10 minutes to plan**
- **20–25 minutes for composing**
- **5–10 minutes to polish your essay**

Experience shows that these steps do not need be taken in the order presented, nor is each step discrete. Rather, they often overlap and blend into each other. While composing your essay, for example, you may also be revising and proofreading. Late in the process, you may weave new ideas into your text or shift the location of ideas. In short, no step really ends until the final period is put into place or the AP proctor calls "Time!"

This book can't tell you exactly how much of the suggested 40-minute writing period to devote to each step. A plan that works for other students may not work for you. In general, however, you won't go wrong by devoting more than half the time—about 25–30 minutes—to composing an essay and no more than 5–10 minutes planning and polishing it.

By now you may have noticed that the basic process of writing a persuasive essay hardly differs at all from that used in writing synthesis or analytical essays. All three require you to read the prompt over and over until you are absolutely sure of what it says and what you are expected to do. The prompt may not turn you on right away, but if you really concentrate on the issue, you may soon be bursting with ideas for your essay.

Argumentative Essay Topics for Practice

SUGGESTED TIME FOR EACH—40 MINUTES

1. *The following statement comes from the writings of the Roman emperor Marcus Aurelius. Read it carefully, and then write an essay that agrees with, modifies, or opposes the author's description of the nature of humankind. Use evidence from your observation, reading, studies, or experience to support your position.*

We are made for cooperation, like feet, like hands, like eyelids, like rows of the upper and lower teeth. To act against one another, then, is contrary to nature; and it is action against one another to be vexed and to turn away.

2. *The paragraph that follows has been adapted from an article about pressures felt by young American women decades ago in the middle of the twentieth century. Read it carefully, and then write an essay that examines the extent to which the author's characterization of the relationship between young American men and women is valid today. Support your views with appropriate evidence.*

The relations between college-bound boys and girls are a tender subject, seldom discussed between the generations. The contemporary sexual mores of young people are so different from those which governed their parents' or teachers' lives that a common meeting ground between them scarcely exists. (It is possible that their parents have forgotten some of the details of their own past experiences.) Girls seldom, if ever, discuss their sexual experiences with their parents, and when they do—unless they are facing a crisis—one cannot escape the impression that the parent-child relationship is a little unhealthy. To be sure, girls often come to college with standards handed to them by their mothers and tacitly upheld by their fathers. Letting a boy kiss you good night, for example, is all right, but preferably not on the first date. Here is where conflict often begins. If the girl is standoffish and stiff, the chances are she will not see the boy again. But this is just what she wants to forestall unless he is a "jerk," and so, partly to secure her aim and partly because she is moved and flattered, she accepts his kisses, and soon after, if she has not already learned, she is taught to "kiss back."

3. *What follows is a well known passage by the seventeenth-century British poet John Donne. Read it carefully, and then write an essay that agrees with, modifies, or opposes Donne's view of man's place in the world. Use appropriate evidence to support your argument.*

No man is an island entire of itself; every man is a piece of the continent, a part of the main. If a clod be washed away by the sea, Europe is the less, as well as if a promontory were, as well as if a manor of thy friend's or of thine own were. Any man's death diminishes me, because I am involved in mankind, and therefore never send to know for whom the bell tolls; it tolls for thee.

4. *To explain why many dramatists and authors of fiction tend to fill their works with disturbed, problem-plagued, and disaffected characters, essayist Roger Rosenblatt said "because defects make for better reading than virtues."*

After considering Rosenblatt's assertion, write an essay that agrees with, modifies, or opposes his explanation for the presence of troubled characters in works of literature. Use appropriate evidence to support your argument.

5. *In a letter to a newspaper columnist known as "The Ethicist," a reader questioned the validity of the so-called Golden Rule, the common principle of ethical behavior, that says you and I should treat others as we would like to be treated.*

   The reader challenged the rule on the grounds that it imposes one person's values and preferences on other people. That is to say, why should it be assumed that others want to be treated as we do? Wouldn't it be far better if the rule said to treat others as they want to be treated?

   What is your opinion? Write an essay that either agrees with the reader's view or one that modifies or disagrees with the reader's point of view. Use evidence from your observation, studies, reading, or experience to support your position.

Arranging Ideas

The best order is the clearest order.

The words you've underlined while reading a passage or prompt, the notes you've written in the margins, the items listed in your outline—these are the raw materials of an essay. Before you begin composing, select the details that will best support your main idea. Discard the others, or better, hold them in reserve—to be used in case one of your selections turns out to be a dud.

Then, arrange those materials. Decide what comes first, second, and third. The best order is the clearest order, the one your reader can follow with the least effort. But, just as a highway map may show several routes from one place to another, there is no single way to get from the beginning to the end of an essay.

No plan is superior to another provided there's a valid reason for using it. The plan that fails is the aimless one, the one in which ideas are presented solely according to when they occurred to you. To guard against aimlessness, rank the ideas in your outline in order of importance. Then work toward your best point, not away from it. Giving away your *pièce de resistance* at the start is self-defeating. Therefore, if you've identified, say, three good rhetorical strategies, save the best one for the end of the essay. Start with your second best, and sandwich your least favorite between the other two. A solid opening draws readers into the essay and creates that all-important first impression, but a memorable ending is even more important. Coming last, it is what readers have fresh in their minds when they assign the essay a grade.

The Formula	
Introductory paragraph	Point 1
Body consisting of three paragraphs	Point 2
Concluding paragraph	Point 3

The Formula

The five-paragraph essay formula is a fundamental, all-purpose plan for arranging ideas into clear, easy-to-follow order. It's a technique you can rely on any time you need to set ideas in order. Its greatest virtue is clarity. Each part has its place and purpose.

You needn't follow the formula slavishly. In fact, professionally written essays rarely adhere to this five-paragraph arrangement. Yet, many essay writers, even those who take a circuitous path between the beginning and end, use some version of it.

But here's a word of caution: the five-paragraph essay is taught so widely in schools that it has almost become a cliché. AP readers will recognize it instantly and may grade it accordingly. The highest scores are usually reserved for essays that demonstrate a particularly strong command of essay-writing techniques. Essays that rely on an obvious organizational formula may not reach that lofty level.

AP Essay Writing Style

Choose your words carefully, of course, and try to adopt a plain, natural style. Don't drag out your SAT vocabulary in an attempt to snow your readers. AP readers won't be impressed by formal, pompous, or elegant writing. Think of them as everyday folks who appreciate straight, plain, everyday language. You have a natural voice. Use it.

Don't be pretentious. Use your natural voice.

AP essays are likely to be more formal than informal. It's inappropriate to be casual when you are analyzing a text, providing quotes, paraphrasing others' words, using the terminology of literary criticism and scholarship. At the same time, though, don't be stuffy or pompous. AP essay readers are old hands at spotting pretense in students' writing.

Just let your genuine voice ring out, although the way you speak is not necessarily the way you should write. Spoken language is often vague, clumsy, repetitive, confused, wordy. Adopt a writing style not unlike the everyday speech of someone who speaks grammatical English, free of the latest cool or hip expressions and clichés. Think of it as the kind of mature speech expected of you in serious conversation, say, during a college interview. Or maybe even the way this paragraph sounds. You could do a lot worse!

Use plain and precise language. Fortunately, English is loaded with simple words that can express the most profound ideas. A sign that says STOP! conveys its message more clearly than one that says CEASE AND DESIST. When a dentist pokes at your teeth, it *hurts*, even if dentists call it "experiencing discomfort." Simple doesn't necessarily mean short, however. It's true that plain words tend to be the short ones, but not always. The word *fid* is short, but it's not plain unless you are a sailor, in which case you'd know that a fid supports the mast on a boat. On the other hand, *spontaneously* is five syllables long. Yet it is a plain and simple word because of its frequent use.

Simple ideas dressed up in ornate words not only obscure meaning but also make writers sound phony, as in:

> Fancy: The epistle states that politicians have a proclivity toward prevarication.
> Plain: The letter says that politicians often lie.

Ernest Hemingway called a writer's greatest gift a "built-in, shock-proof crap detector." Hemingway's own detector worked well. He produced about the leanest, plainest writing in the English language—not that you should try to emulate Hemingway. (That's already been done by countless imitators.) But an efficient "crap detector" of your own will encourage you to choose words only because they express exactly what you mean.

EUPHEMISMS

Of course, there are occasions when the plainest words won't do. When you wish to soften or mitigate painful, unsavory, or objectionable truths, our language offers innumerable euphemisms. For example, there are scores of euphemisms for the verb "to die" (*pass away*, *pass on*, *be deceased*, *rest*, *expire*, *meet one's maker*, and so on), for "bathroom" (*restroom*, *ladies'/men's room*, *W.C.*, *lounge*), and for "drunk," "vomiting," and everything else that might upset a prissy sensibility. Pussyfooting with words has its place. We do it all the time, but in your AP essays resort to euphemisms only when you have a valid reason for doing so.

TIP

Steer clear of language and abbreviations customarily used in text messages and blogs.

Don't interpret this admonition to use plain words as *carte blanche* to use current, everyday slang or street talk in your AP essays. Spoken language, which brims with colorful words and expressions like *chill, pig out, dissed,* and *bummed,* has its place, but its place is not in your AP essay unless you definitely need such lingo to create an effect that you can't produce another way. If you insist on writing like a blogger, that's fine, but don't use quotation marks to call attention to the fact that you can't think of standard or more original words. If, to make a point, you overload your essay with digital slang, such as *Facestalling, YOLO,* and *4ever,* be sure to demonstrate your mastery of conventional English, too, in at least part of the piece. After all, an AP student must be able to write good, standard prose.

Putting Yourself in the Essay

TIP

In AP essays references to yourself are not forbidden, but use them sparingly.

Although it's not forbidden in formal essays to put yourself in the spotlight, custom requires writers to focus on the subject matter, not on themselves. In other words, avoid using first-person pronouns (*I, me, we, us, our, myself, ourselves*). AP readers recognize that in certain contexts such pronouns are appropriate. When writing a personal anecdote to support a claim, for example, using *I* is often preferable to using the more impersonal *one,* as in "When *one* faces a blank page on which to write an AP essay, *one* can feel panic." If, by shunning first-person pronouns, however, your prose becomes stilted or awkward, feel free to use them. In short, use whatever words you need to make your essay interesting and readable.

Varying Sentences

When writing your essay, try to use a variety of sentences to show your awareness that the type, structure, and length of sentences help authors convey meaning and create effects on readers. It's easy to fall into a rut by using the same sentence structure over and over and over. But if you are aiming for a high AP score, vary your sentences. For one thing, variety adds vitality to your prose.

English sentences, as you probably know, are structured in three ways: ***simple, compound, and complex.***

SIMPLE: Metaphors are great.

The sentence is *simple* because it contains one grammatical subject (*Metaphors*) and one verb (*are*). It also states a single main idea.

COMPOUND: Grammar is difficult, but it helps you write well.

The sentence is *compound* because it is made up of two simple sentences joined by a coordinating conjunction (*but*). Other coordinating conjunctions used in compound sentences are *and, yet, or, for, nor,* and *so,* as in:

Grammar is difficult, *and* it drives many people up the wall.
Eliana studied hard, for she wanted a 5 on the AP exam.

Notice that the structure of each of these compound sentences gives roughly equal emphasis to its two main ideas.

COMPLEX: Although he's taking four AP courses, Spencer won't study.

The sentence is *complex* because it is made up of two parts—a simple sentence (*Spencer won't study*) and a dependent clause (*Although he's taking four AP courses*). Because the clause begins with a subordinating conjunction (*Although*), it is called a *subordinate clause*. Subordinate clauses contain ideas related to the complete sentence (called the *independent* or *main* clause) but, compared with the main clause, are usually less important to the meaning of the sentence. Other common subordinating conjunctions include *because, after, before, though, unless, until, whenever,* and *while.*

Not every simple, compound, and complex sentence is structured in the way just described. In fact, variations abound because English is a remarkably flexible language that can be shaped in countless ways, as you'll see below.

Most simple sentences start with the grammatical subject followed by the verb:

Cats (subject) *fall* (verb) asleep in about three seconds.
They (subject) *sleep* (verb) best after eating and cleaning themselves.
I (subject) *wish* (verb) to be a cat in my next life.

A string of sentences with this subject-verb pattern resembles the prose in a grade-school primer—a style that just won't do on an AP essay. To be sure that you write in a more mature and engaging way, analyze one of your recent essays. Do several sentences begin with grammatical subjects? If so, try shifting the subject elsewhere. Try leading off with a prepositional phrase, or with an adverb, adjective, or some other grammatical unit.

The following pairs of sentences show how a subject can be shifted from its customary position:

BEFORE THE SHIFT: Ms. Santero is one of the most popular teachers in the school.
AFTER THE SHIFT: In this school Ms. Santero is one of the most popular teachers.

After a prepositional phrase was added, the subject (*Ms. Santero*) has been moved further along in the sentence.

BEFORE: She taught the novel *Beloved* to our AP English class with enthusiasm.
AFTER: Enthusiastically, she taught the novel *Beloved* to our AP English class.

 TIP

Don't start every sentence with the grammatical subject.

Obviously, the revised sentence begins with an adverb.

> BEFORE: Students were less excited about the book than she was.
> AFTER: Yet, students were less excited about the book than she was.

Well, here the subject (*students*) is stated after an opening connective.

> BEFORE: I loved the book, although it turned out to be an intolerable drag for most of my classmates.
> AFTER: Although the book turned out to be an intolerable drag for most of my classmates, I loved it.

After introducing the sentence with a dependent clause, the writer names the subject, *I*, and then adds the rest of the sentence.

> BEFORE: Ms. Santero pushed the class to find symbolic meaning in various scenes to make the book more meaningful.
> AFTER: To make the book more meaningful, Ms. Santero pushed the class to find symbolic meaning in various scenes.

To revise this sentence the writer begins with a verbal, in this case "to make," the infinitive form of the verb. (Verbals look and feel much like verbs but serve a different function. Verbals, though, come from verbs—hence, their name and their resemblance.)

> BEFORE: I read the book in two days, hoping that it would never end.
> AFTER: Hoping that it would never end, I read the book in two days.

Aiming to diversify sentence openings, the writer starts this sentence with another kind of verbal, known as a *participle*. The *-ing* ending often indicates that a word is a participle.

> BEFORE: I was awed by the tenacity of the characters and absorbed by every soul-stirring syllable of the story.
> AFTER: Awed by the tenacity of the characters, I was absorbed by every soul-stirring syllable of the story.

Determined to try something different, the writer begins the sentence with an adjective that happens to sound like a verb because of its *-ed* ending.

Still another variation to try now and then is the sentence constructed from matched ideas set in juxtaposition. President Kennedy famously used such a sentence to memorable effect in his inaugural speech:

> "Ask not what your country can do for you, ask what you can do for your country."

The power of such sentences lies in the balance of parallel clauses—called a *chiasmus* in grammatical terminology. Each clause could stand alone, but together they express the idea more vigorously. Another example:

> It wasn't that the spirit of the pioneers caught my imagination, it was my imagination that caught the pioneer spirit.

Emphasis can also come from a reversal of customary word order. Out of context, a sentence in which the predicate precedes the subject may seem awkward. But in the right spot, an inverted sentence can leave an indelible mark. "Dull the book is not" packs more wallop than "The book is not dull" or "The book is exciting." In the right context, "Perilous was the climb to the top of the cliff" sounds more ominous than, "The climb to the top of the cliff was perilous." Inverted sentences should be used rarely, however. More than once in an essay diminishes the vigor of each occurrence and may sound silly.

No rule of thumb says that a certain percentage of sentences in an essay ought to be different from the usual subject-verb structure. It really depends on the purpose and style of the essay. But if you find yourself repeating the same sentence pattern, restructure some of your sentences. Your readers are bound to reward you for the effort.

Sentence Types

Our language offers a rich menu of sentence types. Declarative sentences predominate in most essay writing. (Just to refresh your memory, a *declarative* sentence, such as the one you are now reading, simply makes a statement.) But other types of sentences can create all sorts of fascinating effects. Take *interrogative* sentences, for example. (Do you remember that interrogative sentences ask questions?) An interrogative sentence appropriately placed in an essay consisting of declarative sentences can change the pace and rhythm of the prose, underscore an idea, and promote the reader's involvement.

Don't forget about imperative sentences (keep in mind that *imperative* sentences make requests or give commands) and exclamatory sentences (What strong emotion an *exclamatory* sentence can express!).

Furthermore, you can write sentences interrupted at some point by a dash—although some editors and teachers claim that it's not proper to do so in formal prose. Direct and indirect quotations are useful, and on occasion you can drive home a point with a single emphatic word. Excellent!

There's peril, however, in scrambling sentence types for no other reason than to scramble sentence types, for you may end up with a mess on your hands. Be guided by what expresses your ideas most clearly and seems varied enough to interest your readers.

Repetition of Ideas

Repetition can be annoying, but, adroitly used, it adds clout to an idea. When your sweetheart says, "I love you. I love you very much," the repetition intensifies the sentiment. If a coach admonishes his team, "OK, guys, knock it off. I said knock it off," you know he really means it.

The following paragraph may suggest that the writer has a one-track mind:

> In the fall Bethany will be going to college. She is psyched to get out of high school. She is psyched to break away from her small town and live in a big city. She is psyched for meeting new people from all over the country and the world, and she is psyched to get started on a program of studies that she expects will prepare her for law school. But first, she is psyched to take the AP exam.

Every sentence but the first uses the same subject/verb combination. Yet, the overall effect is anything but monotonous. What's memorable is not repetition, but relentlessness. Repeating the verb *psyched* five times emphasizes Bethany's frame of mind. The point could not have been made as emphatically using a different verb in each sentence.

Or take this passage written by an incorrigible bagel freak:

> My taste for bagels knows no bounds. I stop at the bagel shop on my way to school each morning and grab an onion bagel and coffee. Lunch consists of an olive bagel and a couple

TIP

By varying sentences, you'll write more readable essays.

of veggie bagels smeared with cream cheese. At snack time I'm not picky. Any style bagel will do, but I hate to have dinner without a buttered poppy-seed bagel. Before bed I wash down a plain toasted bagel with a glass of milk, and in case I have insomnia, I stash two or three garlic bagels on my nightstand for a tasty middle-of-the-night pick-me-up.

The writer virtually beats you over the head with bagels. But the repetition won't allow you to forget the point—that the writer has eyes not for pizza, not for burritos, not for onion rings—but only for bagels.

A word of caution: Restatements of a word or phrase can also be distracting. Inadvertent repetition obstructs progress by putting useless words in the reader's path. Therefore, stay alert for accidental repetition, as in:

In a corner of the room stood a clock. The clock said four o'clock.
Columbus made three ocean voyages. The voyages took him across the Atlantic Ocean.

Combining such sentences will keep you from ending one sentence and starting the next one with the same words:

The clock in the corner of the room said four.
Columbus made three voyages across the Atlantic.

Sentences can also be plagued with a word or a rhyme that draws attention to itself:

Maybe some people don't have as much freedom as others; but the freedom they do have is given to them for free. Therefore, freedom is proof enough that the best things in life are free.
The members of the assembly remembered that November was just around the corner.

These writers failed to listen to the sound of their words. Had they read their sentences aloud, they may have noticed that the voices were stuck in a groove. In fact, reading your words aloud allows you to step back and examine word sounds (Hold it! Those two words—*aloud* and *allows*—sound jarring and should not be allowed to stand side by side.) Hearing your written words spoken, you're more apt to notice unwanted repetition. Whenever possible, let each of your practice essays cool for a while. Then enlist a friend to read it aloud. Hearing it in another's voice lends objectivity to the process of self-evaluation.

Short and Long Sentences

TIP

To fend off monotony, vary the length of your sentences.

Long sentences (like this one) demand greater effort from readers because they must keep track of more words, modifiers, phrases (not to speak of parenthetical asides), and clauses, without losing the writer's main thought, which may be buried amid any number of secondary, or less important, thoughts, while short sentences are usually easier to grasp. A brief sentence can make a point sharply because all its words concentrate on a single point. Take, for example, the last sentence in this passage:

For three days, my parents and I sat in our SUV and drove from college to college to college in search of the perfect place for me to spend the next four years. For 72 hours we lived as one person, sharing thoughts and dreams, stating opinions about each campus we visited, taking guided tours, interviewing students and admissions officials, asking directions a hundred times, eating together in town after town, and even sleeping in the same motel rooms. But mostly, we fought.

A terse closing sentence following a windy, 46-word sentence produces a mild jolt. Indeed, its point is to startle the reader. The technique is easily mastered but should be used sparingly. Overuse dilutes its impact.

A series of short sentences can be as tiresome as a succession of long ones. A balance works best. If you have strung together four or five equally long (or short) sentences, try to separate, or combine, them. Here, to illustrate, is an overweight sentence that needs demolition:

> In the 1870s, the archaeologist, Heinrich Schliemann, dug in the correct spot and discovered not only one ancient city of Troy, but nine of them, one lying on top of the other, since every few centuries a new city had been built upon the ruins of the old, causing Schliemann to dig right past the layer containing the ruins of the famous city of the Trojan Horse without realizing he had done so, a mistake not corrected until almost fifty years later by Carl Blegen of the University of Cincinnati, by which time, unfortunately, it was too late for Schliemann because he had been dead for forty years.

The sentence is perfectly grammatical, but it carries a big 108-word load. Cut it down to size. Break it into pieces, rearrange it, add verbs, drop an idea or two, change the emphasis and delete words. When you're done, the restyled sentence might sound something like this:

> In the 1870s, the archaeologist, Heinrich Schliemann, dug in the correct spot and discovered not only one ancient city of Troy, but nine of them, one lying on top of the other. He figured out that every few centuries a new city had been built upon the ruins of the old. Without realizing it, he had dug right past the layer he was seeking, the layer containing the ruins of the famous city of the Trojan Horse. His mistake was corrected fifty years later by Carl Blegen of the University of Cincinnati. By then, however, it was too late for Schliemann. He had been dead for forty years.

Likewise, a string of four or five sentences of almost equal length can be combined to create a more balanced and varied paragraph. Here, for instance, is a paragraph, also about an ancient city, made up of short, choppy sentences:

> Pompeii was an ancient city. It belonged to the Roman Empire. It was near the base of Mount Vesuvius. In 79 A.D. the volcano on Vesuvius erupted. Tons of hot, wet ash fell on Pompeii. In less than a day the city was buried. It just vanished. More than seventeen centuries later an Italian peasant found Pompeii. His discovery was accidental. He was digging in a field. His shovel struck the top of a wall. That was two hundred years ago. Pompeii is still being excavated two hundred years later. About two-thirds of the city has been unearthed. It must have been a beautiful city.

With repetition eliminated and some ideas subordinated to others, here is what you get:

> The ancient Roman city of Pompeii lay near the base of Mt. Vesuvius. In 79 A.D. Vesuvius erupted, burying the city with tons of hot, wet ash. In less than a day the city vanished. More than seventeen centuries later an Italian peasant digging in a field with a shovel accidentally struck the top of a wall. He had found Pompeii. Today, 200 years later, the city is still being unearthed. The excavation reveals that Pompeii must have been a beautiful city.

VARYING SENTENCES—A SUMMARY

✓ Use a variety of sentence types: *simple*, *compound*, and *complex*.

✓ Create variety by starting sentences with:

- A prepositional phrase: *From the start, In the first place, At the outset*
- Adverbs and adverbial phrases: *Originally, At first, Initially*
- Dependent clauses: *When you start with this, Because the opening is*
- Conjunctions: *And, But, Not only, Either, So, Yet*
- Adjectives and adjective phrases: *Fresh from, Introduced with, Headed by*
- Verbal infinitives: *To launch, To take the first step, To get going*
- Participles: *Leading off, Starting up, Commencing with*
- Inversions: *Unique is the writer who embarks . . .*

✓ Balance long and short sentences.

✓ Combine a series of very short sentences.

✓ Dismember very long sentences.

Paragraphing

Whoever invented paragraphs deserves a pat on the back because he or she devised a simple way to guide readers through a piece of writing. Each new paragraph alerts readers to get ready for a shift of some kind, just as a car's directional blinker tells other drivers that you're about to turn.

Yet, not every new paragraph signals a drastic change. The writer may simply want to nudge the discussion ahead to the next step. Some paragraphs spring directly from those that preceded them. The paragraph you are now reading, for instance, is linked to the one before by the connecting word *Yet*. The connection was meant to alert you to a change in thought, but it was also intended to remind you that the two paragraphs are related. Abrupt starts may be useful from time to time to keep readers on their toes. But good writers avoid a string of sudden turns that can transform surprise into confusion.

In an essay, paragraphs usually play a primary role and one or more secondary roles. An *introductory paragraph*, for instance, launches the essay and makes the intent of the essay clear to the reader. The *concluding paragraph* leaves the reader with a thought to remember and provides a sense of closure. The majority of paragraphs, however, are *developmental*. They carry forward the main point of the essay by performing any number of functions, among them:

- Adding new ideas to the preceding discussion
- Continuing or explaining in more detail an idea presented earlier
- Reiterating a previously stated idea
- Citing an example of a previously stated idea
- Evaluating an opinion stated earlier
- Refuting previously stated ideas
- Providing a new or contrasting point of view
- Describing the relationship between ideas presented earlier
- Providing background material
- Raising a hypothetical or rhetorical question about the topic

Whatever its functions, a paragraph should contribute to the essay's overall growth. A paragraph that fails to amplify the main idea of the essay should be revised or deleted. Similarly, any idea within a paragraph that doesn't contribute to the development of the paragraph's topic needs to be changed or eliminated.

Topic and Supporting Sentences

As you write your AP essays, be sure to include sentences that contain landmarks to help readers know where they are. Such guiding sentences differ from others because they define the paragraph's main topic, hence their name: *topic sentence*. Topic sentences come in many forms, but what they all have in common is their helpfulness. They are like landmarks that tell readers the direction they'll be going for a while.

Most, but not all, paragraphs contain topic sentences. The topic of some paragraphs is so obvious that to state it would be redundant. For instance, a description of a fast-food restaurant might detail the crowd, the noise, the overflowing garbage cans, the smell of cooking oil, the lines of people, the crumb-strewn formica tables, and so on. A reader would certainly get the picture. To state explicitly "It was a busy day at Burger King" would serve no purpose.

No rule governs every possible use of a topic sentence. A sense of what readers need in order to understand the essay must be your guide. Let topic sentences lead the way. Consider your readers as absentminded wanderers who need frequent reminders of where they are and where they are going. If in doubt, grasp their hands too firmly rather than too loosely. Follow the principle that if there is a way to misunderstand or misinterpret your words, readers are sure to find it.

Developing Paragraphs

Like essays, paragraphs should have a discernible organization. Ideas can be arranged from general to specific, or vice versa. Sequential arrangements make sense for analytical paragraphs. In a cause-and-effect paragraph, logic dictates that the cause precedes the effect, but the opposite may sometimes be preferable. As always, clarity and intent should govern the sequence of ideas.

Writers shun formulas in creating paragraphs, but they generally concur that paragraphs of only one or two sentences are too scanty. Thorough development of an idea calls for several sentences—most of the time, at least. Journalists, however, often write paragraphs consisting of one or two sentences. But most contemporary nonfiction consists of paragraphs of four to eight sentences. Recognizing that readers need frequent breaks, writers these days almost never write paragraphs of a dozen or more sentences.

Poor essays often suffer from lack of development. The writer states ideas and then drops them. You're not apt to do that, though, if you think of your readers as skeptics who doubt that you're on the level unless you prove that you know what you're talking about. An underdeveloped statement, no matter how strongly worded, usually won't do. That's why you must back up your general ideas with specifics, using illustrative material that can be in any number of forms. In an analytical essay, that means referring frequently to the passage. Paraphrase the passage or use direct quotes, but don't let the quotes constitute the bulk of your essay. Rather, state ideas in your own words, then support them with direct or indirect quotations.

Whatever you do, your analysis must be based on something more solid than your intuition or personal preference. The left side of your brain, the logical side, is being examined along with the right, the creative, side. The best essays reveal that both sides of your brain are in good working order.

> Every sentence in a paragraph should help to develop the paragraph's topic.

> **Strategy for Getting on Top of Topic Sentences**
>
> Print out or photocopy an essay you've written recently. On one copy underline all the topic sentences. Let a friend do the same on the second copy. Then compare your answers. If you agree, you can be pretty sure that your topic sentences are doing what they are supposed to do.

> The kind of analytical writing expected on the AP exam is rational discourse, not emotional ranting.

Using Transitions

Picture your readers as tourists in a foreign country and your essay as a journey they are making from one place to another. Because you can't expect strangers to find their own way, you must lead them. Tell them where they are going (the introduction) and remind them of the progress they're making (the body of the essay).

In long essays readers need more reminders than in short ones. To keep readers well informed, you don't need to repeat what you've already written but rather plant key ideas, slightly rephrased, as milestones along the way. (The sentence you just read contains just such a marker. The phrase "*To keep readers well-informed*" cues you to keep in mind the topic of this paragraph—helping readers find their way.) By regularly alluding to the main idea of the paragraphs, you'll keep readers focused and hold their attention from start to finish.

You can help readers along, too, by choosing words that set up relationships between one thought and the next. This can be done with such words as *this*, which actually ties the sentence you are now reading to the previous one. The word *too* in the first sentence of this paragraph serves the same function; it acts as a link between this paragraph and the one before. Fortunately, the English language is brimming with transitional words and phrases for tying sentences and ideas together.

What follows is a collection of common transitional words and phrases grouped according to their customary use. With a bit of thought, you could probably add to the list.

When you **ADD** ideas: *moreover, in addition (to), further, besides, also, and then, then too, again, next, secondly, equally important . . .*

When you make a **CONTRAST**: *however, conversely, in contrast, on the other hand, on the contrary, but, nevertheless, and yet, still, even so . . .*

When you **COMPARE** or draw a **PARALLEL**: *similarly, likewise, in comparison, in like manner, at the same time, in the same vein . . .*

TIP

Do your readers a favor—use transitions to give them a smooth trip through your essays.

When you cite an **EXAMPLE**: *for example, for instance, as when, as illustrated by . . .*

When you show **RESULTS**: *as a result, in consequence, consequently, accordingly, therefore, thus, hence . . .*

When you **REINFORCE** an idea: *indeed, in fact, as a matter of fact, to be sure, of course, in any event, by all means . . .*

When you express **SEQUENCE** or the passing of **TIME**: *soon after, then, previously, not long after, meanwhile, in the meantime, later, simultaneously, at the same time, immediately, next, at length, thereafter . . .*

When you show **PLACES**: *here, nearby, at this spot, near at hand, in proximity, on the opposite side, across from, adjacent to, underneath . . .*

When you **CONCLUDE**: *finally, in short, in other words, in a word, to sum up, in conclusion, in the end, when all is said and done . . .*

You don't need a specific transitional word or phrase to bind every sentence to another. Ideas themselves can create strong links. Notice in the paired sentences below that the underlined words in each second sentence echo an idea expressed in the first.

(1) As a kind of universal language, music unites people from age eight to eighty. (2) <u>No matter how old they are</u>, people can lose themselves in melodies, rhythms, tempos, and endless varieties of sound.

(1) At the heart of *Romeo and Juliet* is a long-standing feud between the Capulets and the Montagues. (2) <u>As enemies</u>, the two families always fight in the streets of Verona.

(1) To drive nails into very hard wood without bending them, first dip the points into grease or soap. (2) <u>You can accomplish the same end</u> by moistening the points of the nails in your mouth or in a can of water.

One of your goals on the AP exam is to assure readers a smooth trip through your essay. Without your help—that is, unless you deliberately tie sentences together with transitions—readers may find themselves lurching from one idea to another. Before long, they'll give up or get lost like travelers on an unmarked road. While not every sentence needs a specific transition, three or four successive sentences without a link of some kind can leave readers wondering whether the trip through your essay is worth taking.

Mini-Workout: Transitions

> **DIRECTIONS:** Use as many transitions as you can while writing paragraphs on the suggested topics below.

1. Write a paragraph on how to do something—drive a car from home to school, pull a practical joke, avoid doing homework, scrub info from your Facebook page, get on the good side of a teacher, give your cat or dog a bath. Use as many SEQUENCE/TIME transitions as possible, but don't overdo it.
2. Write a paragraph detailing a cause and its effect: the cause and effect of good teaching, of a new fad, of stress in high school students, of taking risks, of lying, of a close friendship. Use as many RESULT transitions as you can, but don't go overboard.
3. Write a paragraph that makes a comparison and contrast—the way people respond to pressure, groups in your school, two athletes, then and now, boredom and laziness, two books, a friend who turned into an enemy, an enemy who became a friend. Use as many COMPARISON/CONTRAST transitions as you can, but don't get carried away.
4. Write a paragraph in which you argue for or against an issue—electronic eavesdropping, school dress codes, educational vouchers, censoring the Internet, dieting, restrictions on smoking. Use as many ADDITION transitions as you can, but only where they make sense.

Concluding Your Analytical Essay

At the end of your essay, you can lift your pen off the paper and be done with it. Or, if you have the time, you can present your readers with a little gift to remember you by—perhaps a surprising insight, a bit of wisdom, a catchy phrase—something likely to tease the readers' brains, tickle their funny bones, or make them feel smart.

Choose the gift carefully. It should fit the content, style, and mood of your essay and spring naturally from its contents. Because it comes last, the final paragraph leaves an enduring impression.

TIP

Stay away from summary endings. They insult your reader's intelligence.

A weak, apologetic, or irrelevant conclusion may dilute or even obliterate the effect you tried so hard to create. Above all, *stay away from summary endings.* When an essay is short to begin with, it's insulting to review for readers what is evident on the page in front of them. Readers are intelligent people. Trust them to remember what your essay says.

A catchy conclusion isn't always necessary, but even a short ending may be preferable to none at all. Effective endings leave readers fulfilled, satisfied that they have arrived somewhere. A judiciously chosen ending may sway AP readers to judge your essay somewhat more leniently than otherwise. There are no guarantees, of course, but readers are bound to be touched by a memento of your thinking, your sense of humor, or your vision. Even an ordinary thought, uniquely expressed, will leave an agreeable afterglow.

You might try any one of these common techniques:

- Have a little fun with your conclusion; try to put a smile on your reader's face.
- End with an apt quotation drawn from the essay itself, from the prompt, or from another source.
- Finish by clearly restating your essay's main point but using new words. Changing the wording, in fact, may shed new light on the main idea—a gesture that your readers will appreciate. If appropriate, add a short tag line, a brief sentence that creates a dramatic effect.
- Bring your readers up to date or project them into the future. Say something about prospects for the months or years ahead.

Although an effective conclusion will add luster to an essay, don't feel obliged to add an ending just for the sake of form. Readers will have developed a fairly accurate sense of your writing ability before reaching your essay's last word. Rest assured that a good but incomplete piece of writing will be graded according to what you have done well instead of what you haven't done at all.

Editing and Proofreading Essays

Once you've finished writing your essay, spend whatever time is left editing and proofreading.

Editing for Clarity

Because many words have multiple meanings, do a word-by-word check for clarity. Ask yourself whether a reader could misconstrue a word or find it ambiguous. For example, in an essay about missing teenagers, Paula S. wrote, "The last thing parents should do is talk to their kids." Coming to that sentence, a reader might well wonder whether Paula meant that parents should talk to their kids as a last resort, or that in a list of what parents ought to do, the final step is talking to their kids.

Later in the essay Paula wrote, "Raya told her friend Alexa that she had made a serious mistake by running away from home." Paula certainly understood what she intended to say, but readers can't tell whether Raya took a dim view of Alexa's actions or whether Raya herself had second thoughts about her own flight. Granted, these sentences have been quoted out of context, but the point remains: What may seem perfectly clear to a writer may send a puzzling message to the reader.

That's why you should work hard to arrange your words in the clearest order. Watch for grammatical perils that interfere with meaning, especially **(1) misplaced modifiers, (2) dangling participles**, and **(3) lack of parallelism**—all discussed in the pages that follow.

Misplaced Modifiers

Modifiers are words, phrases, and clauses that tell something about or limit the meaning of a particular word or statement. For example:

> The bedroom had a *broken window*.

The adjective *broken* is a modifier because it tells something about the condition of the *window*. In other words, *broken* "modifies" *window*.

Modifiers must be placed so that they modify the correct words:

> Luke only loves Ruby.

Here *only* modifies the verb *loves*. The modifier is appropriate if Luke feels nothing but love for Ruby—no admiration, no awe, no respect, nor any other emotion. If, however, Luke has but one love, and that love is Ruby, then *only* is misplaced. Properly placed, *only* should come either before or after *Ruby*:

> Luke loves *only* Ruby.   or   Luke loves Ruby *only*.

Another example:

> Nora decided *when she had completed her AP English homework* to watch TV.

In this sentence *when she had completed her AP English homework* is the modifier. But it is hard to tell whether it modifies *decided* or *watch*. If it modifies *decided*, Nora finished her essay and then made a decision to watch TV. If it modifies *watch*, Nora worked on her homework and decided at some point that she would watch TV when she had finished.

> When she had finished her AP English homework, Nora decided to watch TV.
> While doing her AP English homework, Nora decided to watch TV when she had finished.

Now the meaning of both sentences is unambiguous.

Obviously, misplaced modifiers can cloud a writer's intentions. To avoid the problem, place modifiers as close as possible to the words they modify:

> MISPLACED: Diego donated his old car to a charity *that no longer ran well*.

The modifier *that no longer ran well* is too far from *car*, the word it modifies.

> CLEAR: Diego donated his old car *that no longer ran well* to a charity.

Dangling Modifiers

In a sentence words must fit together like pieces of a jigsaw puzzle. Sometimes, a misplaced word looks as though it fits, but it doesn't say exactly what the writer intended.

(1) While running to English class, the bell rang.
(2) Hammering a nail, a crack developed in the board.
(3) When only eight years old, my father warned me about smoking.

The ludicrous meaning of these sentences may not strike you immediately, but look again. Do you see that these sentences describe a surreal world in which bells run to class, cracks hammer nails, and underage fathers dispense advice? The problem is that these sentences try to mate two groups of words that can't go together. The parts are mismatched. After the comma in the first sentence, you'd expect to find out who is running, but you aren't told. Likewise, after the commas in sentences 2 and 3, you are not told who was hammering and who is only eight years old. In short, you're left dangling. Hence, the label *dangling modifier* has been given to this type of construction. To correct the error, add the noun or pronoun to be modified, as in:

> While the boys were running to English class, the bell rang.
> Hammering a nail, Rufus cracked the board.
> When I was eight, my father warned me about smoking.

Rewriting the whole sentence is often the best cure for a dangling modifier, as in:

> DANGLING: While talking on the phone, the stew burned in the pot.
> CLEAR: While I talked on the phone, the stew burned in the pot.

Mini-Workout: Misplaced and Dangling Modifiers

DIRECTIONS: Rewrite any of the following sentences that contain an error in modification. Corrections can be made by shifting words around or revising the whole sentence. Some may be correct.

---

1. The bowling alley lends out shoes to its customers of all sizes.

   _____

2. An old bike was given to a junk man we planned to put in the trash.

   _____

3. At the age of ten, my family and I emigrated from Guatemala to the U.S.

   _____

4. Still sound asleep at noon, my mother thought I was sick.

   _____

5. Totaled beyond repair, Allison knew she'd have to buy another car.

   _____

6. The coach said that canceling the swim meet was the right thing to do under the circumstances.

   _____

7. Used all night to illuminate the steps, I needed new batteries for the flashlight.

    _____

8. A report was submitted about the latest bank heist by the police.

    _____

9. Pausing for a drink of water after the hike, a grizzly bear stood in front of me.

    _____

10. After a quick breakfast, the school bus picked me up at the corner.

    _____

Answers on page 195.

Parallelism

Parallel structure keeps equivalent ideas in the same grammatical form. Here is a sentence that lists the contents of a student's locker:

> The locker held a down jacket, aromatic sweatpants, three sneakers, two left-handed gloves, an unused tuna sandwich, a broken ski pole, a hockey puck, six overdue library books, a disposable camera, and a hiking boot.

Every item listed is an object, each expressed in the same grammatical form: a noun preceded by one or two adjectives. When the student wrote a list of his favorite pastimes, though, the sentence lost its parallelism:

> I like skiing, hiking, to take pictures, and running.

The message is clear, but the phrase "to take pictures" is not grammatically parallel with the other phrases. To revise it, write "taking pictures":

> I like skiing, hiking, taking pictures, and running.

When you structure the pieces of a sentence in parallel form, you put yourself in the company of world-class stylists. Abraham Lincoln, for one, used parallelism at Gettysburg: "We cannot dedicate, we cannot consecrate, we cannot hallow this ground . . . ." And later, ". . . that government of the people, by the people, and for the people shall not perish from the earth." John F. Kennedy used parallelism in his inaugural speech: "Let every nation know, whether it wishes us good or ill, that we shall pay any price, bear any burden, meet any hardship, support any friend, oppose any foe to assure the survival and the success of liberty."

To apply the essential principles of parallel construction to your prose:

- Express all ideas in a series in the same grammatical form, even when the series consists of only two items:

  NOT PARALLEL: Her parents objected to music she played loudly and keeping late hours.

  PARALLEL: Her parents objected to the loud music she played and the late hours she kept.

TIP

The key to parallelism is uniformity—expressing ideas in the same grammatical form.

Here, parallelism is achieved with prepositional phrases, *to the loud music* and *to the late hours*. Each phrase is followed by the pronoun *she* and the past tense of a verb.

After graduation she promised to turn the volume down and to come home earlier.

Each parallel idea consists of an infinitive followed by a noun and an adverb.

■ Use grammatical equivalents to make comparisons and contrasts. When comparing two ideas, for example, express both ideas in phrases, or pair an idea stated in a clause with a second idea also stated in a clause.

FAULTY: They are worried more about public opinion than for what the effect of the proposal may be.

The prepositional phrase *about public opinion* may not be paired with the clause *what the effect of the proposal may be*.

PARALLEL: They are worried more about public opinion than about the effect of the
  proposal.

Parallelism is achieved by pairing two prepositional phrases.

FAULTY: Going out to eat no longer thrills me as much as to cook at home.

The gerund *going out* should not be paired with the infinitive *to cook*.

PARALLEL: Going out to eat no longer thrills me as much as cooking at home.

Parallelism is achieved by pairing two gerunds, *going* and *cooking*.

■ Stay alert for pairs of words that signal the need for parallelism, such as *either/or, neither/ nor, whether/or, both/and*, and *not only/but also*.

Alice will attend *neither* NYU *or* Columbia.

Revise by changing *neither* to *either*, or changing *or* to *nor*. Remember to keep the pair of words close to each other in the sentence. If they are too far apart, your sentence may be hard to follow:

Jake *both* started on the basketball and the volleyball teams.

The signal word *both* is too far removed from the parallel phrase, *basketball and volleyball teams*. Its placement misleads the reader into thinking that the verb *started* is one of the parallel ideas. Correctly worded, the sentence reads:

Jake started on *both* the basketball and the volleyball teams.

■ When an article, a preposition, or a conjunction appears before the first in a series of parallel items, repeat the word before the others in the series.

UNCLEAR: Our mechanic did a better job on my car than his.

Did two mechanics work on the same car or did one mechanic work on two different cars? To clear up the ambiguity, repeat the preposition *on*, as in:

CLEAR: Our mechanic did a better job on my car than *on* his.

Sometimes repeating both a preposition and an article is necessary:

UNCLEAR: Before signing the contract, Tiffany spoke with the president and treasurer of the company.

Did Tiffany speak with one person or with two? Repeating *with the* helps to clarify the meaning:

CLEAR: Before signing the contract, Tiffany spoke with the president and *with the* treasurer of the company.

■ Make sure that parallel ideas are logical equivalents.

ABSURD: Tyler is six feet tall, kind, and a Texan.

Physical features, traits of character, and place of origin are not logically coordinated.

LESS ABSURD: Tyler, a six-foot Texan, is kind.

Still not terribly logical, but at least the revision emphasizes only one of Tyler's qualities—his kindness.

ILLOGICAL: San Diego's *harbor* is reported to be more polluted than any city.

This sentence is meant to compare pollution in the San Diego harbor with pollution in the harbors of other cities, but it fails to achieve its goal. Instead, it illogically compares San Diego's harbor with a city.

LOGICAL: San Diego's *harbor* is reported to be more polluted than the *harbor of any other city.*

ILLOGICAL: Unlike most *cars* on the street, *Anika* has her Subaru washed almost every week.

This sentence is intended to compare Anika's car with other cars on the street, but it manages only to compare Anika to the other cars, an illogical comparison.

LOGICAL: Anika's *Subaru*, unlike *most cars* on the street, is washed almost every week.

A lack of parallelism in phrases and clauses is not just bad form but can cause confusion. Sound parallel structure, in contrast, keeps equivalent ideas in the same grammatical form. Take, for example, a sentence that lists the characteristics of a restaurant in which to have a family birthday party:

We are looking for a place that is private, plenty of space, has a friendly staff, and that people like to look at.

The sentence makes some sense, of course, but it's awkward because the four characteristics are not expressed in parallel form. Instead, they are a mix of an adjective, a phrase, and two clauses. One way to fix the problem is to use only adjectives, as in:

We are looking for a place that is private, spacious, friendly, and attractive.

Or use a series of nouns each preceded by an adjective:

We are looking for a place with total privacy, ample space, a friendly staff, and attractive surroundings.

Mini-Workout: Parallel Structure

> **DIRECTIONS:** Look for faulty parallel structure in the following sentences. Write the correct version of the offending word or phrase in the space provided. Some sentences may be correct.

1. This book not only shows what happens to mentally depressed people but it's all right to seek help.

    _____

2. A more easier and direct route exist between Oakland and San Raphael than the one we took.

    _____

3. Jim is tall, kind, and forward on the basketball team.

    _____

4. Emmett prefers to cook at home rather than going out to eat.

    _____

5. Both angry and disappointment at the team's dismal performance, the coach resigned.

    _____

6. The men haven't decided whether canoeing across the lake would be better than a sailboat.

    _____

7. The wind had not only knocked down the tree but the electric lines came down, too.

    _____

8. After finding a job, she'll get an apartment, continue playing the guitar, and friends will party with her.

    _____

9. Either the mouse will find a quick way into the attic or will gnaw at the siding for days.

    _____

10. City living is exciting, convenient, and provides amazing entertainment.

    _____

Answers on page 196.

Editing for Interest

Your essay will be read by people—real people who know that essays can be lively and interesting. Like readers everywhere, they'll be bored by writing that is dull.

Therefore, try to enliven your prose by:

- ✓ Using *active* instead of *passive* verbs
- ✓ Writing *active* instead of *passive* sentences
- ✓ Omitting needless words
- ✓ Using specific language

Active Verbs

Because *active* verbs describe or show movement, they pump vitality into your prose. *Being* verbs, in contrast, have almost no life in them. Their lifelessness is apparent in the common forms of the verb *to be*:

is	are	was
were	am	has been
had been	have been	will be

> **TIP**
>
> Use active verbs whenever you can.

Being verbs ordinarily join the subject of a sentence to a predicate. They function much like an equal sign in an equation: "Five minus two *is* three" ($5 - 2 = 3$), or "Helena *was* happy" (Helena = happy), or "Your AP score *will be* 5" (That = good news!). Because *being* verbs (and equal signs) lack energy, use active verbs whenever you can.

Yes, it's hard to get along in speech and writing without *being* verbs. But be stingy with them. Check a few of your most recent essays. If more than, say, one out of four sentences uses a form of *to be* as its main verb, try the following revision techniques.

1. **SUBSTITUTE A NEW ACTIVE VERB FOR THE *BEING* VERB:**

    BEING VERB: It is not easy for most students to write immortal essays.

    ACTIVE VERB: Most students struggle to write immortal essays.

2. **EXTRACT AN ACTIVE VERB FROM A NOUN IN THE SENTENCE:**

    BEING VERB: Keizo was the winner of the essay contest.

    ACTIVE VERB: Keizo won the essay contest.

3. **EXTRACT AN ACTIVE VERB FROM AN ADJECTIVE:**

    BEING VERB: My weekend at the beach was enjoyable.

    ACTIVE VERB: I enjoyed my weekend at the beach.

As you delete *being* verbs, you'll probably notice that some sentences resist change. When that happens, turn subjects into verbs and verbs into nouns. Try also to eliminate unnecessary phrases. Full-scale sentence revisions can result in sentences bearing little resemblance to the originals, but verb-swapping often roots out excess verbiage and improves an essay's readability.

Being verbs are not the only verbs that sap the life out of sentences. They share that distinction with several other verbs, including forms of *to have, to come, to go, to make, to move,* and *to get*—verbs with so many different uses that they creep into our speech and writing virtually unnoticed. *Webster's International Dictionary* lists 16 different meanings for the verb *get* and a dozen more for *make* and *move*. It's true that we can hardly get by without these verbs, but use them only if you can swear that no other words will do. Otherwise, trade them in for more vivid verbs, as in:

DULL: The line to the box office *moved* very slowly.

LIVELIER: The line *crept* (*crawled*, *inched*, *poked*) to the box office.

Note that by using a more animated verb, you eliminate the need for "very slowly," which has suddenly become redundant.

DULL: The police officer *gave* drivers permission to turn left on red.

LIVELIER: The police officer *permitted* drivers to turn left on red.

Note that this revision has led not just to a more active sentence but to one that contains fewer words—always a stylistic plus.

Mini-Workout: Active Verbs

> **DIRECTIONS:** Revise each of the following sentences by substituting active verbs for "being" verbs, but try not to change the meaning of the original.

1. Mariana and Leonardo were the highest scorers on the practice AP exam.

   _____

2. Cost is the determining factor in choosing a rug for my bedroom.

   _____

3. It is logical that admission to college is the result of a student's effort and achievement.

   _____

4. The monarchy was over after the Revolutionary War.

   _____

5. Since 9/11 there have been many more terrorist threats.

   _____

6. Chaos is a word that is relevant to my math class.

   _____

7. Everyone is scared of Mr. Gill.

   _____

8. The way to the principal's office is down the next corridor.

   _____

9. There are students who are excellent in chemistry but not in physics.

   _____

10. This novel was the one recommended by the librarian.

    _____

Answers on page 196.

Active and Passive Sentences

To write lively prose, keep in mind the difference between *active* and *passive* sentences. In an active sentence the person or thing performing an action is usually mentioned early in a sentence, so readers know right away who or what you are talking about. In passive sentences the performer of an action is not named or gets less notice than either the receiver of the action or the action itself. For example:

> Two months were spent rehearsing for the concert.

This sentence fails to tell who performed the action—that is, who rehearsed for the concert. The following revision clears up the uncertainty:

> Two months were spent rehearsing for the concert by the marching band.

This version transforms the original, but it still emphasizes the action instead of the performer of the action. To complete the transformation, say something like:

> For two months the marching band rehearsed for the concert.

In the active voice, the performers of the action receive top billing.

Why is the active voice preferable? Mainly because most events in life don't just occur by themselves. Burgers don't just get eaten; people cook and devour them. Marriages don't just happen; couples deliberately go out and marry each other. Goals don't get scored, salmon don't get caught, wallets don't get lost all by themselves. People do these things.

Good essay writers, taking advantage of readers' natural curiosity about others, often strive to make the performer of the action the grammatical subject of their sentences:

> PASSIVE: The award was presented to Hildie by the Art Club.
>
> ACTIVE: The Art Club presented the award to Hildie.
>
> PASSIVE: Ohio State was attended by my brother, my cousin, and three of my uncles.
>
> ACTIVE: My brother, my cousin, and three uncles went to Ohio State.

In some contexts, of course, the actor is unknown or irrelevant. That's when a passive sentence works best. For example:

> PASSIVE: The curtain was raised at 8:30 sharp.
>
> ACTIVE: At 8:30 sharp, a stagehand (or Maryanne, the production assistant) raised the curtain.

TIP

Never use passive where you can use active.

Why?

Active sentences strengthen prose; passive sentences weaken it.

In the passive version, curtain time is the important fact. Who pulled the rope or pushed the button doesn't matter.

Transforming a passive sentence to an active one takes a bit of editing. As you prepare for the AP exam, examine your essays for passive sentences. Change them to active sentences unless you have a very good reason not to.

Mini-Workout: Revising Passive Sentences

> **DIRECTIONS:** Put each of the following sentences into active voice.

1. The backyard was covered by dead leaves.

   _____

2. The situation in Syria was discussed by us.

   _____

3. Friday's quiz was failed because I had been at a play rehearsal every night that week.

   _____

4. Portland was flown to at the start of our weeklong vacation in Oregon.

   _____

5. The Golden Fleece was pursued by Jason and the Argonauts.

   _____

6. The newspaper was fetched by Rex every morning.

   _____

7. The decision to build a fence on the border was made by immigration officials.

   _____

8. Pizza was ordered by more than twenty diners on Saturday night.

   _____

9. Five of Shakespeare's plays were seen by our group in three days.

   _____

10. The voters were urged by the candidate to throw the old mayor out of office.

    _____

Answers on pages 196–197.

Cutting Needless Words

Never use two words when one will do. If it's possible to cut a word out, always cut it out. Tell your readers quickly and directly what you have to say. Brevity works best. Cut out verbiage. Readers value economy.

Stop! Have you noticed that the previous paragraph disregards the very advice it dispenses? Do you see repetition and redundancy? Couldn't the point have been made more succinctly?

Here's a word to the wise:

> You should work through all of the sentences you write by examining each one and crossing out all the words you don't definitely need.

To be precise, that's twenty-four words to the wise—many more than are needed.

> Go through every sentence you write and cross out unnecessary words.

That's better—eleven words of free advice, but still too many. The sentence could be trimmed still further:

> Trim unnecessary words out of every sentence.

This seven-word model is less than a third of the original twenty-four-word clunker. But it can be pared even more:

> Omit needless words.

And still more:

> Cut verbosity.

To make every word count, wring your sentences through this four-step word trimmer:

STEP 1   Look for repetition.

> WORDY: Elena took Jesse to the movies. Jesse is Elena's brother. (10 words)
> TRIMMED: Elena took her brother Jesse to the movies. (8 words)

Granted, cutting 10 words to 8 is not much. But consider that it's a 20 percent reduction, and in a 500-word essay, a 20 percent reduction amounts to 100 words—the equivalent of a whole paragraph.

> WORDY: When Hannah was sixteen years of age she accepted a position at the Moraga Nursery. In this position she learned about plants and about how to handle customers. (28)
> TRIMMED: At sixteen years old, Hannah accepted a position at the Moraga Nursery, where she learned about plants and handling customers. (20)
> RE-TRIMMED: Working at the Moraga Nursery at age sixteen, Hannah learned to handle both plants and customers. (16)

STEP 2   Hunt for phrases that add words but no meaning, such as *the fact that, due to the fact that, at this point in time, at the present time, that being said*, and comparable usages.

> WORDY: Hamlet returned home as a result of his father's death. (10)
> TRIMMED: Hamlet returned home because his father died. (7).
> WORDY: The troops were in danger due to the fact that mines had been planted in the field. (16)
> TRIMMED: The mine field endangered the troops. (6)

TIP

Never use two words when one will do.

Wordy Phrases	Trimmed
what I mean is	I mean
on account of, as a result of	because
in the final analysis	finally
few and far between	few
each and every one	each
this is a subject that	this subject
ten in number	ten
at the age of six years old	at age six
most unique	unique
true fact	fact
biography of her life	biography
in regard to, with regard to, in relation to, with respect to	about

STEP 3 Search for redundancies. Innumerable words are wasted on reiteration of what has already been stated, on repeating the obvious, on restating ideas, on saying the same thing again and again and over, driving readers to the brink of madness.

WORDY: A cloud of black soot rose up to the sky. (10)

Soot, by definition, is black, and rising clouds can only go up.

TRIMMED: A cloud of soot rose to the sky. (8)

WORDY: He had a smile on his face. (7)

Where else but on a face would a smile appear?

TRIMMED: He wore a smile. (4)

WORDY: After carefully scrutinizing the X-ray, Dr. Jackson seemed fully engrossed in her own train of thought. (16)

Scrutinize means "to study carefully," and engrossed means "to think fully." Also, *her own train of thought* is nonsensical because no one can think others' thoughts.

TRIMMED: After scrutinizing the X-ray, Dr. Jackson seemed engrossed in thought. (10)

After you have pared your sentences to the bone, reread what remains and discard still more by tracking down little words like *the, a, an, up, down, its,* and *and.* Even though it may hurt to take out what you worked hard to put in, don't whine. Just grit your teeth and be tough!

STEP 4 Look for telltale words like *which, who, that, thing,* and *all.* They often signify excess verbiage.

WORDY: Tesla was a man who was obsessed by the wonders of electricity. (12)
TRIMMED: The wonders of electricity obsessed Tesla. (6)

Changing the grammatical subject and replacing *was* with an active verb halved the word count.

WORDY: What he most wanted was that the terrorists would release the hostages. (12)
TRIMMED: He most wanted the terrorists to release the hostages. (9)

Mini-Workout: Cutting Needless Words

Part A

DIRECTIONS: Tighten these sentences, but preserve their meaning.
---

1. The biker, a woman named Mary Roe, wrote a book with the title *A Ride Across America*, about biking across America, which she accomplished after riding 90 miles a day in order to prepare for her ride across America.

   _____

   _____

2. There is no reason for the chairperson of the committee, who is Carolyn Welles, to take offense at my suggestion, which is aimed at trying to make the meetings more productive and useful to the entire student body at large.

   _____

   _____

3. Mr. Evans was appointed to be the treasurer of the group in spite of the fact that he had once been arrested and tried and sent to jail for a period of six months for embezzling some money from the business he worked for.

   _____

   _____

4. Harmful criticism is criticism that tears a person down instead of helping the person overcome or deal with a problem.

   _____

   _____

5. All Americans should try to save gasoline, and the best way they can save gasoline all across the country is to cut down on the number of miles they drive when it's really not necessary to drive.

   _____

   _____

Part B

> **DIRECTIONS:** The following paragraph comes from an essay that advocated gaining weight. Please trim its fat.

Such weight-gaining ideas can be used to good advantage by each and every man, woman, and child who is interested in adding pounds of weight to his or her body. They are the latest, most up-to-date set of procedures available anywhere. Owing to the fact that health experts and authorities believe that it is better to be underweight than it is to be overweight, ideas for putting on weight are generally thought to be jokes not taken seriously, which is the reason why such ideas are kept under wraps and not publicized very widely or broadly. Yet, there are many people of all kinds who need to gain weight for a variety of diverse reasons. Here is a quotation that Slim Snyder, who is a graduate of Stanford University, stated during a speech he gave at a meeting of people gathered together at a health conference recently: "Lean people are victims of discrimination, just as obese people are."

_____

_____

_____

_____

_____

_____

_____

_____

_____

_____

Answers on page 197.

Being Specific

Specific words are memorable, while hazy words fade quickly away. Tell your garage mechanic vaguely, "This car is broken," and he'll ask for more information. If a patient in the E.R. says, "I feel pain," a doctor wants to know exactly where it hurts.

In the first draft of an essay for his AP English class, Maccabee S. wrote the following about a day he'd like to forget:

> It was an awful day outside. Everything was going wrong. I felt terrible. Things weren't going well in school. I got a below-par grade on a paper, and I was sure that I had failed my Chem quiz. I also had lots of things to do at home and no time to do them. My mother was in a bad mood, too. She yelled at me for all kinds of things. Then Penny called, and we got into a disagreement. I had trouble with my iPhone, and I couldn't fix it. I went to bed early, hoping that tomorrow would be better.

Reviewing this paragraph a few days later, Maccabee realized the writing begged for more specificity. Yes, the day had been dreadful, but his account needed specific language to prove it. The next draft took care of that:

> On a cold and rainy November day, my life was as miserable as the weather. I felt chills all day, and my throat was sore. In school I got a D on a history paper about the Bubonic Plague, and I was sure that I had failed the chemistry quiz on molecular modeling. The homework was piling up: two lab reports, more than 150 pages to read in Wuthering Heights, a chapter in the history text, and about a hundred new vocabulary words in Spanish. I didn't have time or energy to do it all, especially when my mother started to pick at me about my messy room and the thank you letters I'm supposed to write to my grandparents. Just as she was reminding me that my SAT registration was overdue, Penny called to say that she couldn't come for Thanksgiving after all, so we argued about loyalty and trust and keeping promises. Then she hung up on me. Half an hour later I tried to text her, but my phone was frozen. I tried changing the battery, forcing it into recovery mode, but got nothing but a blank screen. Disgusted, I threw the damn thing across the room. By 9:30 P.M. I fell into bed, hoping that tomorrow would be better.

This version includes many specific details that vividly illustrate the wretchedness of Maccabee's miserable day. Not every paragraph of every essay calls for such detail, but an essay consisting solely of generalities will leave readers at sea.

It's true that vague, shadowy words are easier to think of. But they're often used as a smoke screen to cover up the absence of thought. For example, it's easy to pass judgment on a book by calling it "good" or "interesting." But what readers should be told is precisely why you think so. It's simple to call someone "old" without bothering to show the reader a "round-shouldered, white-haired man hunched in a wheelchair." A student who calls her teacher "ugly" sends a different image of ugliness to each reader. But if the teacher is a "shifty-eyed tyrant who spits when she talks," the specific details create a vivid image. Or if the teacher's personality is ugly, show her cruelly insulting her hapless students.

Of course, it's not essential to back up every generalization with specific details. An essay bogged down in detail can be tedious both to read and to write. Every time you mention *dinner*, you don't have to recite the menu. Excessive analysis is boring, but so is too little. A balance is best. No one can tell you precisely how to achieve that balance. To develop the feel of what seems right takes time and practice, like riding a bike or doing a back flip. In the end, the content and purpose of an essay will have to determine how specific it needs to be.

Specific language is more informative, more interesting, and more desirable.

STRATEGY

To develop the knack of writing specifically, study a written passage that you admire. Pick out both details and broad statements. For practice, use the passage as a model for writing a paragraph of your own.

Context determines how abstract your essay should be. Ask yourself what is most important—giving readers a more detailed account of a general idea or pushing on to more vital matters. Just keep in mind that nobody likes reading essays that fail to deal concretely with anything.

Mini-Workout: Writing Specifically

> **DIRECTIONS:** The following sentences desperately need more specific wording. Please provide the verbal antidote to their vagueness.

1. Missy's score on the AP English exam was high.

   _____

2. Mr. Guzman possesses a variety of values.

   _____

3. Ms. Cronin could care less about my problem doing homework.

   _____

4. Sort of violently, Carrie expressed her anger at the other team's player.

   _____

5. Mitchell studied hard, but to no avail.

   _____

6. Winning the overwhelming approval of the people gave the candidate great satisfaction.

   _____

7. People don't care enough about pollution in the ocean.

   _____

8. My science class is pretty useless.

   _____

9. The twins were very poor when they were growing up.

   _____

10. My parents were happy when I got accepted in college.

    _____

Answers on pages 197–198.

Editing for Standard Usage and Mechanics

Save some editing time to proofread your essays for proper spelling, punctuation, and grammar. You won't be penalized for one or two isolated errors, but AP readers are required to deduct credit from papers crowded with mechanical mistakes.

To minimize writing errors:

- ✓   Write Correct Sentences
- ✓   Use the Correct Verbs
- ✓   Use Adjectives and Adverbs Correctly
- ✓   Choose Correct Pronouns
- ✓   Review Punctuation and Capitalization

Writing Correct Sentences

Time won't permit you to meticulously analyze every sentence in your essays. But if you get into the habit of examining sentences in your practice essays and in other schoolwork, you'll soon purge from your writing the three most common sentence errors:

- ■   **Fragments**—incomplete sentences
- ■   **Run-ons**—two or more improperly joined sentences
- ■   **Comma splices**—two complete sentences separated by a comma

Fragments

Sentence fragments often look remarkably like complete sentences. But looks can be deceptive.

> The bike that Blossom often borrowed.

This fragment appears to have all the characteristics of a sentence: It starts with a capital letter and ends with a period, it conveys a complete thought (*Blossom often borrowed the bike* is a complete thought), and it seems to contain a subject (*Blossom*) and a verb (*borrowed*). What makes it a fragment, though, is that *Blossom* isn't the subject. Rather, *bike* is the subject, and the trouble is that *bike* and the verb *borrowed* don't fit together. A bike, after all, is an inanimate object and can't do any borrowing—at least not in the real world. Clearly, Blossom did the borrowing, but the noun *Blossom* cannot be the subject of the sentence because it is part of the subordinate clause, *that Blossom borrowed*. Therefore, *bike* needs a verb of its own.

> The bike that Blossom often borrowed was stolen.

With the addition of *was stolen*, the sentence is now complete.

Handwriting Matters

Don't be like the would-be bank robber in Antioch, California, who recently handed a teller an unreadable note and fled the bank empty-handed. Sloppy, hard-to-read handwriting is not supposed to count against you on the AP exam, but think of your readers: bogged down in a barely legible essay, they can grow impatient and irritable.

Whether you plan to rob banks or boost your AP score, write legibly. Get into the habit of scrutinizing your penmanship for every letter that doesn't look the way it should. Easier said than done, for sure. But ask a friend to read one of your handwritten essays aloud. Wherever he or she stumbles may be a place where your handwriting needs work.

To determine whether a sentence is complete, uncover its "bare bones." That is, eliminate all its dependent clauses, phrases, and verbals. If what remains is a subject and its verb, it's a complete sentence. If not, it's probably a fragment.

To nail down the subject of long sentences may take some doing, but the bare-bones strategy usually works if you remember that grammatical subjects can never reside in prepositional phrases, dependent clauses, or phrases that interrupt the flow of the sentence.

Beware, too, of sentence fragments that can occur when you use the -*ing* form of a verb. The problem is that it cannot serve as a sentence's main verb—at least not without a helping verb.

FRAGMENT: Leah, at the box office, *selling* movie tickets to the 7:00 show.

CORRECT: Leah, at the box office, *has been selling* movie tickets to the 7:00 show.

The addition of the helping verb *has been* corrects the error. Other helping verbs include *is, was, will be,* and other forms of the verb *to be.*

TO FIND THE "BARE BONES" OF A SENTENCE

STEP 1 Cross out all prepositional phrases, such as *up the wall, around the corner, to the beach, over the counter*. If you eliminate all the prepositional phrases in these sentences, for instance, only the subject and the verb—the "bare bones"—will remain.

COMPLETE SENTENCE: In the middle of the night, Priscilla slept.
BARE BONES: Priscilla slept.

COMPLETE SENTENCE: One of Frieda's friends is in need of help.
BARE BONES: One is.

STEP 2 Delete all the dependent clauses—those parts of sentences that contain a noun and a verb, but that don't qualify as complete sentences because they begin with words and phrases like *although, as, as though, because, before, even though, if, in spite of, regardless of, since, so that, unless, whenever, whether,* and *while*. Other dependent clauses are statements (not questions) that start with *when, where, which, who,* and *what*.

Once the dependent clauses in the following sentences are gone, only the main clauses will remain. That's where to find the bare bones of each sentence.

COMPLETE SENTENCE: Because she missed the bus, Marnie wept.
BARE BONES: Marnie wept.

COMPLETE SENTENCE: While Willie waited for the bus, he studied vocabulary.
BARE BONES: He studied.

STEP 3 Delete interrupters—those parts of sentences that impede the smooth flow of the main idea. Interrupters may be just one word (*however, nevertheless*) or dozens. They're often set off by commas.

COMPLETE SENTENCE: Serena, regardless of the look on her face, rejoiced.
BARE BONES: Serena rejoiced.

COMPLETE SENTENCE: The boat, a sleek white catamaran, sank.
BARE BONES: Boat sank.

COMPLETE SENTENCE: Ryan, who got ticketed for doing 60 in a 30 mph zone, paid the fine.
BARE BONES: Ryan paid.

The process of identifying the bare bones of a sentence is often more complex than that suggested by these examples. But if you practice by carefully peeling away selected sentence parts, you'll eventually lay bare the subject and verb.

Run-on Sentences

A **run-on sentence** consists of two independent clauses with nothing but a blank space between them:

Birthstones are supposed to bring good luck mine has never brought me any.

Fill the gap between *luck* and *mine* by inserting the coordinating conjunction *but*.

Birthstones are supposed to bring good luck, *but* mine has never brought me any.

A comma has also been added because a compound sentence needs a comma between its clauses unless the clauses are very short, as in:

Carla drove but I walked.

Another way to eliminate run-ons is to write two separate sentences:

Birthstones are supposed to bring good luck. Mine has never brought me any.

Or you can use a semicolon, which functions like a period.

Birthstones are supposed to bring good luck; mine has never brought me any.

Note that the initial letter of a sentence that follows a semicolon is never capitalized.

Comma Splices

In a **comma splice**, a comma instead of a period or semicolon is used to join, or splice, two independent sentences.

Othello was fooled by a disloyal friend, he should have known better.

Replace the comma with a period and start a new sentence with *He*, or, use a semicolon:

Othello was fooled by a disloyal friend; he should have known better.

Mini-Workout: Writing Correct Sentences

> **DIRECTIONS:** Look for sentence fragments, run-ons, and comma splices. Use the spaces to identify the error and write the sentence correctly. Some items may contain no error.

1. Because Amy is stressed out about the garbage in the back yard.

   _____

2. St. Petersburg was renamed Leningrad after the Russian Revolution, its original name was restored in the 1990s.

   _____

3. My grandmother is eighty-six years old therefore she walks very slowly.

   _____

4. During the night, the stars that came out like diamonds on black velvet.

   _____

5. There is a belief among superstitious people that birthmarks are caused by influences on the mother before the child is born.

   _____

6. This year's senior class being more involved than last year's.

   _____

7. The American colonists despised the King's tax on British tea they drank Dutch tea instead.

   _____

8. Kayly found a squirrel lying dead in a ditch she didn't tell Kyle.

   _____

9. A biologist working in the field of genetic engineering; involved in the controversy surrounding human cloning.

   _____

10. Use the space below to tell one story about yourself to provide the admissions committee, either directly or indirectly, with an insight into the kind of person you are.

    _____

Answers on page 198.

Using Correct Verbs

Of all the parts of speech, verbs are the most apt to be used incorrectly. As you edit your AP essays, therefore, ask yourself the following three questions:

1. Do all nouns and pronouns agree in number with their verbs?
2. Is every verb in the correct tense?
3. Is every verb in the correct form?

Noun-Verb Agreement A.K.A. Subject-Verb Agreement

Nouns and verbs must agree in *number* and in *person*. A mismatch in number occurs when a singular noun is used with a plural verb, or vice versa. That's why *the tiger were* and *the tigers was* are nonstandard usages.

A mismatch in *person* occurs when the subject is a pronoun and the writer uses a verb of a different person, as in *he are, you is,* and *they am.*

To avoid errors in noun-verb agreement (often called *subject-verb agreement*), it's useful to know the language constructions that most often cause problems:

TIP

Be on the lookout for words inserted between subjects and verbs.

Intervening Words Between the Subject and Verb

Few people make agreement errors when the verb comes right after the subject. But clauses and phrases that come between the noun (i.e., the grammatical subject), or subject, and the verb can sometimes lead you astray:

> *Mail delivery* (singular subject) of today's catalogs and advertisements have been (plural verb) delayed.

The prepositional phrase *of today's catalogs and advertisements* blurs the relationship between subject and verb, and the plural noun *catalogs* can mislead you into using a plural verb. With a correctly matched subject and verb, the sentence reads:

> *Mail delivery* (singular subject) of today's catalogs and advertisements has been (singular verb) delayed.

In short, verbs must agree with the subject, not with words mistakenly thought to be the subject.

Take note, too, that such intervening phrases such as *in addition to, along with, as well as, including,* and other similar phrases don't influence the number of the verb.

> One (singular subject) of Ikuku's stories, in addition to several of her poems, was (singular verb) chosen to be published in the school literary magazine.

Subjects Composed of More Than One Noun or Pronoun

Both singular and plural nouns, when joined by *and*, are called compound subjects and need plural verbs:

> The *picture and the text* (compound subject) *go* (plural verb) inside this box. Several *locust trees and a green mailbox* (compound subject) *stand* (plural verb) outside the house.

Compound subjects thought of as a unit need singular verbs:

> Green *eggs and ham* (compound subject as a unit) is (singular verb) Fannie's favorite breakfast.

Singular nouns joined by *or* or *nor* take singular verbs.

A Coke *or* a Pepsi (two nouns joined by *or*) *is* (singular verb) what I thirst for.

When a subject consists of a singular noun and a plural noun joined by *or* or *nor*, the number of the verb is determined by the noun closer to the verb.

Either a pineapple or some oranges are on the table.
Neither the linemen nor the quarterback was aware of the tricky play.

When a subject contains a pronoun that differs in person from a noun or another pronoun, the verb must agree with the closer subject word.

Neither Meredith nor *you are* expected to finish the work today.
Either he or *I am* planning to work late on Saturday.

When the subject is singular and the predicate noun is plural, or vice versa, the number of the verb is determined by the subject.

The *bulk* of Wilkinson's work *is* two novels and a collection of stories.
Two *novels and a story* are the bulk of Wilkinson's work.

Singular Subjects Containing Words That Sound Plural

The names of certain books (*All the King's Men*), teams (New England Patriots), diseases (mumps), course titles (Robotics), and other singular nouns may sound like plurals because they end in –*s*, but most of the time—although not always—they need a singular verb.

The *news* is good.
Measles is going around the school.

Subjects That Are Sometimes Singular and Sometimes Plural

Collective nouns sound singular but may be plural. A family, for example, is singular. But if you are referring to separate individuals, *family* takes a plural verb.

The *family* (members) *are* arriving for the wedding at different times.

Other collective nouns include *group, crowd, team, jury, soybeans, audience, herd, public, dozen, class, band, flock, majority, committee, heap*, and *lot*. Other words and expressions governed by the same rule are units of time, money, weight, and measurement, and all fractions.

The *jury is* going to decide today.
The *jury are* returning to their homes tomorrow.

Indefinite Pronouns Used as Subjects

Indefinite pronouns such as *everyone, both*, and *any* pose a special problem. Some indefinite pronouns must be matched with singular verbs, some with plural verbs, and some with one or the other, depending on the sense of the sentence. There's no getting around the fact that you need to know which number applies to which pronoun.

1. These words, although they sound plural, get singular verbs: *each, either, neither*, the "ones" (*anyone, no one, everyone, someone*), and the "bodies" (*anybody, everybody, nobody, somebody*).

> *Each* man and woman in the room *gets* only one vote.
> *Everyone* who works hard *is* going to earn an "A."

2. These words get plural verbs: *both, many, few, several*.

> In spite of rumors to the contrary, *both are* on the verge of a nervous breakdown.
> *Several* in the band *are* not going on the trip to Boston.

3. The following words require singular verbs when they refer to singular nouns but plural verbs when they refer to plural nouns: *any, none, some, all, most*.

> Some of the collection is valuable.

In this sentence *some* is singular because it refers to *collection*, a singular noun.

> Some of the bracelets are fake.

Here *some* is plural because it refers to *bracelets*, a plural noun.

A Subject Following the Verb

When the subject of a sentence follows the verb, the verb takes its number from the subject, as usual.

> Behind the building *was* an *alley* (singular subject).
> Behind the building *were* an *alley and a vacant lot* (compound subject).

Mini-Workout: Noun-Verb/Subject-Verb Agreement

> **DIRECTIONS:** In some of the sentences below, verbs fail to agree with nouns. Locate the error and write the correct verb in the space provided. Some sentences may be correct.

1. A long line of cars, trucks, SUVs, and motorcycles were stuck in a traffic jam near the construction zone.

   _____

2. Either my sister or one of her boyfriends have always given me a ride to school.

   _____

3. The Board of Trustees are meeting in Springfield this year instead of in Chicago.

   _____

4. The price of gasoline, in addition to the price of home heating oil, are expected to rise this winter.

   _____

5. Lilah and Lucy started an after-school tutoring service, which have more customers than they can handle.

    _____

6. There is many levels on which a reader will be able to enjoy this book.

    _____

7. Proceeds from the sale of concert tickets is going to help the victims of the hurricane.

    _____

8. The newspaper reports that a rescue team experienced in climbing rugged mountains are expected to arrive at the site of the crash tomorrow morning.

    _____

9. According to school policy, there is to be two security guards stationed in the playground during recess to protect the children.

    _____

10. Many community members say that the promises made by the principal has not brought about the changes that he predicted.

    _____

Answers on page 198.

Using Correct Verb Tenses

Verb tenses convey information about the relative time when an action occurred. To express past action, add *–ed* to the present form: *walk/walked, cry/cried*. To express future action, add *will* before the present tense: *will walk, will cry*. For present perfect, past perfect, and future perfect forms, add *has, have, had,* or *will have*, as in *have walked, has cried, had typed, will have arrived,* and so forth.

Verb tenses permit you to indicate time sequence very precisely. But someone not attuned to distinctions between tenses may say something like this:

> There was a condo where the park was.

The meaning may be clear enough, but to state the idea more accurately, it should read:

> There was a condo where the park *had been.*

The original sentence states that the condo and park were in the same place at the same time—a physical impossibility. Using the past perfect verb *had been*, however, would clearly state that the condo replaced the park.

This is a subtle difference, but sensitivity to such differences helps you to convey meaning more accurately. Familarity with the following conventions governing verb tense will help you avoid errors:

Truisms Are Expressed in the Present Tense Regardless of Other Verbs in the Sentence.

Christmas *is* (present) on December 25th.

Sammy *had been taught* (past perfect) that triangles *contain* (present) 180 degrees.

In Complex Sentences, the Tense of Verbs in the Main Clause and Dependent Clause Must Be in Sequence.

They had driven (past perfect) 20 miles before Chuckie realized (past) that the gas tank was almost empty.

(Because the driving occurred before Chuckie's realization, the past perfect—not the past tense—is needed to show the sequence of events.)

Your teacher believes (present) that you will do (future) well on the AP exam.

In an *If* Clause, Don't Use *Would Have* to Express the Earlier of Two Actions. Instead, Use the Past Perfect.

NO: If Woody *would have studied* more, he would have made the Honor Society.

YES: If Woody *had studied* (past perfect) more, he would have made the Honor Society.

NO: The party would have been better if Watu *would have played* the piano.

YES: The party would have been better if Watu *had played* (past perfect) the piano.

The Tense of Infinitives (*To Eat, To Snow, To Have Eaten, To Have Snowed*, etc.) Is Governed by the Main Verb and by the Meaning of the Sentence.

Eileen was (main verb in past tense) delighted to receive (present infinitive) the award.

(The present infinitive is used because Eileen received the award before she felt happy about getting it.)

When the infinitive refers to a time before the action described by the main verb, the perfect infinitive should be used.

Eileen is (main verb) happy to have received (perfect infinitive) the award.

Adjust Participles (Often Ending in -*ing*) According to the Tense of the Main Verb. When the Participle Describes an Action Occurring Before the Action of the Main Verb, Add *Having* and Then Adjust the Participle.

NO: Working (participle) hard on the essay, Hank opposed cutting the number of words. (Because Hank worked on the essay before he resisted cutting it, the participle needs to be revised.)

YES: *Having worked* hard on the essay, Hank opposed cutting the number of words.

Mini-Workout: Verb Tenses

> **DIRECTIONS:** In these sentences, the underlined verbs may be in the wrong tense. Write the correct verbs in the spaces provided. Some sentences may contain no error.

1. When he talks with his wife, Macbeth <u>felt</u> overcome with guilt.

   _____

2. When they crossed the country by car, they <u>had visited</u> Mount Rushmore.

   _____

3. In the school parking lot, a policeman stops her and <u>asked</u> to see her driver's license.

   _____

4. <u>Writing</u> a poem every week for a year, Quinn finally got one accepted by a literary magazine.

   _____

5. In the afternoon we spotted many friends we <u>saw</u> that morning at the pancake breakfast.

   _____

6. Once the levee had broken, the streets <u>have been</u> flooded.

   _____

Ken: "How are you?"

Bob: "Good, and you?"

Ken: "I'm well, thanks."

Which speaker knows his grammar?

(Answer below)*

_____

7. For anyone with enough brains to have thought about the problem, now <u>is</u> the time to work out a solution.

   _____

8. If Ariane <u>would have stayed</u> home, she would not have missed Eamon's visit.

   _____

9. Marcy kept the promise she <u>has given</u> to Kendra last summer.

   _____

10. The airline pilot <u>expects</u> to have seen the lights of the San Jose airport by now.

    _____

Answers on page 198.

Choosing Adjectives and Adverbs

Errors sometimes occur when an adjective is used where an adverb is required. The reverse—using an adverb in place of an adjective—occurs less often. Check your essay for the proper use of adjectives and adverbs.

Adjectives

Adjectives describe, or modify, nouns and pronouns.

Good is an adjective. Like any adjective, it can be used to descibe a noun, as in *good book, good pie, good night*. That's easy.

Good, along with some other adjectives, causes trouble when used after a verb. Because it won't work after most verbs, avoid using *talks good, sleeps good, writes good*, and so on.

Good, as well as other adjectives, however, can be used after some verbs—those called *linking verbs*, among them, *look, smell, taste, feel, appear, seem, remain*, and all forms of *to be*. So, it's perfectly correct to say *sounds good, feels good*, and *is good*.

What complicates matters is that linking verbs sometimes function as active verbs. *Look*, for instance, is a linking verb when referring to appearance, as in:

> The day *looks* good for flying.

But it is an active verb when it refers to the act of looking, as in:

> Lindsay *looked* sadly at her sick cat.

If you're not sure whether a verb is being used as a linking verb or an active verb, substitute a form of the verb *to be* in its place. If the sentence retains its basic meaning, the verb may well be a linking verb, as in:

> The juice *tastes* good. (The juice *is* good.)
> She will *stay* asleep for a century. (She *will be* asleep for a century.)

Because the second version of each sentence pretty well maintains the meaning of the original, *tastes* and *stay* are linking verbs and may be followed by any adjective you choose: *sour, sweet, tart, spoiled, inactive, torpid, somnolent*, and a zillion more.

Adverbs

Adverbs, often recognizable by their *–ly* endings, usually describe, or modify, verbs, adjectives, or other adverbs. Much of the time they supply the answer to such questions as *How? When? How much? Where? In what sequence? To what exent? In what manner?*

> How does Brodie run? Brodie runs well. (The adverb *well* modifies the verb *run*.)
> How did the grass look? The grass looked mostly brown. (The adverb *mostly* modifies the adjective *brown*.)
> Where did Abigail sit? Abigail sat down. (The adverb *down* modifies the verb *sat*.)
> In what manner did she sit down? She sat down quickly. (The adverb *quickly* modifies the verb *sat*.)

If you ever need to choose between an adjective and an adverb while writing your AP essays, follow this simple two-step procedure:

First: Find the verb and determine whether it is a linking verb.

Second: If it is, use the adjective; if not, use the adverb.

*Both. Neither has made a grammatical error.

Also, if the word modifies an adjective or another adverb, remember to use the adverb. If it modifies a noun or pronoun, use the adjective.

Mini-Workout: Adjectives and Adverbs

> **DIRECTIONS:** Check each of these sentences for faulty use of adjectives and adverbs. Write the correct word in the spaces provided. Some sentences may be correct.

1. Annabelle spoke sincere to Tim when she promised to marry him some day.

   _____

2. Rod always feels shyly about speaking in front of the class.

   _____

3. When the batter got hit in the head, the fans thought he had been hurt bad.

   _____

4. "No problem, Mr. Reynolds, I can do both jobs easy."

   _____

5. The audience remained calmly, even when the hall began to fill with smoke.

   _____

6. Later that day, Kirk and Eliza spoke frankly about their disagreement.

   _____

7. He walked down the corridor completely oblivious to the trail of papers he left behind.

   _____

8. Be sure to shut the door secure because it tends to swing open by itself.

   _____

9. The tyrant looked down cynical on the crowd assembled in the piazza.

   _____

10. The nurse felt bitterly that she had contracted the flu from a patient.

    _____

Answers on page 199.

Using Pronouns Correctly

Skim your essay for pronoun errors. Faulty pronoun usage results most often:

- When pronouns in the wrong "case" are chosen
- When the pronoun reference is unclear or ambiguous
- When pronouns fail to agree in number or gender with their antecedents

Pronoun Case

Most of the time you can probably depend on your ear to tell you what's right and wrong. For example, you'd never say to the bus driver, "Let *I* off at the corner." But you can't always depend on your sense of what sounds right and wrong, especially when pronouns are paired, as in *he and I* and *me and them*. Then, it helps to know that pronouns fall into two groups:

GROUP 1: *I, he, she, they, we, you*

GROUP 2: *me, him, her, them, us, you*

The pronouns in the first group are *nominative case* pronouns and are used in grammatical subjects and predicate nominatives. The second group—*objective case* pronouns—are used everywhere else. Because pronouns, when used in pairs, must come from the same case, "*Him* and *I* went to the movies" is a nonstandard usage.

Any time you need a pair of pronouns, and you know that one of them is correct, pick the other from the same group. If you don't know either pronoun, here's a handy rule of thumb to follow: Substitute *I* or *me* for one of them. If *I* seems to fit, choose pronouns from Group 1; if *me* fits better, use Group 2.

Elvis asked that (he, him) and (she, her) practice handstands.

If you insert *me* in place of one of the pronouns, you'll get:

Elvis asked that me practice handstands.

Because no one would say that seriously, *I* must be the word that fits. So the pronouns you need come from Group 1, and the sentence should read:

Elvis asked that he and she practice handstands.

Use objective case pronouns in phrases that begin with prepositions, as in:

<u>between</u> *you* and *me*,
<u>to</u> Rhyana and *her*
<u>among</u> *us* women

A FEW MORE PRINCIPLES OF PRONOUN CASE

- Use objective case pronouns when the pronoun refers to a person to whom something is being done:

  Taylor invited *him* to the prom.

  The waiter gave *her* and *me* a piece of cake.

- To find the correct pronoun in a comparison, complete the comparison using the verb that would follow naturally:

  Rennie runs faster than *she* (runs).

  A woman such as *I* (am) could solve the problem.

- When a pronoun appears side by side with a noun (*we* boys, *us* women), deleting the noun will help you pick the correct pronoun:

  (*We, Us*) seniors decided to take a day off from school in late May. (Deleting *seniors* leaves <u>We</u> decided to . . .).

  This award was presented to (*we, us*) students by the faculty. (Deleting *students* leaves *award was presented to <u>us</u> by the* . . .).

- Use possessive pronouns (*my, our, your, his, her, their*) before a *gerund*, a noun that looks like a verb because of its *-ing* ending.

  Her asking the question shows that she is alert. (*Asking* is a gerund.)

  Mother was upset about *your* opening the presents too soon. (*Opening* is a gerund.)

Gerunds

What is a gerund? It's a verb form that ends in –*ing* and is used as a noun.

> *Fishing* is my grandpa's favorite pastime.
> He started *fishing* as a boy in North Carolina.
> As a result of all that *fishing* he hates to eat fish.

In all three sentences the gerund is derived from the verb *to fish*. Don't confuse gerunds with the participle form of verbs, as in:

> PARTICIPLE: *Fishing* from the bank of the river, my Grandpa caught a catfish.
> GERUND: *Fishing* from the bank of a river is my Grandpa's greatest pleasure.

Not every noun with an *-ing* ending is a gerund. Sometimes it's just a noun, as in *thing, ring, spring*. At other times, -*ing* words are verbs; in particular, they're participles that modify pronouns in the objective case.

> I hope you don't mind *my* intruding on your conversation (Here *intruding* is a gerund.)
> I hope you don't mind *me* intruding on your conversation. (Here *intruding* is a participle.)

Mini-Workout: Pronoun Case

> **DIRECTIONS:** Find the pronoun errors in the following sentences. Write the correct pronoun in the space provided. Some sentences may be correct.

1. Josh took my brother and I to the magic show last night.

   _____

2. He said that in my pocket I would find $10 in change to split between me and Lucy.

   _____

3. The waiter promised to hold the table for we girls.

   _____

4. Him and me took turns on the treadmill.

   _____

5. They refused to let we boys into the arena without reservations.

   _____

6. When the coins fell out of his sleeve, the audience laughed even harder than us.

   _____

7. Him falling asleep at the wheel caused the accident.

   _____

8. Did you stay as long as they at the dance?

   _____

9. I never spoke with them—neither he nor his brother.

   _____

10. If I were him, I'd practice for a long time before the next performance.

   _____

Answers on page 199.

Pronoun References

Check the reference of every pronoun in your essay. Be certain that each refers clearly to its antecedent—usually a noun or another pronoun. Avoid the confusion that results when no clear tie exists or when a pronoun seems to refer to more than one antecedent:

The librarian told Sophia that it was *her* responsibility to shelve the books.

Who is responsible? The librarian or Sophia? It's impossible to tell because the pronoun *her* may refer to either of them. Revised, the sentence reads:

The librarian told Sophia that one of her responsibilities as a library clerk was to shelve books.

A sentence containing two or more pronouns with ambiguous references can be especially troublesome and unclear:

Mike became a good friend of Morgan's after *he* helped *him* repair *his* Toyota.

Whose car needed fixing? Who helped whom? To answer these questions, the sentence needs to be rewritten:

Mike and Morgan became good friends after Morgan helped Mike repair *his* Toyota.

This version is better, but it's still uncertain who owned the car. One way to set the meaning straight is to use more than one sentence:

When Morgan needed to repair his Toyota, Mike helped him do the job. Afterward, Mike and Morgan became good friends.

To be correct, a pronoun should refer directly and clearly to a specific noun or another pronoun, or it should refer by implication to an idea. Such implied references frequently involve the pronouns *it, they*, and *you*, and the relative pronouns *which, that*, and *this*, and cause trouble mostly when the pronoun is used to refer to rather general or ambiguous ideas, as in:

Homeless people allege that the city is indifferent to their plight, *which* has been disproved.

What has been disproved? That an allegation was made? That the city is indifferent? The intended meaning is unclear because *which* has no distinct antecedent. To clear up the uncertainty, the sentence might read:

Homeless people allege that the city is indifferent to their plight, but the allegation has been disproved.

Finally, don't use pronouns to refer to possessives, as in:

In Eminem's latest hit, he stumbles over several words.

The pronoun *he* obviously refers to Eminem, but the word *Eminem* doesn't appear in the sentence. Because the possessive noun *Eminem's* is not a grammatical equivalent to *Eminem*, the revised sentence should be:

In his latest hit, Eminem stumbles over several words.

Mini-Workout: Pronoun References

> **DIRECTIONS:** Revise the following sentences to eliminate pronoun reference problems. Some sentences may be correct

1. Mira loves to text and spends most of her spare time doing it.

   _____

2. Juan answered the test questions, collected his pens and pencils, and handed them in.

   _____

3. In Fitzgerald's *The Great Gatsby*, he writes about the American Dream.

   _____

4. Its economy is a mess, but Greece will weather the crisis.

   _____

5. When teens loiter outside the theater on Friday night, they give you a hard time.

   _____

6. His father let him know he had only an hour to get to the airport.

   _____

7. Zachary has been interested in playing major league baseball, and he aspires to be one someday.

   _____

8. Rob has a part-time job at the boatyard and spends every summer on the water, which lies at the root of his interest in going to Annapolis.

   _____

9. If someone buys an old used car, he better be ready to pay for repairs.

   _____

10. After the interview, Alonzo told Rick that he thought Colgate University was a good place for him to spend the next four years.

   _____

Answers on page 199.

Pronoun-Antecedent Agreement

Finally, take a look at the agreement between all the pronouns and their antecedents. Do they agree in gender, number, and person? Problems frequently occur with so-called *indefinite pronouns* like *everyone, anyone*, and *nobody*—singular words that should usually be followed by singular pronouns. Sometimes such words are meant as plurals, however, and should be followed by plural pronouns. (See the earlier discussion on noun-verb agreement, page 169.)

Singular pronouns should have singular antecedents; plural pronouns, plural antecedents. Note the problem of pronoun-antecedent agreement in these sentences:

> Everybody is sticking to *their* side of the story
> Anybody can pass this course if *they* study hard.
> Neither teacher plans to change *their* policy regarding late papers.

Properly stated, the sentences should read:

> Everybody is sticking to *his* side of the story.
> Anybody can pass this course if *she* studies hard.
> Neither teacher plans to change *his* policy regarding late papers.

Some people, objecting to the use of specific gender pronouns, prefer the cumbersome and tacky phrase "he or she," but most good writers avoid using it.

Still other words may sound singular but are plural in certain contexts:

> The jury will render *its* verdict tomorrow./The jury will return to *their* homes tomorrow.
> The senior class posed for *its* picture./The senior class had *their* portraits taken for the yearbook.

THE PROBLEM OF *NONE*

Heads often get scratched about the use of the indefinite pronoun *none*. Is it singular or is it plural?

Much of the time it's singular because of its meaning, *not one*, as in:

Three lost jackets were turned in, but *none* was (singular verb) Joanie's.

Every house on the block has a garage; *none* has (singular verb) a car parked inside.

When *none* is followed by a prepositional phrase with a plural meaning, however, usage varies. Some authorities claim that *none* should always be treated as singular. Others argue that it depends on the noun or pronoun the word refers to:

Sophie says she's had many boyfriends, but *none* of them was (singular verb) in love with her.

Here the writer has made a general statement about all of Sophie's ex-beaus. Yet, according to some experts, *none* should be followed by a singular verb. Only when it would be ridiculous to regard it as singular should it be a plural, as in:

None of the children *meet* (plural verb) in the schoolyard during lunch period.

A plural verb is used here because it makes no sense to say that one child *meets* in the schoolyard at lunch.

Similarly:

A survey of all the residents showed that *none were* (plural verb) in favor of changing the rule.

To use a singular verb would be like saying, absurdly, *all one of them*.

Mini-Workout: Pronoun Agreement

> **DIRECTIONS:** Look for errors of agreement between pronouns and antecedents in the sentences below. Use the spaces provided to write the correct pronoun or, if necessary, to revise the sentence. Alter only those sentences that contain errors.

1. The English teacher announced that everyone in the class must turn in their term papers no later than Friday.

   _____

2. The Army, which paid soldiers large bonuses to re-enlist when their tours of duty were over, changed their policy when the budget was cut.

   _____

3. The library put their collection of rare books on display.

   _____

4. Each of my sisters have their own smartphone.

   _____

5. In that class, our teacher held conferences with us once a week.

   _____

6. Everyone on the girls' field hockey team worked as hard as they could to win the championship.

   _____

7. The teacher dictates sentences in French, and each of the students write it down in English and hand it in.

   _____

8. Each horse in the procession followed their riders down to the creek.

   _____

9. The school's chess team has just won their first match.

   _____

10. The person elected to the class presidency will find that the faculty and administration will cooperate with them and help them succeed.

    _____

Answers on pages 199–200.

Punctuation

There are many reasons why you should know how to punctuate. One of them is that error-free AP essays tend to earn higher scores than those crowded with mistakes. It happens that the AP essay instructions single out "*appropriate . . . punctuation* in communicating the argument" as one of the criteria used for scoring essays. Because the AP bigwigs take punctuation seriously, you should, too. The next few pages cover the basics of everyday punctuation.

Apostrophes

Apostrophes are used in only three places:

1. **Contractions** such as *won't, it's, could've*, and *where's*. Apostrophes mark places where letters have been omitted.
2. In **plurals** of letters, signs, or numbers, as in *A's* and *B's*, the *1960's*, and *10's* and *20's*, although many experts simplify matters by writing *1960s, Ps* and *Qs*, and so forth.

3. In **possessive nouns** such as the *student's class, women's room,* and in indefinite pronouns such as *anybody's guess.* When the noun is plural and ends in *s,* put the apostrophe after the *s,* as in *leaves' color* and *horses' stable.* Some possessive forms use both an apostrophe and *of,* as in *a friend of the family's;* some others that specify time, space, value, or quantity also require apostrophes, as in *a week's time, a dollar's worth, at my wit's end.*

Commas

Commas divide sentences into parts, clarify meaning, and prevent confusion.

1. Use a comma to signal a **pause,** as in:

   NO PAUSE: After brushing his teeth gleamed.
   PAUSE: After brushing, his teeth gleamed.

   Commas are needed after some introductory words and in forms of address:

   Well, you can open it whenever it's convenient.
   The letter will be waiting for you at home, *Jimmy.*

2. Commas set off words that **interrupt the flow** of a sentence, as in

   Izzie, *regrettably,* was omitted from the roster.
   Linh, *on the other hand,* was included.

   Commas separate information not essential to the meaning of the sentence:

   The lost hikers, *who had come from New Jersey,* found shelter in a cave.
   The three bikers, *using an out-of-date road map,* arrived two hours late.

   Commas set off **appositives**:

   Samantha, *the prosecutor,* entered the courtroom.
   The judge, *Mr. Peterson,* presided at the trial.

3. Commas separate the clauses of a **compound sentence**:

   The competition is stiff, but it won't keep Rhyana from winning.
   Yamil had better call home, or he'll be in big trouble.

4. Commas separate items in a **series**:

   Rosie's car needs *new tires, a battery, a muffler, and an oil change.*
   It was a wonder that Milan could sit through the *long, boring, infantile, and ridiculous* lecture.

   Some writers prefer to skip the comma before the last item in a series, but just in case clarity may suffer, it can't hurt to put it in.

5. Commas separate parts of **addresses, dates, and place names**:

   Who lives at 627 West 115th Street, New York, NY?"
   Brian was born on May 27, 2001, the same day as Maya.
   Dave has lived in Madison, Wisconsin; Seattle, Washington; and Eugene, Oregon.

   Note that each location in the last example already contains a comma. So, semicolons were added between the items to avoid confusion.

6. Commas separate quotations from attributions in **dialogue**.

   John said, "Close the window."
   "I want it open," protested Ben.

Semicolons

Semicolons may be used between closely related sentences, in effect, shortening the pause that would naturally occur between two separate sentences:

> Mother was worried; her daughters never stay out this late.

> The momentum was building; she couldn't be stopped now.

A caution: Because semicolons function like periods, use them only between independent clauses or in a series in which one or more items contain a comma, as in:

> On his trek, Norwood met Noah, a carpenter from Maine; Dr. Jones, a pediatrician from St. Louis; Jonathan, an airline pilot; and me, of course.

Quotation Marks

Quotation marks usually surround direct quotations, as in:

> As the author of the passage pointed out, "George Washington, when naked, weighed at least two hundred pounds."

Quotation marks also enclose the titles of poems, stories, chapter headings, essays, magazine articles, and other short works. Don't use them for longer works. Novels, plays, films, and magazine titles should be underlined in handwritten essays and italicized when they appear in print.

Avoid calling attention to clichés, trite expressions, or slang terms by using quotation marks. Rewrite instead, using fresh, original language.

Finally, quotation marks may enclose words that express the silent thoughts of a character, as in:

> Carlos glanced at his watch. "I'm going to be late," he thought.

Periods and commas are placed inside closing quotation marks. Question marks and exclamation points go outside the quotation mark unless they are part of the quote itself.

> "When will the seminar start?" asked Regis.

> Do you understand the meaning of the concept "The end justifies the means"?

Mini-Workout: Punctuation

Part A. Possessives

> **DIRECTIONS:** Check your mastery of possessives by writing the correct possessive form of the italicized word in the space provided. Some items may be correct.

1. *Liams* reason was personal. _____

2. The future of *Americas* foreign policy is being debated. _____

3. *Teams* from all over the county have gathered at the stadium. _____

4. Luis isn't at all interested in *womens* issues. _____

5. The *girls* locker room is downstairs, but the *boys* is upstairs. _____

6. We are invited to the *Andersons* house for New *Years* Eve. _____

7. All of the *Rosses* are going out to eat. _____

8. Have you seen *Silas's* iPad, which he left here yesterday? _____

9. Both of the *computers* keyboards need repair. _____

10. He'll be back in one *months* time. _____

Part B. Commas and Semicolons

> **DIRECTIONS:** In the sentences below insert or remove commas and semicolons as necessary. Some sentences may be correct.

1. While Buddy was riding his bike got a flat tire.

2. The mail carrier did not leave the package for Valerie was not at home.

3. After doing homework Mikey as you might expect texted with friends until midnight.

4. His work criticized many commonly held beliefs however and it was strictly censored.

5. The car, that ran into mine at the intersection, was an SUV.

6. I need Google maps of Boston; and Portland, Maine.

7. The people who live by the water must be prepared for occasional flooding.

8. The boat, was 75 feet long and 18 feet wide, its mast was about 80 feet tall.

9. To anyone interested in flying planes hold endless fascination.

10. Jacob and Owen left alone for the weekend invited all their friends to a party.

Answers on page 200.

Sample Analytical Essays

What follows is a typical analytical essay question along with four student responses written by hand under testing conditions: a time limit, no access to a dictionary or other books, and a certain amount of tension. By reading the essays and a reader's comments, you will see what it takes to earn a 6, the highest score. Read the weaker essays, too. They'll alert you to some pitfalls to avoid when you write essays of your own.

Question

SUGGESTED TIME—30 MINUTES

> **DIRECTIONS:** The passage below is the complete text of a theater review by Henry James entitled "Mr. Henry Irving's Macbeth." It was published in a London newspaper in 1875. After reading it carefully, write a well-organized essay that defines James's rhetorical purpose and analyzes some of the strategies he employs to achieve it.

Mr. Henry Irving's Macbeth, which, on the actor's first appearance in the part in London some six weeks ago, produced not a little disappointment in the general public, seems to have been accepted as an interesting if not a triumphant attempt,

Line and is exhibited to audiences numerous if not overflowing, and deferential if not

(5) enthusiastic. Considering the actor's reputation, indeed, the very undemonstrative

attitude of the spectators at the Lyceum is most noticeable. Mr. Irving's acting is, to
my mind, not of a kind to provoke enthusiasm, and I can best describe it by saying
that it strikes me as the acting of a very superior amateur. If Mr. Irving were somewhat younger, and if there existed in England any such school of dramatic training
(10) as the Conservatoire of Paris, any such exemplary stage as the Théâter Français, a
discriminating critic might say of him: "Here is an aspirant with the instincts of an
artist, and who, with proper instruction, may become an actor." But, thanks to the
absence of a school and of any formidable competition, success has come easily
to Mr. Irving, and he has remained, as the first tragic actor in England, decided-
(15) ly incomplete and amateurish. His personal gifts—face, figure, voice, enunciation—
are rather meagre; his strong points are intellectual. He is ingenious, intelligent, and fanciful; imaginative he can hardly be called, for he signally fails to give their great imaginative
value to many of the superb speeches he has to utter. In declamation he is decidedly flat;
his voice is without charm, and his utterance without subtlety. But he has thought out his
(20) part, after a fashion of his own, very carefully, and in the interest of his rendering of it lies
in seeing a spare, refined man, of an unhistrionic—or a rather sedentary—aspect, and
with a thick, unmodulated voice, but with a decided sense of the picturesque, grappling
in a deliberate and conscientious manner with a series of great tragic points. This hardly
gives an impression of strength, of authority, and it is not for force and natural magic that
(25) Mr. Irving's acting is remarkable. He has been much criticized for his conception of his
part—for making Macbeth so spiritless a plotter before his crime, and so arrant a coward
afterward. But in the text, as he seeks to emphasize it, there is a fair warrant for the line he
follows. Mr. Irving has great skill in the representation of terror, and it is quite open to him
to have thrown into relief this side of his part. His best moment is his rendering of the scene
(30) with the bloody daggers—though it must be confessed that this stupendous scene always
does much toward acting itself. Mr. Irving, however, is here altogether admirable, and his
representation of nature trembling and quaking to its innermost spiritual recesses really
excites the imagination. Only a trifle less powerful is his scene with Banquo's ghost at the
feast, and the movement with which, exhausted with vain bravado, he muffles his head
(35) in his mantle and collapses beside the throne. Mr. Irving has several points in common
with Edwin Booth, and belongs to the same general type of actor; but I may say that if, to
my thinking, Edwin Booth comes nearer to being a man of genius, I find Mr. Irving more
comfortable to see. Of Miss Bateman, who does Lady Macbeth, the less said the better. She
has good-will and a certain superficial discretion; but a piece of acting and declaiming of
(40) equal pretensions, more charmless in an artistic way, it has not been my fortune to behold.

Lilah's Response
(Printed as it was written)

Either Henry James was depressed or trying to have fun when he wrote this review of Macbeth with Mr. Henry Irving playing the lead. He could have been in a cynical mood because he doesn't have a single praiseworthy thing to say about the performance or about the audience or about Mr. Irving as an actor. However, the review is witty in a mean sort of way and probably caused laughter among the readers of the newspaper that printed it in 1875. But James might have put humor into his review in order to prevent himself from sounding like a total curmudgeon.

So how did James amuse his readers and destroyed Mr Irving at the same time? First, he wrote the entire review in one paragraph which contains an evaluation of five different topics with respect to the performance of Macbeth. He covers the audience, Mr. Irving's training and acting ability, his physical features and voice, his portrayal of Macbeth, and then at the end he writes about the performance by Miss Bateman in the role of Lady Macbeth. The last two sentences about Miss Bateman are the nastiest ones of all. After the criticism about Mr. Irving, he brings his sarcastic wit to a climax by saying "the less said the better," but then he immediately contradicts his own statement by delivering a knock-out punch with these words: "She has good will . . . but a piece of acting and declaiming of equal pretentions, more charmless in an artistic way, it has not been my fortune to behold." The other things he talks about in the review also come under his brutal criticism in a variety of ways. For example, the audience is called "deferential," implying that they are there more out of duty and respect for the lead actor than because they have any intellectual interest in seeing Macbeth. The general public says the production is "interesting," which is an "interesting" way to put it because when someone doesn't want to say something negative but can't find a positive statement to make "interesting" is the euphemism they use.

When James begins to write about Mr. Irving's acting, he says it is as good as "a very superior amateur," a devastating putdown for a professional actor. The word "amateur" has a negative connotation not only for professionals but also for amateurs because the word suggests incompetence. The insult is compounded in lines 14–15 when James says he is "decidedly incomplete and amateurish." The reason that James gives for Irving's poor acting is related to the education received by English actors. In England there is no school or theater that trains actors the way they do in France. In a way, that excuses Mr. Irving's acting ability due to his country being unable to train him properly.

Now that James has criticized Irving's acting ability and England's deficiency in training actors, he focuses on Irving's physical features and voice and finds both unacceptable, using negative words like "meagre," "flat" and "without charm," and "without subtlety." Then he plays with the word "remarkable," saying that "Mr. Irving's acting is remarkable" (line 25). That could mean the the acting is good or even excellent, but James surprises the reader by using it ironically. What he means but doesn't' say is the acting is remarkably bad.

As he turns his attention to Irving performing Macbeth's part, James finds something good to say about the way Irving played the scene with the bloody daggars. But he undercuts his praise by adding that the scene is so stupendous that it "does much toward acting itself," meaning that the scene is so strong that it helps the actor, including one as bad as Mr. Irving, to perform well. Finally, now that he has almost destroyed Irving's acting. James can't resist one more insulting criticism by describing Irving seeing Banquo's ghost. In that scene Irving is "altogether admirable," but he is really not since he "trembles and quakes . . . muffles his head in his mantle and collapses beside the throne." (lines 31—35) What James is implying that Irving is over-acting and over-emoting: he is playing the part as if he was cast in a melodrama or TV soap.

The readers of this essay in London most likely got a laugh out of James's sarcastic humor, but it's a kind of negative humor because it is given at the expense of an actor whose reputation will be smeared by James's superior tone.

Your impressions: _____

_____

_____

_____

Comment to Lilah from an AP Reader

Aside from a few distracting errors in style and mechanics (more attentive proofreading would no doubt have helped), and an out-of-place allusion to a TV soap opera, your essay is a model of insight and focus. It captures the essence of James's review and analyzes in impressive detail how the author manages to be simultaneously funny and, as you say, devastating. Using apt and specific textual examples, you show how James first attacks Irving and then softens the onslaught by blaming England for the poor man's ineptitude. You also point out correctly that James saves his most brutal assault for Miss Bateman, whose performance exceeds Irving's in its deficiences. The language in your essay not only conveys a sensitive reading of the passage but shows an awareness that diction—the use of "curmudgeon," "euphemism," and "melodrama," to cite a few well-chosen words—is essential to a mature and readable style. References to James's readers in both the opening and concluding paragraphs endow your essay with a sense of unity not always evident in AP essays.

SCORE: 5

Kevin's Response

(Printed as it was written)

Based on the theater review entitled "Mr Henry Irving's Macbeth," Henry James was a sophisticated writer and a strict judge of performers on the stage. His sophistication comes through in his diction, the syntaxes of his sentences, the structure of the passage and a use of irony. His strictness is illustrated by saying only the most critical things about two performers, one being Henry Irving and the second being Miss Bateman, who plays Lady Macbeth. He dismisses Miss Bateman with a wave of his hand by saying "the less said the better" Obviously, to write about her performance is giving it more attention than it deserves. As a matter of fact, James said that he'd never seen a more charmless piece of acting in his life.

James saves most of his abuse for Mr. Irving's Macbeth, using a whole thesaurus of negative words and phrases to describe it, including "very superior amateur," "may become an actor," "decidedly incomplete and amateurish," "fails to give great imaginative value to many of the superb speeches," "without charm," "without subtlety," and many others. He begins the review with some general commentary about the apathetic audience and about Mr. Irving's poor training as an actor. These generalizations are followed up with specific details about his looks, in particular his face and figure, and about his very poor voice, which is "thick" and "unmodulated."

By going from general to specific, he uses a very convincing structure. He introduces general ideas to the reader, getting them ready to find out more, and then wham! he provides the concrete evidence to back up his opinions. He describes Mr. Irving's weaknesses as an actor followed by an evaluation of his performance in playing the role of Macbeth. James agrees with other critics that Irving has made Macbeth a "spiritless plotter before his crime, and so arrant a coward afterward." (lines 26–27).

In terms of syntax, James likes to say things by stating the negative of the reverse of what he wants to say (litotes). For example, he uses "interesting if not triumphant" and "audiences numerous if not overflowing." This kind of sentence structure would appeal to a more sophisticated reader than if he came right out a said the performance was a flop and the audience was small.

The author's irony, however, gives the passage a tone that illustrates his opionion. He quotes an imaginary critic, who is probably James himself in disguise in lines 11–12, who might say "Here is an aspirant with the instincts of an artist, and who, with proper instruction, may become an actor." This is James's way of giving criticism. He makes a negative comment but uses words that seem positive or encouraging but they are not. Later in the same way he gives the impression that he is praising Irving's "representation of terror," but it is really damning with faint praise because he then slaps him down by saying that any actor can make the stupendous scene with the bloody daggers exciting. Finally, there is a comparison made between Irving and an actor named Edwin Booth, who is "nearer to being a man of genius" than Irving (line 37). Again, he is implying something insulting, namely that Irving is definately not a man of genius.

Your impressions: _____

_____

_____

_____

Comment to Kevin from an AP Reader

The introductory paragraph provides an accurate but conventional blueprint for the essay to follow. True to your word, you deal with each rhetorical feature in turn, and ably support your assessment of James as "a sophisticated writer and strict judge."

Your discussion of structure, complete with the dramatic "wham!" carefully explains the effects of using details to support generalizations. In addition, your analysis of James's diction, introduced with a delightful conceit ("whole thesaurus of negative words and phrases") is thorough and well documented.

Not so, however, the paragraph on syntax. Aside from misidentifying the rhetorical device—James uses antitheses, not litotes—you fail to support the dubious assertion that sophisticated readers prefer one kind of sentence structure to another. You put the essay back on track in the last paragraph, however, by serving up several astute examples of James's irony.

Although you demonstrate an ability to express ideas clearly and forcefully, the essay doesn't exhibit the level of effective writing expected of the very best papers.

SCORE: 4

Danielle's Response

(Printed as it was written)

My mother is British and so my parents go to England every year and go to plays in London. My great grandfather whose name was David Chambers was the owner of a noodle factory near London and could have read the review "Mr Henry Irving's Macbeth" in the London newspaper in 1875. (I don't know if he went to the theater, but he might of gone because he was pretty rich and dressed in elegant clothes in a photo of him and his wife (my great grandmother Jennie) that we have at home on our dining room wall.) If he saw the review by Henry James, he would not have wasted his time and money on going to see <u>Macbeth</u> in the theater.

So Henry James succeeded in accomplishing his purpose. He told readers not to bother with the play because it was "not a little disappointment" as he wrote in line 2.

In all ways, Macbeth was a flop. Henry James uses language that would turn anyone off to the play. For example, he writes about the "undemonstrative attitude of the spectators," meaning the audience. That means they just sat there probably bored out of their minds and maybe didn't even applaud the performance of Mr. Irving and especially Lady Macbeth played by an actress named Miss Bateman.

Mr. Irving strikes the author as "the acting of a very superior amateur," a humorous way to say it because the word <u>amateur</u> is as a surprise at the end of the phrase. <u>Superior</u> sounds like a compliment, but <u>amateur</u> contridicts the compliment. I suppose that readers of the newspaper would find that funny also and would probably enjoy reading the review more than going to the play because the review is filled with comments that could get readers to chuckle or maybe even laugh, while the play would put them to sleep, which I can sympathize with when we read it last year in English class.

"Here is an aspirant with the instincts of an artist, and who, with proper instruction, may become an actor." If that's not a put down, I don't know what it is. It is an awful but also funny remark to say about an actor who is trying to play the lead. Then he adds "His personal gifts—face, figure, voice, enunciation—are rather meagre." Another insult that readers would enjoy.

They'd also get a charge out of the image of a "spare, refined man, of an unhistrionic (?) or rather sedentary-aspect, and with a thick, unmodulated voice, but with a decided sense of the picturesque, grappling in a deliberate and conscientious manner with a series of great tragic points." (lines 21–23)

Henry James then delivers the final blow by saying "Mr. Irving's acting is remarkable" in line 25, but he means remarkably bad, not remarkable good.

At the end of the review James does the same thing he did before when he says that Miss Batemen acting the part of Lady Macbeth is "charmless in an artistic way." A funny phrase because charmless is negative while artistic is positive, and the contradiction is suppose to make a reader laugh. In the last line (40) Henry James concludes his irony by saying "it has not been my fortune to behold" when he really means misfortune because he is referring to Miss Batemen's terrible performance.

Obviously, I don't know if my gtreat-grandfather read this review but he would probably enjoyed it more than this performance of Macbeth.

Your impressions: _____

_____

_____

_____

Comment to Danielle from an AP Reader

The essay has a distinctive edge over most other essays written in response to this question because of the interesting link you've made with your family history. Imagining that the review may have been read by your relatives helps to make the passage a living document and serves to identify the author's purpose—to entertain readers while also encouraging them to stay away from that production of *Macbeth*.

To your credit, you point out several features of the passage that were meant to amuse readers, not an easy task when the author is Henry James, known for his elegant but convoluted style of writing. Your analysis is perceptive, although you rely on quotations rather heavily—too heavily, in fact. Quoted material is crucial in an analytical essay, but in some places, where it would have been better to use your own words, quotes dominate the text.

Your more-than-adequate analysis of the passage is limited to its humor, but the writing is marked by a rather undisciplined syntax, especially by sentences that go on and on. There are few sentence errors, to be sure, but it's a chore to wade through excessively drawn-out sentences.

Marginal control of sentence structure and sentence length detracts from what could have been a more effective essay.

SCORE: 3

Franklin's Response

(Printed as it was written)

In 1875 Henry James wrote a theater review that was published in a London newspaper. It was about Macbeth, Shakespearen play with Mr. Henry Irving receiving top billing as the character Macbeth. The play opened six weeks before the review appeared in the newspaper.

The "general public" which is the name James gives to the audience thought the play was "interesting." They were probably interested in seeing the murder of the king by Macbeth and Lady Macbeth and other things like the three witches and having a whole forest move when the actors put branches in their helmets pretending to be trees.

The public also liked the scene with the bloody daggars when Macbeth came out of the king's room with them and Lady Macbeth called him a coward and takes the daggars back inside and smears blood on the two servants who are supposed to look like they killed the king. Another great scene is when Banquo's ghost comes to the bancquet. The review in line 33 says it was "powerful".

James says the interest of the play was more than what they thought about Mr. Henry Irving. They think he is a "very superior amateur" actor in line 8. James says that he is too old for the part of Macbeth, who should be younger than about 35 or 40 since he and Lady Macbeth have no children, but he should be old enough to be a general in the king's army. In the performance "his voice is without charm" meaning it is dull and flat as if he was reciting the lines from memory and doesn't have an idea of how to build them up with expression and emotion. He (line 22) also has a "think, unmodulated voice".

The performance also has some good things to it. "Mr. Irving has great skill in the presentation of terror." This is important in the play because Macbeth is fighting for his life after Lady Macbeth sleepwalks and comitts suicide. He is scared of Macduff because he has killed his wife and children and when he hears that Macduff did not have natural childbirth and was ripped out of his mother's womb instead he knows that he is soon about to meet his own doom. Macbeth also shows terror at the banquet where Banquo comes in as a ghost and only Macbeth can see him. During that scene Mr. Henry Irving "muffles his head in his mantle and collapses beside the throne (34–35)".

In conclusion, James is full of criticism about the acting of Mr. Henry Irving. He contradicts himself in lines 37–38 when he says that "I find Mr. Irving more comfortable to see". So, it is like James did not really make a decision to like the play or not. The good things and the bad things cancel each other out like an acid and a base in chemistry and the end result is neutral.

Your impressions: _____

_____

_____

_____

Comment to Franklin from an AP Reader

To conclude that Henry James is "neutral" about this production of *Macbeth* suggests that you have misread the passage. Although the author manages to squeeze one or two half-hearted compliments into the review, the tone of James's remarks is mainly sarcastic and disparaging.

Your essay also suggests that you have a weak grasp of literary analysis. Although you are obviously aware of the need to paraphrase key ideas and include quotations, the essay summarizes the content of the passage more than it analyzes the author's diction, tone, imagery, and so forth.

That you are familiar with *Macbeth* is evident. Indeed, the detail with which you discuss certain events in the play demonstrates that, had you been asked to discuss the events of the play, you might have written a winning essay. But here you have overstepped the boundaries of the task and filled the essay with irrelevancies.

Your essay is competently organized, although using the opening paragraph to rephrase the prompt deprives you of an opportunity to say something fresh and appealing. The writing, while grammatically sound, is generally wordy, ungraceful, and mechanically flawed.
SCORE: 2

Answer Key to Mini-Workouts

Misplaced and Dangling Modifiers, pages 150–151
Answers may vary.

1. The bowling alley lends out shoes of all sizes to its customers.

2. An old bike we planned to put in the trash was given to a junk man.

3. When I was ten, my family and I emigrated from Guatemala to the United States.

4. Having found me sound asleep at noon, my mother thought I was sick.

5. After totaling the car beyond repair, Allison knew she'd have to buy another one.

6. Correct

7. Used all night to illuminate the steps, the flashlight needed new batteries.

8. A report was submitted by the police about the latest bank heist. (The original sentence is correct if the police have been busy robbing banks.)

9. Pausing for a drink of water after the hike, I found a grizzly bear standing in front of me.

10. The school bus picked me up at the corner after I had a quick breakfast.

Mini-Workout: Parallel Structure, page 154

Answers will vary.

1. but explains that it's all right to seek help

2. An easier and more direct route

3. plays forward on the basketball team

4. go out to eat

5. both angry and disappointed

6. better than taking a sailboat

7. knocked down not only the tree

8. and party with friends

9. The mouse will either find a quick way into the attic or gnaw

10. and amazingly entertaining

Active Verbs, pages 156–157

Answers will vary.

1. Mariana and Leonardo scored highest on the practice AP exam.

2. Cost determines my choice of bedroom rug.

3. Logic dictates that a student's effort and achievement govern college admission.

4. The Revolutionary War ended the monarchy.

5. Terrorist threats multiplied after 9/11.

6. The word "chaos" applies to my math class.

7. Mr. Gill scares everyone.

8. The next corridor leads to the principal's office.

9. Some students excel in chemistry but not in physics.

10. The librarian recommended this novel.

Revising Passive Sentences, page 158

Answers will vary.

1. Dead leaves covered the back yard.

2. We discussed the situation in Syria.

3. Because I had been at a play rehearsal every night that week, I failed the quiz.

4. We flew to Portland at the start of our weeklong vacation in Oregon.

5. Jason and the Argonauts pursued the Golden Fleece.

6. Rex fetched the newspaper every morning.

7. Immigration officials decided to build a fence on the border.

8. More than 20 diners on Saturday night ordered pizza.

9. Our group saw five of Shakespeare's plays in three days.

10. The candidate urged the voters to throw the old mayor out of office.

Cutting Needless Words, pages 161–162

Part A

Answers may vary.

1. Mary Roe wrote *A Ride Across America*, a book about her cross-country bike ride. To train for her feat, she biked 90 miles a day.

2. My suggestion for making meetings more productive and relevant to all students needn't offend the chairperson, Carolyn Welles.

3. Even though he spent six months in prison for embezzlement, Mr. Evans was appointed treasurer of the group.

4. Harmful criticism hurts more than it helps.

5. By reducing unnecessary driving, Americans everywhere can save gasoline.

Part B

Avoiding discrimination is but one of many reasons for people to gain weight, according to Stanford University graduate Slim Snyder, who, at a recent conference on health, said, "Lean people are victims of discrimination, just as obese people are." Fortunately, many up-to-date weight-gaining procedures are widely available. But they are ridiculed and kept well hidden because health experts agree that being lean is preferable to being obese.

Writing Specifically, page 164

Answers will vary.

1. Missy earned a 5 on the AP English exam.

2. Mr. Guzman insists that students study an hour every night, that they be punctual to class, and that they regard math as the epitome of logical thinking.

3. When I told Ms. Cronin that I'm kept from doing homework by driving my brother to piano lessons or Little League, by yearbook meetings on Tuesdays, by work for Peer Leaders and SADD, and by my part-time job at the florist, she muttered, "That's *your* problem."

4. "Get out of my face," Carrie snarled as she punched the Tigers' goalie in the nose.

5. Mitchell's reward for six hours at his desk studying chemistry was a big fat F on the quiz.

6. After winning by a 3 to 1 margin, the senator-elect grinned from ear to ear and told her supporters that she was ready to work in their behalf.

7. Countries bordering the Indian Ocean dump garbage, sewage, and other hazardous waste products into the sea.

8. In science we talk about experiments, but we can't do them because we don't have any equipment.

9. Joey and Teddy, the family twins, couldn't go out at the same time until they were 16 because they shared the same pair of shoes.

10. The acceptance letter thrilled my parents. Their worried looks suddenly disappeared, they stopped nagging me about homework, and because the question had been answered, they never again asked what would become of me.

Writing Correct Sentences, page 168

Answers may vary.

1. Amy is stressed out about the garbage in the back yard.

2. St. Petersburg was renamed Leningrad after the Russian Revolution. Its original name was restored in the 1990s.

3. My grandmother is 86 years old; therefore, she walks very slowly.

4. During the night, the stars came out like diamonds on black velvet.

5. Correct

6. This year's senior class is more involved than last year's.

7. The American colonists despised the king's tax on British tea; they drank Dutch tea instead.

8. Kayly found the squirrel lying dead in a ditch, but she didn't tell Kyle.

9. A biologist working in the field of genetic engineering can get involved in the controversy surrounding human cloning.

10. Correct

Noun-Verb/Subject-Verb Agreement, pages 171–172

1. was stuck   The subject is *line*, a singular noun.

2. has given   The construction *either . . . or* needs a singular verb.

3. is meeting   The subject *Board* is a singular noun.

4. is expected   The subject is *price*, a singular noun.

5. which has   The pronoun *which* refers to *service*, a singular noun.

6. There are   The subject is *levels*, a plural noun.

7. are going   The subject *Proceeds* is a plural noun.

8. is expected   The noun *team* to which the verb refers is singular.

9. are to be   The subject *guards* is plural.

10. have not been   The noun *promises* is plural.

Verb Tenses, page 174

1. feels   6. were

2. visited   7. No error

3. asks   8. had stayed

4. No error   9. had given

5. had seen   10. expected

Adjectives and Adverbs, page 176

1. sincerely

2. shy

3. badly

4. easily

5. calm

6. Correct

7. Correct

8. securely

9. cynically

10. bitter

Pronoun Case, page 179

1. me

2. Correct

3. us

4. He and I

5. us

6. we

7. His falling

8. Correct

9. him

10. he

Pronoun References, page 181

Answers will vary.

1. Mira loves texting and spends most of her spare time doing it.

2. Juan answered the test questions and handed them in. Then he collected his pens and pencils.

3. In *The Great Gatsby* Fitzgerald writes about the American Dream.

4. Correct

5. When teens loiter outside the theater on Friday night, the police give you a hard time.

6. Nate was told by his father, "I have only an hour to get to the airport."

7. Zachary aspires to play major league baseball someday.

8. Rob wants to go to Annapolis because he has a part-time job at the boatyard and spends every summer on the water.

9. Anyone who buys an old used car better be ready to pay for repairs.

10. After the interview, Alonzo told Rick, "I think Colgate University is a good place for you to spend the next four years."

Pronoun Agreement, pages 183–184

Answers will vary.

1. all the students in the class

2. its policy

3. its collection

4. has her own smartphone

5. Correct

6. as she could

7. write them down . . . and hand them in

8. All the horses

9. its first match.

10. will find the faculty and administration cooperative and supportive.

Punctuation, 186–187

A. Possessives

1. Liam's

2. America's

3. Correct

4. women's

5. girls'

6. Andersons'

7. Correct

8. Silas's

9. computers'

10. month's

B. Commas and Semicolons

1. While Buddy was riding, his bike got a flat tire.

2. The mail carrier did not leave the package, for Valerie was not at home.

3. After doing homework, Mikey, as you might expect, texted with friends until midnight.

4. His work criticized many commonly-held beliefs, however, and it was strictly censored.

5. The car that ran into mine at the intersection was an SUV.

6. I need Google maps of Boston and Portland, Maine.

7. The people who live by the water must be prepared for occasional flooding.

8. The boat was 75 feet long and 18 feet wide; its mast was about 80 feet tall.

9. To anyone interested in flying, planes hold endless fascination.

10. Jacob and Owen, left alone for the weekend, invited all their friends to a party.

5
Practice Tests

INSTRUCTIONS: Each test in this section lasts 3 hours and 15 minutes.

As you take each test, allow yourself one hour to answer the multiple-choice questions. Use the answer sheet provided.

Then take a five-minute break and answer the essay questions. Write your essays on standard 8½" × 11" composition paper. Before you write the essays, set aside a 15-minute reading period. During that time, you may read all the essay questions, study the sources for question 1 (the synthesis essay), and plan what you are going to say. At the end of 15 minutes take out lined paper and begin to write. The suggested writing time for each essay is 40 minutes.

When you are finished, check your answers with the Multiple-Choice Answer Key that follows each exam. Read the answer explanations for both the questions you missed and those you answered correctly.

To rate your essays, use the Essay Self-Scoring Guide provided with each test.

Worksheets are also provided at the end of each test to help you determine your total score.

ANSWER SHEET
Practice Test 1

Multiple-Choice Questions

Time—1 hour

1. Ⓐ Ⓑ Ⓒ Ⓓ Ⓔ   13. Ⓐ Ⓑ Ⓒ Ⓓ Ⓔ   25. Ⓐ Ⓑ Ⓒ Ⓓ Ⓔ   37. Ⓐ Ⓑ Ⓒ Ⓓ Ⓔ
2. Ⓐ Ⓑ Ⓒ Ⓓ Ⓔ   14. Ⓐ Ⓑ Ⓒ Ⓓ Ⓔ   26. Ⓐ Ⓑ Ⓒ Ⓓ Ⓔ   38. Ⓐ Ⓑ Ⓒ Ⓓ Ⓔ
3. Ⓐ Ⓑ Ⓒ Ⓓ Ⓔ   15. Ⓐ Ⓑ Ⓒ Ⓓ Ⓔ   27. Ⓐ Ⓑ Ⓒ Ⓓ Ⓔ   39. Ⓐ Ⓑ Ⓒ Ⓓ Ⓔ
4. Ⓐ Ⓑ Ⓒ Ⓓ Ⓔ   16. Ⓐ Ⓑ Ⓒ Ⓓ Ⓔ   28. Ⓐ Ⓑ Ⓒ Ⓓ Ⓔ   40. Ⓐ Ⓑ Ⓒ Ⓓ Ⓔ
5. Ⓐ Ⓑ Ⓒ Ⓓ Ⓔ   17. Ⓐ Ⓑ Ⓒ Ⓓ Ⓔ   29. Ⓐ Ⓑ Ⓒ Ⓓ Ⓔ   41. Ⓐ Ⓑ Ⓒ Ⓓ Ⓔ
6. Ⓐ Ⓑ Ⓒ Ⓓ Ⓔ   18. Ⓐ Ⓑ Ⓒ Ⓓ Ⓔ   30. Ⓐ Ⓑ Ⓒ Ⓓ Ⓔ   42. Ⓐ Ⓑ Ⓒ Ⓓ Ⓔ
7. Ⓐ Ⓑ Ⓒ Ⓓ Ⓔ   19. Ⓐ Ⓑ Ⓒ Ⓓ Ⓔ   31. Ⓐ Ⓑ Ⓒ Ⓓ Ⓔ   43. Ⓐ Ⓑ Ⓒ Ⓓ Ⓔ
8. Ⓐ Ⓑ Ⓒ Ⓓ Ⓔ   20. Ⓐ Ⓑ Ⓒ Ⓓ Ⓔ   32. Ⓐ Ⓑ Ⓒ Ⓓ Ⓔ   44. Ⓐ Ⓑ Ⓒ Ⓓ Ⓔ
9. Ⓐ Ⓑ Ⓒ Ⓓ Ⓔ   21. Ⓐ Ⓑ Ⓒ Ⓓ Ⓔ   33. Ⓐ Ⓑ Ⓒ Ⓓ Ⓔ   45. Ⓐ Ⓑ Ⓒ Ⓓ Ⓔ
10. Ⓐ Ⓑ Ⓒ Ⓓ Ⓔ   22. Ⓐ Ⓑ Ⓒ Ⓓ Ⓔ   34. Ⓐ Ⓑ Ⓒ Ⓓ Ⓔ
11. Ⓐ Ⓑ Ⓒ Ⓓ Ⓔ   23. Ⓐ Ⓑ Ⓒ Ⓓ Ⓔ   35. Ⓐ Ⓑ Ⓒ Ⓓ Ⓔ
12. Ⓐ Ⓑ Ⓒ Ⓓ Ⓔ   24. Ⓐ Ⓑ Ⓒ Ⓓ Ⓔ   36. Ⓐ Ⓑ Ⓒ Ⓓ Ⓔ

Practice Test 1

Section I

TIME: 1 HOUR

DIRECTIONS: *Questions 1–11.* Carefully read the following passage and answer the accompanying questions.

The passage below is excerpted from a memoir published in the mid-20th century.

Passage 1

You can live a lifetime and, at the end of it, know more about other people than you know about yourself. You learn to watch other people, but you never watch yourself because you strive against loneliness. If you read a book, or shuffle a deck of cards, or care for a dog, you
Line are avoiding yourself. The abhorrence of loneliness is as natural as wanting to live at all. If
(5) it were otherwise, men would never have bothered to make an alphabet, nor to have fashioned words out of what were only animal sounds, nor to have crossed continents—each man to see what the other looked like.

Being alone in an aeroplane even for so short a time as a night and a day, irrevocably alone, with nothing to observe but your instruments and your own hands in semi-darkness,
(10) nothing to contemplate but the size of your small courage, nothing to wonder about but the beliefs, the faces, and the hopes rooted in your mind—such an experience can be as startling as the first awareness of a stranger walking by your side at night. You are a stranger. It is dark already and I am over the south of Ireland. There are the lights of Cork and the lights are wet; they are drenched with Irish rain, and I am above them and dry. I am above them
(15) and the plane roars in a sobbing world, but it imparts no sadness to me. I feel the security of solitude, the exhilaration of escape. So long as I can see the lights and imagine the people walking underneath them, I feel selfishly triumphant, as if I have eluded care and left even the small sorrow of rain in other hands.

It is a little over an hour now since I left Abingdon, England. Wales and the Irish Sea are
(20) behind me like so much time used up. On a long flight distance and time are the same. But there had been a moment when Time stopped—and Distance too. It was the moment I lifted the blue-and-silver Gull from the aerodrome, the moment the photographers aimed their cameras, the moment I felt the craft refuse its burden and strain toward the earth in sullen rebellion, only to listen at last to the persuasion of stick and elevators, the dogmatic
(25) argument of blueprints that said she *had* to fly because the figures proved it. So she had flown, and once airborne, once she had yielded to the sophistry of a draughtsman's board, she had said, "There, I have lifted the weight. Now, where are we bound?"—and the question had frightened me.

We are bound for a place thirty-six hundred miles from here—two thousand miles of it
(30) unbroken ocean. Most of the way it will be night. We are flying west with the night. So there
behind me is Cork; and ahead of me is Berehaven Lighthouse. It is the last light, standing
on the last land. I watch it, counting the frequency of its flashes—so many to the minute.
Then I pass it and fly out to sea.

The fear is gone now—not overcome nor reasoned away. It is gone because something
(35) else has taken its place; the confidence and the trust, the inherent belief in the security of
land underfoot—now this faith is transferred to my plane, because land has vanished and
there is no other tangible thing to fix faith upon. Flight is but momentary escape from the
eternal custody of earth. . . .

(1942)

1. The rhetorical purpose of using the second-person pronoun "you" in the opening lines of the
   passage is meant primarily to

   (A) explain how difficult it is for people to understand themselves.
   (B) show that the speaker refuses to admit she's thinking of herself.
   (C) create the effect that the writer is addressing "you," the reader.
   (D) indicate that the narrator is giving advice to an undefined audience.
   (E) comment on the human experience, particularly the narrator's own.

2. In lines 3–4, the speaker makes a hypothetical statement about loneliness primarily to

   (A) make a point about the dynamics of interpersonal relationships.
   (B) introduce the idea that pain is part of the human condition.
   (C) account for the need to be active in various endeavors.
   (D) generalize about why we are interested in stories of other people.
   (E) provide examples of everyday activities.

3. In line 9 and after, the writer constructs three sentences that begin with "nothing to (*followed
   by a verb*) but. . . ." The effect of this repetition is best described by which of the following?

   (A) It simulates the monotony often experienced on long, uneventful airplane flights.
   (B) It heightens readers' anticipation to learn what the narrator will substitute for the
       rejected verb.
   (C) It adds surprise to the narrative, an element meant to entertain readers.
   (D) It dramatizes a crucial motif of the passage—the narrator's sense of discovery.
   (E) It adds to the adventure of crossing three thousand miles of water in a small airplane.

4. The rhetorical purpose of switching from second-person to first-person narration in line 12 is
   mainly to

   (A) explain the meaning of "You are a stranger" (line 12).
   (B) indicate that until then the narrator hasn't been thinking only about herself.
   (C) give an example of the "abhorrence of loneliness" (line 4).
   (D) emphasize that the narrator acknowledges how alone she now really is.
   (E) prove that the narrator is an accomplished pilot.

5. The rhetorical function of the phrase "sobbing world" (line 15) is primarily to

(A) describe the rain outside the airplane.
(B) suggest the pulsating sounds of the airplane engine.
(C) explain the sadness of lonely people.
(D) reveal the narrator's affection for the Irish people far below.
(E) indicate that flying serves as a release from everyday cares.

6. In context, lines 8–18 ("Being alone . . . in other hands) could be used to support which of the following claims about the writer's tone?

(A) Her tone while describing her solitude in the sky is buoyant.
(B) Her tone when looking down at cities below is sentimental.
(C) She adopts an awed tone when referring to the darkness outside.
(D) She adopts a nonchalant tone when contemplating her courage.
(E) She adopts a reverent tone when referring to people on the ground below.

7. The sentence in line 20 ("On a long . . . same") has all of the following rhetorical functions EXCEPT

(A) to present information about the way pilots tend to think.
(B) to introduce the anecdote that follows in lines 20–28.
(C) to illustrate how pilots on long solo flights sometimes may become disoriented.
(D) to help contrast the tedium of long-distance flying with the thrill of taking off.
(E) to explain the phrase "like so much time used up" (line 20).

8. Which of the following best characterizes the writer's decision to undertake a long solo flight?

(A) The irony of flying solo in order to escape loneliness
(B) The need to overcome fears of inadequacy
(C) A means to escape from routine
(D) An effort to assuage feelings of self-doubt about her capabilities
(E) An amorphous desire to make a name for herself

9. All of the following interpretations explain the rhetorical purpose in line 21 of capitalizing "Time" and "Distance" EXCEPT

(A) to support the narrator's previous claim that on long flights "distance and time are the same" (line 20).
(B) to indicate that suddenly becoming airborne is the equivalent of a metaphysical moment that, in effect, transforms reality.
(C) in the context, to emphasize the significance of the moment when the plane became airborne.
(D) to imply that during a solo flight Time and Distance assume the stature of a deity in the mind of a pilot.
(E) to suggest that Time and Distance become virtually palpable during the experience of flying solo.

10. In the third paragraph (lines 19–28), which of the following rhetorical strategies is most prominent?

   (A) Emphasizing sensual imagery
   (B) Using abstract generalizations
   (C) Mixing facts and impressions
   (D) Appealing to authority
   (E) Employing periodic sentences

11. The primary rhetorical effect of the paragraph in lines 29–33 is to

   (A) satisfy readers' curiosity about the purpose of the flight.
   (B) build admiration for the narrator by describing her ambitious flight plan.
   (C) enrich the passage by contrasting the narrator's impressions with factual material.
   (D) give credence to such ideas as "the exhilaration of escape" (line 16) and feeling "selfishly triumphant" (line 17).
   (E) indirectly explain with facts and figures what motivates the narrator to fly.

DIRECTIONS: *Questions 12–25.* Carefully read the following passage and answer the accompanying questions.

This is an excerpt from a speech made by a British nobleman who served in the government of Queen Victoria late in the 19th century.

Passage 2

It is no doubt true that we are surrounded by advisers who tell us that all study of the past is barren except insofar as it enables us to determine the laws by which the evolution of human societies is governed. How far such an investigation has been up to the present
Line time fruitful in results I will not inquire. That it will ever enable us to trace with accuracy the
(5) course which States and nations are destined to pursue in the future, or to account in detail for their history in the past, I do not believe.

We are borne along like travelers on some unexplored stream. We may know enough of the general configuration of the globe to be sure that we are making our way toward the ocean. We may know enough by experience or theory of the laws regulating the flow of liq-
(10) uids, to conjecture how the river will behave under the varying influences to which it may be subject. More than this we can not know. It will depend largely upon causes which, in relation to any laws which we are ever likely to discover, may properly be called accidental, whether we are destined sluggishly to drift among fever-stricken swamps, to hurry down perilous rapids, or to glide gently through fair scenes of peaceful cultivation.

(15) But leaving on one side ambitious sociological speculations, and even those more modest but hitherto more successful investigations into the causes which have in particular cases been principally operative in producing great political changes, there are still two modes in which we can derive what I may call "spectacular" enjoyment from the study of history.

There is first the pleasure which arises from the contemplation of some great historic
(20) drama, or some broad and well-marked phase of social development. The story of the rise, greatness, and decay of a nation is like some vast epic which contains as subsidiary episodes the varied stories of the rise, greatness, and decay of creeds, of parties, and of statesmen. The imagination is moved by the slow unrolling of this great picture of human mutability, as it

is moved by contrasted permanence of the abiding stars. The ceaseless conflict, the strange
(25) echoes of long-forgotten controversies, the confusion of purpose, the successes which lay
deep the seeds of future evils, the failures that ultimately divert the otherwise inevitable
danger, the heroism which struggles to the last for a cause foredoomed to defeat, the wick-
edness which sides with right, and the wisdom which huzzas at the triumph of folly—fate,
meanwhile, through all this turmoil and perplexity, working silently toward the predestined
(30) end—all these form together a subject the contemplation of which we surely never weary.

But there is yet another and very different species of enjoyment to be derived from the
records of the past, which require a somewhat different method of study in order that it may
be fully tasted. Instead of contemplating, as it were, from a distance, the larger aspects of the
human drama, we may elect to move in familiar fellowship amid the scenes and actors of
(35) special periods.

We may add to the interest we derive from the contemplation of contemporary politics, a
similar interest derived from a not less minute and probably more accurate knowledge of some
comparatively brief passage in the political history of the past. We may extend the social circle
in which we move—a circle perhaps narrowed and restricted through circumstances beyond
(40) our control—by making intimate acquaintances, perhaps even close friends, among a society
long departed, but which, when we have once learnt the trick of it, it rests with us to revive.

It is this kind of historical reading which is usually branded as frivolous and useless, and
persons who indulge in it often delude themselves into thinking that the real motive of their
investigation into bygone scenes and ancient scandals is philosophic interest in an impor-
(45) tant historical episode, whereas in truth it is not the philosophy which glorifies the details,
but the details that make tolerable the philosophy.

12. The speaker's rhetorical intent in the first sentence of the passage (lines 1–3) is made evident
by all of the following EXCEPT

(A) to convey a sense of authority.
(B) to make a connection with his audience by saying "we" and "us."
(C) to assure his audience that he's attuned to their beliefs and values.
(D) to acknowledge that they are people of some stature.
(E) to capture the audience's attention using hyperbole.

13. In the first paragraph, the speaker makes two negative statements: "I will not inquire" and "I
do not believe." Which of the following best explains the speaker's rhetorical goal in saying
what he won't do and doesn't believe?

(A) To win the audience's confidence by speaking frankly
(B) To surprise his listeners by challenging the status quo
(C) To impress the audience with his decisiveness
(D) To reveal to the audience the obstreperous side of his personality
(E) To prepare his listeners to hear some distressing news

14. In lines 4–6 of the passage, which of the following traits of character best describes the rhetorical effect the speaker is likely to leave on his audience?

(A) That he is unwilling to take risks
(B) That he recognizes his limitations
(C) That he is proud of his accomplishments
(D) That he is an honorable public servant
(E) That he is a relentless seeker of truth

15. Which of the following best describes the rhetorical effect of lines 4–6?

    (A) It reiterates the thesis of the passage.
    (B) It explains the gap between historical theory and historical fact.
    (C) It provides evidence that supports the previous generalization.
    (D) It casts doubt on the validity of some common assumptions.
    (E) It confirms the speaker's authority to speak on the subject of the passage.

16. Considering the rhetorical imagery in the second paragraph (lines 7–14), which of the following is the best interpretation of the speaker's position on the nature of governmental policies and planning?

    (A) Anyone responsible for carrying out governmental plans should be ready to change them at any time.
    (B) Good governmental policies will survive in spite of various pressures to change them.
    (C) There is no way to assure the success of even the most carefully wrought plans and policies.
    (D) The amount of uncertainty about the future negates the necessity for planning ahead.
    (E) It's in the nature of things that expectations for the future, however meritorious, will invariably be thwarted by countervailing forces.

17. The primary rhetorical purpose of the speaker's extended analogy in lines 7–14 is to

    (A) offer a fresh perspective on a commonly accepted belief.
    (B) win the audience's favor with a lively and amusing parable.
    (C) show that serious academic controversies have a light side.
    (D) demonstrate that some academic theories need not be taken literally.
    (E) ridicule a widely accepted historical principle.

18. The speaker's primary rhetorical intent in the third paragraph (lines 15–18) is to

    (A) heighten the audience's anticipation to hear what he will say about political change.
    (B) present an exemplary argument against "sociological speculations."
    (C) induce his listeners to think more deeply about the causes of "great" political upheavals.
    (D) dismiss customary ways of studying history in favor of a sensational new way.
    (E) persuade the audience that learning history is not only worthwhile but also fun.

19. Which of the following best describes the exigence of the fourth paragraph (lines 19–30)?

    (A) To describe the appeal of history over the ages
    (B) To define the benefits of knowing about the past
    (C) To stress the unpredictability of human events
    (D) To highlight the vast sweep of history
    (E) To pinpoint reasons why history needs to be studied

20. In context, lines 19–30 could be used to support which of the following statements about the speaker's tone?

   (A) His tone when discussing the impermanence of nations is ponderous.
   (B) His tone when discussing humankind's enduring conflicts is melancholy.
   (C) He acquires an enthusiastic tone when discussing the variety of human experience.
   (D) He adopts a bitter tone when dealing with the evil that men do.
   (E) He uses a jubilant tone when speaking about the permanence of the stars.

21. The speaker's dominant rhetorical technique in lines 19–30 is to

   (A) overwhelm the audience with fleeting references to an abundance of historical events.
   (B) romanticize history as a series of captivating, often inexplicable stories.
   (C) exaggerate the significance of ordinary events.
   (D) suggest that the sweep of history is too complex to be fully understood by one individual.
   (E) imply that the audience is fortunate to be alive at the present time.

22. The main rhetorical function of the fifth paragraph (lines 31–35) is best described as

   (A) an acknowledgment that some periods of history are more significant than others.
   (B) an apology for having thus far ignored a number of "special periods" of history.
   (C) an attempt to assuage the misgivings of some audience members.
   (D) an effort to refocus the audience's attention.
   (E) a gesture of good will to non-historians in the audience.

23. While encouraging his listeners to become informed about the past (lines 39–40), the speaker embeds a parenthetical remark ("a circle . . . beyond our control") in order to suggest that

   (A) the passage of time inevitably makes data increasingly hard to retrieve.
   (B) historical archives are a good source of information.
   (C) much of the past can be reconstructed by examining contemporary conditions.
   (D) an absence of informants caused by time, distance, or death should not be a deterrent.
   (E) limiting the topic increases the chances of a comprehensive understanding of a historical period.

24. The rhetorical intent of the last sentence in the passage (lines 42–46) is mainly to

   (A) impress the audience with highly charged diction such as "frivolous" and "useless."
   (B) praise the audience for its interest in the philosophy of history.
   (C) point out a misconception related to the study of history.
   (D) arouse the listeners' curiosity by making reference to "ancient scandals."
   (E) leave behind a thoughtful definition of "truth" by using a paradoxical counterclaim.

25. The speaker's shift in pronoun usage—from "I" (first person singular) in lines 1–6, to "we" (first person plural) in lines 7–41, and finally to "their" (third person) in lines 42–46)—may best be described as

(A) a device for increasing the effectiveness of his argument.

(B) a rhetorical trick designed to hold his listeners' attention.

(C) a plan to be persuasive by keeping the audience off balance.

(D) a method for defusing potential objections to his message.

(E) a rhetorical technique meant to project an image of all-inclusiveness.

DIRECTIONS: *Questions 26–33.* Carefully read the following passage and answer the accompanying questions.

The passage below, adapted from an essay written in the mid-twentieth century, offers a glimpse of science through the ages.

Passage 3

(1) When you consider the whole historical evolution of science, it might be divided three ways: antiquity; classical science, starting with the Renaissance; and modern science, which started at the turn of the twentieth century. (2) In the West, for example, for more
Line than two-thousand years, scientists subscribed to a classification system devised by the
(5) Greek physician, Hippocrates. (3) His theory was that one's innate psych-physical consti-tution was determined by the relative predominance within one's body of one of the four "humors"—blood, phlegm, black bile, and yellow bile. (4) This humoral pathology persisted into the nineteenth century. (5) What best qualifies the science of antiquity, however, is the naïve faith in the perfection of our senses and reasoning.
(10) (6) What man saw was the ultimate reality. (7) Everybody, being by necessity the center of their universe, knew there was no doubt that ours is a flat earth and man is the center. (8) There is an "up" and "down," an absolute space, as expressed in Euclidean geometry. (9) Human reasoning was thought to lead to more reliable results than crude trial and experi-ment, as reflected by the dictum of Aristotle that a big stone falls faster than a small one. (10)
(15) What is remarkable about this statement is not that it is wrong, but that it never occurred to Aristotle to try it. (11) He probably would have regarded such a proposal as an insult.

(12) Around two millennia later the Renaissance arrived. (13) It was a great awakening. (14) The Western mind experienced something new. (15) It was the time when Galileo, a boisterous young man, lived in Italy. (16) One day he climbed a leaning tower while carry-
(20) ing a big stone as well as a smaller one. (17) He dropped both of them off the top, but first he had asked friends to stand at the bottom and observe which stone landed first. (18) They arrived at the same instant.

(20) This same man, doubting the perfection of his senses, later built a telescope to improve the range of his eyes, and thus discovered the rings of Saturn and the satellites of
(25) Jupiter. (21) This was a dramatic discovery. (21) Galileo was but one of the first swallows of an approaching spring. (22) Somewhat earlier, Copernicus had already concluded that it was not absolutely necessary to suppose that the sun rotates around the earth; it could be

the other way around. (23) Johannes Kepler agreed. (24) Using simple observation, reason
ing, and careful measurement, the earth was found to move around the sun, not vice-versa.

(30)   (25) Somewhat later Antony van Leeuwenhoek, a greengrocer at Delft, in Holland,
improved the range of his senses by building a microscope. (26) With it he discovered a
new world of living creatures too small to be seen by the naked eye. (27) Thus began the
science which I will call "classical," which reached its peak with Sir Isaac Newton, who with
the concept of gravitation, made a coherent system of the universe.

(35)   (28) This classical science replaced divine whims by natural laws, corrected many previous errors, and extended man's world into both the bigger and smaller dimensions, but it
introduced nothing new that man could not "understand." (29) By the word "understand"
we simply mean that we can correlate the phenomenon in question with some earlier
experience of ours. (30) If I tell you that it is gravitation which holds our globe in the sun,
(40) you will say "I understand," though nobody knows what gravitation is. (31) All the same, you
"understand" because you know that it is gravitation which makes apples fall, and you have
all seen apples fall before.

     (32) For several centuries, this classical science had little influence on everyday life. (33)
Soon after, the scientific community began to speak optimistically about finding the secret
(45) of life. (34) It became obvious over time that the secret of life was not to be had by a little
casual experimentation, and that life in today's terms appeared to arise only through the
medium of pre-existing life.

     (35) Yet, if science was not to be embarrassed by some kind of mind-matter dualism, the
emergence of life had, in some way to be accounted for. (36) Nevertheless, as years passed,
(50) the secret remained locked in its living jelly, in spite of larger microscopes and more formidable means of dissection. (37) The mystery was heightened because it was discovered
that the supposedly simple amoeba was already a complex, self-operating chemical factory.

     (38) With the failure of many efforts, science was left in the half-embarrassing position of
having to postulate theories of living origins which it could not demonstrate, or at the very
(55) least they thought the next generation would be in a position to do so. (39) Around the end
of the nineteenth century (1896), two mysterious discoveries signified the arrival of a new
period, the period of modern science. (40) One was that of Wilhelm Roentgen, who discovered new rays which could penetrate through solid matter. (41) The other was the discovery
of radioactivity by Antoine Henri Becquerel, a discovery which shook the solid foundation
(60) of our universe, built of indestructible matter.

26. The writer wants the first sentence of the passage (reproduced below) to catch the reader's
     interest and provide a succinct introduction to its topic.

         When you consider the whole historical evolution of science, it might be divided three
         ways: antiquity; classical science, starting with the Renaissance; and modern science,
         which started at the turn of the twentieth century. In the West, for example

     Which version of the underlined section of the passage best achieves this goal?

     (A) (as it is now)
     (B) Today's scientists argue that their discipline has had three important periods in history:
     (C) The history of science is composed of three periods:
     (D) The history of science may well be summarized by dividing it into three periods—
     (E) Science has a history comprising three distinctive periods, namely:

27. In order to provide a more effective transition between sentences 1 and 2, the writer wants to replace part or all of the underlined section of sentence 2 (reproduced below).

> *In the West, for example, for more than two-thousand years,* scientists subscribed to a classification system devised by the Greek physician, Hippocrates.*

In the context, which would be the best choice?

(A) At first,

(B) For above two-thousand years in the West,

(C) During more than two-thousand years, in antiquity

(D) For example, during antiquity, which lasted more than two-thousand years,

(E) In antiquity, a period longer than two-thousand years,

28. The writer wants to highlight the primary features of the science in antiquity, and also add to the coherence of the discussion. To do so, the writer plans to revise sentence 5 (reproduced below)

> *What qualifies the science of antiquity is the naïve faith in the perfection of our senses and reasoning.*

Which version most effectively serves this purpose?

(A) What epitomized the science of antiquity is the naïve faith in the perfection of our senses and reasoning.

(B) What best characterized the science of antiquity, however, was the naïve faith in the perfection of our senses and reasoning.

(C) However, the best quality of the science of antiquity was the naïve faith in the perfection of man's senses and reasoning.

(D) What best characterizes the science of antiquity, however, may have been the naïve faith in the perfection of our senses and reasoning.

(E) What best characterizes the science of antiquity, however, was a belief, however innocent, in the perfection of our senses and of our reasoning.

29. After reading the draft of the passage, the writer singled out an excerpt (reproduced below) to be revised without altering its essential meaning.

> *(12) Around two millennia later the Renaissance arrived. (13) It was a great awakening. (14) The Western mind experienced something new. (15) It was the time when Galileo, a boisterous young man, lived in Italy. (16) One day he climbed a leaning tower while carrying a big stone as well as a smaller one. (17) He dropped both of them off the top, but first he had asked friends to stand at the bottom and observe which stone landed first.*

Which version of sentences 12–17 best achieves those objectives?

(A) After about two-thousand years, the arrival of the Renaissance seemed to awaken the Western mind. Take as an example a boisterous young man in Italy. Galileo by name, one day he decided to carry two stones—one was big and one was small—up to the very top of a leaning tower. After previously having asked friends to observe which stone landed on the pavement first, he dropped them simultaneously.

(B) Two thousand years later, during that great awakening of the Western mind now called the Renaissance, Galileo, a boisterous young Italian, climbed a leaning tower carrying two stones, one big and one small. Having asked companions to observe which stone landed first, he dropped them simultaneously.

(C) Approximately two thousand years afterward, upon the arrival of the Renaissance, a great awakening took place in Western minds. Take, for example, the case of a young boisterous Italian named Galileo. To illustrate that the Western mind had experienced a new transformation, one day Galileo climbed up a leaning tower while carrying both a big stone and a smaller stone. From the top of the tower, he dropped both of them, but first he had asked friends to stand at the bottom and report to him which stone hit the ground first.

(D) Approximately two thousand years afterward, upon the arrival of the Renaissance, a great awakening took place in Western minds. Take, for example, the case of a young, boisterous Italian named Galileo. As an example that the Western mind had experienced something new, one day he tried an experiment and climbed a leaning tower carrying a big stone and a smaller one. He dropped both of them off the top, but first he had asked friends to stand at the bottom and watch for which one landed first.

(E) Around two millennia later the Renaissance came into history. It was a great awakening. The Western mind experienced something new. It was the time when Galileo, a boisterous Young man, lived in Italy. One day he climbed to the top of a leaning tower. He carried both a big stone and a smaller one. From the top he dropped both of them at the same moment. Beforehand, however, he had asked a couple of friends to stand at the bottom and to observe which stone landed first.

30. In sentence 21 the writer claims that the sighting of the planets' features was "dramatic." But left unsaid is what made it so. Which of the following sentences provides the best explanation?

(A) This was a dramatic discovery as a result of no one knew that the rings and moons existed before.

(B) This was a dramatic discovery because no one had seen the features and moons earlier.

(C) This was a dramatic discovery because nobody knew they had been there before.

(D) This was a dramatic discovery since the true facts about the rings and moons were not known before.

(E) This was a dramatic discovery; the rings and moons surprised everybody.

31. Sentences 23 and 24 (reproduced below) tell us that Kepler supported Copernicus's findings.

> *(23) Johannes Kepler agreed. (24) Using simple observation, reasoning, and careful measurement, the earth was found to move around the sun, not vice-versa.*

Which of the following versions best establishes the writer's position on the nature of Kepler's contribution to the expansion of scientific knowledge?

(A) (as it is now)

(B) Kepler confirmed Copernicus's theory. Using simple observation, reasoning, and careful measurement, the earth was found to move around the sun, not vice-versa.

(C) Kepler confirmed Copernicus's theories that the earth moved around the sun using simple observation, reasoning, and careful measuring, not vice-versa.

(D) Kepler used simple observation, reasoning, and careful measurement to prove that the earth moved around the sun, not vice-versa.

(E) With the use of observation, reasoning, and careful measurement, the sun was found by Kepler to support Copernicus's theory about the earth's movement.

32. An attentive reading of the passage suggests a disconnect in thought between sentences 32 and 33 (reprinted below).

> *(32) For several centuries, this classical science had little influence on everyday life. (33) Soon after, the scientific community began to speak optimistically about solving the secret of life.*

Which of the following sentences would best fill that gap?

(A) At that moment qualified scholars and researchers began to speak optimistically about solving the secret of life.

(B) By the beginning of the 1900s, and then during two wars and the Great Depression, you'd hardly hear a peep about it.

(C) In search of funding, researchers appealed to government and private sources.

(D) An intellectual elite, however, wanted to look deeper into Nature's cooking pot.

(E) On philosophical and moral grounds, some religious and conservative groups began an effort to squelch research.

33. The writer wants to add a phrase at the start of sentence 37 (reproduced below), adjusting the capitalization as needed, to set up a comparison with the idea expressed in sentence 36.

> *The mystery had been heightened because it was discovered that the supposedly simple amoeba was already a complex, self-operating chemical factory.*

Which of the following achieves this purpose?

(A) As it happened,
(B) Furthermore,
(C) What is more,
(D) Fortuitously,
(E) By contrast,

DIRECTIONS: *Questions 34–40.* Carefully read the following passage and answer the accompanying questions:

The passage below is a draft.

Passage 4

(1) The history of music until about 200 A.D. is shrouded in darkness because there is virtually no extant music and little was written about it by the ancients. (2) The journey that jazz has taken can be traced with reasonable accuracy. (3) That it ripened most fully
Line in New Orleans seems beyond dispute, although there are a few misguided deviants who
(5) support other theories of its origin. (4) Even before jazz, for most New Orleanians, music wasn't a luxury as it often is elsewhere. (5) It was a necessity. (6) Throughout the nineteenth century, diverse ethnic and racial groups—French, Spanish, and African, Italian, German, and Irish—found common cause in their love of music. (7) European folk and African-Caribbean elements merged with a popular American mainstream, causing a cultural revo-
(10) lution that spread far and wide.

(8) Just after the beginning of the new century, jazz began to emerge as part of a broad musical revolution. (9) It encompassed ragtime, blues, spirituals, marches, and the popular fare of "Tin Pan Alley." (10) It also reflected the profound contributions of people of African heritage to this new and distinctly American music. (11) Clearly, the need for an audience
(15) was obvious for it to succeed. (12) Then, of course, there was talent for the production of it—also essential, too. (13) Moreover, success was required for there to be a favorable audience to receive and support it.

(14) Before long the local urge for musical expression was powerful. (15) Anything that could be twanged, strummed, beaten, blown, or stroked was likely to be exploited for its
(20) musical usefulness. (16) For a long time the washboard was a highly respected percussion instrument, and the nimble fingers of Baby Dodds and others showed sheer genius on that workaday, washday utensil. (17) What's more, dancing had long been a mainstay of New Orleans nightlife, and jazz performers gave dancers what they wanted. (18) During earlier decades, string bands, led by violinists, had co-managed dance work. (19) They offered

(25) waltzes, quadrilles, and polkas to a polite dancing public. (20) Around 1895, however, jazz pioneers Buddy Bolden and Bunk Johnson arrived on the scene. (21) They blew their cornets in the street and in funeral parades. (22) From there it was a small step to take their music into the dance halls and clubs of their uncommonly vital city.

(23) The early development of jazz in New Orleans was also connected to the commu-
(30) nity life of the city, as seen in brass band funerals, music for picnics in parks or ball games, Saturday night fish fries, and Sunday camping along the shores of Lake Ponchartrain. (24) There were also red-beans-and-rice banquets on Mondays and nightly dances at neighborhoods all over town. (25) This spirit or emotional content connected the performer to the audience. (26) It offered a musical communication in which all parties could
(35) participate.

(27) By the turn of the twentieth century, instrumentation borrowed from both brass marching bands and string bands was predominant. (28) It consisted of a front line of cornet, clarinet, and trombone, and with a rhythm section of guitar, bass, and drums. (29) Dance audiences, especially the younger ones, however, craved more excitement. (30)
(40) Gradually, the emergence of ragtime, blues and, later, jazz began to satisfy the demand. (31) Musicians began to redefine roles, moving away from sight-reading toward playing by ear. (32) The 1890s represented the culmination of a century of music making in the city and around the country.

(33) Stories of the twenties in Chicago and elsewhere are almost too familiar to need
(45) repeating here. (34) What seems pertinent is to observe that jazz gravitated toward a particular kind of environment in which its existence was not only possible but, seen in retrospect, probable. (35) On the south side of Chicago during the twenties the New Orleans music continued an unbroken development. (36) It is not by coincidence that the decade of the 1920s has come to be known as "The Jazz Age." (37) This was the time when jazz became
(50) fashionable, as part of the youthful revolution in morals and manners that come with the "return to normalcy" following World War I.

(38) Americans were now more urbanized, affluent and entertainment-oriented than ever before. (39) The music industry was quick to take advantage of the situation. (40) In 1921, 100 million phonograph records were produced in the United States (compared
(55) to 25 million in 1914). (41) Two years later production remained high at 92 million, setting a trend which continued for the better part of the decade (until the impact of radio). (42) This prosperity relied heavily on the demand of records for dancers. (43) They could be used at home for practicing the latest steps, including such exotic dances as the Shimmy, the Charleston, and the more utilitarian Fox Trot, also known as "the
(60) businessman's bounce."

34. In order to give the passage greater coherence, the writer wants to add a phrase at the beginning of sentence 2 (reproduced below) that, adjusting for the necessary capitalization, will create a meaningful link to the idea expressed in sentence 1.

    The journey that jazz has taken can be traced with reasonable accuracy.

    Which of the following best achieves this goal?

    (A) On the contrary,
    (B) In the same vein,
    (C) On the other hand,
    (D) Nevertheless,
    (E) Meanwhile,

35. After reviewing the draft of this passage, the writer thinks that readers may find that the tone of sentence 3 (reproduced below) is too harsh.

    That it ripened most fully in New Orleans seems beyond dispute, although <u>there are a few misguided deviants who support other theories of its origin</u>.

    Which of the following versions of the underlined text best expresses the meaning and also maintains the overall tone of the passage?

    (A) Long-term doubts still persist.
    (B) Not everyone agrees.
    (C) Opinions of some cultural historians state other views.
    (D) There are schools of thought varying on the issue.
    (E) Skeptics are serious about doubting the claim.

36. In sentence 7 (reproduced below) which of the following versions of the underlined text best establishes the writer's position on an important theme in the passage?

    European folk and African-Caribbean elements merged with a popular American mainstream, <u>causing a cultural revolution that spread far and wide.</u>

    (A) (as it is now)
    (B) inspiring "good time" music delivered in a rollicking, sometimes rough, manner.
    (C) creating a sound that appealed to young musicians because it was fun.
    (D) a sound so addictive that many musicians never again played anything else.
    (E) a combination that made New Orleans a perfect venue for jazz to take seed and thrive.

37. To make the prose more coherent, the writer wants to revise sentences 11–13 (reproduced below) and at the same time maintain their essential meaning.

    (11) Clearly, the need for an audience was obvious for it to succeed. (12) Then, of course, there was talent for the production of it—also essential, too. (13) Moreover, success was required for there to be a favorable audience to receive and support it.

    Which of the following versions best achieves those goals?

    (A) Obviously, the music's success needs an enthusiastic, supportive audience that needs to hear that new kind of music, and a production crew that know what they're doing.
    (B) It is clear that success depended on a favorable audience needing, supporting, and wanting to hear the music produced in a talented way.
    (C) Clearly, a receptive audience is needed for success. Also a talent to produce the music.
    (D) Success for this brand of music clearly depended on a need for it, a talent to produce it, and an audience to receive it.
    (E) Above all, an audience is needed. Also essential are talented production crews, but most of all a desire to listen and to support it in the future.

38. The writer wants sentence 14 (reproduced below) to function as a smooth transition between paragraphs.

    Before long the local urge for musical expression was powerful.

    Which of the following best serves the writer's purpose?

    (A) (keep it as it is)
    (B) As luck would have it, fans of jazz rejoiced.
    (C) Fortunately for jazz fans, all those requirements were met.
    (D) Jazz fans, it seems, got their wishes.
    (E) Looking back at the situation, this was a turning point in jazz history.

39. To provide additional information, the writer may want to add the following sentence to the discussion in either the fifth or the sixth paragraph (lines 36–46).

    At the same time, it was widely reported that Scott Joplin was producing ragtime on his piano at the Maple Leaf Club in Sedalia, Missouri; and in Memphis, W.C. Handy was evolving his own spectacular conception of the blues.

    Where would the sentence best be placed?

    (A) Before sentence 32
    (B) After sentence 32, but not in the next paragraph
    (C) In the new paragraph after sentence 32
    (D) After sentence 33
    (E) After sentence 34

40. The writer wants to add information to support the main purpose of the passage. All of the following sentences would help achieve that goal EXCEPT which one?

(A) Recordings made by the Original Dixieland Jazz Band strongly influenced the spread of jazz throughout the South and beyond.

(B) Despite the impact of racial segregation at the time, many jazz groups consisted only of black musicians.

(C) While sheet music continued to be an important medium for the popularity of new music, phonograph records were far superior.

(D) Within six months of its release, over a million recordings had been sold, thus fusing the New Orleans sound with the term "jazz" in a commercial world.

(E) Chicago became a destination for many jazz musicians who left New Orleans in search of new ideas and venues with new audiences.

DIRECTIONS: *Questions 41–45.* Carefully read the following passage and answer the accompanying questions.

The passage below is a draft.

Passage 5

(1) Research in the field of earthquake engineering is required, especially in places with a high to moderate seismic activity like California. (2) The lessons learned not only in 1906 but also during the 1957 and 1989 San Francisco quakes have shown the devastat-
Line ing effects, although at longer distances than previously known, due to extensive periods
(5) of shear waves. (3) Hence, earthquake engineering research must become a priority, driven mainly by the need to predict future quakes, but also to find solutions for mitigating their effects.

(4) This sort of interest in research did not exist on April 18, 1906, when a powerful earth-quake centered just off the coast grabbed San Francisco by the throat at 5:12 A.M. and nearly
(10) shook it to death. (5) The magnitude 7.8 quake arrived in two pulses, the second more pow-erful than the first. (6) "It hurled my bed against an opposite wall, and smashed the win-dows. (7) Glass shards covered the floor," wrote Emma Burke, the wife of a local attorney. (8) Above all, she recalled the deafening noise. (9) It was intense. (10) It grew increasingly louder and louder. (11) There was the crash of dishes. (12) And pictures fell from the walls.
(15) (13) There was the rattle of the flat tin roof, too. (14) "Actually," she noted long afterwards, "the groaning and the straining of the building itself made such a roar that no one noise could be distinguished."

(15) The tragedy was compounded by the great number of people and buildings which were concentrated along the path of the fault. (16) The destruction caused by the quake
(20) and the ensuing fire in the Italian Quarter resulted in the complete loss of much of the city, including the Italian Quarter, which, like other parts of the city hit by the disaster, had been reduced to a knotted, tangled mass of bent steel frames, charred bricks, and ashes. (17) In North Beach, only a small part of the community remained. (18) The Italians

on Telegraph Hill, occupied by large numbers of Italians had been luckier than most, *(25)* although they suffered losses since insurance companies were not interested in insuring remote areas of the Hill. (19) The scattered fire hydrants and water cisterns were not to be found east of Dupont Street, and the insurance companies were not willing to gamble. (20) It was reported in the Italian press that some 20,000 Italians lost their homes in the conflagration.

(30)   (21) One of the priests from the church of Sts. Peter and Paul had managed to save the consecrated host, vestments, and holy vessels. And said Mass under the inflamed sky. After the fires died, the Italians quietly returned to North Beach and tried to find the confidence to rebuild Little Italy.

(22) Approximately five to six hundred Italians had definitely left SF due to this tragic *(35)* event, while over six thousand new immigrants arrived and helped the survivors clear the ruins. (23) Seven hundred building permits were granted to North Beach Italian residents and businessmen to expedite the construction of the Colony. (24) Several real estate firms, such as the J. Cuneo Realtors in North Beach, demonstrated their confidence in the determination of the Italians. (25) This hastened the rebuilding process.

41. Which of the following sentences, if placed before sentence 1, would both attract readers' attention and provide an effective introduction to the ensuing paragraph?

    (A) Most people who have experienced an earthquake don't want to do it again.
    (B) After one disastrous day in April 1906, a single scientific principle became self-evident:
    (C) For safety and feelings of well-being, seismic hazard assessment is a necessity everywhere on earth.
    (D) The earthquake risk implication for many regions in the U.S. and throughout the world is alarming.
    (E) Losses from natural hazards like earthquakes are rapidly growing, and the projected trends are unsustainable.

42. The writer wants to include a word or more at the beginning of sentence 4 (reproduced below), adjusting for capitalization as needed, in order to give the passage a more personal tone.

    This sort of research and concern did not exist on April 18, 1906, when a powerful earthquake centered just off the coast grabbed San Francisco by the throat at 5:12 a.m. and nearly shook it to death.

    Which of the following would best achieve that purpose?

    (A) Because
    (B) Without any doubt,
    (C) Certainly,
    (D) With regret,
    (E) Alas,

43. The writer portrays Emma Burke's experience (sentences 9–14) using several short sentences (reproduced below) written as though each event had been discrete. Without changing the basic meaning, the writer now wants to revise the text to suggest that those incidents occurred as one brief but frightening cataclysm.

> *(9) It was intense. (10) It grew increasingly louder and louder. (11) There was the crash of dishes. (12) And pictures fell from the walls. (13) There was the rattle of the flat tin roof, too. (14) "Actually," she noted long afterwards, "the groaning and the straining of the building itself made such a roar that no one noise could be distinguished."*

Which version of those sentences best achieves that goal?

(A) It grew louder and louder—terrifyingly so—when all at once dishes and pictures crashed to the floor, the tin roof rattled, and the building itself strained and groaned.

(B) The terrifying noise was intense when all of a sudden our dishes crashed to the floor and pictures fell off the walls as the rattling of the flat tin roof and the strain and groan of the building was frightening.

(C) The intense noises were terrifying and grew suddenly louder with the crash of dishes and pictures on the wall while the building's tin roof rattled and the building itself strained and groaned.

(D) The increasingly loud noise grew louder and louder as dishes fell from the shelves and pictures dropped to the floor, just as the rattle of the flat tin roof, the groaning and straining of the building itself intensified the terrifying noise.

(E) Adding to the terror was the intensifying noise of crashing dishes, pictures falling, the rattling of the flat tin roof, and the building itself straining and groaning.

44. The writer wants to add more information to the third paragraph (sentences 15–29) to support the main intent of the paragraph. All of the following pieces of evidence would help to fulfill this purpose EXCEPT which one?

(A) The burning of hazardous material and its effects on health

(B) Statistics about injuries, hospital admissions, and deaths

(C) The complete shutdown of transportation systems and its consequences

(D) A map showing population density throughout the city

(E) Hair-raising stories about couriers who worked in zones without communications

45. The writer notices a gap in continuity between sentences 24 and 25 (reproduced below), and for the sake of coherence wants to provide an appropriate idea to fill it.

> *Several real estate firms, such as the J. Cuneo Realtors in North Beach, demonstrated their confidence in the determination of the Italians. This hastened the rebuilding process.*

Which of the following choices best meets that goal?

(A) Mortgage rates for new home purchases were deliberately left low.

(B) The company held fun-filled fundraising events to publicize the plight of many Italian families.

(C) They invested $400,000 in the reconstruction of apartments, stores, flats, and business offices.

(D) Zoning laws were discussed at public meetings of the City Council.

(E) To show good will, several Italian real estate agents were hired.

Section II

Three Essay Questions

TIME: 2 HOURS AND 15 MINUTES

Write your essays on standard 8½″ × 11″ composition paper. At the exam you will be given a bound booklet containing 12 lined pages.

Essay Question 1

SUGGESTED TIME:

15 MINUTES FOR READING THE QUESTION AND SOURCES

40 MINUTES FOR WRITING AN ESSAY

Many people worldwide devote huge amounts of time, money, and energy opposing the use of animals in laboratory research. Many others take the view that animals should be used in research for the overall benefit of humankind.

Carefully read the following six sources, including the material that introduces each source. Then, in an essay that synthesizes at least three of the sources, take a position on the claim that animals should be used in research for the overall benefit of humankind.

Source A (AALAS)
Source B (PETA)
Source C (Pie graph)
Source D (Derbyshire)
Source E (Nuffield)
Source F (Haggarty)

Instructions:

- Respond to the prompt with a thesis that may establish a line of reasoning.
- Provide evidence from at least three of the provided sources to support the thesis. Indicate clearly the sources used through direct quotation, paraphrase, or summary. Sources may be cited as Source A, Source B, etc., or by using the descriptions in parentheses.
- Explain the relationship between the evidence and the thesis.
- Demonstrate an understanding of the rhetorical situation.
- Use appropriate grammar and punctuation in communicating the argument.

Source A

"What Benefits Have Come from Medical Research Using Animals?" American Association for Laboratory Animal Science (AALAS), *www.foundation.aalas.org*

The following comes from the website of a foundation that provides funding to promote awareness of research in animal care and animal contributions to biomedical research, safety testing, and education.

. . . Today's children routinely receive a vaccine that provides a lifetime of protection against polio. Children are also immunized against typhus, diphtheria, whooping cough, smallpox, and tetanus. Untold millions of people around the world are healthy because of these vaccines made possible through animal research.

Diabetes is another example of the importance of biomedical research. Approximately 6.2% of the population (17 million people) has diabetes. Nearly 1 million new cases of diabetes are diagnosed every year, and based on death certificate data, diabetes contributed to 209,664 deaths in 1999 alone. Without insulin treatments to regulate blood sugar levels, many more diabetics would die. Dogs were crucial to the research that identified the cause of diabetes, which led to the development of insulin. . . .

The importance of animal research to those suffering from heart and circulatory diseases cannot be overlooked. About 50 million Americans age six and older have high blood pressure, which can cause strokes, heart attacks, and heart disease. Research involving animals has helped identify the causes of high blood pressure and develop more effective drugs to control the problem. Other research has resulted in treatments for strokes and heart attacks that save thousands of lives and reduce recovery time. Dogs have been especially important to researchers who developed open-heart surgery, pacemakers, and heart transplants. These techniques have revolutionized therapy for people who have severe heart disease.

Source B

"Using Animals for Medical Testing Is Unethical and Unnecessary," *The Ethics of Medical Testing*, an online academic journal, 2012.

The following has been excerpted from an article prepared by People for the Ethical Treatment of Animals (PETA), the world's largest animal rights organization, with two million members and supporters.

Millions of animals suffer and die needlessly every year in the United States as they become subjects for medical testing and other horrible experiments. Although most people assume such activity is necessary to advance medical science, in reality it does very little to improve human health. The results of animal testing do not directly transfer to humans, and such results can be easily manipulated. . .

Diseases that are artificially induced in animals in a laboratory are never identical to those that occur naturally in humans. Because animal species differ from one another biologically in many significant ways, it becomes even more unlikely that animal experiments will yield results that will be correctly interpreted and applied to the human condition in a meaningful way.

For example, according to former National Cancer Institute director Dr. Richard Klausner, "We have cured mice of cancer for decades, and it simply didn't work in humans." And although at least 85 HIV/AIDS vaccines have been successful in nonhuman primate studies, as of 2010, every one of nearly 200 preventive and therapeutic vaccine trials has failed to demonstrate benefit to humans.

Source C

"Numbers of Animals Used in Research in the United Kingdom," Home Office (2004), *Statistics of Scientific Procedures on Living Animals,* Great Britain, 2003.

The pie graph below comes from a British government agency.

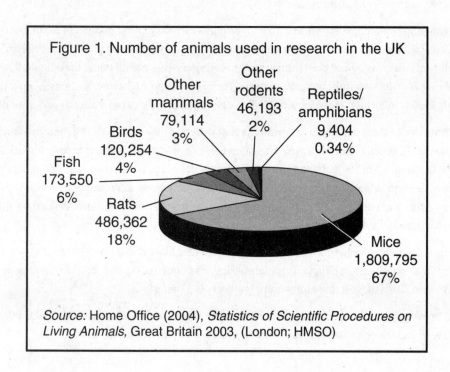

Figure 1. Number of animals used in research in the UK

Other mammals 79,114 3%

Other rodents 46,193 2%

Reptiles/ amphibians 9,404 0.34%

Birds 120,254 4%

Fish 173,550 6%

Rats 486,362 18%

Mice 1,809,795 67%

Source: Home Office (2004), *Statistics of Scientific Procedures on Living Animals,* Great Britain 2003, (London; HMSO)

Source D

Stuart Derbyshire, Ph.D., "Animal Experimentation," Speech at Edinburgh Book Festival, August 19, 2002.

Below are excerpts from a talk given at a book festival by a faculty member in the School of Psychology, University of Birmingham.

. . . Ongoing research with a wide variety of animals includes investigations of AIDS, cancer, heart disease, cystic fibrosis, and muscular dystrophy. The development of artificial arteries, the possibility of reversing spinal cord injury, and the aging process are all being investigated using animal models. The best hopes to cure malaria, Parkinson's and Alzheimer's diseases, epilepsy, clinical obesity, infertility, and a variety of birth defects all rely on current animal experiments.

Without doubt there are many experiments that will fail or lead to no useful therapy—such is the nature of all science. But to suggest that scientists are pointlessly pursuing experiments and models that do not work is just wrong-headed. The process of peer review and grant allocation certainly has its problems, but it is not that bad! If there were good alternatives to animals that worked better or as well, for less money and hassle, scientists would use them. We can be stubborn but we are not totally bananas.

. . . Tom Regan and Richard Ryder argue that animals are like us, that they share with us the capacity for seeing, hearing, believing, remembering, and anticipating and for experiencing pleasure and pain. They suggest that animals are "subjects of a being."

But, in every important sense, they are flat out wrong. Animals and humans do not think alike, feel alike, or experience alike. Humans and animals are not on the same scale.

Source E

"The Ethics of Research Involving Animals: A Guide to the Report," Nuffield Council on Bioethics, May 25, 2005.

The following is excerpted from a report issued by a foundation that studies and reports on ethical issues involving biological and medical research.

The question of defining the moral status of humans and animals often arises in the debate on research involving animals. Are humans morally more important than all animals? Is there a sliding scale with humans at the top and the simplest animals at the bottom? Or are humans and animals morally equal?

We suggest that the proper moral treatment of a being depends on the characteristics it possesses, rather than simply on the species to which it belongs. We identify five morally relevant features:

- Sentience (the capacity to feel pleasure and pain)
- Higher cognitive capacities (for example, the ability to use language and learn complicated tasks, such as making and using tools)
- The capacity to flourish (the ability to satisfy species-specific needs)
- Sociability (being a member of a community)
- Possession of a life (attributing value to life itself)

What weight should be given to each of the morally relevant features in considering whether or not research is acceptable? Are there factors to be weighed against human benefit? Should they be understood as absolute constraints? For example, should any use of animals that are capable of suffering be prohibited, or only the use of those that have higher cognitive capacities?

Many people seem to support a "hybrid" approach. This involves a combination of laying down definite limits for what should and should not happen (for example: "animals with higher cognitive capacities such as chimpanzees should never be used in research") and weighing up the costs and benefits of a particular action (for example, "research that causes minimum pain to a mouse is acceptable if it helps to ascertain the safety of an important and frequently used chemical").

Source F

Clare Haggarty, "Animals in Scientific Research: The Ethical Argument," National Anti-Vivisection Society, *www.navs.org*

The following comes from the website of an organization devoted to protecting animals and their rights.

The worst atrocity we inflict upon animals condemned to scientific research may be the act of removing them from the natural habitat, or breeding them in captivity, and then placing them in the artificial environment of a laboratory cage, where they have no hope of having the kind of life nature intended for them.

In the end, we as a society have a choice. Do we treat our fellow creatures with cruelty and callousness? Or with compassion, respect and justice? As humans, we have the freedom to make that choice. With this freedom comes the moral obligation to make responsible decisions.

Animals have no such choice. Because they cannot say no, they are completely vulnerable to whatever the researcher has in store for them, no matter how much pain and suffering is involved. Animals are unable to understand or claim their right to be alive, to be free from pain and suffering, and fulfill their biological potential. Therefore, it is up to humans to recognize and protect those rights for them, just as we are morally obligated to protect infants, the developmentally disabled, and the mentally ill.

It has been said that the moral progress of our society can be measured by the way it treats animals. Animal experimentation—an institutionalized form of exploitation—stands in the way of moral progress. Now is the time to extend our sphere of ethical concern to all creatures.

Essay Question 2

SUGGESTED TIME: 40 MINUTES

(This question counts as one-third of the total score for Section II.)

> Here are two passages from the essays of the renowned physicist Albert Einstein. After reading them carefully, write an essay that analyzes and compares Einstein's use of language and rhetoric in each.
>
> **Instructions:**
> - Respond to the prompt with a thesis that may establish a line of reasoning.
> - Select and use evidence to develop and support the line of reasoning.
> - Explain the relationship between the evidence and the thesis.
> - Demonstrate an understanding of the rhetorical situation.
> - Use appropriate grammar and punctuation in communicating the argument.

Passage A

Physics deals with "events" in space and time. To each event belongs, besides its place coordinates x, y, z, a time value t. The latter was considered measurable by a clock (ideal periodic process) of negligible spatial extent. This clock C is to be considered at rest at one
Line point of the coordinate system, e.g., at the coordinate origin ($x = y = z = 0$). The time of an
(5) event taking place at a point P (x,y,z) is then defined as the time shown on the clock C simultaneously with the event. Here the concept "simultaneous" was assumed as physically meaningful without special definition. This is a lack of exactness which seems harmless only since with the help of light (whose velocity is practically infinite from the point of view of daily experience) the simultaneity of spatially distant events can apparently be decided
(10) immediately.

Passage B

I am convinced there is only one way to eliminate these grave ills, namely through the establishment of a socialist economy, accompanied by an educational system which would be oriented toward social goals. In such an economy, the means of production are owned by society itself and are utilized in a planned fashion. A planned economy, which adjusts produc-
(15) tion to the needs of the community, would distribute work to be done among all those able to work and would guarantee a livelihood to every man, woman and child. The education of the individual, in addition to promoting his own innate abilities, would attempt to develop in him a sense of responsibility for his fellow men in place of the glorification of power and success in our present society.
(20)   Nevertheless, it is necessary to remember that a planned economy is not yet socialism. A planned economy as such may be accompanied by the complete enslavement of the individual. The achievement of socialism requires the solution of some extremely difficult socio-political problems: is it possible, in view of the far-reaching centralization of political and economic power, to prevent bureaucracy from becoming all-powerful and overweening?
(25) How can the rights of the individual be protected and therewith a democratic counterweight to the power of the bureaucracy be assured?

Essay Question 3

SUGGESTED TIME: 40 MINUTES

(This question counts as one-third of the total score for Section II.)

> The statement below is from the German poet Goethe. It might be applied to schools, government, social services, business, even to families—anyplace, really, where people interact with each other. Is Goethe just expressing an unattainable principle of human behavior, or does his ideal have real-life applicability? In a well-organized essay, comment on the validity of Goethe's statement as a realistic guide to personal relationships. To support your point of view, you may draw evidence from your reading, studies, observation, and personal experience.
>
> **Instructions:**
>
> - Respond to the prompt with a thesis that may establish a line of reasoning.
> - Select and use evidence to develop and support the line of reasoning.
> - Explain the relationship between the evidence and the thesis.
> - Demonstrate an understanding of the rhetorical situation.
> - Use appropriate grammar and punctuation in communicating the argument.

"Treat people as if they were what they ought to be and you help them to become what they are capable of being."

END OF PRACTICE TEST 1

ANSWER KEY
Practice Test 1

Answers to Multiple-Choice Questions

1. **E**	13. **C**	25. **A**	37. **D**
2. **C**	14. **B**	26. **C**	38. **D**
3. **D**	15. **D**	27. **E**	39. **C**
4. **D**	16. **C**	28. **B**	40. **B**
5. **E**	17. **A**	29. **B**	41. **B**
6. **A**	18. **D**	30. **E**	42. **E**
7. **C**	19. **A**	31. **D**	43. **A**
8. **A**	20. **C**	32. **D**	44. **D**
9. **A**	21. **B**	33. **A**	45. **C**
10. **C**	22. **D**	34. **C**	
11. **C**	23. **D**	35. **B**	
12. **E**	24. **C**	36. **E**	

Summary of Answers in Section I (Multiple-Choice)

Number of correct answers _____

Use this information when you calculate your score for this exam. See page 241.

Answer Explanations to Multiple-Choice Questions

Passage 1—An excerpt from Beryl Markham, *West with the Night*

1. **(E)** By using "you" the narrator generalizes human experience, but she's really just thinking about what she has learned.

2. **(C)** Because loneliness is foremost in her mind, the speaker declares that much of human activity is motivated by the desire to avoid such feelings.

3. **(D)** The "story" in the passage takes place inside the narrator's head. It is dominated by discoveries about herself and ruminations about, among other things, loneliness, sights seen far below, and the behavior of the aircraft itself.

4. **(D)** Until the switch in pronoun person, the narration is rooted in the past and in what the speaker has discovered about herself. The switch in pronoun occurs just after having realized how isolated she's become, when she calls herself a stranger.

5. **(E)** Piloting a plane provides the "security of solitude, the exhilaration of escape" (lines 15–16). These feelings contrast with the cares of the world below and "the small sorrow of rain" (line 18). Choices (C) and (D) may be implied by the rain, but the narrator is literally and figuratively above it all and feeling "selfishly triumphant" (line 17).

6. **(A)** The narrator is happily startled (lines 11–12) and exhilarated (line 16) by the experience of being aloft and alone.

7. **(C)** The sentence explains why the distance is compared to "so much time used up." To some extent it also serves other functions, but it does not show that equating time and distance is a sign of pilot disorientation.

8. **(A)** For someone subscribing to the notion that abhorrence of loneliness is a common human frailty, it seems contradictory to set off alone on such a journey. But that's just the point. Her flight is just the sort of enterprise that keeps loneliness at bay.

9. **(A)** All the other choices are feasible interpretations, but not (A), which, in the context, is virtually impenetrable.

10. **(C)** After reciting the facts about where she is and what she sees, the narrator dramatizes the feelings and thoughts evoked by the experience of lifting the aircraft into the sky. The passage may contain elements named by the other choices, but in this specific context, they are less noteworthy than (C).

11. **(C)** Having concentrated on the emotional dimensions of flying solo, the writer has chosen to enhance the narrative with facts and figures.

Passage 2—An excerpt from Arthur James, Earl of Balfour, "On the Benefits of Reading" (1887)

12. **(E)** The speaker's intentions are made clear by his self-assured tone, the allusion to "advisers," the use of first-person pronouns, and the phrase "no doubt." To win the confidence of his audience, he may deliberately be avoiding hyperbole or other unsettling rhetoric.

13. **(C)** The speaker is about to challenge the conventional theory that we must learn about the past in order to avoid repeating its mistakes in the future. His words suggest that for him it's a dead issue.

14. **(B)** In spite of his decisiveness, the speaker expresses reservations about being able to predict how any country will behave, indicating a realistic awareness of what he can and cannot do.

15. **(D)** As suggested by the first two sentences, the main subject of the passage is the traditional claim that studying the past enables us to better plan the future. In the third sentence, the speaker questions the credibility of that theory.

16. **(C)** The speaker poetically likens a nation's future to the experience of waterborne travelers who encounter unforeseen obstacles that may or may not permit safe arrival at a specific destination.

17. **(A)** All the choices have some merit, but the speaker's over-the-top focus on the random flow of water is meant to open minds to a new way of thinking about history.

18. **(D)** By rejecting the notion that historic events are most useful as a key to predicting the future, the speaker indirectly prepares his listeners to accept a new and "spectacular" approach to history—or at least to give it a try.

19. **(A)** The speaker is supporting his claim that studying history can be spectacularly enjoyable.

20. **(C)** The speaker seems energized by the drama of the "vast epic" that tells the story of mankind through the ages.

21. **(B)** The text is crowded with references to stories, epics, controversies, heroism, fate, subject of contemplation, and other appealing allusions.

22. **(D)** The speaker intends to broaden his remarks to include events of the present as well as "special periods" of the past.

23. **(D)** The speaker asserts that historians, if they are determined, can make "close friends" even among the "long departed."

24. **(C)** In the climax of the passage, the speaker challenges the observation that history buffs believe their interest in the past is based on philosophy. Rather, he asserts, the lure of history is generated by the details.

25. **(A)** Shifts in pronoun usage enable the speaker, first, to introduce himself, then to speak on behalf of himself and everyone else in the audience, and finally to criticize others—that crowd of "frivolous," "useless," and self-delusional readers and thinkers.

Passage 3—The History of Science

26. **(C)** This version is not only the most succinct, but also is stated as an inarguable fact that matches the straightforward content of the passage.

27. **(E)** This choice logically introduces a discussion of the earliest period of science. (A) is ambiguous. (B) is awkwardly worded. (C) and (D) misplace the emphasis on the length of the period rather than on what occurred at the time.

28. **(B)** The goal is accomplished by a new choice of words and the proper placement and punctuation of the transitional word "however."

29. **(B)** combines sentences, removes needless words, and includes all the essential details. It is the most readable version of the text.

30. **(E)** Each of the other choices is faulty in some way: (A) is awkwardly worded. (B) uses the wrong verb tense. (C) contains a pronoun with an ambiguous antecedent. (D) includes the redundancy "true facts."

31. **(D)** All the other choices suffer from misplaced-modification errors.

32. **(D)** is the only choice that provides continuity in the narrative.

33. **(A)** is the best answer because the writer is trying to intensify the problem in order to show what a remarkable achievement it was for science, if not to unlock the secret of life, at least to begin to understand it better.

Passage 4—The Development of Jazz

34. **(C)** is the best choice because it sets up a contrast between ancient music and jazz. (A) is not appropriate because it implies—incorrectly—that sentence 1 is in some way contentious. Likewise, the other choices are irrelevant in the context.

35. **(B)** makes the point and neutralizes the text without casting aspersions on naysayers. Other choices are awkwardly expressed or contain redundancies.

36. **(E)** coincides with the content of the passage, the evolution of jazz in New Orleans. The other choices pertain to matters found elsewhere in the passage, or not at all.

37. **(D)** is written concisely. It also uses parallelism in a way that promotes clarity. Other choices are wordy, vague, or awkwardly expressed.

38. **(D)** According to the previous paragraph, all the conditions for jazz to flourish had been met, much to the delight of jazz fans.

39. **(C)** The sentence serves as a detail that follows the claim that new music was being heard "around the country." The next paragraph also discusses music heard elsewhere, although its focus is on Chicago.

40. **(B)** The racial make-up of jazz groups, doubtlessly vital to the history of jazz, is not mentioned in this passage. All the other choices contain information that touches on topics discussed in the passage.

Passage 5—San Francisco Earthquake

41. **(B)** is the only choice that qualifies. The reference to a particular day is meant to arouse curiosity, and the subject matter leads directly into the sentence that follows.

42. **(E)** works best as an expression of the writer's dismay about the lack of understanding about earthquakes at the time. (D), while also a phrase suggesting displeasure, is weaker than (E) and also requires an indication of who is regretful, as in "With regret, I . . . ."

43. **(A)** captures the essence of the experience most effectively. Other choices are weakened by wordiness, redundancies, lack of parallelism, and other flaws.

44. **(D)** All the other choices are evidence of the earthquake's destructiveness.

45. **(C)** The added sentence eliminates the gap in meaning by explaining just how the realty company came to the aid of the Italian community and thereby enabled homes to be built more quickly.

Answers to Essay Questions

For an overview of how essays are graded, turn to "How Essays Are Read and Evaluated," page 37.

Although answers to the essay questions will vary greatly, the following descriptions suggest a possible approach to each question and contain ideas that could be used in a response to the question. Perhaps your essay contains many of the same ideas. If not, don't be alarmed. Your ideas may be at least as insightful, or even more so, as those below.

Essay Question 1

On this issue, it's unusual to take an extreme position, although those who do probably come down on the side of animal protection. But not always.

Some Arguments In Favor of Using Animals for Research:

- Millions of people owe their good health to vaccines developed with the help of animals. (Source A)
- Many diseases, from diabetes to heart disease, can be treated with drugs developed in laboratories using animals. (Source A)
- The vast majority of animals used in research—mice and rats—are of a lower order than humans and most other mammals. (Source C)
- Animals and humans should not be equated because they are not on the same scale; humans are special. (Source D)

Some Arguments Against Using Animals for Research:

- The results of animal testing do not directly transfer to humans. (Source B)
- Literally millions of animals are used in research in just one year in just one country—England. (Source C)
- Employing animals for research should not be undertaken without considering several morally relevant features, among them the cognitive level of the animal. (Source E)
- The treatment of animals in the lab is cruel and callous. (Source F)
- The moral position of a society can be measured by the way its animals are treated. (Source F)

Essay Question 2, Based on Passages by Albert Einstein

Although the two passages were written by the same person, they are dramatically different from each other. In the first, Einstein explains a phenomenon in physics, a world in which he is very much at home. Much of the passage is factual, precise, and impersonal. He writes, for example, "The latter was considered measurable . . . ," using a passive construction in order to avoid using the first person. The technical nature of the passage is evident in several symbols and formulas and in the specialized language of physics, e.g., "negligible spatial extent" and "the simultaneity of spatially distant events."

Unlike the first passage, the second is written speculatively. Gone are the voice of authority and the technical language and formulas—replaced herein by vague generalizations couched in the language of economics and sociology. Consider such phrases as "an educational system . . . oriented toward social goals," and "the education of the individual . . . would attempt to develop . . . a sense of responsibility." This sort of language may sound good, but it lacks substance. It's jargon, plain and simple. We are hearing the views of someone who may be a thoughtful human being, but the words resemble empty platitudes. Instead of stating his case forcefully, Einstein resorts to the repeated use of "would," a word that suggests tentativeness. Had he been more confident and well-informed on the topic, his language would have reflected greater certainty. He would have been better served by using "will," a far more decisive word.

Essay Question 3, Based on a Statement by Goethe

The task in this question is to support, challenge, or qualify Goethe's statement. If you agree with Goethe, your essay should contain examples—possibly in anecdotal form—of people living up to expectations because they were treated with respect and dignity. You may remember a time, for example, when you were treated like an adult, and so you behaved like one, or, in contrast, because you were treated as a child, you acted silly or immature.

If you cannot subscribe to Goethe's point of view, you should cite examples of people being treated well but acting badly. A striking example occurred not long ago when a high school student in New York murdered his English teacher after the teacher had gone out of his way to help the student deal with both academic and personal problems. One could argue, of course, that because this case was an aberration, it cannot reasonably support a generalization about human behavior. In fact, beware of drawing any broad conclusions based on a single event or example— both in your essay writing and in life.

How to Score the Essays

The following essay-scoring guidelines apply to all three essays on the exam. The maximum score on an essay is 6; the minimum, 0.

Points are awarded in three categories:

1. Thesis (0–1 point)
2. Evidence and Commentary (0–4 points)
3. Sophistication (0–1 point)

THESIS (0–1 point)

No credit is given for an absent, erroneous, or incoherent thesis or one that merely restates or paraphrases the essay prompt.

One point is awarded for a thesis that states or strongly implies a reasonable interpretation of the issue raised by the prompt for Essay #1, the synthesis essay. Similarly, for Essay #2 one point is given for a reasonable thesis related to rhetoric in the given passage. For Essay #3 add a point for a thesis that clearly articulates a position on the issue raised by the prompt.

EVIDENCE AND COMMENTARY (0–4 points)

No points are given for restating the thesis in different words or for material irrelevant to the prompt.

One point is earned for evidence that tends to help develop the thesis.

Two points are given for evidence that clearly supports the thesis but may not add significantly to the writer's line of reasoning.*

Three points are awarded in Essay #1 for evidence that supports the thesis and also begins to show how source material supports your point of view. Give three points for evidence in Essay #2 that identifies and offers some analysis of rhetoric in the passage. Likewise, in Essay #3, give three points for specific evidence that helps to develop an argument for or against the main idea expressed by the prompt.

Four points indicate that you have consistently and effectively included compelling evidence to support all claims in a line of reasoning and also have clearly employed at least three sources to strengthen your position on the given issue (Essay #1), identified ample relevant evidence of rhetoric in the given passage (Essay #2), and cited compelling evidence to support your argument in favor of or against the given issue (Essay #3).

SOPHISTICATION (0–1 point)

No credit is given for ideas, however discerning, that you mention but don't develop.

One point is awarded for the development of ideas that broaden an interpretation of the issue (Essay #1), cite and explain significant rhetorical features of the passage (Essay #2), and discuss the opinions expressed in the given passage (Essay #3) by one or more of the following:

   (a) Identifying and discussing complexities or tensions in the text.
   (b) Illuminating an interpretation of the work by situating it within a broader context.
   (c) Suggesting alternative interpretations of the work.
   (d) Employing a consistently vivid and persuasive writing style.

Use of Standard English: No specific credit is given for the use of standard English. Readers are bound to be favorably impressed, however, by well-expressed, economical, virtually error-free prose.

---

*The term **"line of reasoning"** refers to the means by which an idea or thesis is supported. For instance, an essay may focus on the writer's choice of words, use of logic, sequence of ideas, or even the essay's title in order to validate the thesis. A poor line of reasoning exists when there is a gap between the thesis and the evidence presented.

Essay Evaluation Worksheet

In the spaces below enter the number of credits earned in each category. See pages 238–239 for detailed scoring guidelines.

	Essay 1 Synthesis Essay	Essay 2 Analytical Essay	Essay 3 Argumentative Essay
Category			
Thesis (0–1)			
Evidence and Commentary (0–4)			
Sophistication (0–1)			
TOTAL SCORE ON EACH ESSAY (0–6)			

Enter each essay score on the Test Score Worksheet.

Test Score Worksheet

Use this page to calculate your score on the AP English Language Practice Test 1.

SECTION 1. Multiple-Choice Questions

STEP A Enter the number of correct answers (out of 45) _____

SECTION 2. Essay Questions

STEP B Transfer your essay scores (0–6) from your Essay Evaluation Worksheet.

Essay 1 (Synthesis) _____   Essay 2 (Analysis) _____   Essay 3 (Argumentative) _____

Add the three essay scores _____   (This is your Essay Raw Score.)

STEP C Multiply Essay Raw Score by 3.055 _____

For your Final Essay Score, round to the nearest whole number. _____

SECTION 3. Composite Score

To determine your Composite Score, add the figures from STEP A and STEP C.

STEP A _____   +   STEP C _____   =   Composite Score _____

SECTION 4. Convert Composite Score to AP Test Score

Composite Score	AP Grade
90–100	5
68–89	4
36–67	3
13–35	2
1–12	1

_____

AP essays are ordinarily judged in relation to other essays written on the same topic at the same time. Therefore, the scores you assign yourself for these essays may not be the same as the scores you would earn on an actual exam.

ANSWER SHEET
Practice Test 2

Multiple-Choice Questions

Time—1 hour

1. Ⓐ Ⓑ Ⓒ Ⓓ Ⓔ   13. Ⓐ Ⓑ Ⓒ Ⓓ Ⓔ   25. Ⓐ Ⓑ Ⓒ Ⓓ Ⓔ   37. Ⓐ Ⓑ Ⓒ Ⓓ Ⓔ

2. Ⓐ Ⓑ Ⓒ Ⓓ Ⓔ   14. Ⓐ Ⓑ Ⓒ Ⓓ Ⓔ   26. Ⓐ Ⓑ Ⓒ Ⓓ Ⓔ   38. Ⓐ Ⓑ Ⓒ Ⓓ Ⓔ

3. Ⓐ Ⓑ Ⓒ Ⓓ Ⓔ   15. Ⓐ Ⓑ Ⓒ Ⓓ Ⓔ   27. Ⓐ Ⓑ Ⓒ Ⓓ Ⓔ   39. Ⓐ Ⓑ Ⓒ Ⓓ Ⓔ

4. Ⓐ Ⓑ Ⓒ Ⓓ Ⓔ   16. Ⓐ Ⓑ Ⓒ Ⓓ Ⓔ   28. Ⓐ Ⓑ Ⓒ Ⓓ Ⓔ   40. Ⓐ Ⓑ Ⓒ Ⓓ Ⓔ

5. Ⓐ Ⓑ Ⓒ Ⓓ Ⓔ   17. Ⓐ Ⓑ Ⓒ Ⓓ Ⓔ   29. Ⓐ Ⓑ Ⓒ Ⓓ Ⓔ   41. Ⓐ Ⓑ Ⓒ Ⓓ Ⓔ

6. Ⓐ Ⓑ Ⓒ Ⓓ Ⓔ   18. Ⓐ Ⓑ Ⓒ Ⓓ Ⓔ   30. Ⓐ Ⓑ Ⓒ Ⓓ Ⓔ   42. Ⓐ Ⓑ Ⓒ Ⓓ Ⓔ

7. Ⓐ Ⓑ Ⓒ Ⓓ Ⓔ   19. Ⓐ Ⓑ Ⓒ Ⓓ Ⓔ   31. Ⓐ Ⓑ Ⓒ Ⓓ Ⓔ   43. Ⓐ Ⓑ Ⓒ Ⓓ Ⓔ

8. Ⓐ Ⓑ Ⓒ Ⓓ Ⓔ   20. Ⓐ Ⓑ Ⓒ Ⓓ Ⓔ   32. Ⓐ Ⓑ Ⓒ Ⓓ Ⓔ   44. Ⓐ Ⓑ Ⓒ Ⓓ Ⓔ

9. Ⓐ Ⓑ Ⓒ Ⓓ Ⓔ   21. Ⓐ Ⓑ Ⓒ Ⓓ Ⓔ   33. Ⓐ Ⓑ Ⓒ Ⓓ Ⓔ   45. Ⓐ Ⓑ Ⓒ Ⓓ Ⓔ

10. Ⓐ Ⓑ Ⓒ Ⓓ Ⓔ   22. Ⓐ Ⓑ Ⓒ Ⓓ Ⓔ   34. Ⓐ Ⓑ Ⓒ Ⓓ Ⓔ

11. Ⓐ Ⓑ Ⓒ Ⓓ Ⓔ   23. Ⓐ Ⓑ Ⓒ Ⓓ Ⓔ   35. Ⓐ Ⓑ Ⓒ Ⓓ Ⓔ

12. Ⓐ Ⓑ Ⓒ Ⓓ Ⓔ   24. Ⓐ Ⓑ Ⓒ Ⓓ Ⓔ   36. Ⓐ Ⓑ Ⓒ Ⓓ Ⓔ

Practice Test 2

Section I

TIME: 1 HOUR

> **DIRECTIONS:** *Questions 1–13.* Carefully read the following passage and answer the accompanying questions.

The passage comes from the quill of a renowned essayist of the 16th century.

Passage 1

I am not excessively fond of salads or fruit, with the exception of melons. My father hated every kind of sauce; I like them all. Eating too much makes me uncomfortable; but in respect of its properties I am not yet very certain that any kind of food disagrees with me.

Line Nor have I noticed that I am affected by full or new moons, by autumn or spring.

(5)　　We are subject to fickle and inexplicable changes. For example, radishes, which I first found to agree with me, afterwards disagreed, and now they agree again. In several things I have found my stomach and palate to vary in the same way: I have changed more than once from white wine to claret, and back again from claret to white wine.

I have a dainty tooth for fish, and the meatless days are my meat-days; my fasts are my

(10) feasts. Besides, I believe that it is, as some people say, more easily digested than meat. As it goes against my conscience to eat meat on fish-days, so my taste rebels against mixing meat and fish; the difference seems to me too wide.

From my youth up I have occasionally skipped a meal; either to sharpen my appetite for the next day (for, as Epicurus used to fast and make lean meals in order to accustom

(15) his greed to dispense with plenty, I do so, on the contrary, in order to train my greed to take better advantage of plenty and to enjoy it more cheerfully); or I used to fast to keep my strength for the performance of some mental or bodily action; for both my body and mind are made cruelly sluggish by repletion. . . . To cure my ailing digestion, I say that we should not so much look to what we eat as to whom we eat with.

(20)　　To me no dressing is so acceptable, and no sauce so appetizing, as that derived from good company. I think it is more wholesome to eat more at leisure with a good friend, and less, and to eat oftener. But I would give hunger and appetite their due; I should take no pleasure in dragging through three or four wretched repasts a day, restricted by doctors' orders. Who will assure me that I can recover at supper-time the good appetite I had this

(25) morning? Let us old men especially take the first opportunity that comes our way. Let us leave the making of dietaries to doctors and almanac makers . . . .

I do not cover my legs and thighs more in winter than in summer: simple silk hose. For the relief of my colds I gave way to the habit of keeping my head warmer, and my belly on account of the colic. But in a few days my ailments became accustomed to them and scorned

(30) my ordinary precautions: from a cap I advanced to a kerchief, and from a bonnet to a lined hat. The wadding of my doublet is now only ornamental. All that would be of no avail unless I added a hare's skin or a vulture's plumage, with a skull-cap for the head. Continue this gradual progress and you will go a long way. I shall take care not to do so, and would gladly go back to where I began, if I dared. "Have you developed a new ailment? Is the remedy no

(35) longer of any avail? You have grown accustomed to it? Then try another." In this way they ruin their health who allow themseves to be fettered by enforced rules, and superstitiously adhere to them; they need more and more, and after that more again. There is no end.

1. Which of the following best describes the rhetorical function of the last sentence of the first paragraph (line 4)?

   (A) It helps to establish the speaker's credentials as an expert on the topic of the passage.
   (B) It challenges a commonly held superstition to be discussed later in the passage.
   (C) It introduces a major theme in the passage.
   (D) It refers to an old saying about the consequences of overeating.
   (E) It creates a rhetorical link between paragraph 1 and the first sentence of paragraph 2.

2. The writer's rhetorical purpose in alluding in line 4 to "full and new moons" and also to seasons of the year is primarily to

   (A) acknowledge his awareness that some foods are not available all the time.
   (B) admit that some common superstitions may have merit.
   (C) confess that he's occasionally fallen prey to irrational decision making.
   (D) ridicule the notion that the moon and seasons guide our eating decisions.
   (E) reject the idea that food choices need to vary according to the months and seasons.

3. Describing his culinary preferences in lines 1–8, the writer's primary purpose is to

   (A) outline standards for pleasurable eating.
   (B) stress that regularly changing one's diet is good for you.
   (C) flaunt his tendency to change his diet whenever he wants.
   (D) urge the members of his audience to vary their food choices.
   (E) describe a diet that his audience may do well to emulate.

4. The speaker's references to radishes and to claret (lines 5–8) function in all the following ways EXCEPT to

   (A) prove the validity of the second paragraph's topic sentence.
   (B) identify the changes that the speaker has experienced.
   (C) define the word "fickle" (line 5).
   (D) add to the litany of the speaker's personal quirks.
   (E) hint that the speaker has switched from a serious to an ironic tone.

5. The description of the speaker's "dainty tooth for fish" (line 9) contributes to the unity of the passage by

   (A) contrasting the tastes of two different foods.
   (B) adding further details to the speaker's self-portrait.
   (C) condemning those who do not observe meatless days.
   (D) drawing a parallel between different kinds of cooking.
   (E) commenting on the absurdity of the speaker's taste in food.

6. Which of the following best describes the rhetorical function of lines 21–25?

    (A) They serve as a transition between the paragraphs that come both before and after.

    (B) They support the speaker's assertion that he likes all sauces (line 2).

    (C) They provide evidence contrary to material in the previous paragraph.

    (D) They reiterate an idea presented in a previous paragraph.

    (E) They state a logical conclusion based on statements in the previous paragraph.

7. The writer's main rhetorical purpose in lines 22–26 (starting with "But I would give hunger . . .") is to argue that

    (A) his advanced age accounts in part for his culinary eccentricities.

    (B) the amount one eats is more important than what one eats.

    (C) one should give physicians their due as responsible guides regarding what one should and should not eat.

    (D) after a lifetime of eating whatever he desired, there is no reason to change now.

    (E) "doctors and almanac makers" (line 26) help people like the speaker to age gracefully.

8. In order to leave a rhetorical effect on his audience, the speaker overstates some of his thoughts. In context, which of the following excerpts is the idea most exaggerated?

    (A) "from white wine to claret, and back again" (line 8)

    (B) "body and mind are made cruelly sluggish" (lines 17–18)

    (C) "three or four wretched repasts a day" (line 23)

    (D) "from a bonnet to a lined hat" (lines 30–31)

    (E) "a hare's skin and a vulture's plumage" (line 32)

9. Drawing contrasts is an effective rhetorical strategy. The principal contrast drawn by the speaker throughout the passage is between

    (A) theory and fact.

    (B) conventions and individual preferences.

    (C) old wives' tales and modern practices.

    (D) youth and old age.

    (E) restraint and freedom.

10. In context, which of the following statements accurately describes the writer's tone?

    (A) His tone when discussing salads and fruits (line 1) is hypercritical.

    (B) He uses a vacillating tone when talking about radishes (lines 5–6).

    (C) When the subject is meat and fish (lines 11–12), he adopts a peevish tone.

    (D) The tone of his comment on skipping meals (line 13) is conciliatory.

    (E) The tone of his reference to dinner companions (lines 20–21) is compassionate.

11. The rhetoric in the passage creates a portrait of a man who can best be described as

    (A) shamelessly self-absorbed.

    (B) well educated.

    (C) adaptable to change.

    (D) cultured and sophisticated.

    (E) pious and self-righteous.

12. The passage as a whole can best be described as

   (A) an authority's prescription for a better diet.
   (B) an anecdote about old-fashioned eating customs.
   (C) an account of one man's culinary preferences.
   (D) a comparison of the speaker and his father.
   (E) a reflection on unhealthful eating habits.

13. In the context of the passage, all of the following excerpts contain the same rhetorical device EXCEPT

   (A) "I first found to agree with me, afterwards disagreed" (lines 5–6).
   (B) "changed . . . from white wine to claret, and back again" (lines 7–8).
   (C) "not so much look to what we eat as to whom we eat with" (line 19).
   (D) "eat more at leisure with a good friend, and less, and to eat oftener" (lines 21–22).
   (E) "they need more and more, and after that more again." (line 37).

DIRECTIONS: *Questions 14–24.* Carefully read the following passage and answer the accompanying questions.

This passage by a 20th-century author is an excerpt from an essay about Henry David Thoreau's Walden.

Passage 2

Allen Cove, Summer, 1954

    Walden is an oddity in American letters. It may well be the oddest of our distinguished oddities. For many it is a great deal too odd, and for many it is a particular bore. I have not found it to be a well-liked book among my acquaintances, although usually spoken of with

Line respect, and one literary critic for whom I have the highest regard can find no reason for

(5) anyone's giving *Walden* a second thought. To admire the book is, in fact, something of an embarrassment, for the mass of men have an indistinct notion that its author was a sort of Nature Boy.

    I think it is of some advantage to encounter the book at a period in one's life when the normal anxieties and enthusiasms and rebellions of youth closely resemble those of

(10) Thoreau in that spring of 1845 when he borrowed an ax, went out to the woods, and began to whack down some trees for timber. Received at such a juncture, the book is like an invitation to life's dance, assuring the troubled recipient that no matter what befalls him in the way of success or failure he will always be welcome at the party—that the music is played for him, too, if he will but listen and move his feet. In effect, that is what the book is—an

(15) invitation, unengraved; and it stirs one as a young girl is stirred by her first big party bid. Many think it is a sermon; many set it down as an attempt to rearrange society; some think it none of these.

    It still seems to me the best youth's companion yet written by an American, for it carries a solemn warning against the loss of one's valuables, it advances a good argument for

(20) traveling light and trying new adventures, it rings with the power of positive adoration, it contains religious feeling without religious images, and it steadfastly refuses to record bad news. If our colleges and universities were alert, they would present a cheap pocket

edition of the book to every senior upon graduating, along with his diploma, or instead of it. Even if some senior were to take it literally and start felling trees, there could be worse

(25) mishaps: the ax is older than the Dictaphone* and it is just as well for a young man to see what kind of chips he leaves before listening to the sound of his own voice. And even if some were to get no further than the table of contents, they would learn how to name eighteen chapters by the use of only thirty-nine words and would see how sweet are the uses of brevity.

(30)   If Thoreau had merely left us an account of a man's life in the woods or if he had simply retreated to the woods and there recorded his complaints about society, or even if he had contrived to include both records in one essay, *Walden* would probably not have lived a hundred years. As things turned out, Thoreau, very likely without knowing quite what he was up to, took man's relation to Nature and man's dilemma in society and man's capacity

(35) for elevating his spirit and he beat all these matters together, in a wild free interval of self-justification and delight, and produced an original gourmet omelette from which people can draw nourishment in a hungry day. Walden is one of the vitamin-enriched American dishes.

       If it were a little less good than it is, or even a little less queer, it would be an abominable

(40) book. Even as it is, it will continue to baffle and annoy the literal mind and all those who are unable to stomach its caprices and imbibe its theme. Certainly, the plodding economist will continue to have rough going if he hopes to emerge from the book with a clear system of economic thought. Thoreau's assault on the Concord society of the mid-nineteenth century has the quality of a modern Western: he rides into the subject at top speed, shooting

(45) in all directions. Many of his shots ricochet and nick him on the rebound, and throughout the melee there is a horrendous cloud of inconsistencies and contradictions, and when the shooting dies down and the air clears, one is impressed chiefly by the courage of the rider and by how splendid it was that somebody should have ridden in there and raised all that ruckus.

(50)   When he went to the pond, Thoreau struck an attitude deliberately. But posturing was not to draw the attention of others to him but rather to draw his own attention more closely to himself. "I learned this at least by my experiment: that if one advances confidently in the direction of his dreams, and endeavors to live the life which he has imagined, he will meet with a success unexpected in common hours." The sentence has the power to resuscitate

(55) the youth drowning in a sea of doubt. I recall my exhilaration upon reading it many years ago, in a time of hesitation and despair. It restored me to health. And now in 1954 when I salute Henry Thoreau on the hundredth birthday of his book, I am merely paying off an old score—or an installment on it.

A type of tape recorder often used in offices to dictate letters and memos.

14. The writer's intent of the opening paragraph (lines 1–7) is mainly to

   (A) acknowledge that *Walden* is not an easy read.
   (B) admit that *Walden* is not his favorite book.
   (C) raise the reader's curiosity about what makes *Walden* an "oddity."
   (D) prod readers into making up their own minds about the book's success.
   (E) prepare readers for a devastating review of Thoreau's book.

15. The rhetoric in lines 10–11, describing what he did in the spring of 1845, implies mainly that Thoreau

   (A) had a specific plan of action in mind.
   (B) was determined to make a name for himself.
   (C) acted impulsively.
   (D) had a devil-may-care attitude.
   (E) had energy to spare.

16. In the second paragraph (lines 8–17), which of the following best characterizes the writer's position on the relevance of reading *Walden* at a young age?

   (A) The book is "like an invitation" (lines 11–12). It can be accepted, ignored, or turned down.
   (B) Because he was a young man when he went into the woods, Thoreau serves as a role model for young readers.
   (C) Although not all young people are rebels, enough of them are to make *Walden* a kind of handbook for youth.
   (D) On principle, thoughtful young readers may be unable to accept Thoreau's ideas.
   (E) Thoreau offers youthful readers a plan for figuring out their place in the world.

17. By using the locution "began to whack down some trees" (lines 10–11) the writer intends mainly to

   (A) illustrate that Thoreau was typical of young men going through the "normal" stages of life alluded to in line 9.
   (B) support his assertion in line 7 that Thoreau was a "sort of Nature Boy."
   (C) characterize the free-spirited personality of young Henry Thoreau.
   (D) switch the tone of the passage from generally cerebral to more down-to-earth and physical.
   (E) editorialize on how attitudes toward trees changed between 1845 and 1954, when the passage was written.

18. Which of the following best describes the writer's exigence in the passage?

   (A) The mixed messages that *Walden* sends to young readers
   (B) Thoughtful commentary on how to live a productive and satisfying life
   (C) The need for universal truths
   (D) The serenity and grandeur that can be found in nature
   (E) The dictum that to understand the world one must retreat from it

19. In context, the third paragraph (lines 18–29) can be used to support which of the following claims about the writer's tone?

   (A) His tone when discussing *Walden*'s function as a book for young people is hyperbolic.
   (B) His tone when mentioning religion is disapproving.
   (C) He uses a reverent tone when referring to colleges and universities.
   (D) When referring to felling trees he adopts a sentimental tone.
   (E) He adopts an ironic tone when discussing *Walden*'s table of contents.

20. By figuratively likening *Walden* to an "original gourmet omelette," (line 36) the writer intends to convey the idea that Thoreau's work

   (A) may not suit all tastes.
   (B) appeals mostly to sophisticates.
   (C) is a basic treatment of the subject but tends to be effete.
   (D) is comprised largely of a harmonious mix of quality ingredients.
   (E) is more than a little pretentious.

21. The writer's opinions about *Walden* in lines 39–49 are primarily meant to

   (A) reiterate the wide disparities in readers' views of the book.
   (B) confuse the reader as a means to stimulate curiosity.
   (C) prepare prospective readers for a challenging but stimulating ride.
   (D) entice readers with the promise of an unusual experience.
   (E) argue that contradictions in the book don't impede understanding it.

22. Which of the following best describes the rhetorical effect of the writer's frequent use of "if . . . then" sentence construction, as in lines 22, 30, *et al.?*

   (A) It heightens the validity of the conclusions drawn by the writer.
   (B) It enhances the unity of the passage.
   (C) It uses the text of the passage to echo *Walden*'s theme, an alternate lifestyle.
   (D) It reflects the conviction and sincerity of the writer.
   (E) It transforms the writer's opinions into facts.

23. Which of the following excerpts does the writer use specifically to support an assertion made early in the passage that readers of *Walden* should be young?

   (A) "it advances a good argument for traveling light" (lines 19–20)
   (B) "it steadfastly refuses to record bad news" (lines 21–22)
   (C) "to see what kind of chips he leaves before listening to the sound of his own voice" (lines 25–26)
   (D) "his shots ricochet and nick him on the rebound" (line 45)
   (E) "not to draw the attention of others to him but rather to draw his own attention more closely to himself" (lines 51–52)

24. The writer's purpose in the last paragraph (lines 50–58) can best be described as an effort to

   (A) vicariously relive his experience reading *Walden*.
   (B) inform his audience that Thoreau's initial motives for telling the story of his life in the woods changed over time.
   (C) express gratitude to Thoreau for writing an autobiographical story.
   (D) inspire his audience to read *Walden* because long ago it had life-altering effects on him.
   (E) advise young readers that *Walden* offers *wise* counsel to help them overcome self-doubt.

DIRECTIONS: *Questions 25–32.* Carefully read the following passage and answer the accompanying questions.

The passage below is a draft.

Passage 3

(1) For an artist to achieve the highest position in the history of human culture, they must have a number of circumstances going their way. (2) It must be a significant moment in cultural history and in the development of the craft. (3) Ludwig van Beethoven was born into a family of professional musicians in Bonn in the Rhineland. (4) He learned the rudiments of music from his father and was later taught by the best musicians in the court. (5) From the first, his genius impressed all with whom he came in contact.

(6) The first decade of his career was characterized by youthful exuberance, by a proud consciousness of his own powers. (7) Then, just as he was beginning to realize his ambitions, fate struck a staggering blow. (8) He, who had been hailed as the most promising musician of his time, began to lose his hearing.

(9) Fifty-seven years later, as a crusty old bachelor, so deaf he couldn't hear his own music played by a full orchestra, yet still able to hear thunder, he shook his fist at the roaring heavens for the last time and died. (10) He died as he had lived, challenging God and defying the universe. (11) He was Defiance Incarnate. (12) For instance, encountering a Grand Duke and his court in public, his hat was jammed down on his head while striding through the aristocratic entourage. (13) He had the manners of a disobliging steamroller (most steamrollers are abjectly obliging and conciliatory); and he was rather less particular about his dress than a scarecrow. (14) In fact, he was once arrested as a tramp because the police authorities refused to believe that such a tatterdemalion could be a famous composer, much less a temple of the most turbulent spirit that ever walked the streets of Vienna, Europe's musical capital.

(15) Beethoven was only nineteen when the French Revolution electrified Europe. (16) That event aroused visions of liberty, fraternity and equality that he carried with him for the rest of his life. (17) It struck at the heart of the established order. (18) Young Beethoven, a rebel by temperament, became one of thousands all over Europe to whom revolutionary stirrings held out the promise of a new order. (19) He adopted as his motto the thoroughly republican sentiment, "Freedom above all!"

(20) That Beethoven's spirit was turbulent is beyond question. (21) The impetuous fury of his strength, which he could quite easily contain and control but often would not, goes

(30) beyond anything of the kind to be found in the works of other composers. (22) No other composer has ever melted his hearers into complete sentimentality by the tender beauty of his music, comprised of serene and memorable themes and motifs that are typically Beethovian. (23) Nobody but Beethoven could govern Beethoven; and when, as it happened when the fit was on him, he deliberately refused to govern himself.

25. In order to begin the passage with a standard English sentence that is both related to the text and accords with the writing style and tone of the passage that follows, which of the following would be the best replacement for the underlined section of sentence 1 (reproduced below)?

    For an artist to achieve the highest position in the history of human culture, they must have a number of circumstances going their way.

    (A) circumstances should be lined up
    (B) they should have circumstances in their corner
    (C) a number of circumstances must coincide
    (D) the circumstances for him or her must be right
    (E) similar circumstances and conditions should prevail

26. The writer wants an effective transition between sentences 2 and 3 (reproduced below)—that is, between the opening of the passage and the introduction of the person who'll be the focus of the passage.

    (2) It must be a significant moment in cultural history and in the development of the craft. (3) Ludwig van Beethoven was born into a family of musicians in Bonn in the Rhineland.

    Which of the following best achieves that purpose?

    (A) Prayers were answered precisely during the heyday of two famous classical composers, Haydn and Mozart.
    (B) Somebody appeared in the history of music at precisely the right time.
    (C) At the time there were several candidates.
    (D) These conditions were ideally filled with the arrival of an Olympian figure in musical history.
    (E) It seems that the circumstances were outstanding at this significant moment.

27. In sentence 14 (reproduced below), which of the following versions of the underlined text coincides with the writer's portrait of Beethoven?

    In fact, he was once arrested as a tramp because the police authorities refused to believe that such a tatterdemalion could be a famous composer, much less a temple of the most turbulent spirit that ever walked the streets of Vienna, Europe's musical capital.

    (A) (no change)
    (B) believed that every man must be the master of his own fate
    (C) suffered through childhood with an overbearing alcoholic father
    (D) found expression in pure sound
    (E) acquired numerous musical jobs, among them, an assistant organist in a chapel

28. The writer wants to add emphasis to the claim made in sentence 11 (reproduced below), adjusting capitalization as necessary, to give greater credence to the evidence that follows.

>   *He was Defiance Incarnate.*

Which of the following best achieves that goal?

(A) Yes, he definitely was Defiance Incarnate.
(B) Unquestionably, he was Defiance Incarnate.
(C) Was he Defiance Incarnate? Absolutely!
(D) Indeed, he was often referred to as "Defiance Incarnate."
(E) Everybody used to call him Defiance Incarnate.

29. To back up the claim made in sentence 11, the writer wants to revise sentence 12 (reproduced below) by providing a pertinent anecdote.

>   *For instance, encountering the Grand Duke and his court in public, his hat was pulled down over his ears while striding through the aristocratic entourage.*

Which of the following versions of sentence 12 best serves the purpose?

(A) (no change)
(B) To prove the point, his hat was defiantly pulled down over his ears one day when he strode through the aristocratic Grand Duke and his court after meeting them in the street one day.
(C) One day, for example, he encountered the Grand Duke and his court in the street. Not only didn't he step aside, he pulled his hat down over his ears and strode right through the middle of the entourage.
(D) One day, to cite a for instance, Beethoven encountered the Grand Duke and his aristocrat court in public. Defiantly, then, he strode through the entourage and pulled down his hat to cover his ears.
(E) One day, the Grand Duke and his court encountered Beethoven in public. Defiantly, he pulled his hat over his ears and strode directly through the aristocratic entourage.

30. The writer is thinking about adding the following sentence to the fourth paragraph (sentences 15–19) to provide more information about Beethoven's life.

>   *Although Vienna was a far cry from Paris, no place is wholly insulated against time.*

Where would the sentence best be placed?

(A) (leave it out)
(B) Before sentence 15
(C) After sentence 15
(D) After sentence 16
(E) After sentence 17

31. In sentence 22 (reproduced below) the writer wants to provide a convincing detail to illustrate Beethoven's impetuosity.

    No other composer has ever melted his hearers into complete sentimentality by the tender beauty of his music, <u>comprised of serene and memorable themes and motifs that are typically Beethovian</u>.

    Which version of the underlined text accomplishes this goal?

    (A) (as it is now)
    (B) exploiting various sounds created by instruments that had been used since the Renaissance
    (C) regularly employing traditional tempos and rhythms for both soloists and the string and brass sections of the orchestra
    (D) and then suddenly turned on them and mocked them with derisive trumpet blasts for being such fools
    (E) often writing musical passages that have become instantaneously recognizable by classical music devotees

32. The writer wants to end with a thought that brings closure to the passage and also reflects its content. Which of the following best accomplishes that goal?

    (A) That's the way most geniuses are.
    (B) Naturally, he didn't follow this pattern in every sonata, quartet, concerto, and symphony he wrote.
    (C) Meanwhile, however, he made musical history.
    (D) You might say that the world is a better place because of that.
    (E) He was ungovernable.

DIRECTIONS: *Questions 33–39.* Carefully read the following passage and answer the accompanying questions.

The passage is the first draft of a speech to be delivered at a conference of state and local highway safety officials in 1954, when the construction of America's interstate highway system was being planned.

Passage 4

Good morning, ladies and gentlemen:

(1) A privilege accorded me is that of coming to this meeting in order to extend to each and every one of you a sincere welcome on behalf of the Government of the United States. (2) The purpose of our meeting is one that is essentially local or community-based. (3) But when any
Line particular activity in the United States takes 38,000 American lives in one year, it is transformed
(5) like a national problem of the first importance.

(4) I refer, of course, to the horrific annual death toll on our nation's streets and highways.
(5) This conference has been called, and you have heeded the call with an understanding between us that this is not merely a local and community problem. (6) It is a problem for all

of us, from the highest to the lowest echelon of government and for every citizen of our great

(10) land. (7) Studies of traffic fatalities contain startling statistics, among them one that seems especially dire: (8) During the past fifty years, traffic accidents killed more people than wars.

(9) We have organizations and laws that presumably work effectively to promote safety on the road—or at least try to minimize the danger. (10) But you will probably agree, in view of the loss of lives, the bodily harm, and the incalculable suffering of victims and their sur-

(15) vivors, we haven't done enough. (11) Obviously, it is now a long-standing problem which by its nature has no easy solutions.

(12) The building of the biggest infrastructure project in American history, the proposed interstate highway system, will not only improve driving safety, but will also be of huge benefit to the United States economy. (13) Throughout the country, road-building companies

(20) are already starting to hire thousands of workers.

(14) Best of all, however, it will save lives because safety is of primary importance. (15) The roadways will be smooth and wide, with landscaped dividers separating lanes of opposing traffic. (16) There will be limited access. (17) In rural areas, entrances and exits may be dozens or more miles apart. (18) Imagine, too, that you and your family might drive from

(25) Maine to Florida or from New Jersey to Texas, and never meet a stop light.

(19) Of course all of us recognize that the reality of this idealized vision is still years away. (20) After today's meeting, most of us will get into our cars, pull out of the parking lot and face the driving hazards and hardships of today. (21) Yet each one of you can contribute something to traffic safety in your community, whether you are driving a car or crossing

(30) the street.

(22) Everyone starts learning basic safety skills and attitudes from their families. (23) Children are taught to look both ways, a habit that lasts a lifetime. (24) After all, safety is an essential part of parenting, and family roles help permanently to shape people's lives. (25) I do believe, as is often said, that "It takes a village . . . ." In other words, both families and com-

(35) munities can foster not only safe driving habits but also pedestrian awareness. (26) Organized community groups command respect and thereby win the support of everyone who values public safety. (27) Public opinion will do the rest.

33. The speaker wants to greet the audience (sentence 1, reproduced below) in a cordial, concise, business-like manner.

> *A privilege accorded me is that of coming to this meeting in order to extend to each and every one of you a sincere and cordial welcome on behalf of the Government of the United States.*

Which of the following versions best achieves that purpose?

(A) (as it is)

(B) It is a high honor and distinct personal privilege to welcome you here this morning on behalf of the government of the United States.

(C) Hello and welcome. Thanks a lot for accepting your government's invitation to this conference. We really appreciate you being here today.

(D) You have come from all corners of America to be here today. When you go back home, I hope you'll feel so very, very thrilled that you had come here to this meeting.

(E) I am happy to see you here today and thank you, on behalf of our government, for coming to this important conference.

34. The purpose of sentences 2 and 3 (reproduced below) is to justify the convening of the conference.

> *(2) The purpose of our meeting is one that is essentially local or community-based. (3) But when any particular activity in the United States takes 38,000 American lives in one year, it is transformed like a national problem of the first importance.*

Which of the following versions of the underlined section does that most effectively?

(A) (as it is)
(B) the priority about how to resolve it needs a change
(C) its character changes it into a first-rate national problem
(D) the results are being felt across the country
(E) it becomes a nation-wide concern

35. The speaker wants to add a word or phrase at the start of sentence 5 (reproduced below), adjusting for capitalization as needed, to set up a cause-and-effect relationship with the idea in sentence 4.

> *This conference has been called, and you have heeded the call with an understanding between us that it is not merely a local and community problem.*

Which of the following best achieves this goal?

(A) For this purpose only,
(B) In the interests of halting the carnage,
(C) Between us,
(D) Consequently,
(E) To support the government's cause,

36. While reading this draft, the writer thinks that the meaning of sentence 8 (reproduced below) may be misunderstood or misinterpreted.

> *During the past fifty years, traffic accidents killed more people than wars.*

Which of the following versions of the underlined text would solve that problem?

(A) (as it is)
(B) wars had killed fewer people than traffic accidents.
(C) the chances of dying in traffic accidents are greater than those in war.
(D) deaths in traffic accidents outnumbered deaths in war.
(E) more deaths occur in traffic accidents than occur in war.

37. Between the third and fourth paragraphs—i.e., between sentences 11 and 12 (reproduced below)—the writer, for the sake of coherence, wants to add a sentence with two functions: first, to serve as a transition between paragraphs and, second, also to introduce the topic of the new paragraph.

> *(11) Obviously, it is now a long-standing problem which by its nature has no easy solutions.*

> *(12) The building of the biggest infrastructure in American history, the proposed interstate highway system, will not only improve driving safety, but will also be of huge benefit to the United States economy.*

Which of the following best serves that purpose?

(A) No sensible person can honestly say, well, all we need are more traffic cops, more traffic lights, safer cars, and tougher licensing requirements.

(B) However, under the leadership of our president, this bleak picture will soon begin brightening.

(C) But the U.S., the most resourceful country on earth, ten years ago led the world into the Atomic Age and ended World War II.

(D) At this time in our history, such a dilemma is positively archaic, and we have no choice but to deal with it intelligently.

(E) The time is ripe for government officials to sit down with auto-industry manufacturers and unions and do something about it.

38. In sentence 13 (reproduced below), the writer wants to provide a convincing argument why the new road system will be an economic boon to the country.

> *Throughout the country, <u>road-building companies are already starting to hire thousands of workers.</u>*

Which version of the underlined text best accomplishes this goal?

(A) (as it is)

(B) people with city jobs will no longer have to live in the city.

(C) as more people drive, automobiles will come with many more built-in safety features and lower gas prices.

(D) tourists will stop along the highway to buy gas, have picnics, and see the sights.

(E) the system will allow people to cross long stretches of countryside in a hurry.

39. The writer wants to add the following sentence to the last paragraph (sentences 22–27).

> *Teens, sometimes reluctantly, emulate their parents' safety habits.*

Where would the sentence best be placed?

(A) (leave it out)

(B) Before sentence 23

(C) After sentence 23

(D) After sentence 24

(E) After sentence 25

DIRECTIONS: *Questions 40–45.* Carefully read the following passage and answer the accompanying questions.

The passage is a draft of an op-ed piece that the writer wants published in a local newspaper.

Passage 5

(1) What a relief it was six years ago, to be promoted to work in the office of the superintendent after a decade grappling with fifth-graders as a classroom teacher. (2) For the first time I got the opportunity to do something about educational issues from pre-K to 12th
Line grade that had long plagued our district.

(5)   (3) Over time, I observed changes that adversely affected the level of education in our schools. (4) I had seen them, been part of them—and above all grew tired of them. (5) But as the superintendent, I am super-confident that we—meaning you the citizens of Springhill, and we, the staff of our schools—are up to the task of raising the standards we hold dear.

(6) I don't question for a moment why I wanted this responsibility, even as I'm tasked
(10) with making budget reductions even while the district is so under-resourced. (7) I love this community deeply, and I'm inspired daily by educators' dedication and our children. (8) I know our district has had its challenges. (9) But I also know that we're ready to re-write the story.

(11) It's time we finally address these issues; from systemic financial challenges and
(15) under-enrollment, to teacher retention and quality schools across Springhill. (12) I'm committed to fundamentally changing how the district does business, and ready for every opportunity to rethink and reallocate where we spend money for Springhill's students. (13) Change will be difficult, but the outcome makes it imperative: high-quality community schools in every neighborhood!

(20)   (14) Our ability to invest more in our schools is on the horizon. (15) Looking at the overall picture of the future, the bottom line that lies ahead will require a series of re-arrangements of school configurations. (16) Such changes can be expansions to larger facilities. (17) Closures that will de-inventory some of the district's present-day existing buildings. (18) Last but not least, consolidations to be rolled out more or less about five years down the
(25) road.

(19) It will be tough, painful work, but by making difficult decisions now, we will create conditions that will better serve our children long into the future. (20) If we don't make these changes, we run the risk of the state taking control of our schools, an action that could have dire consequences. (21) I believe from the bottom of my heart that it's possible to serve
(30) all students and I am ready to set the trajectory to secure this future for our children. (22) To make this happen, we need to make sure and guarantee that every school is adequately staffed and has sufficient resources. (23) Above all, we must have high-quality teachers, administrators and support personnel whom we compensate competitively. (24) A faction in the community strongly opposes regular pay increases, asserting that annual salaries are
(35) already too high for a ten-month job that includes weeks of vacation time.

(25) Being the superintendent is not a one-person show, so I invite the community to the table for this dialogue. (26) Please reach out to me if you'd like to be part of the solution for the future of Springhill's schools. (27) I work for you, and I am listening.

40. Which of the following sentences, if placed before sentence 1, would capture the interest of readers and provide an effective introduction to the topic of the passage?

    (A) As a parent myself, I'm interested in making our schools as good as they can be.
    (B) Now, in my sixth year as superintendent of Springhill's schools, you probably want to know our plans for the future.
    (C) When I became superintendent of the Springhill School District, it was a dream come true, even though I knew the road ahead would be tough.
    (D) I was born and raised in Springhill, where I attended school from K to 12.
    (E) The urge to be a school superintendent is like having an itch so annoying you've got to scratch it.

41. After sentence 3, the writer wants to cite a symptom of the district's educational decline. Which of the following would best achieve that goal?

    (A) Twelfth graders graduating from high school got accepted more at state institutions than at private and prestigious ones.
    (B) Greater college acceptances occurred from state institutions than from prestigious, private ones.
    (C) Prestigious private institutions accepted fewer seniors than did state universities and colleges.
    (D) In the past, 80 to 90 percent of our Honor Society seniors were accepted at prestigious private colleges; this year the percentage fell to 60.
    (E) Applicants to state colleges and universities received acceptances larger in quantities than prestigious, private institutions.

42. The writer is concerned about the ambiguity of sentence 9 (reproduced below).

    But I also know that we're ready to re-write the story.

    In the context, which of the following interpretations best articulates and is also most consistent with the main point of the passage?

    (A) (leave it as it is)
    (B) Nevertheless, it's time to go where our district has never gone before.
    (C) But let us not forget the past while planning for the future.
    (D) However, we can use lessons of the past to plan the future.
    (E) But don't dwell on the past; instead, focus on the future.

43. The writer thinks that sentences 15–18 (reproduced below) form a vague, longwinded, jargon-filled, hard-to-follow statement.

    (15) Looking at the overall picture of the future, the bottom line that lies ahead will require a series of re-arrangements of school configurations. (16) Such changes can be expansions to larger facilities. (17) Closures that will de-inventory some of the district's present-day existing buildings. (18) Last but not least, consolidations to be rolled out more or less about five years down the road.

    In the context, which of the following versions best eliminates the writer's concerns and also supports the basic meaning of the passage?

    (A) To meet the demands of the next five years, the district must expand, combine, and eliminate some of its facilities.
    (B) Looking five years into the future, some of the district's buildings will require expansion, elimination, or re-configuration.
    (C) Planning for the next five years must include re-configuring the district's facilities by expanding, eliminating, or re-configuring some of them.
    (D) The meeting of demands during the next five years necessitates that some district buildings will be required to being expanded, eliminated, or re-configured.
    (E) Within the next five years' time, some district buildings must undergo expansion, elimination, or re-configuration to meet future demands.

44. At the end of sentence 20 (reproduced below) the writer wants to provide a persuasive argument for avoiding a state takeover of the schools.

    If we don't make these changes, we run the risk of the state taking control of our schools, <u>*an action that could have dire consequences.*</u>

    Which version of the underlined text best accomplishes this goal?

    (A) a condition that would force the district to abandon plans to reduce class sizes and expand after-school tutorial and enrichment programs.
    (B) a step that will encourage the growth and expansion of charter schools.
    (C) an action that is very damaging to democracy in our district.
    (D) a move that is likely to cause discontent and conflict in our school community.
    (E) a policy that nullifies laws saying and guaranteeing every child the right to a free education.

45. The writer wants to rebut the claim alleged in sentence 24 that teachers are overpaid. Which one of the following ideas would be *least* effective in achieving this purpose?

    (A) Reading a letter of gratitude from the parent of a child who received after-school help in writing a college application essay from her English teacher
    (B) A personal anecdote about having been a teacher and buying classroom supplies because of the school's limited budget
    (C) Citing statistics about the hours that teachers spend commuting because they can't afford to live in the district
    (D) A description of a third-grade class in which nine of thirty-two children speak languages other than English at home
    (E) Explaining that a third of the district's teachers are paying off student loans

Section II

Three Essay Questions

TIME: 2 HOURS AND 15 MINUTES

Write your essays on standard 8½" × 11" composition paper. At the exam you will be given a bound booklet containing 12 lined pages.

Essay Question 1

SUGGESTED TIME:
15 MINUTES FOR READING THE QUESTION AND SOURCES
40 MINUTES FOR WRITING AN ESSAY

According to recent polls, one out of three U.S. teenagers who use mobile devices, access the Internet, or join social networks, such as Facebook, have at least once found themselves subject to insulting and potentially harmful bullying from malicious, mean-spirited school-mates. Although most victims ignore this so-called cyberbullying, some students experience harmful emotional reactions. They may refuse to go to school, or perhaps suffer from anxiety, fear, depression, and insomnia. In a few tragic cases, teenagers have committed suicide.

Because cyberbullying usually occurs off campus during non-school hours, schools must decide whether to take action against bullies or whether to let the community handle the problem.

Carefully read the following seven sources, including the material that introduces each source. Then, in an essay that synthesizes at least three of the sources, take a position on the claim that schools should track down and punish students for off-campus cyberbullying.

Source A (Kids)
Source B (CRF)
Source C (Kim)
Source D (Cartoon)
Source E (Willard)
Source F (Hsu)
Source G (Chart)

Instructions:

- Respond to the prompt with a thesis that may establish a line of reasoning.
- Provide evidence from at least three of the provided sources to support the thesis. Indicate clearly the sources used through direct quotation, paraphrase, or summary. Sources may be cited as Source A, Source B, etc., or by using the descriptions in parentheses.
- Explain the relationship between the evidence and the thesis.
- Demonstrate an understanding of the rhetorical situation.
- Use appropriate grammar and punctuation in communicating the argument.

Source A

"Stop Cyberbullying," *www.stopcyberbullying.com*, Wired Kids, accessed from the Web, July 31, 2010.

Below are excerpts from an online article published by a project that bills itself as the world's largest Internet safety, help, and education organization.

What is cyberbullying, exactly?

"Cyberbullying" is when a child, preteen or teen is tormented, threatened, harassed, humiliated, embarrassed or otherwise targeted by another child, preteen or teen using the Internet, interactive and digital technologies or mobile phones.

. . . Children have killed each other and committed suicide after having been involved in a cyberbullying incident.

. . . When schools try and get involved by disciplining the student for cyberbullying actions that took place off-campus and outside school hours, they are often sued for exceeding their authority and violating the student's free speech rights. They also often lose. . . . They can also educate the students on cyber-ethics and the law. If schools are creative, they can sometimes avoid the claim that their actions exceeded their legal authority for off-campus cyberbullying actions. We recommend that a provision is added to the school's acceptable use policy reserving the right to discipline the student for actions taken off-campus if they are intended to have an effect on a student or they adversely affect the safety and well-being of a student while in school. This makes it a contractual, not a constitutional, issue.

Source B

"The Legality of School Responses to Cyberbullying," Constitutional Rights Foundation, Chicago. Posted by *www.deliberating.org*, 2007.

The following passage comes from a document published on the website of an organization that studies issues related to education and the law.

The First Amendment to the U.S. Constitution states, "Congress shall make no law . . . abridging the freedom of speech." However, the Supreme Court has ruled in several cases that schools can limit student speech. In the 1969 Tinker decision, for example, the Court decided that schools could prohibit student speech if it "materially and substantially interfere[d] with the requirements of appropriate discipline in the operation of the school."

. . . Recent lower court decisions have addressed harassment via Internet technologies. . . . In the majority of decisions, the courts ruled that a school could not discipline a student for inappropriate off-campus e-mail unless that student brought the speech to school. Given the courts' reluctance to limit off-campus student speech, U.S. school officials, parents, and legislators have addressed cyberbullying in other ways. For example, in Vermont . . . a new state law requires that public schools establish bullying prevention procedures. Some schools have added a provision to their acceptable use policies that students must sign. These policies authorize schools to "discipline students for actions taken off campus if they are intended to have an effect on a student or they adversely affect the safety and well-being of a student while in school . . . . "Additionally, some parents and students have successfully argued that cyberbullies violated civil or criminal laws by, for example, intentionally inflicting emotional distress or committing a hate crime.

Source C

Victoria Kim, "Suit Blends Internet, Free Speech, School," *Los Angeles Times*, August 3, 2008.

The following passage is excerpted from a newspaper article by a staff writer for the Los Angeles Times.

On a sunny May afternoon, teenagers dismissed from a Beverly Hills middle school gathered outside a restaurant four blocks away and gossiped about their friends.

Amid lots of giggling, the conversation among the eighth-graders . . . was dominated by an unflattering assessment of a girl at school, who was called a "spoiled brat" and a "slut."

. . . What may have been just another middle school moment became a serious headache for school officials when one of the students uploaded the conversation as a video on *YouTube.com*. Because of the Internet posting, Beverly Vista School officials found themselves grappling with their responsibility to ensure a student's well-being and the ambiguous limits of their authority on the Web.

Citing "cyber-bullying" concerns, school administrators suspended for two days the student who uploaded the video, without disciplining others in the recording. The suspended student sued the school district, saying her free-speech rights were violated.

"The speech for which the plaintiff was punished was not 'student speech' at all and cannot be regulated or controlled by the defendants," attorneys wrote in the suit.

> [The court agreed. In December 2009, the judge said that the school violated the student's First Amendment rights. He added that the girl's actions were juvenile and inappropriate, but they did not cause serious enough disruption on campus to warrant administrative action.]

In an Idaho case . . . parents sued a school district for its failure to intervene in their daughter's harassment, which included, among other things, spreading photos and rumors on the Internet about the girl's sexual orientation. The court sided with the school, saying officials did not have "substantial control" over the dissemination of the photos.

Source D

Clive Edwards, Cartoon on cyberbullying.

The image below is an unpublished cartoon created by a freelance cartoonist in 2010.

Source E

Nancy Willard, "School Response to Cyberbullying and Sexting," Center for Safe, Responsible Internet Use, August 2, 2010.

The following passage has been adapted from an article by attorney Nancy Willard, a widely recognized authority on responsible Internet use.

Jessica Logan, a senior at an Ohio high school, had sent nude photos of herself to a boyfriend. After the relationship ended, her ex-boyfriend sent the photos to other female students at Logan's school, after which the image went "viral" and was distributed to many students. This resulted in months of harassment and teasing for Logan.

Logan hanged herself one month after her graduation. Logan's parents filed suit against the high school and several other defendants, alleging that the school and local police did not do enough to protect their daughter from harassment.

A very significant challenge in this regard is what has been happening in some schools when police officers overreact. News reports of students involved in sexting who have been hauled off in handcuffs are exceptionally disturbing. The highly predictable consequence of this police overreaction is to place the student depicted at exceptionally high risk of intense harassment by peers. This could place the student at high risk of suicide. Such actions will also make it exceptionally difficult for school officials to prevent sexual harassment—for which schools could be held liable.

School officials must assert authority over actions that might take place on their campus that could cause emotional harm to students. It is entirely unnecessary, even if law enforcement response might be appropriate, to have students hauled from school in handcuffs.

Source F

Cindy Hsu, "N.J. School District Set to Battle Cyber Bullies," HD2, *wcbs.com*, August 1, 2008.

The following is adapted from a news item published on the website of CBS News.

A local school district is trying to protect its students from cyberbullies, even when they attack from home. CBS 2 HD has learned how the school is cracking down and making the bullies the target.

. . . School officials . . . now have the authority to take action, even when the cyber attacks are off school grounds.

"When a kid is at home on his home computer, then he's not totally isolated from the school," Dr. James Patterson said. "It used to be, as you know, the Internet is an area of basically free speech, but free speech has some restrictions to it."

Experts argue that the free speech argument should take a back seat to threats of physical violence. . . . "Cyber-bullying is a big deal. It's leading to significant emotional distress of young people," said Nancy Willard of the Center for Safe and Responsible Internet Use.

. . . Teachers are now obligated to report cases of cyberbullying to school officials. Students tell CBS 2 HD, they need all the help they can get.

"I think it's a good idea because if they don't take action, it's just going to keep happening and people are going to get hurt," Montclair High School senior Carole Johnson said.

As far as the punishment for cyberbullying, school officials say bullies could face suspension or law enforcement could be called in for extreme cases.

Source G

"Cyberbullying Facts and Statistics for 2016–2018"

The chart below shows the results of a worldwide survey conducted by the research group, Comparitech. *www.comparitech.com*

Percentage of Parents that Report Their Child Has Been a Victim of Cyberbullying. 2011–2018 Survey Results

Country	2018	2016	2011
India	37	32	32
Brazil	29	19	20
United States	26	34	15
Belgium	25	13	12
South Africa	26	25	10
Malaysia	23	—	—
Sweden	23	20	14
Canada	20	17	18
Turkey	20	14	5
Saudi Arabia	19	17	18
Australia	19	20	13
Mexico	18	20	8
Great Britain	18	15	11
China	17	20	11
Serbia	16	—	—
Germany	14	9	7
Argentina	14	10	9

Essay Question 2

SUGGESTED TIME: 40 MINUTES

(This question counts as one-third of the total score for Section II.)

Read the following passage, an excerpt from an email written to friends and family by an American soldier fighting in Iraq, 2003–2004. Then write an essay in which you analyze the rhetorical strategies used by the author to explain his experience and convey his attitude toward that experience.

Instructions:

- Respond to the prompt with a thesis that may establish a line of reasoning.
- Select and use evidence to develop and support the line of reasoning.
- Explain the relationship between the evidence and the thesis.
- Demonstrate an understanding of the rhetorical situation.
- Use appropriate grammar and punctuation in communicating the argument.

I know a number of you have been curious about what it's like over here, so we are going to take a small mental voyage. First off, we are going to prepare our living area. Go to your vacuum, open the canister, and pour it all over you, your bed, clothing, and your personal effects. Now roll in it until it's in your eyes, nose, ears, hair, and . . . well, you get
(5) the picture. You know it's just perfect when you slap your chest and cough from the dust cloud you kicked up. And so, there is no escape, trust me. You just get used to it.

OK, pitch a tent in your driveway, and mark off an area inside it along one wall about six feet by eight feet (including your bed). Now pack everything you need to live for four months—without Wal-Mart—and move in. Tear down the three walls of your tent seen from
(10) the street and you have about as much privacy as I have.

If you really want to make this accurate, bring in a kennel full of pugs; the smell, snoring, and social graces will be just like living with my nine tentmates. Also, you must never speak above a whisper because at all times at least four of your tentmates will be sleeping. That's where the flashlight comes in handy; you are going to use it to navigate a pitch-dark tent,
(15) 24 hours a day.

Time for hygiene. Walk to the nearest bathroom. In my case, it's a thousand-foot trudge over loose gravel. Ever stagger to the john at 0400? Try it in a frozen rock garden. Given the urges that woke you at this hour, taking the time to put on your thermals and jacket might not be foremost in your mind. But halfway there, it's too late. So dress warmly. It gets
(20) really freakin' cold here at night.

I don't even feel like talking about the latrine experience. All I have to say is that, after the first time, I went back to the tent and felt like either crying or lighting myself on fire to remove the filth.

Essay Question 3

SUGGESTED TIME: 40 MINUTES

(This question counts as one-third of the total score for Section II.)

> The paragraph below comments on the tendency of human beings to think about and plan for the future. After reading it, write a well-organized essay that states and develops your views on the usefulness of planning for the future. Use appropriate evidence from your reading, experience, or observations to support your argument.
>
> **Instructions:**
>
> - Respond to the prompt with a thesis that may establish a line of reasoning.
> - Select and use evidence to develop and support the line of reasoning.
> - Explain the relationship between the evidence and the thesis.
> - Demonstrate an understanding of the rhetorical situation.
> - Use appropriate grammar and punctuation in communicating the argument.

It's human nature to plan, dream, and think about the future. In fact, most students go to school and college with the presumption that they are being prepared for what lies ahead. On the other hand, some people think it's foolish and wasteful to be anything but wary about the future because our vision is limited, and unexpected events and conditions will inevitably cause us to be disappointed. Such people prefer to live for the present, to make the most of what exists here and now and to avoid wasting time with concerns about uncontrollable things to come. In your opinion, is it more worthwhile to concentrate on the present or use our energies to shape our future?

END OF PRACTICE TEST 2

ANSWER KEY
Practice Test 2

Answers to Multiple-Choice Questions

1.	E	13.	E	25.	C	37.	B
2.	D	14.	C	26.	D	38.	A
3.	C	15.	C	27.	D	39.	C
4.	E	16.	A	28.	C	40.	E
5.	B	17.	C	29.	C	41.	D
6.	D	18.	B	30.	A	42.	B
7.	A	19.	E	31.	D	43.	A
8.	E	20.	D	32.	E	44.	A
9.	B	21.	C	33.	E	45.	E
10.	B	22.	A	34.	E		
11.	A	23.	C	35.	B		
12.	C	24.	D	36.	D		

Summary of Answers in Section I (Multiple-Choice)

Number of correct answers _____

Use this information when you calculate your score for this exam. See page 280.

Answer Explanations to Multiple-Choice Questions

Passage 1—An excerpt from Michel de Montaigne, "The Enjoyment of Living"

1. **(E)** Because it is too early in the passage to know whether (B) and (C) might be correct, search first for a rhetorical link between the first two paragraphs: although the speaker begins by discussing his eating preferences—the ostensible subject of the passage—he adds thoughts about other matters. In the second paragraph, prior to returning to his culinary preferences, he picks up where he left off—with a general statement about change. In effect, the intimate rhetorical relationship between the two sentences in question eliminates the other choices as reasonable answers.

2. **(D)** Although the writer says in line 4 that he has not "noticed" the effect of "full and new moons," etc., he is implying that to be influenced by phases of the moon is just plain stupid.

3. **(C)** The writer appears proud of himself for the alacrity with which he alters his diet to suit himself.

4. **(E)** The paragraph begins with its topic sentence. The rest supports it. It also performs the functions shown in (B), (C), and (D). There is no evidence that the speaker's tone has shifted.

5. **(B)** The explanation contributes to the image of the speaker as a gentleman with well-defined culinary tastes. The other choices refer to eating but not specifically to the speaker's predilections for certain foods.

6. **(D)** According to the previous paragraph, one's dining companions at a pleasurable meal are at least as important as the quality of the food. Lines 20–21 reiterate that sentiment.

7. **(A)** Age is very much on the writer's mind throughout the passage. He discusses his long-past youth (lines 13–19) and alludes to "old men," (line 25), as well as to various quirks and ailments common to seniors (lines 27–37).

8. **(E)** In the sixth paragraph (lines 27–37) the speaker describes his methods for staying warm. He knows how ridiculous it would be to resort to "a hare's skin or a vulture's plumage." Yet he uses the term to emphasize the lengths to which he would go to remain comfortably warm. The other choices may overstate the truth but not to the degree of Choice (E).

9. **(B)** In neither food nor health care do the speaker's preferences conform to conventional practice. Choices other than (B) are vaguely implied, but they don't describe the principal contrasts made in the passage.

10. **(B)** The writer has an on-again-off-again relationship with radishes. None of the other choices is valid.

11. **(A)** Although there are elements of all the choices—except (C), perhaps—the man's extraordinary self-adulation is apparent throughout the passage. He uses words such as *I, me, my*, and *our* in great abundance.

12. **(C)** In context the passage is a description of how the speaker manages to lead a pleasurable life by acceding to his whims and fancies. Here and there allusions to other choices appear, but only (C) describes the passage as a whole.

13. **(E)** Each of the incorrect choices consists of contrasting phrases that emphasize movement or progress from one stage or set of conditions to another. Only (E), while structurally similar to the other choices, denotes intensified rather than contrasting progress.

Passage 2—An excerpt from E.B. White, "A Slight Sound at Evening"

14. **(C)** is a rhetorical device common not just to book critics but to others as well: identify liabilities before lauding strengths.

15. **(C)** To some extent, each of the choices has some validity. Line 9, however, specifies that Thoreau was driven by "the normal anxieties and enthusiasms and rebellions of youth."

16. **(A)** The writer can't presume to know or predict *Walden's* impact, except to say that the book is sure to stimulate many different responses.

17. **(C)** *Walden* is essentially the story of the archetypical free spirit. Whacking down trees is just the sort of impulsive thing such a person might do.

18. **(B)** The writer touts the advantages of encountering *Walden* during one's youth (lines 8–29), for it gives a "good argument for traveling light and trying new adventures," among many other things.

19. **(E)** The entire paragraph touts *Walden's* many virtues. The book, he suggests, ought to be handed out instead of a diploma to college graduates. Even the table of contents gets a nod of approval. In fact, he observes wryly that the table of contents is worth reading because it contains a writing lesson—namely, omit needless words.

20. **(D)** This choice reiterates and emphasizes the writer's opinion stated in various places throughout the passage (see lines 18–22 and 39–49) that *Walden* is rich in ideas and broad in scope.

21. **(C)** The lines in question could send some readers fleeing from *Walden*, but the writer may lure some of them back with claims starting in line 47 that one will be "impressed chiefly by the courage of the rider," etc.

22. **(A)** By using the logic of "if . . . then" propositions, writers add to the persuasiveness of their arguments.

23. **(C)** The quotation alludes to the trees chopped down in youth (lines 10–11) as well as to an office Dictaphone (line 25) used later, when one is more established in life. Clearly, the "chips" precede the "voice."

24. **(D)** is the best answer, although (B), (C), and (E) are at least partly valid.

Passage 3—Adapted from Joseph Machlis, "The Music of Beethoven"

25. **(C)** is the best choice. (A) is ambiguous and uses the same sort of jargon as the original; (B) uses a pronoun that disagrees with its antecedent; (D) contains awkward usage; and (E) contains a redundancy.

26. **(D)** provides a sensible and coherent connection between the two sentences. The other sentences contain worthy thoughts but fail to provide an appropriate transition.

27. **(D)** Because the writer is focused mainly on the musical passions of Beethoven, the other choices are of marginal relevance.

28. **(C)** All the choices assert Beethoven's defiance, but (C), by forcefully answering a question, has dramatic impact.

29. **(C)** is the best answer because, unlike the others, it states the facts with no ambiguities, misplaced modifiers, pronoun reference errors, or excessive verbiage.

30. **(A)** The sentence adds nothing substantive to the paragraph, and besides, it is more or less self-evident.

31. **(D)** describes a tactic that creates the impression of a brash, capricious musical style—although in reality every note had been carefully thought out.

32. **(E)** Restating the main theme of the passage, this terse conclusion also reiterates the point of the last paragraph.

Passage 4—A speech about driving safety

33. **(E)** The greeting is purposeful, friendly, and, above all, appropriate for the occasion.

34. **(E)** The syntax, diction, and meaning in all but (E) are awkward, vague, or beside the point.

35. **(B)** best serves the purpose by alluding directly to the death toll that thus far has been the speaker's main concern.

36. **(D)** makes an unambiguous comparison between deaths in traffic and deaths in war. The other choices contain faulty comparisons or problems with verb tense or noun-verb agreement.

37. **(B)** gracefully bridges the two paragraphs with a transitional sentence that works rhetorically by planting just a hint of what's to come.

38. **(A)** is the only choice that explicitly describes an economic benefit.

39. **(C)** places the sentence in logical, chronological sequence.

Passage 5—An op-ed essay by a public school district superintendent

40. **(E)** Choice (E) is a clever and witty comment that may appeal to readers. It could, however, undermine the tone of a passage meant to deliver a serious message. Besides, sentence 1 already contains a touch of humor—just enough, perhaps, to entice the audience to continue reading.

41. **(D)** is best because it is written in standard English. The other choices are flawed by such weaknesses as awkward, unidiomatic expression, lack of parallelism, faulty comparison, and redundancy. (Whether the statement proves the speaker's point is another matter.)

42. **(B)** While acknowledging the challenges of the past, the speaker refuses to let the district yield to them and wants to break new ground—in other words, change the "story" of Springhill's school system.

43. **(A)** is the most concise and accurate rendering of the statement. The others suffer variously from jargon, modification problems, awkwardness of expression, and repetition. It has none of the deficiencies of the other choices.

44. **(A)** is the most forceful argument because it cites a specific impact that a state takeover would impose on the district's children.

45. **(E)** is the least effective because it is a problem that is unrelated to being teacher.

Answers to Essay Questions

For an overview of how essays are graded, turn to "How Essays Are Read and Evaluated," page 37.

Although answers to the essay questions will vary greatly, the following descriptions suggest a possible approach to each question and contain ideas that could be used in a response to the question. Perhaps your essay contains many of the same ideas. If not, don't be alarmed. Your ideas may be at least as insightful, or even more so, as those below.

Essay Question 1

Some Arguments In Favor of School-Administered Punishment for Cyberbullying:

- Schools have the authority to discipline students whose actions on or off the campus adversely affect the safety and well-being of other students. (Sources B and C)
- Schools should have the power to prevent activities that inflict emotional distress on students. (Source B)
- Giving a school the authority to punish helps to eliminate ambiguities in the law by establishing precedents for other schools to follow. (Source C)
- A school's authority to punish can serve as a warning to all students that cyberbullies will be held accountable for their actions. (Source D)
- Awareness of the school's right to punish for cyberbullying is likely to reduce the amount of cyberbullying among students. (Source F)

Some Arguments Against School-Administered Punishment for Cyberbullying:

- Schools may be sued for violating students' right to free speech. (Source A)
- Schools' actions should be limited to educating students on cyber-ethics and the law. (Source A)
- Schools may overstep their rightful authority to discipline students. (Sources A and B)
- Schools that punish cyberbullies may be sued if they fail to mete out penalties for every incident of harassment. (Source C)
- Doling out large numbers of penalties for cyberbullying can interfere with learning. (Source D)
- Cyberbullying in the form of sexting may require the intervention of law-enforcement authorities, which can place depicted students at a higher risk of harassment by peers. (Source E)

Essay Question 2, Based on a Passage by Edward P. Gyokeres

The author intends to recreate his experience in Iraq for a homefront audience that he assumes has no idea what it's like being a soldier in a war zone. As he tells his story, the author addresses the reader as "you," a device that establishes intimacy between himself and the recipients of his e-mail. In addition, he speaks frankly and informally, using the common, down-to-earth parlance of a soldier—for example, "personal effects" (line 4), "0400" (line 17), "really freakin' cold" (line 20).

The author could easily have summarized his life in Iraq by stating simply, "It's wretched." Instead, however, he tries to make the account as vivid as possible by employing the rhetorical device of a "small mental voyage" (line 2). Rather than tell what he sees, feels, hears, and smells, he helps his readers recreate the experience by instructing them to do outrageous things with everyday objects: empty the contents of a vacuum cleaner bag onto yourself, tear apart the walls of a small tent you've set up on your driveway, and so forth.

Recognizing that a reader's imaginings will leave a more powerful impression than any words he can write, the author deliberately avoids going into minute detail, interjecting instead ". . .well, you get the picture" (lines 4–5) and "trust me" (line 6). He uses a similar tactic at the end of the passage by briefly describing his nighttime "latrine experience." Again, he stops short of piling on details, saying, "I don't even feel like talking about" it (line 21). Again, he expects that a reader's imagination will fill in the blanks. But just in case, he describes what happened after returning to his tent: He feels the urge to light himself on fire, a claim that may seem like hyperbole. But everything in his existence is so dreadful that readers might well believe he means it.

Essay Question 3, Based on the Choice Between Preparing for the Future and Living for the Present

Should preparing for the future trump living for the here and now?
This is a question that in one form or other you probably face every day. One clear-cut response is that only an irresponsible hedonist would snub the future in favor of the present. Or you might think just the opposite: Live it up now and let the future take care of itself. A third alternative, of course, says that neither extreme works in all situations and that individuals must choose which path to follow based on various criteria applicable to themselves.

If you lean toward seizing the day, you might argue that when unique opportunities, either trifling or weighty, come along, you ought to grab them immediately rather than wait and later kick yourself for passing them by. Using a rationale such as *tempus fugit* (time flies . . . i.e., don't waste time), you might explain why, say, it's sometimes more important to hang out with friends than to study for tomorrow's math test. Or, more consequentially, why might it be better to take time off after high school to chase your dreams rather than go directly to college? To justify such a choice you might argue that change occurs so rapidly and unpredictably that preparing for a distant goal—say, a particular job or profession—is a gamble at best because when the future comes that job or profession may have changed or even disappeared.

On the other hand, an equally compelling case could be made in support of the standard advice that success comes to those who work hard, follow the rules, and practice, practice, practice. The very fact that you are preparing for an AP exam suggests that to some extent you subscribe to those sentiments.

Whatever your position, your essay's main idea needn't be supported by your personal preferences. You might draw evidence instead from the experience of others, both real and imaginary. Take the character Macbeth, for example. Egged on by his wife, he impulsively murders the king, never bothering to contemplate the potential aftereffects. Conversely, Hamlet suffers dire consequences by ruminating too long and hard before taking steps to avenge his father's death. Even history can be instructive. Within months of testing the atom bomb during World War II, the United States dropped bombs on two Japanese cities, killing over 200,000 civilians. Days later the war came to an end. Nevertheless, the president, Harry Truman, was vilified for acting rashly—especially for failing to give the enemy a chance to surrender before unleashing the bombs' deadly power. Truman's supporters declared, however, that the bombing ultimately saved countless lives by eliminating the need to invade the Japanese homeland.

You might also tap contemporary events to support your point of view. Climate change, for instance, raises the question of whether immediate action is needed to slow it down, or whether time, being on our side, allows the world to wait for the development of new and effective technologies to help solve the problem.

Regardless of your position, be mindful of the need to include substantial, detailed evidence to support your claims, and that an in-depth discussion of the issue is far better than a broad, scatter-shot approach.

How to Score the Essays

The following essay-scoring guidelines apply to all three essays on the exam. The maximum score on an essay is 6; the minimum, 0.

Points are awarded in three categories:

1. Thesis (0–1 point)
2. Evidence and Commentary (0–4 points)
3. Sophistication (0–1 point)

THESIS (0–1 point)

No credit is given for an absent, erroneous, or incoherent thesis or one that merely restates or paraphrases the essay prompt.

One point is awarded for a thesis that states or strongly implies a reasonable interpretation of the issue raised by the prompt for Essay #1, the synthesis essay. Similarly, for Essay #2 one point is given for a reasonable thesis related to rhetoric in the given passage. For Essay #3 add a point for a thesis that clearly articulates a position on the issue raised by the prompt.

EVIDENCE AND COMMENTARY (0–4 points)

No points are given for restating the thesis in different words or for material irrelevant to the prompt.

One point is earned for evidence that tends to help develop the thesis.

Two points are given for evidence that clearly supports the thesis but may not add significantly to the writer's line of reasoning.*

Three points are awarded in Essay #1 for evidence that supports the thesis and also begins to show how source material supports your point of view. Give three points for evidence in Essay #2 that identifies and offers some analysis of rhetoric in the passage. Likewise, in Essay #3, give three points for specific evidence that helps to develop an argument for or against the main idea expressed by the prompt.

Four points indicate that you have consistently and effectively included compelling evidence to support all claims in a line of reasoning and also have clearly employed at least three sources to strengthen your position on the given issue (Essay #1), identified ample relevant evidence of rhetoric in the given passage (Essay #2), and cited compelling evidence to support your argument in favor of or against the given issue (Essay #3).

SOPHISTICATION (0–1 point)

No credit is given for ideas, however discerning, that you mention but don't develop.

One point is awarded for the development of ideas that broaden an interpretation of the issue (Essay #1), cite and explain significant rhetorical features of the passage (Essay #2), and discuss the opinions expressed in the given passage (Essay #3) by one or more of the following:

(a) Identifying and discussing complexities or tensions in the text.
(b) Illuminating an interpretation of the work by situating it within a broader context.
(c) Suggesting alternative interpretations of the work.
(d) Employing a consistently vivid and persuasive writing style.

Use of Standard English: No specific credit is given for the use of standard English. Readers are bound to be favorably impressed, however, by well-expressed, economical, virtually error-free prose.

---

*The term **"line of reasoning"** refers to the means by which an idea or thesis is supported. For instance, an essay may focus on the writer's choice of words, use of logic, sequence of ideas, or even the essay's title in order to validate the thesis. A poor line of reasoning exists when there is a gap between the thesis and the evidence presented.

Essay Evaluation Worksheet

In the spaces below enter the number of credits earned in each category. See page 278 for detailed scoring guidelines.

	Essay 1 Synthesis Essay	Essay 2 Analytical Essay	Essay 3 Argumentative Essay
Category			
Thesis (0–1)			
Evidence and Commentary (0–4)			
Sophistication (0–1)			
TOTAL SCORE ON EACH ESSAY (0–6)			

Enter each essay score on the Test Score Worksheet.

Test Score Worksheet

Use this page to calculate your score on the AP English Language Practice Test 2.

SECTION 1. Multiple-Choice Questions

STEP A Enter the number of correct answers (out of 45) _____

SECTION 2. Essay Questions

STEP B Transfer your essay scores (0–6) from your Essay Evaluation Worksheet.

Essay 1 (Synthesis) _____   Essay 2 (Analysis) _____   Essay 3 (Argumentative) _____

Add the three essay scores _____   (This is your Essay Raw Score.)

STEP C Multiply Essay Raw Score by 3.055 _____

For your Final Essay Score, round to the nearest whole number. _____

SECTION 3. Composite Score

To determine your Composite Score, add the figures from STEP A and STEP C.

STEP A _____   +   STEP C _____   =   Composite Score _____

SECTION 4. Convert Composite Score to AP Test Score

Composite Score	AP Grade
90–100	5
68–89	4
36–67	3
13–35	2
1–12	1

_____

AP essays are ordinarily judged in relation to other essays written on the same topic at the same time. Therefore, the scores you assign yourself for these essays may not be the same as the scores you would earn on an actual exam.

ANSWER SHEET
Practice Test 3

Multiple-Choice Questions

Time—1 hour

1. Ⓐ Ⓑ Ⓒ Ⓓ Ⓔ   13. Ⓐ Ⓑ Ⓒ Ⓓ Ⓔ   25. Ⓐ Ⓑ Ⓒ Ⓓ Ⓔ   37. Ⓐ Ⓑ Ⓒ Ⓓ Ⓔ

2. Ⓐ Ⓑ Ⓒ Ⓓ Ⓔ   14. Ⓐ Ⓑ Ⓒ Ⓓ Ⓔ   26. Ⓐ Ⓑ Ⓒ Ⓓ Ⓔ   38. Ⓐ Ⓑ Ⓒ Ⓓ Ⓔ

3. Ⓐ Ⓑ Ⓒ Ⓓ Ⓔ   15. Ⓐ Ⓑ Ⓒ Ⓓ Ⓔ   27. Ⓐ Ⓑ Ⓒ Ⓓ Ⓔ   39. Ⓐ Ⓑ Ⓒ Ⓓ Ⓔ

4. Ⓐ Ⓑ Ⓒ Ⓓ Ⓔ   16. Ⓐ Ⓑ Ⓒ Ⓓ Ⓔ   28. Ⓐ Ⓑ Ⓒ Ⓓ Ⓔ   40. Ⓐ Ⓑ Ⓒ Ⓓ Ⓔ

5. Ⓐ Ⓑ Ⓒ Ⓓ Ⓔ   17. Ⓐ Ⓑ Ⓒ Ⓓ Ⓔ   29. Ⓐ Ⓑ Ⓒ Ⓓ Ⓔ   41. Ⓐ Ⓑ Ⓒ Ⓓ Ⓔ

6. Ⓐ Ⓑ Ⓒ Ⓓ Ⓔ   18. Ⓐ Ⓑ Ⓒ Ⓓ Ⓔ   30. Ⓐ Ⓑ Ⓒ Ⓓ Ⓔ   42. Ⓐ Ⓑ Ⓒ Ⓓ Ⓔ

7. Ⓐ Ⓑ Ⓒ Ⓓ Ⓔ   19. Ⓐ Ⓑ Ⓒ Ⓓ Ⓔ   31. Ⓐ Ⓑ Ⓒ Ⓓ Ⓔ   43. Ⓐ Ⓑ Ⓒ Ⓓ Ⓔ

8. Ⓐ Ⓑ Ⓒ Ⓓ Ⓔ   20. Ⓐ Ⓑ Ⓒ Ⓓ Ⓔ   32. Ⓐ Ⓑ Ⓒ Ⓓ Ⓔ   44. Ⓐ Ⓑ Ⓒ Ⓓ Ⓔ

9. Ⓐ Ⓑ Ⓒ Ⓓ Ⓔ   21. Ⓐ Ⓑ Ⓒ Ⓓ Ⓔ   33. Ⓐ Ⓑ Ⓒ Ⓓ Ⓔ   45. Ⓐ Ⓑ Ⓒ Ⓓ Ⓔ

10. Ⓐ Ⓑ Ⓒ Ⓓ Ⓔ   22. Ⓐ Ⓑ Ⓒ Ⓓ Ⓔ   34. Ⓐ Ⓑ Ⓒ Ⓓ Ⓔ

11. Ⓐ Ⓑ Ⓒ Ⓓ Ⓔ   23. Ⓐ Ⓑ Ⓒ Ⓓ Ⓔ   35. Ⓐ Ⓑ Ⓒ Ⓓ Ⓔ

12. Ⓐ Ⓑ Ⓒ Ⓓ Ⓔ   24. Ⓐ Ⓑ Ⓒ Ⓓ Ⓔ   36. Ⓐ Ⓑ Ⓒ Ⓓ Ⓔ

Practice Test 3

Section I

TIME: 1 HOUR

> **DIRECTIONS:** *Questions 1–13.* Carefully read the following passage and answer the accompanying questions.

The passage is an excerpt from an essay by a 19th-century American author.

Passage 1

But it is mostly my own dreams I talk of, and that will somewhat excuse me for talking of dreams at all. Everyone knows how delightful the dreams are that one dreams one's self, and how insipid the dreams of others are. I had an illustration of the fact, not many evenings ago,
Line when a company of us got telling dreams. I had by far the best dreams of any; to be quite
(5) frank, mine were the only dreams worth listening to; they were richly imaginative, delicately fantastic, exquisitely whimsical, and humorous in the last degree; and I wondered that when the rest could have listened to them they were always eager to cut in with some silly, senseless, tasteless thing that made me sorry and ashamed for them. I shall not be going too far if I say that it was on their part the grossest betrayal of vanity that I ever witnessed.

(10) But the egotism of some people concerning their dreams is almost incredible. They will come down to breakfast and bore everybody with a recital of the nonsense that has passed through their brains in sleep, as if they were not bad enough when they were awake; they will not spare the slightest detail; and if, by the mercy of Heaven, they have forgotten something, they will be sure to recollect it, and go back and give it all over again with added
(15) circumstance. Such people do not reflect that there is something so purely and intensely personal in dreams that they can rarely interest anyone but the dreamer, and that to the dearest friend, the closest relation or connection, they can seldom be otherwise than tedious and impertinent. The habit husbands and wives have of making each other listen to their dreams is especially cruel. They have each other quite helpless, and for this reason
(20) they should all the more carefully guard themselves from abusing their advantage. Parents should not afflict their offspring with the rehearsal of their mental maunderings in sleep, and children should learn that one of the first duties a child owes its parents is to spare them the anguish of hearing what it has dreamed about overnight. A like forbearance in regard to the community at large should be taught in the first trait of good manners in public schools,
(25) if we ever come to teach good manners there.

Certain exceptional dreams, however, are so imperatively significant, so vitally important, that it would be wrong to withhold them from the knowledge of those who happened not to dream them, and I could scarcely forgive myself if I did not, however briefly, impart

them. It was only last week, for instance, that I found myself one night in the company of
(30) the Duke of Wellington, the great Duke, the Iron one, in fact; and after a few moments of
agreeable conversation on topics of interest among gentlemen, his Grace said that now, if I
pleased, he would like a couple of those towels. We had not been speaking of towels, that I
remember, but it seemed the most natural thing in the world that he should mention them
in the connection, whatever it was, and I went at once to get them for him. At the place
(35) where they gave out towels, and where I found some very civil people, they told me that
what I wanted was not towels, and they gave me instead two bath-gowns, of rather scanty
measure, butternut in color, and Turkish in texture. The garments made somehow a very
strong impression upon me, so that I could draw them now, if I could draw anything, as they
looked when they were held up to me. At the same moment, for no reason that I can allege, I
(40) passed from a social to a menial relation to the Duke, and foresaw that when I went back to
him with those bath-gowns he would not thank me as one gentleman to another, but would
offer me a tip as if I were a servant. . . .

     This seemed to end the whole affair, and I passed on to other visions, which I cannot recall.

1. Which of the following best describes the writer's exigence in the passage?

    (A) Increasing resentment and antagonism between social classes
    (B) The innate shortsightedness of upper-class people
    (C) The unwillingness of some people to cast off their own misperceptions
    (D) The insensitive ways in which people often treat one another
    (E) How personal ambition can destroy compatibility between friends

2. In lines 2–3 ("Everyone knows . . . dreams of others are"), the speaker's rhetorical intent is primarily to

    (A) please the members of audience by confiding in them.
    (B) impress the audience with the depth of his understanding of the subject.
    (C) utter a controversial truth for the audience to ponder.
    (D) demonstrate that he has given the matter of dreams a great deal of thought.
    (E) engage the audience by stating a view with which they are likely to agree.

3. In context, lines 4–10 ("I had by far . . . almost incredible") could be used to support all of the following claims about the speaker's tone EXCEPT

    (A) He adopts a reverent tone when describing the nature of his own dreams.
    (B) His tone is reproachful when describing others who like to talk about their dreams.
    (C) When describing the qualities of his own dreams he uses a self-serving tone.
    (D) When describing his own dreams, the speaker assesses them realistically.
    (E) His tone when describing the content of other people's dreams is derisive.

4. In context, the rhetorical intent of the sentence in line 10 ("But the egotism . . . incredible") is primarily to

    (A) attract the attention of those who enjoy analyzing their own and others' dreams.
    (B) prepare the audience for an illustrative anecdote about "incredible" egotism.
    (C) reinforce the depth of the speaker's alienation from reality.
    (D) reveal the speaker's insights into human behavior.
    (E) suggest that dream interpretation is an inexact science.

5. Which of the following best describes the rhetorical function of the sentence (lines 10–15) in the second paragraph?

    (A) It provides details to support the preceding generalization.
    (B) It reiterates the main idea of the passage.
    (C) It presents an alternative view of the passage's main subject.
    (D) It undercuts an assertion made in the first paragraph.
    (E) It introduces a question to be answered later in the passage.

6. All of the following excerpts from the passage contribute to the speaker's emotive intent EXCEPT

    (A) "how insipid the dreams of others are" (line 3).
    (B) "silly, senseless, tasteless thing" (lines 7–8).
    (C) "grossest betrayal of vanity" (line 9).
    (D) "will not spare the slightest detail" (line 13).
    (E) "tedious and impertinent" (line 18).

7. In the second paragraph (lines 10–25), the speaker sketches out the behavior of "some people" mainly to

    (A) make the point that dreamers are subject to excessive vanity.
    (B) argue that dreams can be a source of conflict and anguish in human relationships.
    (C) stress that accurate accounts of dreams are unusually rare.
    (D) illustrate that dreams encourage erratic and ludicrous behavior.
    (E) advise the audience to be discreet when recounting their dreams to others.

8. The last sentence of the second paragraph (lines 23–25) can best be described as

    (A) a generalization followed by a specific example.
    (B) a suggestion followed by a reason for it.
    (C) a statement about a cause and its effect.
    (D) a reasonable assumption and logical conclusion.
    (E) a recommendation followed by an editorial comment.

9. At the start of the third paragraph (line 26) the writer uses "however," in order to

    (A) contradict an idea stated earlier about teaching children good manners in school.
    (B) introduce an alternative point of view about recitations about one's dreams.
    (C) assert that a skill can be acquired to assure that listeners will be rapt when hearing about a dream.
    (D) remind the audience that not all dreams, as stated in lines 7–8, are "silly," "senseless," and "tasteless."
    (E) reassure the audience that he still has a great deal of importance to say.

10. That the speaker declares that some dreams "are so imperatively significant, so vitally important" (lines 26–27) is ironic mainly because

   (A) the speaker has been railing against the telling of dreams.
   (B) some dreams are "exceptional" (line 26).
   (C) the speaker has characterized dreams as "intensely personal" (lines 15–16).
   (D) irrational events occur in dreams as well as in reality.
   (E) people rarely remember their dreams.

11. In the context of the passage, all of the following phrases refer to the same idea EXCEPT

   (A) "first duties a child owes to its parents" (line 22).
   (B) " . . . if we ever come to teach good manners" (line 25).
   (C) "agreeable conversation on topics of interest among gentlemen" (line 31).
   (D) "civil people" (line 35).
   (E) "thank me as one gentleman to another" (line 41).

12. The speaker's report of his nighttime encounter with the Duke of Wellington (lines 29–42) contributes to the overall unity of the passage in which one of the following ways?

   (A) As proof of the fleeting nature of dreams
   (B) As a deliberate example of a "silly, senseless, tasteless thing" (lines 7–8)
   (C) As a description of the speaker's social status
   (D) As evidence that dreams leave permanent impressions on the dreamer
   (E) As an illustration of the speaker's conviction that accounts of his own dreams are "worth listening to" (line 5)

13. The use of an ellipsis at the end of line 42 is meant to suggest that the speaker

   (A) thinks it's been a mistake to recount this particular dream.
   (B) suddenly discovered that he's humiliated himself.
   (C) has experienced a failure of memory.
   (D) has been rendered speechless by a strong emotional reaction.
   (E) regrets that he misrepresented the truth.

DIRECTIONS: *Questions 14–23.* Carefully read the following passage and answer the accompanying questions.

The passage below is part of a talk delivered by T. S. Eliot, a renowned 20th-century poet.

Passage 2

I hold no diploma, certificate, or other academic document to show that I am qualified to discuss this subject. I have never taught anybody of any age how to enjoy, understand, appreciate poetry, or how to speak it. I have known a great many poets, and innu-

Line merable people who wanted to be told that they were poets. I have done some teaching,

(5) but I have never "taught poetry." My excuse for taking up this subject is of wholly different origin. I know that not only young people in colleges and universities, but secondary school children also, have to study, or at least acquaint themselves with, poems by living poets; and I know that my poems are among those studied. This fact brings some

welcome supplement to my income; and it also brings an increase in my correspondence,
(10) which is more or less welcome, though not all the letters get answered. These are the
letters from children themselves, or more precisely, the teenagers. They live mostly in
Britain, the United States, and Germany, with a sprinkling from the nations of Asia. It is
in a spirit of curiosity, therefore, that I approach the subject of teaching poetry: I should
like to know more about these young people and about their teachers and the methods
(15) of teaching.

For some of my young correspondents seem to be misguided. Sometimes I have been
assigned to them as a "project," more often they have made the choice themselves—it is
not always clear why. (There was one case, that of an Egyptian boy, who wanted to write a
thesis about my work, and as none of my work was locally available and as he wanted to
(20) read it, asked me to send him all my books. That was very exceptional, however.) Very often
the writers ask for information about myself, sometimes in the form of a questionnaire. I
remember being asked by one child whether it was true that I only cared to associate with
lords and bishops. Sometimes a photograph is asked for. Some young persons seem to want
me to provide them with all the material for a potted biography, including mention of my
(25) interests, tastes, and ways of amusing myself. Are these children studying poetry, or merely
studying poets? Very often they want explanations, either of a whole poem ("what does it
mean") or of a particular line or phrase; and the kind of question they ask often suggests
that their approach to that poem has been wrong, for they want the wrong kind of explanation, or ask questions which are simply unanswerable. Sometimes, but more rarely, they are
(30) avid for literary sources, which would seem to indicate that they have started too early on
the road to Xanadu.

Now, when I was young, this sort of thing did not happen. I did study English at school,
beginning, thank God, with grammar, and going on to "rhetoric"—for which also I am
grateful. And we had to read a number of set books of prose and verse—mostly in school
(35) editions which made them look peculiarly unappetizing. But we never were made to read
any literature which could be called "contemporary."

No. Not only were we not encouraged to take an interest in the poetry actually being
written, but even had we been, I doubt whether we should have thought of entering into
correspondence with the authors. Some of the juvenile correspondence I receive seems to
(40) be instigated by the teachers, but the greater part does not. Indeed, some of my letters, I
suspect, are inspired by a desire to score off the teacher in the hope of getting some statement from the horse's mouth which will be a direct contradiction of what has been taught.
(I confess that this last type of letter is one which I sometimes take pleasure in answering—
when the teacher seems to have been wrong.) But my point is that this pressure upon the
(45) poet from young people who have been compelled to read his work is a modern phenomenon. I don't believe that Tennyson and Browning, Longfellow and Whittier (to say nothing
of Poe and Whitman, poets whose works we did not study) were embarrassed by juvenile
correspondence choking up their letter boxes. The teaching of the contemporary literature,
the introduction of the young to poetry by living poets, is something that came about in my
(50) time without my being aware of what was happening.

14. The speaker's rhetorical purpose in the opening paragraph (lines 1–10) is primarily to

   (A) win the audience's sympathy.
   (B) highlight the divisions between poetic theory and practice.
   (C) raise doubts about his qualifications to talk about the topic.
   (D) disabuse the audience of preconceptions about his expertise or his stature as a poet.
   (E) introduce the audience to the subject he intends to talk about.

15. Which of the following best accounts for setting the phrase "taught poetry" in quotation marks (line 5)?

   (A) The speaker means to ridicule the notion that poetry writing can be taught.
   (B) The speaker believes that teaching poetry is a fanciful—or at least a questionable—enterprise.
   (C) The quotation marks indicate that the speaker is being ironic.
   (D) The punctuation suggests that the speaker has never been successful in teaching others how to write poems.
   (E) The quoted phrase has become a cliché among teachers of poetry.

16. In the opening paragraph (lines 1–15), which of the following best characterizes the speaker's justification for choosing the topic of his talk?

   (A) His teaching experience—although limited—has been exceptionally gratifying.
   (B) Students apparently have an interest in contemporary poets.
   (C) He has been charmed by young people's attention to his poetry.
   (D) He is intrigued by the lives of youngsters who have written him letters.
   (E) He is puzzled by the rationale behind the letters written to him by students.

17. In the context of the passage, all of the following excerpts contribute to the speaker's main purpose EXCEPT

   (A) "I have done some teaching . . ." (line 4).
   (B) "welcome supplement to my income" (lines 8–9).
   (C) "an increase in my correspondence" (line 9).
   (D) "only cared to associate with lords and bishops" (lines 22–23).
   (E) "my interests, tastes, and ways of amusing myself" (lines 24–25).

18. Based on lines 26–31, which of the following best characterizes the speaker's position on the relevance of his topic for teachers of poetry?

   (A) Because the standards for understanding poetry are relatively diffuse, teachers can enrich students' comprehension by adding poets' biographical information.
   (B) By accepting the criticism he offers, teachers will help students explicate poems more thoroughly.
   (C) By adopting the speaker's viewpoint, teachers can alter the widespread belief that a poem has a specific meaning or message.
   (D) After considering the speaker's views, teachers should regularly ask students to justify or explain their interpretations of poems.
   (E) Acknowledging that the speaker's opinions are valid, a poetry teacher ought to encourage students to write poems of their own.

19. In the second paragraph (lines 16–31), the speaker describes communications he has received from students primarily to

(A) illustrate the shortcomings of being an acclaimed poet.
(B) record dismay over what constitutes the study of poetry in schools.
(C) commend young people for the depth of their knowledge and appreciation of poetry.
(D) question the decision of teachers to concentrate on the works of living poets.
(E) express concern that teaching poetry in schools is often counterproductive.

20. Which of the following best characterizes the rhetorical function of the first sentence of the third paragraph (line 32)?

(A) It provides a logical transition between the third and fourth paragraphs.
(B) It restates the main idea of the previous paragraph.
(C) It bolsters the main point of the third paragraph.
(D) It introduces a change in the speaker's attitude toward the topic of the passage.
(E) It briefly summarizes the main idea of the passage.

21. In context, all of the following describe the speaker's rhetorical intent in using the expression "thank God" (line 33) EXCEPT

(A) to indicate that he is a devout, God-fearing individual.
(B) to suggest that writing letters to poets is less valuable than studying grammar.
(C) to express skepticism about the usefulness of some current educational practices.
(D) to imply that knowledge of grammar is essential to a good education.
(E) to encourage his audience to master English grammar.

22. In context, lines 37–50 ("No. Not only . . . what was happening") could be used to support which of the following claims about the speaker's tone?

(A) His tone when discussing poetry being written at the time is sentimental.
(B) He adopts a mischievous tone when discussing reasons why some students wrote letters to him.
(C) He adopts a critical tone in describing the pressure often placed upon modern-day poets.
(D) He uses a skeptical tone when musing on the experience of poets of the past.
(E) His tone is disgruntled when acknowledging that he'd been unaware that students had been learning about contemporary poets.

23. Based on the diction in lines 46–48 ("I don't . . . letter boxes"), which of the following best characterizes the speaker's feelings about his role as a contemporary poet?

(A) Pressure to make a living as a poet
(B) Satisfaction about his success
(C) Envy of Tennyson, Browning, and other poets of old
(D) Regret over time spent responding to young people's letters
(E) A mix of embarrassment and delight over being singled out as a source of wisdom

> **DIRECTIONS:** *Questions 24–31.* Carefully read the following passage and answer the accompanying questions.

The passage below has been adapted from a psychological research report, dated 2019. It is a draft.

Passage 3

(1) Humans are secretive creatures with brains adept at concealing information. (2) Yet surprisingly, little research has been done on the psychology of secrets—particularly, whether how common it is to have and keep them? (3) The results of them? (4) And the
Line toll they take on us. (5) "For a long time, secrecy was thought to be too difficult to study, in
(5) part because you'd have to convince people to open up about their most closely guarded thoughts," says J. Barrow, a social psychologist at Manitoba University.

(6) But ever since 2015 Barrow has conducted a series of studies on the subject of personal secrecy with a boldly simple strategy: he just asks people to confess their deepest secrets. (7) His project, during which thousands of people have been surveyed, has gener-
(10) ated numerous insights: for example, that 97 percent of US adults are concealing at least one uncomfortable fact about themselves at any given time. (8) Moreover, a large share of people have up to a dozen significant secrets weighing on them. (9) The most secretive among us are less satisfied with their personal relationships, such as housewives feeling trapped and stifled.

(15) (10) "Going into this work, I wasn't sure how forthcoming people would be," says Barrow. (11) "But our participants seemed eager to open up." (12) The response during a similar study at Columbia University in the 1990s was almost identical.

(13) Many of the secrets divulged to Barrow's team involve sex. (14) The most common secret, researchers found, is having romantic thoughts about a person other than one's
(20) partner. (15) That is followed closely by cheating and various forms of emotional infidelity, like maintaining clandestine contact with an ex. (16) Among the secrets that weigh the most heavily on people, the surveys show, are those that concern mental health, a past traumatic experience, and body image. (17) "The more we think that secrets reflect poorly on who we are, the more shame we feel and the more we ruminate on them," says Barrow.

(25) (18) The researchers have also examined the psychological impact of keeping secrets. (19) In the past, studies have suggested that highly secretive people are less happy because it is mentally exhausting to continually lie and censor oneself in social situations. (20) But Barrow's work has challenged this analysis, showing that for most people the stress of concealing secrets does not significantly affect their well-being. (21) The real emotional burden
(30) of secrecy, he has found, is social isolation. (22) "If there is a really important thing going on in your life but you have chosen to hold it back from other people, you are building a wall between yourself and others," he says. (23) "This will make you feel alone and disconnected, which over time will take an emotional toll."

(24) One study found that if someone confesses a secret to at least one other person, he
(35) or she can find some relief. (25) "Even if the secret is kept from everybody else, talking to one person about it can make a world of difference," Barrow says, "even if that person is a stranger."

24. The writer wants the text of the introductory paragraph to be in standard written English. Which of the following versions best achieves that goal and also preserves the paragraph's basic meaning?

(A) (as it is now)

(B) Humans are secretive creatures. Their brain is adept at concealing information. Surprisingly enough, little research has been done on the psychology of secrets—particularly, on whether how common it is to have and keep them and what the results are, such as the toll they take on us.

(C) Humans are secretive creatures with brains adept at concealing information. Yet surprisingly little research has been done on the psychology of secrets—particularly, such questions as whether how common it is to harbor and keep them? The results of them? And what toll they take on us?

(D) Humans are secretive creatures with brains adept at concealing information. Yet, surprisingly, little research has been done on the psychology of secrets—in particular, whether or not it is common to have them and keep them? And their results? And the toll they take on us?

(E) Secretive creatures like humans have brains adept at concealing information. Yet, surprisingly little research has been done on the psychology of secrets: in particular, how common it is to have them, keep them, and at what toll.

25. In sentence 9 (reproduced below) which of the following versions of the underlined text best establishes the writer's position on the main argument of the passage?

The most secretive among us are less satisfied with their personal relationships, such as housewives feeling trapped and stifled.

(A) (as it is now)

(B) and suffer from problems that have no specific name but amounted to crushing boredom

(C) which cause discontent, and even though they play out their assigned roles in life, they feel dead inside

(D) less productive at work, and at a higher risk for anxiety, depression, and other health problems

(E) creating a sense that the individual has no awareness of an authentic self-image

26. In sentence 12 (reproduced below), the writer wants to provide a convincing explanation for why respondents were willing to reveal their secrets.

The response during a similar study at Columbia University in the 1990s was almost identical.

Which version of the text best accomplishes this goal?

(A) (as it is now)

(B) In our lonely, atomized society, we simply turn in desperation to anyone who'll listen.

(C) Evidently, they wanted to unburden themselves.

(D) Compared to older people, young men and women are less sensitive to the protocol of personal boundaries.

(E) Interviewers had been carefully screened to determine whether they had secrets of their own.

27. The writer is thinking about replacing sentence 13 (reproduced below) with a new sentence that will serve as a transition between paragraphs and also capture the audience's interest in the material that follows.

    Many of the secrets divulged to Barrow's team involve sex.

    Which of the following best achieves that objective?

    (A) (as it is now)
    (B) The secrets divulged during interviews held over two years' time pertained to several different areas of interest.
    (C) Barrow's team found that both men and women were equally forthcoming in revealing their secrets.
    (D) Among the most prominent topics discussed during interviews were money, family relations, sex, shopping, and friends.
    (E) As they talked, many respondents expressed fears that they would be perceived as chronic whiners who felt sorry for themselves.

28. To augment the discussion, the writer wants to add the following sentence to the fifth paragraph (sentences 18–23).

    The real emotional burden of secrecy, he has found, is social isolation.

    Where would the sentence best be placed?

    (A) Before sentence 19
    (B) After sentence 19
    (C) After sentence 20
    (D) After sentence 21
    (E) After sentence 22

29. The writer wants to add more information to the fifth paragraph (sentences 18–23) to support its main point. All of the following pieces of evidence help to achieve that purpose EXCEPT which one?

    (A) Wealth and fame are no antidotes to private feelings of inadequacy.
    (B) For solace, keepers of secrets may turn to drinking and drugs.
    (C) People withdraw from social situations in order to ease anxieties.
    (D) People isolate themselves out of fear that they may inadvertently disclose secrets.
    (E) Maintaining privacy is feeling secure.

30. The writer wants to add an idea after sentence 23 (reproduced below) that, adjusting for capitalization as needed, will serve as a bridge to the next paragraph.

    "This will make you feel alone and disconnected, which over time will take an emotional toll."

    Which of the following choices will best accomplish this goal?

    (A) True loneliness is a kind of spiritual emptiness, a feeling of superfluousness.
    (B) Community, on the other hand, is based on mutual affection.
    (C) Barrow's research also suggests that this self-destructive habit can be broken.
    (D) Psychologists like Barrow say the hardest thing to cure is an individual's effort to self-cure.
    (E) It is said that militants join terrorist groups to experience a sense of belonging.

31. The writer wants to add more information to the last paragraph (sentences 24–25) to build the main argument of the paragraph. All of the following pieces of evidence help to achieve this purpose EXCEPT which one?

(A) Confiding to non-intimates may facilitate honesty because the interviewer's feelings about you matter less than those of a good friend.

(B) Respondents may crave approval from an interviewer seen as some sort of authority figure.

(C) Experienced interviewers know how to establish trust and break down respondents' inhibitions.

(D) With support and guidance, a person can be empowered to break a pattern of obsessive thinking and begin to cope with secrets.

(E) Long-suffering respondents may be grateful for an interviewer with a sympathetic ear.

DIRECTIONS: *Questions 32–38.* Carefully read the following passage and answer the accompanying questions.

The passage is an excerpt from the draft of a newspaper story, dated September 2017.

Passage 4

(1) The growth in space satellites is being spurred not only by advances in miniaturization, low-cost electronics and rocketry but by the absence of worldwide guidelines for the uses of space. (2) This month, a single rocket launched from India recklessly flung 104
Line small "satellites" into space, each about the size of a Starbucks Trenta Cold Mocha Cookie
(5) Crumble Frappuccino. (3) Swarms of such minuscule instruments—hard to track and hard to dodge—increase the risk of collision for the world's vital communication, navigation and defense satellites. (4) Within a few years there might be another 20,000 or so small craft launched into a narrow band of space around the Earth, more than ten times the number of all working satellites presently in orbit. (5) By then traffic jams will heighten the hazards
(10) of junk encircling the Earth. (6) The US Air Force tracks 23,000 objects in orbit the size of a baseball or larger—most of them derelict rocket parts, decommissioned spacecraft and assorted pieces of wreckage.

(7) Emphasis must be placed on the ethical uses of space, or harm will inevitably befall the international space station, the Hubble Space Telescope and hundreds, or soon to be
(15) thousands, of satellites used for communications, national security, weather-forecasting and navigation. (8) The Satellite Industry Association estimates that about $127 billion in annual revenue from satellite services is vulnerable.

(9) Traveling at orbital speeds up to 17,000 miles an hour, even an aluminum pellet one centimeter wide packs the kinetic equivalent of a 400-pound safe moving at 60 miles an
(20) hour. (10) Last year, a scrap barely bigger than a grain of salt blew a hole in the European Space Agency's Sentinel 1-B satellite, knocking off five pieces that narrowly missed a nearby satellite. (11) More recently, something jolted the AMC9 telecommunications satellite owned by Luxembourg-based SES, disrupting data and broadcast services over the U.S. and Mexico.

(25)   (12) Unchecked, the growing debris in orbit "might make some regions of space unusable in the future, and that would impact everybody—everybody who uses a mobile phone, who gets television signals, who relies on weather forecasts," says Holger Krag, head of the European Space Agency's Space Debris Office. (13) "In other words, nearly everyone."

         (14) Parts that don't burn up in re-entry hit the Earth. (15) Aerospace industries try to
(30) predict where they will land. (16) When, in 2016, China's Tiangong-1 space lab stopped functioning and began to fall, it appeared to be headed to an area in the eastern United States, including most of Maryland and northern Virginia, nearly all of Pennsylvania and New Jersey. (17) Chinese technicians on the ground tried to control the craft's engines and significantly slow its descent. (18) "Firing the engines will have to be done at a specific
(35) moment so that it would reenter the atmosphere and substantially burn up over a large, unpopulated region of the southern Pacific Ocean," the European Space Agency (ESA) advised. (19) "Any surviving pieces would fall into the ocean, far from any populated areas." (20) However well meant, ESA's advice came too late because in the meantime, the spacecraft had died. (21) Teams on the ground could no longer control it. (22) It wasn't possible
(40) to give even an approximation of impact zone until just a short time before re-entry. (23) Most scientists didn't worry. (24) The odds of getting hit by a piece of the space station were extraordinarily low, about 1 million times smaller than winning a Powerball jackpot—and that's only if you lived in one of the "high-risk" areas. (25) Ultimately, the ESA estimated even lower odds: 1 in 300 trillion.

(45)   (26) Lottie Williams was unique as she walked through a park in 1997 in Tulsa, Oklahoma. (27) She was hit by a falling piece of space junk. (28) A strange tap hit her on the shoulder. (29) She also heard a piece of the Delta II rocket hit the ground. (30) Nobody else had been hit by a piece of space junk before she did. (31) "The weight was comparable to an empty soda can," she told Fox News. (32) "It looked like a piece of fabric except that when
(50) you tapped it, it sounded metallic."

         (33) Two decades earlier, in July 1979, Americans watched the sky in awe as Skylab, America's first manned space station, plunged to the Earth. (34) While some feared being hit by space junk, others celebrated and turned the event into a commercial opportunity. (35) There were several Skylab parties, and one hotel in Charlotte, North Carolina, even
(55) designated itself an official crash zone, featuring a painted target.

32. The writer wants to add the following sentence to the first paragraph (sentences 1–6) in order to support the paragraph's main argument.

    Some aerospace experts claim the presence of literally millions of hazardous "splinters," most of them too small to track.

    Where would the sentence best be placed?

    (A) Before sentence 3
    (B) After sentence 3
    (C) After sentence 4
    (D) After sentence 5
    (E) After sentence 6

33. The writer is concerned that the tone of sentence 2 (reproduced below) may be too glib.

> *This month, a single rocket launched from India flung 104 small satellites into space, each about the size of* <u>a Starbucks Trenta Cold Mocha Cookie Crumble Frappuccino</u>.

Which of the following versions of the underlined text provides the most appropriate introduction to the passage?

(A) (as it is now)
(B) a can of Coca Cola
(C) an astronaut's headgear
(D) an embroidered kids' lunch bag
(E) one-quarter of an unabridged dictionary

34. The writer wants to add a phrase at the beginning of sentence 3 (reproduced below), adjusting for capitalization, if necessary, to show the cause-and-effect relationship between sentences 2 and 3.

> *Swarms of small satellites—hard to track and hard to dodge—increase the risk of collision for the world's vital communication, navigation, and defense satellites.*

Which of the following best achieves that purpose?

(A) Accordingly, therefore,
(B) Resultfully,
(C) Subsequently,
(D) Meanwhile,
(E) Consequently,

35. In sentence 7 (reproduced below), which of the following versions of the underlined text best establishes the writer's position on the main argument of the passage?

> <u>*Emphasis must be placed on the ethical uses of space, or*</u> *harm will inevitably befall the international space station, the Hubble Space Telescope and hundreds, or soon to be thousands, of satellites used for communications, national security, weather-forecasting and navigation.*

(A) (as it is now)
(B) With the privatization of space exploration still in its infancy,
(C) Unless a gentlemen's agreement of understanding by like-minded countries is signed,
(D) Barring a pact by the world's countries to monitor and impose strict rules of access to certain areas of space,
(E) Russia, Japan, the U.S., and other countries must pledge to mend their careless ways or

36. Which of the following sentences, if placed before sentence 14 (reproduced below), would serve as a transition between paragraphs, appeal to the audience, and provide the most effective introduction to the topic of the next paragraph?

    Parts that don't burn up in re-entry hit the Earth.

    (A) (as it is now)
    (B) While it may sound like a bad April Fools' Day prank, pieces of space junk, some the size of a bus, sometimes fall out of the sky.
    (C) When an orbiting satellite fails, what to do about it is a question that space scientists have long pondered.
    (D) A satellite that no longer works is called, of all things—"space junk."
    (E) A system called "Controlled Re-Entry" is often used to bring broken satellites back to the Earth's surface.

37. Because of the length and content of the fifth paragraph (sentences 14–25), the writer is thinking about adding a topic sentence to the paragraph. Which of the following would serve best that purpose?

    (A) (leave the paragraph as it is)
    (B) How to deal with space debris has occasionally been a worrisome issue.
    (C) The prospect of a catastrophic crash by an uncontrollable space vehicle into a populated area has created far more anxiety than circumstances warranted.
    (D) Considering the minuscule odds of an inoperative spacecraft crashing to Earth in a populated area, people's fears were exaggerated beyond all reason.
    (E) Sophisticated technology put satellites into orbit around the Earth but failed to account for people's inevitable fears concerning the potential consequences of technical failure.

38. After proofreading the passage, the writer wants to revise sentences 26–30 (reproduced below) for greater coherence and economy of expression.

    (26) Lottie Williams was unique as she walked through a park in 1997 in Tulsa, Oklahoma. (27) She was hit by a falling piece of space junk. (28) A strange tap hit her on the shoulder. (29) She also heard a piece of the Delta II rocket hit the ground. (30) Nobody else had been hit by a piece of space junk before she did.

    In the context, which of the following versions of the text best accomplishes the goal?

    (A) Walking through a park in Tulsa, Oklahoma, in 1997, a piece of a Delta II rocket hit Lottie Williams on the shoulder before landing on the ground. In history, no other person before that was hit with a piece of space junk.
    (B) In 1997, Lottie Williams made history by walking through a Tulsa, Oklahoma, park and having a falling piece of a Delta II rocket hit the ground after tapping her on the shoulder—an unusually unique experience.
    (C) A piece of the Delta II rocket gave Lottie Williams, who was walking through a Tulsa, Oklahoma, park at the time in 1997, an opportunity to become the first person ever to be struck on the shoulder by a space junk fragment.
    (D) Lottie Williams is the only person in history known to be hit by falling space junk. In 1997, as she walked through a park in Tulsa, Oklahoma, she felt a strange tap on her shoulder and heard something hit the ground. It was a piece of the Delta II rocket.
    (E) Humankind experienced something unique in 1997 at a time when Lottie Williams was taking a walk in a park in Tulsa, Oklahoma. A piece of a Delta II rocket hit her shoulder before it landed on the ground. Nobody before or since has had the same thing happen to them.

> **DIRECTIONS:** *Questions 39–45.* Carefully read the following passage and answer the accompanying questions.

This passage is a draft of a contemporary newspaper column on maintaining good health.

Passage 5

(1) Everyone knows how important it is to maintain good physical and mental health. A wealth of research indicates that escaping to a neighborhood park, hiking through the woods or spending a weekend by the lake can lower a person's stress levels, decrease blood
Line pressure and reduce the risk of asthma, allergies, diabetes, cardiovascular problems and at
(5) the same time improve mental health and increase life expectancy. (2) That explains why doctors around the world prescribe time in nature as a means of improving and maintaining their patients' health.

(3) One question has remained: (4) How long or how frequently should you experience the great outdoors in order to reap its great benefits? (5) Is there a recommended dose? (6)
(10) Just how much nature is enough?

(7) According to a paper published in *Science Journal*, the answer is about 120 minutes each week. (8) The study examined data from nearly 20,000 people in Britain who participated in a two-year survey from 2014 to 2016. (9) All were asked to record their activities each week. (10) It found that people in urban, rather than natural, environments were
(15) forced to use much of their energy to overcome the effects of constant stimulation. (11) Thirty, sixty, or even ninety minutes in nature did not leave as significant an impact, and what's more, five hours a week in nature offered no additional health benefits.

(12) "What really amazed us was that this was true for all groups of people," said Dr. M. P. Greene, an environmental specialist who led the study. (13) "Two hours a week was the
(20) threshold for both men and women, older and younger adults, different ethnic groups, people living in rich as well as poor areas, and even for those living with long term illnesses." (14) It did not matter how close people lived to recreational spaces or how often they frequented them, as long as they accumulated two hours of outdoor time by the end of the week. (15) "Nature is not like a pill you get prescribed by your doctor that you have to take in small doses
(25) every day," Dr. Greene said. (16) "What matters most is that you're able to fit it into your lifestyle." (17) In cities, of course, there are fewer natural landscapes or parks to visit every day, an excuse Dr. Greene has heard more than once. (18) But they can still get the same benefits by taking a long walk on one day and a visit to a recreational area on a weekend.

(19) Dr. R. Petrocelli, a California internist, often prescribes outdoor time to her patients,
(30) who come mostly from low-income settings. (20) Monthly, in fact, she leads group outings in the Bay Area's hills and beaches. (21) "When you go to a park with your family, there are so many good things that can happen," Dr. Petrocelli says. (22) "Children get to play and be physically active. They get to socialize, and they get some stress relief." (23) Adults experience the same benefits.

(35) (24) But teasing out the exact causes of these health benefits is necessary; many people already are burdened by health expenses that they can't afford but can't be avoided. (25) Does being outdoors encourage physical activity? (26) Or are healthier, happier people simply more likely to spend time outdoors? (27) The answers are elusive. Much of the existing evidence is based on an arguably too simplistic either-or dichotomy.

(40)   (28) Still, nature prescriptions are growing in popularity. (29) In Sweden, *friluftsliv*, the term for living close to nature, is so ingrained in everyday life—from commuting by bike to relaxing in lakeside saunas—that there are tax breaks offered as incentives for the lifestyle. (30) And last year, the national hospital system in Scotland began urging doctors at some medical practices to write prescriptions for outdoor activities as a routine part of patient care.

(45)   (31) "This study will help clinicians like me better advise patients," Dr. Greene said. And, he added, "It provides a realistic target that most people can achieve. Low cost and low risk, it's just what the doctor ordered."

39. The writer is thinking about replacing sentence 1 (reproduced below) with another sentence that would both capture the audience's interest and provide an effective introduction to the passage.

> *Everyone knows how important it is to maintain good physical and mental health.*

Which of the following would best serve that purpose?

(A) (as it now is)

(B) Heart disease is the leading cause of death among American men.

(C) Statistics show that for several years obesity has been an ongoing problem in the United States.

(D) Here's a fact: Spending time outdoors, especially in green spaces, is good for you.

(E) When one has a sedentary lifestyle, there are many ways for a person's health and well-being to erode.

40. In sentence 10 (reproduced below) the writer wants to provide convincing evidence to show that spending time in nature has salutary effects on health. Which version of the underlined text best accomplishes this objective?

> *It found that* <u>people in urban, rather than natural, environments were forced to use much of their energy to overcome the effects of constant stimulation.</u>

(A) (as it is now)

(B) natural environments captured people's attention while simultaneously eliciting feelings of pleasure.

(C) the green leaf pigment called chlorophyll, the one link between the sun and life, is evidently essential to the flow of perpetual energy to our minds and bodies.

(D) people whose weekly outdoor time amounted to two or more hours felt energized and relaxed, slept better, and were generally pleased to be alive.

(E) being in nature is restorative because natural environments help people feel a sense of escape from the stressful demands of life.

41. The writer wants to add a phrase at the start of sentence 11 (reproduced below), adjusting the capitalization as needed, to set up a comparison with the idea discussed in sentence 10.

    Thirty, sixty, or even ninety minutes in nature did not leave as significant an effect. . . .

    Which of the following best achieves that objective?

    (A) even so,
    (B) when all is said and done, however,
    (C) by the same token,
    (D) conversely,
    (E) on the other hand,

42. In sentence 18 (reproduced below), which of the following versions best supports the writer's position on the main argument of the passage?

    But they can still get the same benefits by taking a long walk on one day and a visit to a recreational area on a weekend.

    (A) (as it is now)
    (B) But Dr. Greene tells patients they can still get the same benefits by taking a long walk on one day and making a trip to a recreational area on a weekend.
    (C) But a long walk on one day and a trip to a recreational area on weekends has the same effect.
    (D) Irregardless, Dr. Greene claims they can still get the same benefits from a long walk on one day and a trip to a recreational area on a weekend.
    (E) However, the benefits available to them by taking a long walk on one day or making a trip to a recreational area on a weekend.

43. In sentence 24 (reproduced below), the writer wants to describe what is needed for greater understanding of why being in nature is healthful.

    But teasing out the exact causes of these health benefits is necessary; <u>many people already are unavoidably burdened by health expenses that they can't afford but can't be avoided.</u>

    Which version of the underlined text best accomplishes this goal?

    (A) (as it is now)
    (B) at present, the existing evidence base is purely speculative.
    (C) tracking habits and responses over a period of time could shed light on the possible mechanisms.
    (D) anything that gets people off the couch and away from screens is bound to be helpful.
    (E) health care providers and insurance companies, among others, are instrumental in keeping down the cost of care.

44. In the next paragraph (sentences 28–30), the writer wants to expand the argument for more reliable data about the relationship between nature and people's health. Which of the following pieces of evidence would best serve as an introduction to this topic?

    (A) Today's trend toward urbanization means that much of the world's population spends less time exposed to natural environments.

    (B) "Our study on the effects of natural environments looks at a specific point in time," says Carl Masak, a researcher at Norway's Institute of Sport and Health Sciences in Oslo.

    (C) According to existing evidence, during the last decade people's understanding of the relationship between health and the environment has been in a state of flux.

    (D) Indeed, if the postulated causal relationship between natural environments and health is correct, access to national, state, and local parks should be free of charge.

    (E) Since 2009, behavioral and physiological responses to nature have attracted the attention of numerous Ph.D. candidates at universities around the world.

45. In the next-to-last paragraph of the passage (sentences 28–30), the writer wants to provide further evidence to support the claim, made in sentence 28, that nature prescriptions are becoming not only more common but even essential to a comprehensive health plan for an individual. Which of the following pieces of evidence would best achieve this purpose?

    (A) An announcement by the AMA (American Medical Association) that doctors should routinely consider recommending outdoor experiences to their patients

    (B) The publication of a best-selling book containing the accounts of two dozen gravely ill men and women whose health returned to normal after a prescribed regimen of outdoor activities

    (C) A report on the effectiveness of the "healing forest" created for stressed-out citizens of South Korea

    (D) A month-long public-service infomercial campaign broadcast on social media to highlight the health benefits of outdoor activity

    (E) The development by the National Institutes of Health of age-appropriate guidelines—like those for weekly exercise—for experiences in natural settings

Section II

Three Essay Questions

TIME: 2 HOURS AND 15 MINUTES

Write your essays on standard 8½″ × 11″ composition paper. At the exam you will be given a bound booklet containing 12 lined pages.

Essay Question 1

SUGGESTED TIME:
15 MINUTES FOR READING THE QUESTION AND SOURCES
40 MINUTES FOR WRITING AN ESSAY

Individuals and groups are invited into many high schools to inform students about colleges and job opportunities. By law, such schools must also allow representatives from the armed forces to talk with students about joining the military. Not everyone supports this policy. Peace groups as well as many parents, for instance, would like to change the law in order to keep military recruiters out of the schools.

Carefully read the following seven sources, including the material that introduces each source. Then, in an essay that synthesizes at least three of the sources, take a position on the issue that a law denying military recruiters access to students on high school campuses should be passed.

Source A (ACLU)
Source B (Inouye)
Source C (*Debate.org*)
Source D (Cartoon)
Source E (Hawk)
Source F (Hardcastle)
Source G (Miralao)

Instructions:

- Respond to the prompt with a thesis that may establish a line of reasoning.
- Provide evidence from at least three of the provided sources to support the thesis. Indicate clearly the sources used through direct quotation, paraphrase, or summary. Sources may be cited as Source A, Source B, etc., or by using the descriptions in parentheses.
- Explain the relationship between the evidence and the thesis.
- Demonstrate an understanding of the rhetorical situation.
- Use appropriate grammar and punctuation in communicating the argument.

Source A

"Q & A About Military Recruitment at High Schools," ACLU of Washington, *www.aclu-wa.org*, September 14, 2007.

This passage is excerpted from an online article prepared by the American Civil Liberties Union, a group devoted to protecting the constitutional rights of all Americans.

Are schools required to allow military recruiters on campus?

. . . [L]aws require high schools to give military recruiters the same access to the campus as they provide to other persons or groups who advise students about occupational or educational options. Therefore, if a school does not have any on-campus recruiting by employers or colleges, it is not required to have on-campus military recruiting. For example, if a school has a job fair with booths for many employers, it must offer a booth to military recruiters.

Can peace groups or military counseling groups get equal time as military recruiters?

Nothing would prevent a school from allowing peace groups to come on campus if it wished. Whether peace groups could require the school to provide access against its wishes depends on whether the school has created a public forum for that kind of expression. . . .

Can I prevent my school from giving contact information to military recruiters?

The law requires schools to release basic contact information about students (called "directory information") to military recruiters. However, schools are required to honor a family's request that such information not be provided.

Source B

Arlene Inouye, "Should Military Recruiters Be Allowed on School Campuses?" *California Teachers Association Educator*, May 2013, *www.cta.org*.

Below is an excerpt from an article by a Los Angeles teacher who coordinates CAMS (Coalition for Alternatives to Militarism in Our Schools).

   Public schools should not be the recruiting grounds for young people to be subjected to sophisticated, persuasive marketing techniques designed to sell them on joining the military. . . . Military recruitment is about the indoctrination of our young in a culture that glamorizes war and violence. Recruiters use deception and false promises to entice students who feel like they have few or no options. We call this the "poverty draft." The lure of the military particularly impacts youth of color, and more middle-class families as college becomes less affordable.

   I witnessed Marine recruiters promising students from working-poor families a way to be "successful," go to college, buy a home for their parents and make their families proud. They promise male students a way to manhood, strength and independence. They promise females the best of all worlds: supervision and independence that will help them build strength of character. Recruiters know how to market the military in a way that speaks to the dreams and hopes of these young people.

   . . . If we are a society that values our young, it is imperative we stop allowing the military to give them false and misleading information. It is wrong for the military to be afforded legitimacy and authority in our schools without also providing the truth about what it means to experience war.

Source C

"Should the Military Be Allowed to Recruit in Public Schools?" *Debate.org*, © 2013.

According to the keepers of Debate.org, their website is a place "where intelligent minds from around the world come to debate online and read the opinions of others."

I enlisted at the start of my senior year in high school—the best decision I ever made. I knew I wasn't going to college if I didn't join. (No money and lack of drive hurt my GPA.)

Now that I've left active duty, I'm a much better student. I'm focused, I'm driven, and I'm a lot more respectful of others. I'm a better person and I would not be this way if a recruiter had not visited my high school.

Military experience has opened doors for me and for those like me who have limited or even no options after high school. It turns boys and girls into men and women.

Every enlistee I ever met knew they were going to war, and 99% accepted it. Why? you may ask. Because they are the few who are willing to step up and fight, unlike those who hide behind those who fight.

So don't cry that high school students are easy targets for the propaganda spread by military recruiters. Think about it: Colleges do the exact same thing as military recruiters do.

—*Submitted by "Wild Bill," a U.S. Marine, 2006–2011*

Source D

"EP," "Military Recruitment Day," SouthWest Organizing Project, *swop.net*, Albuquerque, NM. Accessed from Google Images, July 2010.

This cartoon comes from the SouthWest Organizing Project, which works to empower communities to realize racial and gender equality as well as social and economic justice.

Source E

Ruby Hawk, "Military Recruitment in High Schools," *Socyberty.com.*, February 15, 2010.

This is excerpted from a position paper posted on the website of a group that publishes articles online on social issues from human psychology to politics and education.

The United States has long been against recruitment of child soldiers in other countries. So why do we have military recruiters going to high schools lecturing kids about all the advantages of joining the military? The pressure put on these students by aggressive recruiters has been unconscionable. Misconduct by recruiters includes deception, false promises, and hassling these kids at school and home. How can we call it volunteering when these youths are hounded and tricked into the service?

. . . [T]he U.S. continues its strategy to recruit youngsters under 17, and fails to protect 17 year olds from aggressive abusive recruitment. The ACLU [American Civil Liberties Union] also found that the U.S. military tactics targets kids from low income families. Last year a U.N. committee called on the U.S. to end military training in public schools and to stop targeting low income students and other venerable [*sic*] economic groups for military service.

In Georgia, violations are continuing. Federal law compels high schools to disclose student records of juniors and seniors, including students under 17, to military recruiters. Parents can sign and submit a form asking that the data be withheld, but many schools do not make that information available to parents. . . .

Source F

Mike Hardcastle, "What Should You Do After High School? A Look at Your Postgraduate Choices." *about.com*, accessed August 2010.

The passage consists of excerpts from an article posted online by a group that dispenses practical advice to teenagers.

Military life is for you if you thrive in a strict and structured environment, like helping people, have a sense of adventure and want to travel. ROTC [Reserve Officers Training Corps] is also a way to pay for university and ensure that you will have a job immediately after graduation.

Military life is not for everyone. Military service often puts you in high-risk situations and your life is often in danger even if you are not in a war zone. Depending on what type of service you choose even training can carry life-or-limb risks. Also, it is common for military service people to engage in peacekeeping missions that are anything but peaceful.

Whether you are deployed to a recognized war zone like the Middle East or are sent on a peacekeeping mission, a military career carries unusual risks. It also has incredible benefits. You get to see the world because military life involves travel. . . . You also get to learn crazy-fun skills that can't be learned anywhere else without having to pay for it like: skydiving, scuba diving, piloting aircraft, driving heavy-armored equipment, target shooting, to name a few. You don't just work in the military. It is a way of life. As the commercials state, it is really the toughest job you will ever love.

. . . While there is nothing wrong with jumping right in to the workforce after high school, be wary of accepting just any old job in order to bring home a paycheck. While you are still young you have so many opportunities to take advantage of that working in a dead end job or accepting a seemingly high paying position with no future is simply a waste. This is your life; make the best of it.

Source G

Sidney Miralao, "Military Recruiters Are Exploiting High School Students' Financial Insecurities," *Research and Commentary*, August 14, 2020

The passage contains excerpts from an article published online by Inequality.org., *an organization that focuses on economic inequality.*

. . . There's a group of outsiders in schools we should be wary of: the U.S. military.

Schools have become goldmines for recruiting future soldiers. . . . Recruiters at my high school set up shop in the cafeteria. For two hours they would sit through four different lunch periods and give their spiel to whoever was curious enough to stop at their station.

Recruiters use their omnipresence on campus to build relationships and trust in all kinds of different ways. They may offer to chaperone homecoming events, timekeep at football games, or even give lectures in history and government classes.

All the while, they paint a glamorous picture of life in the military. Promises of scholarships and a chance to earn honor and respect around the world are very compelling to 17-year-olds, especially those with not a lot of options.

That's key. Recruiters deliberately exploit the financial and social insecurities of teenagers to enlist more soldiers. A RAND Corporation study, for example, found that nearly 57 percent of students at public high schools with ROTC programs relied on free or reduced-price lunch—about 10 percent more than schools without them.

Finally, four years of studies by the Resistance Center in Massachusetts found that Black, Hispanic, Indigenous, and low-income students were overrepresented among the enlistees most often put into harm's way.

. . . These practices are nothing less than predatory. Research reveals numerous physical and mental health risks from joining the military at a young age—including higher rates of substance abuse, depression, PTSD, and suicide. Students' rights to health care, education, housing, and citizenship, among other military "perks," should not have to be earned by putting their lives on the line.

Essay Question 2

SUGGESTED TIME: 40 MINUTES

(This question counts as one-third of the total score for Section II.)

> What follows is part of an essay, "Our March to Washington," written by Theodore Winthrop (1828–1861) about going off to fight in the Civil War. Carefully read the excerpt and then write an essay that analyzes the rhetorical strategies Winthrop used to convey his feelings about the experience.
>
> **Instructions:**
> - Respond to the prompt with a thesis that may establish a line of reasoning.
> - Select and use evidence to develop and support the line of reasoning.
> - Explain the relationship between the evidence and the thesis.
> - Demonstrate an understanding of the rhetorical situation.
> - Use appropriate grammar and punctuation in communicating the argument.

At three o'clock in the afternoon of Friday, April 19, we took our peacemaker, a neat twelve-round brass howitzer, down from the Seventh Regiment Armory, and stationed it in the rear of the building. The twin peacemaker is somewhere near us, but entirely hidden by
Line this enormous crowd.

(5)   An enormous crowd! of both sexes, of every age and condition. The men offer all kinds of truculent and patriotic hopes; the women shed tears, and say, "God bless you, boys."

This is a part of the town where baddish cigars prevail. But good or bad, I am ordered to keep all away from the gun. So the throng stands back, peers curiously over the heads of its junior members, and seems to be taking the measure of my coffin.

(10)   At a great house on the left, as we pass the Astor Library, I see a handkerchief waving for me. Yes! it is she who made the sandwiches in my knapsack. They were a trifle too thick, as I afterwards discovered, but otherwise perfection. Be these my thanks and the thanks of hungry comrades who had bites of them!

At the corner of Great Jones Street we halted for half an hour,—then, everything ready,
(15) we marched down Broadway.

It was worth a life, that march. Only one who passed, as we did, through that tempest of cheers, two miles long, can know the terrible enthusiasm of the occasion. I could hardly hear the rattle of our own gun-carriages, and only once or twice the music of our band came to me muffled and quelled by the uproar. We knew now, if we had not before divined it, that our great
(20) city was with us as one man, utterly united in the great cause we were marching to sustain.

This grand fact I learned by two senses. If hundreds of thousands roared it into my ears, thousands slapped it into my back. My fellow-citizens smote me on the knapsack, as I went by at the gun-rope, and encouraged me each in his own dialect. "Bully for you!" alternated with benedictions, in the proportion of two "bullies" for one blessing.

(25)   I was not so fortunate as to receive more substantial tokens of sympathy. But there were parting gifts showered on the regiment, enough to establish a variety-shop. Handkerchiefs, of course, came floating down upon us from the windows like a snow. Pretty little gloves pelted us with love-taps. The sterner sex forced upon us pocket-knives new and jagged, combs, soap, slippers, boxes of matches, cigars by the dozen and the hundred, pipes to
(30) smoke shag and pipes to smoke Latakia,[1] fruit, eggs, and sandwiches. One fellow got a new purse with ten bright quarter-eagles.

---
[1] *a type of tobacco*

Essay Question 3

SUGGESTED TIME: 40 MINUTES

(This question counts as one-third of the total score for Section II.)

> The following passage was written by Sidney Smith (1771–1845), an English clergyman known as the wittiest man of his time. It has been adapted from Smith's review of *The Book of Fallacies* by Jeremy Bentham, published in London in 1824.
>
> Once you have read the passage, write an essay in which you support, refute, or qualify Smith's claim that to invoke our ancestors as a justification to act in a certain way is to rely on an "absurd and mischievous" fallacy. Use evidence from your reading, study, observation, or personal experience to develop your argument.
>
> **Instructions:**
>
> - Respond to the prompt with a thesis that may establish a line of reasoning.
> - Select and use evidence to develop and support the line of reasoning.
> - Explain the relationship between the evidence and the thesis.
> - Demonstrate an understanding of the rhetorical situation.
> - Use appropriate grammar and punctuation in communicating the argument.

There are a vast number of absurd and mischievous fallacies, which pass readily in the world for sense and virtue, while in truth they tend only to fortify error and encourage crime. Mr. Bentham has enumerated the most conspicuous of these in the book before

Line us . . .

(5)   OUR WISE ANCESTORS—*The Wisdom of Our Ancestors—The Wisdom of the Ages— Venerable Antiquity—Wisdom of Old Times*—This mischievous and absurd fallacy springs from the grossest perversion of the meaning of words. Experience is certainly the mother of wisdom, and the old have, of course, greater experience than the young; but the question is who are the old? and who are the young?

(10)   Of *individuals* living at the same period, the oldest has, of course, the greatest experience; but among *generations* of men the reverse is true. Those who come first (our ancestors) are the young people, and have the least experience. We have added to their experience the experience of many centuries; and, therefore, as far as experience goes, are wiser and more capable of forming an opinion than they were. The real feeling should be, *not*

(15) can we be so presumptuous as to put our opinions in opposition to those of our ancestors? but can such young, ignorant, inexperienced persons as our ancestors necessarily were, be expected to have understood a subject as well as those who have seen so much more, lived so much longer, and enjoyed the experience of so many centuries?

END OF PRACTICE TEST 3

ANSWER KEY
Practice Test 3

Answers to Multiple-Choice Questions

1.	**D**	13.	**B**	25.	**D**	37.	**A**
2.	**E**	14.	**D**	26.	**C**	38.	**D**
3.	**D**	15.	**B**	27.	**A**	39.	**D**
4.	**C**	16.	**E**	28.	**B**	40.	**D**
5.	**A**	17.	**D**	29.	**A**	41.	**E**
6.	**D**	18.	**C**	30.	**C**	42.	**B**
7.	**B**	19.	**B**	31.	**D**	43.	**C**
8.	**E**	20.	**A**	32.	**E**	44.	**C**
9.	**B**	21.	**A**	33.	**B**	45.	**E**
10.	**A**	22.	**B**	34.	**E**		
11.	**A**	23.	**C**	35.	**D**		
12.	**E**	24.	**E**	36.	**A**		

Summary of Answers in Section I (Multiple-Choice)

Number of correct answers _____

Use this information when you calculate your score for this exam. See page 320.

Answer Explanations to Multiple-Choice Questions

Passage 1—An excerpt from William Dean Howells' "I Talk of Dreams"

1. **(D)** Through much of the passage the speaker laments the indignities he has suffered, especially when he tells others about his dreams.

2. **(E)** It may not be universal, but the speaker's view of dreams is not uncommon. One's own dreams are generally more interesting to ourselves than are the dreams of others.

3. **(D)** The speaker is egregiously hypocritical, or even delusional. That is, he has retreated into a world of unreality, allowing himself to think more highly of himself than is warranted.

4. **(C)** Even this early in the passage, because the audience is likely to be aware of the speaker's state of mind, the sentence contributes another dimension to his self-portrait.

5. **(A)** In the first sentence of the paragraph, the speaker generalizes about the incredible "egotism of some people." In the next sentence, he explains exactly what he means.

6. **(D)** In each of the incorrect choices, the speaker includes adjectives meant to arouse negative feelings about the content of others' dreams. Choice (D) is the exception because it refers not to the dreams but rather to the behavior of the dreamer.

7. **(B)** The paragraph consists largely of examples of adverse consequences brought on by recitations of dreams.

8. **(E)** The verb "should be taught" is a clue that the speaker is proposing a course of action. In the second clause, the speaker adds a gratuitous slur.

9. **(B)** The word prepares the audience for a discussion of the speaker's own dreams, which he believes to be in a class by themselves.

10. **(A)** After criticizing people for imposing their dreams on others, it is ironic that the speaker is about to do just what he insists should not be done—tell the story of a dream.

11. **(A)** All the phrases except one allude to acceptable customs and behavior observed by members of a certain social class. The allusion to a child's "duties" is different because it refers to obligatory behavior.

12. **(E)** By telling about his dream, the speaker supports his claim, made in the first paragraph, that unlike the dreams of others, his own dreams are worth hearing about. Although (B) may seem like a reasonable choice, it is a flawed answer because it refers specifically to the dreams of other people.

13. **(B)** The speaker's original intent is to impress the audience with a story about his association with the lofty Duke of Wellington. By the end, of course, the duke has demeaned him, much to the speaker's embarrassment. (A) is a reasonable answer but is less specific than (B).

Passage 2—An excerpt from T. S. Eliot, "On Teaching the Appreciation of Poetry"

14. **(D)** The speaker presents himself as an ordinary person, not as a distinguished authority on either the art of poetry or the teaching of it. Choice (E) is a reasonable answer, but in comparison to (D) is too general.

15. **(B)** The quotation marks indicate the speaker has doubts that poetry can be taught effectively, if at all.

16. **(E)** The speaker explains in lines 12–13: "It is in a spirit of curiosity . . . that I approach the subject of teaching poetry." He also wants to know more about the young people, their teachers, and the current teaching methods (lines 13–15).

17. **(D)** All the other choices are examples of the ordinary concerns and occupations of everyday people. The speaker includes them in the passage to portray himself as a regular person rather than an illustrious, larger-than-life poet.

18. **(C)** The speaker's criticism focuses on students being subjected to types of questions and certain approaches that are "wrong" because they presuppose that there will always be right and wrong answers.

19. **(B)** The latter half of the paragraph critiques teachers' focus on poets and on having students seek precise answers about the meanings of poems.

20. **(A)** The sentence marks a slight change in the direction of the passage. By using the phrase "this sort of thing" the speaker ties paragraph 3 to what he intends to say in paragraph 4. The paragraphs are specifically linked to each other, too, by allusions to childhood: "too early" in paragraph 2 and "when I was young" at the start of paragraph 3.

21. **(A)** To some degree, all the choices except (A) are implied by the speaker's brief interjection.

22. **(B)** The speaker admits to being slightly amused to be in cahoots with students who want to prove that their teachers had misinterpreted one of his poems.

23. **(C)** With such usages as "embarrassed by juvenile correspondence" (lines 47–48) and "choking up . . . letter boxes" (line 48), the speaker conveys a sense of longing for a time when poets could devote themselves exclusively to being poets.

Passage 3—An excerpt from "Frontiers of Research and Discovery," an anonymously written report on keeping secrets

24. **(E)** This version eliminates awkward expression, unorthodox mechanics, repetition, and redundancy.

25. **(D)** uses a series of grammatically parallel phrases to develop the idea of pervasive dissatisfaction among people who harbor secrets.

26. **(C)** Is the only logical explanation. The other reasons might have merit if more information had been given about how respondents were chosen and interviews conducted.

27. **(A)** Although none of the choices stands out as a truly effective transitional sentence, each of them could serve that purpose. As for capturing the audience's interest, however, (A), which highlights sex, wins hands down. (D) also mentions sex, but its allure is diminished by all of the other topics.

28. **(B)** The sentence develops the idea stated in sentence 19 that the stress of concealing secrets doesn't significantly affect a person's well-being. Rather, the real emotional toll is social isolation.

29. **(A)** The paragraph's main idea relates to the emotional burdens borne by socially isolated people. Except for (A), all the choices to one degree or another touch on that idea.

30. **(C)** The paragraph in question takes up the subject of alleviating, or even eliminating, the symptoms of despair created by loneliness. Therefore, (C) provides an apt transition between paragraphs.

31. **(D)** The principle is valid, but of all the choices it is the least effective in explaining why respondents willingly revealed their secrets.

Passage 4—An excerpt adapted from a newspaper story draft about satellites in space, 2019

32. **(E)** The writer has organized the paragraph more or less sequentially according to the size of various objects—from the deliberate insertion of satellites into orbit to the unwelcome presence of hazardous baseball-sized objects. In this context, the sentence in question, which discusses millions of "hazardous splinters too small to track," fits best at the end of the paragraph.

33. **(B)** offers the simplest and easiest-to-grasp (hence, most appropriate) image.

34. **(E)** is the best choice to indicate that one event is the cause of another. (B) is not a standard English idiom. The other choices may be appropriate but are less precise than the correct one.

35. **(D)** spells out what the writer believes needs to be done to prevent catastrophe in space. The other choices are either irrelevant or too vague to solve the problem.

36. **(A)** The sentence serves all three functions. An argument could be made for (B), however, because of its engaging references to April Fools' Day and pieces of junk "the size of a bus." Despite its appeal, however, (B) adds little substance to the passage.

37. **(A)** All the choices except (A) accurately describe the substance of the paragraph. Any one of them, therefore, might serve as the topic sentence. Because the overall meaning and intent of the paragraph are relatively transparent, however, a separate topic sentence may be superfluous. But if the writer insisted on adding one, (B) would be the most reasonable choice.

38. **(D)** avoids the wordiness, awkward expression, grammatical flaws, and incoherence of both the original and other versions.

Passage 5—An excerpt adapted from a newspaper column draft on good health, 2019

39. **(D)** An abrupt opening statement such as this one has a good chance of attracting readers' attention. It not only introduces the first paragraph but also summarizes the entire passage. The other choices are basically commonplace ideas unlikely to generate much interest. Nor do they relate very closely to the content of the entire passage.

40. **(D)** Although all the choices refer in some way to the salutary effects of nature, (D) names the very benefits that were the focus of the study.

41. **(E)** Using (E) as a transition, the writer contrasts the experiences of those who did and those who didn't spend a certain period of time out-of-doors.

42. **(B)** is the best choice because it relates directly to the exigence of the passage and avoids writing errors found among the others, including faulty diction, verb choice, pronoun person, pronoun reference, sentence fragment, and parallel structure.

43. **(C)** is the only choice that proposes a course of action to determine why natural environments seem to enhance mental and physical health.

44. **(C)** suggests that because no consistently reliable data are available, there is a need for more research on the subject.

45. **(E)** A set of guidelines developed by a world-class authority like the NIH is the most convincing evidence.

Answers to Essay Questions

For an overview of how essays are graded, turn to "How Essays Are Read and Evaluated," page 37.

Although answers to the essay questions will vary greatly, the following descriptions suggest a possible approach to each question and contain ideas that could be used in a response to the question. Perhaps your essay contains many of the same ideas. If not, don't be alarmed. Your ideas may be at least as insightful, or even more so, as those below.

Essay Question 1

Some Arguments <u>In Favor</u> of Changing the Law That Gives Military Recruiters Access to Students in High Schools:

- The quality of enlistees is high [implying that recruiting in high schools is unnecessary]. (Source A)
- Recruiters use questionable methods to sway young and impressionable students into joining the military. (Source D)
- Military recruitment is about the indoctrination of young people in a culture that glamorizes war and violence. (Source B)
- The United States has a tradition of deploring the recruitment of very young soldiers in other countries. (Source E)
- Military recruiters use highly persuasive and often deceptive sales pitches that target low-income and non-college-bound students. (Sources E and G)

Some Arguments <u>Against</u> Changing the Law That Gives Military Recruiters Access to Students in High Schools:

- The law is fair because it provides equal access to high school students by employers, colleges, and the military. (Source A)
- Families of students can exercise the right to withhold student contact information from military recruiters. (Source A)
- Military experience opens doors for young men and women who face limited options after high school. (Source C)
- Military recruiters should be welcome in schools because their techniques are no different from those used by college recruiters. (Source C)
- Non-college-bound students can be given useful information about the vast educational and other opportunities available to service men and women. (Source F)
- Because the armed forces consist overwhelmingly of high school graduates, the system must be working. Knowing that high school graduation is a requirement for enlistment, more students may stay in school instead of dropping out. (Source G)

Question 2, Based on an Excerpt from Theodore Winthrop's "Our March to Washington," 1861

The first-person narrator of this episode is a young man on his way to war. He and his regiment are parading through a city where people have gathered to send them off.

First he is assigned to keep onlookers away from a large cannon, a howitzer, named a "peace-maker." Whether he is aware of the irony of applying that label to a machine of war remains unclear, but in all likelihood he isn't, because he seems too caught up in the spirit of the moment.

Indeed, he is impressed by the size of the cheering crowd. Twice he uses the phrase "enormous crowd" (lines 4 and 5), once with an exclamation point for additional emphasis. He notes the men's expressions of "truculent and patriotic hopes" (line 6). He also notices that the "women shed tears and say, 'God bless you, boys'" (line 6), but he seems unmindful of the feelings that evoke such responses. In other words, this is not a time for subtle observation or reflection. Yet, he reads in the faces of onlookers that they seem "to be taking the measure of my coffin" (line 9). In other words, before continuing his description of the parade, the speaker senses briefly the dark implications behind the noisy celebration.

"It was worth a life, that march" (line 16), he says, an opinion that can be interpreted in two ways. It could mean simply that the march was an experience of a lifetime. On the other hand, it suggests that the speaker knows that he, as well as many of his comrades, will soon be giving up their lives—a thought reinforced by the phrase "terrible enthusiasm" (line 17), in which "terrible" seems to be used in the sense of "terrifying" or "horrible," although at that time the word also carried a connotation of "awe-inspiring."

What is more, the speaker uses the term "tokens of sympathy" (line 25) for the small gifts—handkerchiefs, gloves, combs, soaps, etc.—that the crowd bestows on the troops. In a sense, this could also be the speaker's way of drawing attention to the discrepancy between the sacrifice he and his comrades may be about to make in battle and the trivial price paid by the people left behind. Or the seemingly insignificant gifts may also be interpreted as more personal expressions of support.

On one level, then, the passage is a rather superficial depiction of a typical farewell march of troops going to fight. On a deeper level, though, readers are privy to the apprehension felt by one young soldier. His fears and anxieties are presented not as blatant statements but by hints and indirections. Like most of the crowd—more inclined to shout "'bullies'" than "benedictions" (line 24)—he puts up a brave front at a time of great peril and uncertainty.

Question 3, Based on Sidney Smith's Review of *The Book of Fallacies*

If you were to agree with Smith, your essay might begin with a rationale such as this: Young people need to make decisions on their own. Self-reliance is a sign of maturity. Therefore, on the verge of adulthood, the young will disregard the wisdom of the past. Beyond that, you could probably name several situations and endeavors in which young people are likely to be better informed than their elders. When it comes to modern electronic and digital technology, for instance, it's a truism that the young folks are far more savvy than the geezers. The same principle applies to such everyday activities as going to bed and getting up in the morning. Traditional wisdom says, "Early to bed and early to rise . . . ," but modern youth knows better. They have the advantage of research into enzymes and body chemistry showing that most teenagers, biologically, tend to function more efficiently later in the day than early in the morning. No doubt you can think of additional ways in which to support Smith's surprising assertion that our ancestors are "the young people, and have the least experience."

If, on the other hand, you choose to poke holes in Smith's argument, you might cite several examples of how old-time wisdom and experience are valid today. You might argue, for instance, that governmental decisions and policies must be based on historical evidence. From World War II, the world learned, if nothing else, to be far more alert to the threats of genocide. From Iran and Afghanistan, America has presumably learned to be wary of political and military quagmires. In crisis after crisis, the wisdom of America's founders has proved to be a solid foundation for decision-making. In addition, ancient religious texts thousands of years old still serve as moral compasses for individuals as well as groups. Back in the 17th century, Rouchefoucauld said, "Nothing is given so profusely as advice," and, "The true way to be deceived is to think oneself more clever than others"—just two pieces of wisdom among countless others that are as apt today as they were generations ago.

Or let your essay take the middle ground between these two extremes. A strong case could be made that the past can serve as a beacon in some areas of life, but is hopelessly irrelevant in others. Certainly our ancestors can teach us little about treating cancer or AIDS. Their knowledge of diseases, health, nutrition, and genetics now seems quaint. Their understanding of the physical world was relatively primitive. But, when it comes to common sense about character and human relations, getting and spending money, morals and values, and so on, the wisdom of "old times" may still be instructive and useful.

How to Score the Essays

The following essay-scoring guidelines apply to all three essays on the exam. The maximum score on an essay is 6; the minimum, 0.

Points are awarded in three categories:

1. Thesis (0–1 point)
2. Evidence and Commentary (0–4 points)
3. Sophistication (0–1 point)

THESIS (0–1 point)

No credit is given for an absent, erroneous, or incoherent thesis or one that merely restates or paraphrases the essay prompt.

One point is awarded for a thesis that states or strongly implies a reasonable interpretation of the issue raised by the prompt for Essay #1, the synthesis essay. Similarly, for Essay #2 one point is given for a reasonable thesis related to rhetoric in the given passage. For Essay #3 add a point for a thesis that clearly articulates a position on the issue raised by the prompt.

EVIDENCE AND COMMENTARY (0–4 points)

No points are given for restating the thesis in different words or for material irrelevant to the prompt.

One point is earned for evidence that tends to help develop the thesis.

Two points are given for evidence that clearly supports the thesis but may not add significantly to the writer's line of reasoning.*

Three points are awarded in Essay #1 for evidence that supports the thesis and also begins to show how source material supports your point of view. Give three points for evidence in Essay #2 that identifies and offers some analysis of rhetoric in the passage. Likewise, in Essay #3, give three points for specific evidence that helps to develop an argument for or against the main idea expressed by the prompt.

Four points indicate that you have consistently and effectively included compelling evidence to support all claims in a line of reasoning and also have clearly employed at least three sources to strengthen your position on the given issue (Essay #1), identified ample relevant evidence of rhetoric in the given passage (Essay #2), and cited compelling evidence to support your argument in favor of or against the given issue (Essay #3).

SOPHISTICATION (0–1 point)

No credit is given for ideas, however discerning, that you mention but don't develop.

One point is awarded for the development of ideas that broaden an interpretation of the issue (Essay #1), cite and explain significant rhetorical features of the passage (Essay #2), and discuss the opinions expressed in the given passage (Essay #3) by one or more of the following:

(a) Identifying and discussing complexities or tensions in the text.
(b) Illuminating an interpretation of the work by situating it within a broader context.
(c) Suggesting alternative interpretations of the work.
(d) Employing a consistently vivid and persuasive writing style.

Use of Standard English: No specific credit is given for the use of standard English. Readers are bound to be favorably impressed, however, by well-expressed, economical, virtually error-free prose.

---

*The term **"line of reasoning"** refers to the means by which an idea or thesis is supported. For instance, an essay may focus on the writer's choice of words, use of logic, sequence of ideas, or even the essay's title in order to validate the thesis. A poor line of reasoning exists when there is a gap between the thesis and the evidence presented.

Essay Evaluation Worksheet

In the spaces below enter the number of credits earned in each category. See pages 317–318 for detailed scoring guidelines.

	Essay 1 Synthesis Essay	Essay 2 Analytical Essay	Essay 3 Argumentative Essay
Category			
Thesis (0–1)			
Evidence and Commentary (0–4)			
Sophistication (0–1)			
TOTAL SCORE ON EACH ESSAY (0–6)			

Enter each essay score on the Test Score Worksheet.

Test Score Worksheet

Use this page to calculate your score on the AP English Language Practice Test 3.

SECTION 1. Multiple-Choice Questions

STEP A Enter the number of correct answers (out of 45) _____

SECTION 2. Essay Questions

STEP B Transfer your essay scores (0–6) from your Essay Evaluation Worksheet.

Essay 1 (Synthesis) _____   Essay 2 (Analysis) _____   Essay 3 (Argumentative) _____

Add the three essay scores _____   (This is your Essay Raw Score.)

STEP C Multiply Essay Raw Score by 3.055 _____

For your Final Essay Score, round to the nearest whole number. _____

SECTION 3. Composite Score

To determine your Composite Score, add the figures from STEP A and STEP C.

STEP A _____   +   STEP C _____   =   Composite Score _____

SECTION 4. Convert Composite Score to AP Test Score

Composite Score	AP Grade
90–100	5
68–89	4
36–67	3
13–35	2
1–12	1

_____

AP essays are ordinarily judged in relation to other essays written on the same topic at the same time. Therefore, the scores you assign yourself for these essays may not be the same as the scores you would earn on an actual exam.

ANSWER SHEET
Practice Test 4

Multiple-Choice Questions

Time—1 hour

1. Ⓐ Ⓑ Ⓒ Ⓓ Ⓔ   13. Ⓐ Ⓑ Ⓒ Ⓓ Ⓔ   25. Ⓐ Ⓑ Ⓒ Ⓓ Ⓔ   37. Ⓐ Ⓑ Ⓒ Ⓓ Ⓔ

2. Ⓐ Ⓑ Ⓒ Ⓓ Ⓔ   14. Ⓐ Ⓑ Ⓒ Ⓓ Ⓔ   26. Ⓐ Ⓑ Ⓒ Ⓓ Ⓔ   38. Ⓐ Ⓑ Ⓒ Ⓓ Ⓔ

3. Ⓐ Ⓑ Ⓒ Ⓓ Ⓔ   15. Ⓐ Ⓑ Ⓒ Ⓓ Ⓔ   27. Ⓐ Ⓑ Ⓒ Ⓓ Ⓔ   39. Ⓐ Ⓑ Ⓒ Ⓓ Ⓔ

4. Ⓐ Ⓑ Ⓒ Ⓓ Ⓔ   16. Ⓐ Ⓑ Ⓒ Ⓓ Ⓔ   28. Ⓐ Ⓑ Ⓒ Ⓓ Ⓔ   40. Ⓐ Ⓑ Ⓒ Ⓓ Ⓔ

5. Ⓐ Ⓑ Ⓒ Ⓓ Ⓔ   17. Ⓐ Ⓑ Ⓒ Ⓓ Ⓔ   29. Ⓐ Ⓑ Ⓒ Ⓓ Ⓔ   41. Ⓐ Ⓑ Ⓒ Ⓓ Ⓔ

6. Ⓐ Ⓑ Ⓒ Ⓓ Ⓔ   18. Ⓐ Ⓑ Ⓒ Ⓓ Ⓔ   30. Ⓐ Ⓑ Ⓒ Ⓓ Ⓔ   42. Ⓐ Ⓑ Ⓒ Ⓓ Ⓔ

7. Ⓐ Ⓑ Ⓒ Ⓓ Ⓔ   19. Ⓐ Ⓑ Ⓒ Ⓓ Ⓔ   31. Ⓐ Ⓑ Ⓒ Ⓓ Ⓔ   43. Ⓐ Ⓑ Ⓒ Ⓓ Ⓔ

8. Ⓐ Ⓑ Ⓒ Ⓓ Ⓔ   20. Ⓐ Ⓑ Ⓒ Ⓓ Ⓔ   32. Ⓐ Ⓑ Ⓒ Ⓓ Ⓔ   44. Ⓐ Ⓑ Ⓒ Ⓓ Ⓔ

9. Ⓐ Ⓑ Ⓒ Ⓓ Ⓔ   21. Ⓐ Ⓑ Ⓒ Ⓓ Ⓔ   33. Ⓐ Ⓑ Ⓒ Ⓓ Ⓔ   45. Ⓐ Ⓑ Ⓒ Ⓓ Ⓔ

10. Ⓐ Ⓑ Ⓒ Ⓓ Ⓔ   22. Ⓐ Ⓑ Ⓒ Ⓓ Ⓔ   34. Ⓐ Ⓑ Ⓒ Ⓓ Ⓔ

11. Ⓐ Ⓑ Ⓒ Ⓓ Ⓔ   23. Ⓐ Ⓑ Ⓒ Ⓓ Ⓔ   35. Ⓐ Ⓑ Ⓒ Ⓓ Ⓔ

12. Ⓐ Ⓑ Ⓒ Ⓓ Ⓔ   24. Ⓐ Ⓑ Ⓒ Ⓓ Ⓔ   36. Ⓐ Ⓑ Ⓒ Ⓓ Ⓔ

Practice Test 4

Section I

TIME: 1 HOUR

DIRECTIONS: *Questions 1–13.* Carefully read the following passage and answer the accompanying questions.

The passage is an excerpt from a book about the Mississippi River written late in the nineteenth century.

Passage 1

The Mississippi is well worth reading about. It is not a commonplace river, but on the contrary is in all ways remarkable. Considering the Missouri its main branch, it is the longest river in the world—four thousand three hundred miles. It seems safe to say that it is also
Line the crookedest river in the world, since in one part of its journey it uses up one thousand
(5) three hundred miles to cover the same ground a crow would fly over in six hundred and seventy-five. It discharges three times as much water as the St. Lawrence, twenty-five times as much as the Rhine, and three-hundred and thirty-eight times as much as the Thames. No other river has so vast a drainage-basin; it draws its water supply from twenty-eight states and territories; from Delaware on the Atlantic seaboard, and from all the country
(10) between that and Idaho on the Pacific slope—a spread of forty-five degrees of longitude. The Mississippi receives and carries to the Gulf water from fifty-four subordinate rivers that are navigable by steamboats, and from some hundreds that are navigable by flats and keels. The area of its drainage-basin is as great as the combined areas of England, Wales, Scotland, Ireland, France, Spain, Portugal, Germany, Austria, Italy, and Turkey; and almost all this
(15) wide region is fertile; the Mississippi valley, proper, is exceptionally so.

It is a remarkable river in this: that instead of widening toward its mouth, it grows narrower; grows narrower and deeper. From the junction of the Ohio to a point half-way down to the sea, the width steadily diminishes, until, at the "Passes," above its mouth, it is but a little over half a mile. At its junction of the Ohio, the Mississippi's depth is eighty-seven feet;
(20) the depth increases gradually, reaching one hundred and twenty-nine just above its mouth.

An article in the New Orleans *Times-Democrat*, based on reports of able engineers, states that the river annually empties four hundred and six million tons of mud into the Gulf of Mexico—which brings to mind Captain Marryat's rude name for the Mississippi—"the Great Sewer." This mud, solidified, would make a mass a mile square and two hundred and
(25) forty-one feet high.

The mud deposit gradually extends the land—but only gradually; it has extended it not quite a third of a mile in the two hundred years which have elapsed since the river took its place in history. The belief of the scientific people is that the mouth used to be at Baton

Rouge, where the hills cease, and the two hundred miles of land between there and the Gulf

(30) was built by the river. This gives us the age of that piece of country, without any trouble at all—one hundred and twenty-thousand years. Yet, it is much the youthfulest batch of country that lies around there anywhere.

The Mississippi is remarkable in still another way—its disposition to make prodigious jumps by cutting through narrow necks of land, and this straightening and shortening itself. More

(35) than once it has shortened itself thirty miles at a single jump! These cut-offs have had curious effects: they have thrown several river towns out into the rural districts, and built up sand-bars and forests in front of them. The town of Delta used to be three miles below Vicksburg; a recent cut-off has radically changed the position, and Delta is now *two miles above* Vicksburg.

Both of these river towns have been retired to the country by just that cut-off. A cut-off

(40) plays havoc with boundary lines and jurisdictions: for instance, a man is living in the state of Mississippi today, a cut-off occurs tonight, and tomorrow the man finds himself and his land over on the other side of the river, within the boundaries and subject to the laws of the state of Louisiana. Such a thing, happening in the upper river of the old times, could have transferred a slave from Missouri to Illinois and made a free man of him.

(45) The Mississippi does not alter its locality by cut-offs alone: it is always changing its habitat *bodily*—is always moving bodily *sidewise*. At Hard Times, Louisiana, the river is two miles west of the region it used to occupy. As a result, the original site of that settlement is not now in Louisiana at all, but on the other side of the river, in the state of Mississippi. *Nearly the whole of that one thousand three hundred miles of old Mississippi river which La*

(50) *Salle floated down in his canoes, two hundred years ago, is good solid dry ground now.* The river lies to the right of it, in places, and to the left of it in other places.

(But enough of these examples of the mighty stream's eccentricities for the present. Let us drop the Mississippi's physical history, and say a word about its historical history—so to speak):

The world and the books are so accustomed to use, and over-use, the word 'new' in con-

(55) nection with our country, that we early get and permanently retain the impression that there is nothing old about it. We do of course know that there are several comparatively old dates in American history, but the mere figures convey to our minds no just idea, no distinct realization, of the stretch of time which they represent. To say that De Soto, the first white man who ever saw the Mississippi River, saw it in 1542, is a remark which states a fact without interpret-

(60) ing it: it is something like giving the dimensions of a sunset by astronomical measurements, and cataloguing the colors by their scientific names;—as a result, you get the bald fact of the sunset, but you don't see the sunset. It would have been better to paint a picture of it.

The date 1542, standing by itself, means little or nothing to us, but when the Mississippi was first seen by a white man, less than a quarter of a century had elapsed since Francis I.'s defeat at

(65) Pavia; since the death of Raphael and Martin Luther's placarding of the Ninety-Five Theses—the act which began the Protestant Reformation. When De Soto took his glimpse of the river, Ignatius Loyola was an obscure name; the order of the Jesuits was not yet a year old; Michelangelo's paint was not yet dry on the Sistine Chapel ceiling; Mary Queen of Scots was not yet born, but would be before the year closed. Catherine de Medici was a child; Elizabeth of England was not yet in

(70) her teens; Calvin, Benvenuto Cellini, and the Emperor Charles V. were at the top of their fame, and each was manufacturing history after his own peculiar fashion. The sixteenth century, too, found the absurd chivalry business in full feather, and the joust and the tournament the frequent pastime of titled fine gentlemen. All around, religion was in a peculiarly blooming condition; the Spanish Inquisition was roasting, and racking, and burning, with a free hand. Elsewhere,

(75) nations were being persuaded to holy living by the sword and fire; in England, Henry VIII. had

suppressed the monasteries, burnt a bishop or two, and was getting his English reformation and his harem effectively started.

When De Soto stood on the banks of the Mississippi, it was still two years before Luther's death; Rabelais was not yet published; 'Don Quixote' was not yet written; Shakespeare was (80) not yet born; a hundred long years must still elapse before Englishmen would hear the name of Oliver Cromwell. Unquestionably the discovery of the Mississippi is a datable fact which considerably mellows and modifies the shiny newness of our country, and gives her a most respectable outside-aspect of rustiness and antiquity. De Soto merely glimpsed the river, then died and was buried in it by his priests and soldiers. One would expect the priests (85) and the soldiers to multiply the river's dimensions by ten—the Spanish custom of the day—and thus move other adventurers to go at once and explore it. On the contrary, their narratives when they reached home, did not excite that amount of curiosity. The Mississippi was left unvisited by whites during a term of years which seems incredible in our energetic days. One may 'sense' the interval to his mind, after a fashion, by dividing it up in this way: (90) After De Soto glimpsed the river, a fraction short of a quarter of a century elapsed, and then Shakespeare was born; lived a trifle more than half a century, then died; and when he had been in his grave considerably more than half a century, the *second* white man saw the Mississippi. In our day we don't allow a hundred and thirty years to elapse between glimpses of a marvel. If somebody should discover a creek in the county next to the one that (95) the North Pole is in, Europe and America would start fifteen costly expeditions thither: one to explore the creek, and the other fourteen to hunt for each other.

1. Which of the following best describes the writer's exigence in the opening paragraph (lines 1–15) of the passage?

(A) The role of the Mississippi River in the history of the United States
(B) The singular qualities of the Mississippi River, a unique geographical phenomenon
(C) The commercial importance of the Mississippi River to the cities and states through which the river flows
(D) How the Mississippi River affects people living on or near its banks
(E) The uniqueness of America's dependence on the Mississippi River

2. On which of the following rhetorical features does the writer primarily depend to support the assertion made in the first sentence of the passage: "*The Mississippi is well worth reading about.*"?

(A) Cause and effect
(B) Citation of statistical data
(C) Comparison and contrast
(D) A logical progression of ideas
(E) Highly connotative diction

3. The rhetorical effect of the writer's decision to spell out numbers (e.g., "three-hundred and thirty-eight" as in line 7) instead of using numerals ("338") could be used to support all of following claims EXCEPT

(A) it impedes superficial skimming of the passage.
(B) it adds a sense of the substance to the statistics.
(C) it facilitates the memorization of the numbers.
(D) it endows the passage with an aura of momentousness.
(E) it subtly simulates the prodigious dimensions of the river.

4. In the third paragraph (lines 21–25), the writer's rhetorical purpose for introducing the *Times-Democrat* newspaper story about the river is primarily to

   (A) reinforce the assertion made in line 16 that the river is "remarkable."
   (B) imply that, because the status of the river is constantly in flux, the latest changes are newsworthy.
   (C) serve as an appropriate lead-in to the derogatory comment by Captain Marryat (line 23).
   (D) imply that the river is critical to the economy and well-being of New Orleans.
   (E) add to the veracity of the information provided by the passage.

5. In context, lines 28–35 ("The belief . . . a single jump") could be used to support which of the following claims about the author's attitude toward the subject of the passage?

   (A) The river and its environs are like a living, willful creature.
   (B) The river is an example of nature imitating art.
   (C) The river's history provides clues to how the Earth originally came to exist.
   (D) The river's unpredictability makes it a force of nature to be constantly observed and carefully measured.
   (E) It is risky, if not foolhardy, for people to settle and build homes alongside the river.

6. In the paragraph (lines 45–51), the writer introduces a hypothetical scenario primarily to

   (A) compare the impotence of humans to the power of nature.
   (B) raise readers' awareness of nature's potential cruelty.
   (C) illustrate that natural phenomena sometimes have unexpected consequences.
   (D) imply that manmade law will never take precedence over natural law.
   (E) make a point about nature's overall indifference toward humankind.

7. In the parenthetical sentence (lines 52–53), all of the following describe the writer's rhetorical intentions EXCEPT

   (A) to reach out to readers whose attention to the passage may be flagging.
   (B) to maintain the informal, conversational tone of the passage.
   (C) to assure readers that the passage has a broader sweep than the subject's eccentricities.
   (D) to suggest that there are more reasons why the Mississippi River is a unique treasure.
   (E) to prepare readers for a change in the focus of the passage.

8. In the ninth paragraph (lines 54–62), the writer asserts that the adjective "new" to describe America is overused on the grounds that

   (A) stereotypical historical and cultural notions change very slowly, if at all.
   (B) little of importance occurred in America until it was "discovered" by Europeans late in the 15th century.
   (C) recorded history deliberately omitted events occurring in the Western Hemisphere.
   (D) until the United States became independent, historians of Western civilization viewed North America as little more than a barbaric wasteland.
   (E) some values now called "American" originated in antiquity.

9. In lines 58–62 of the passage, the writer uses an analogy in order to convey the idea that

   (A) being the first white man to see the river is of no particular importance.
   (B) precisely which white man first saw the Mississippi River will never be known for sure.
   (C) history has bestowed on De Soto more honor than he deserves.
   (D) historical facts are often not facts at all but approximations of truth.
   (E) the event's meaning will become discernible only with the passage of time.

10. Lines 63–81, list events that occurred near the time when De Soto first sighted the river later to be called the Mississippi. The writer includes that information primarily to

    (A) stress how long it has been since white men have known about the river.
    (B) imply the historical significance of De Soto's encounter with the river.
    (C) add detail and color to enliven the main idea of the passage.
    (D) indicate that the Western Hemisphere was unknown to populations across the sea at the time.
    (E) suggest the importance of the river in the settling of the North American continent.

11. In the context, lines 63–77 ("The date 1542 . . . effectively started") could be used to support which of the following claims about the writer's tone?

    (A) His tone when alluding to certain women (lines 68–70) is sexist.
    (B) His tone when referring to events that had not yet occurred by 1542 is dismissive.
    (C) His tone when alluding to famous figures of the time is condescending.
    (D) He adopts a nostalgic, admiring tone toward the customs of chivalry.
    (E) He adopts a scoffing, jeering tone when discussing the anti-religious practices of the Spanish Inquisition.

12. In the last paragraph (lines 78–96), which of the following best characterizes the writer's view on why the word "new" is improperly used to describe America?

    (A) Americans' conception of time has accelerated during the centuries since America was discovered and settled.
    (B) It was often necessary to differentiate the "new" world (America) from the "old" (Europe and the East).
    (C) As the pace of life speeds up, one's sense of "the old" and "the new" becomes increasingly blurry.
    (D) The passage of time has been compressed because notable historical events occurred infrequently.
    (E) Different cultures conceive of time in a multitude of different ways.

13. In the last paragraph (lines 78–96), which of the following best characterizes the writer's assessment of humanity's basic nature?

    (A) Because of technology, humanity has become accustomed to an accelerated pace of life.
    (B) Humanity has tended to become more aggressive with the passage of time.
    (C) Adaptability to changing circumstances is one of humanity's great strengths.
    (D) Competition between both individuals and groups has come to drive human progress.
    (E) As civilization progresses, basic changes occur in understanding what it means to be human.

> **DIRECTIONS:** *Questions 14–25.* Carefully read the following passage and answer the accompanying questions.

The passage is an excerpt from the speech delivered in 1994 by Nelson Mandela on the occasion of his inauguration as the president of South Africa.

Passage 2

Friends, comrades and my fellow South Africans, I greet you in the name of peace, democracy and freedom for all. As I did four years ago, after being released from more than twenty-seven years in prison, I stand before you not as a prophet but as a humble servant of
Line you, the people. Your tireless and heroic sacrifices have made it possible for me to be here
(5) today. I therefore place the remaining years of my life in your hand.

This is indeed a joyous time for the human spirit. I am delighted by the overwhelming and continuing support of the African National Congress. To all of those who worked so hard through many decades, I thank you and honor you. To the people of South Africa and the world who are watching: My presidency is your victory, too. I shall never forget how you
(10) worked for years to help end apartheid, and how at the time of the presidential election I watched, along with all of you, as the tens of thousands of our people stood patiently in long queues for many hours, some sleeping on the open ground overnight, waiting to cast a momentous vote. South Africa's heroes are legend across the generations. But it is you, the people, who are our true heroes.

(15) On this day of rejoicing, I extend my sincere and warmest gratitude to the millions of my compatriots and those in every corner of the land who cast their ballots for the future of our country. I send special greeting to the people of Cape Town, this city which has been my home for three decades. For decades, your mass marches and other forms of support served as a constant source of strength not only to me but to countless victims of persecution.

(20) I salute the African National Congress. It has fulfilled our every expectation in its role as leader of the great march to freedom. I also salute the National Union of South African students and, of course, the women of the Black Sash, a movement that has non-violently helped countless families to overcome the oppression of apartheid. We note with pride that you have acted as the conscience of white South Africa. Even during the darkest days in the
(25) history of our struggle, you held the flag of liberty high.

I extend my greetings to the working class of our country. Your organized strength is the pride of our movement. You remain the most dependable force in the struggle to end exploitation and oppression. I pay tribute to the many religious communities who carried the campaign for justice forward when the organizations for our people were silenced. On
(30) this occasion, we thank the world community for their great contribution to the anti-apartheid struggle. Without your support our struggle would not have reached this advanced stage. The sacrifice of the frontline states will be remembered by South Africans forever.

Today, we are entering a new era for our country and its people. Today, we celebrate not the victory of party, but a victory for all the people of South Africa. Perhaps it was history that
(35) ordained that it be here, at the Cape of Good Hope, that we should lay the foundation stone of our new nation. For it was here at this Cape, over three centuries ago, that there began the fateful convergence of the peoples of Africa, Europe and Asia on these shores. It was to this peninsula that the patriots, among them many princes and scholars of Indonesia, were

dragged in chains. It was on the sandy plains of this peninsula that the first battles of the epic
(40) wars of resistance were fought.

When we look out across Table Bay, the horizon is dominated by Robben Island, whose
infamy as a dungeon I endured for more than two decades. Built to stifle the spirit of freedom as old as colonialism in South Africa, for three centuries that island was seen as a place
to which outcasts could be banished. The names of those who were incarcerated on Robben
(45) Island are a roll call of resistance fighters and democrats spanning over three centuries. If
indeed this is a Cape of Good Hope, that hope owes much to the spirit of that legion of fighters and others of their caliber.

We have fought for a democratic Constitution since the 1880s. Ours has been a quest
for a Constitution freely adopted by the people of South Africa, reflecting their wishes and
(50) their aspirations. The struggle for democracy has never been a matter pursued by one race,
class, religious community or gender among South Africans. In honoring those who fought
to see this day arrive, we honor the best sons and daughters of all our people. We can count
amongst them Africans, coloreds, whites, Indians, Muslims, Christians, Hindus, Jews—all of
them united by a common vision of a better life for the people of this country.

(55) It was that vision that inspired us in 1923 when we adopted the first ever Bill of Rights
in this country. That same vision spurred us to put forward the African Claims in 1946. It is
also the founding principle of the Freedom Charter we adopted as policy in 1955, which in
its very first lines places before South Africa an inclusive basis for citizenship.

In the 1980s the African National Congress was still setting the pace, being the first major
(60) political formation in South Africa to commit itself firmly to a Bill of Rights, which we published in November, 1990. These milestones give concrete expression to what South Africa
can become. They speak of a constitutional, democratic, political order in which, regardless
of color, gender, religion, political opinion or sexual orientation, the law will provide for
the equal protection of all citizens. They project a democracy in which the government,
(65) whomever that government may be, will be bound by a higher set of rules, embodied in the
Constitution, and will not be able to govern the country as it pleases.

Democracy is based on the majority principle. This is especially true in a country such as
ours where the vast majority have been systematically denied their rights. At the same time,
democracy also requires that the rights of political and other minorities be safeguarded. In
(70) the political order we have established there will be regular, open and free elections, at all
levels of government—central, provincial and municipal. There shall also be a social order
which respects completely the culture, language and religious rights of all sections of our
society and the fundamental rights of the individual.

The task at hand will not be easy. But you have mandated us to change South Africa from
(75) a country in which the majority lived with little hope, to one in which they can live and
work with dignity, with a sense of self-esteem and confidence in the future. The cornerstone
of building a better life of opportunity, freedom and prosperity is the Reconstructive and
Development Program. This needs unity of purpose. It needs action. It requires us all to
work together to bring an end to division, an end to suspicion and build a nation united in
(80) our diversity.

The people of South Africa have spoken in these elections. They want change! And
change is what they will get. Our plan is to create jobs, promote peace and reconciliation,
and to guarantee freedom for all South Africans. Your government will tackle the widespread poverty so pervasive among the majority of our people. By encouraging investors
(85) and the democratic state to support job creating projects in which manufacturing will play

a central role, we will try to change our country from a net exporter of raw materials to one that exports finished products. The government will devise policies that encourage and reward productive enterprise among the disadvantaged communities—African, colored, and Indian. By easing credit conditions we can assist them to make inroads into the productive
(90) and manufacturing spheres and break out of the small-scale distribution and development of our battered society.

While we are and shall remain fully committed to the spirit of a government of national unity, we are determined to initiate and bring about the change that our mandate from the people demands. We place our vision of a new constitutional order for South Africa on the
(95) table not as conquerors, prescribing to the conquered. We speak as fellow citizens to heal the wound of the past with the intent of constructing a new order based on justice for all.

This is a challenge that faces all South Africans today, and it is one to which I am certain we will all rise.

In conclusion, I wish to quote my own words during my trial so many years ago in 1964.
(100) They are as true today as they were then: I have fought against white domination and I have fought against black domination. I have cherished the ideal of a democratic and free society in which all persons live together in harmony and with equal opportunities. It is an ideal which I hope to live for and to achieve. But if needs be, it is an ideal for which I am prepared to die.

14. Which of the following best describes the speaker's rhetorical purpose in the first paragraph of the passage (lines 1–5)?

(A) To present himself as a living example of South Africa's ideals and values
(B) To remind the audience of how thoroughly South Africa's politics has been changed in recent years
(C) To convey both a sense of personal modesty as well as enormous pride in and appreciation for the support of his countrymen
(D) First, to thank his listeners for the honor of being chosen their president and, second, to pledge that he will serve them well
(E) To express his support of basic human rights such as the freedom to live in peace

15. In the second paragraph (lines 6–14), which of the following ideas best supports the speaker's goal of making his topic relevant to people both inside and outside South Africa?

(A) The speaker alludes to a joyous celebration of "the human spirit" (line 6).
(B) All who supported the abolition of apartheid can now turn their energies to supporting other worthy causes.
(C) While apartheid has been abolished in South Africa, beware of apartheid-like conditions in places all over the world.
(D) Only time will tell whether apartheid will be forever dead, temporarily damaged, or still active in other countries.
(E) For their untiring effort and numerous sacrifices, anti-apartheid forces, whoever and wherever they are, must be acknowledged as heroic figures.

16. In line 12, the speaker alludes to "long queues" and "sleeping on the open ground" largely to

    (A) describe how avidly the people wanted him to be their president.
    (B) lament the chaos that developed when people misunderstood voting procedures.
    (C) deplore the hardships voters faced while preparing to cast their ballots.
    (D) emphasize the people's desire to live in a democratic society.
    (E) suggest how seriously the people took their hard-won right to vote.

17. In context, lines 15–32 ("On this day . . . forever") could be used to support all of the following claims about the speaker's tone EXCEPT

    (A) his tone when discussing the people who voted in the last election is flattering.
    (B) his tone when addressing the citizens of Cape Town is appreciative.
    (C) he adopts a hopeful tone in approaching the subject of his speech.
    (D) he uses a tone of gratitude when referring to laborers and other blue-collar types of people.
    (E) he uses a reverent, admiring tone when discussing anti-apartheid groups.

18. In the fourth paragraph (lines 20–25), the speaker structures his salute to students and women in which one of the following ways?

    (A) By comparing and contrasting two different groups
    (B) By defining groups into a general class and then providing details to distinguish one group from another
    (C) By classifying items into categories according to a consistent principle
    (D) By citing a cause and its effects
    (E) By using an analogy to draw comparisons between two unlike concepts

19. Which of the following best characterizes the main rhetorical function of the fifth paragraph of the passage (lines 26–32)?

    (A) To support with specific examples a generalization made in a previous paragraph
    (B) To develop the main theme of the passage
    (C) To augment the roster of contributors to freedom in the new South Africa
    (D) To assure the people that those who fought and sacrificed themselves for freedom will be long remembered
    (E) To prepare the audience for an inspiring lesson about the history of the country

20. All of the following account for the speaker's musings in lines 34–40 ("Perhaps it was history . . . were fought") about why this site is a fitting place for his presidential inauguration EXCEPT

    (A) Robben Island is visible just across the bay.
    (B) the immediate area has symbolic value for the anti-apartheid movement.
    (C) a cape named "Good Hope" is an appropriate venue for an event of this character.
    (D) the African slave trade began here during the seventeenth century.
    (E) the place has played a significant role in the speaker's personal history.

21. All except which one of the following excerpts from the passage supports the speaker's idea that the new South Africa derives it's strength from the blending together of divergent peoples?

    (A) "the working class of our country" (line 26)
    (B) "all the people of South Africa" (line 34)
    (C) "convergence of the peoples of Africa, Europe and Asia" (line 37)
    (D) "the best sons and daughters" (line 52)
    (E) "social order" (line 71)

22. In the context of the passage, which of the following best explains the rhetorical purpose of placing the sixth paragraph (lines 33–40) and seventh paragraphs (lines 41–47) in sequence?

    (A) By alluding to a grim chapter in the country's history, the speaker wants the audience to be grateful for all he has done for them.
    (B) The speaker wants to advocate the preservation of Robben Island as a memorial to those who suffered there.
    (C) The two paragraphs juxtapose extreme conditions in the history of South Africa.
    (D) The two paragraphs illustrate personal experiences in the life of the speaker.
    (E) Both paragraphs support the assertion that South Africa's best years are about to begin.

23. Which of the following best describes the writer's exigence in lines 48–73 of the passage?

    (A) The decades-long efforts to develop equality among all the people of South Africa
    (B) The government's responsibility to determine fair guidelines for citizenship
    (C) The principle that government rules and policies are always subject to the will of the people
    (D) The concept that no person may be above the law
    (E) That democracy is the best form of government for assuring the contentment and good will of the people

24. Which of the following best describes the difference, if any, between the speaker's main purpose in the eleventh paragraph (lines 67–73) and his main purpose in the twelfth paragraph (lines 74–80)?

    (A) The first paragraph satisfies the audience's hunger for practical information; the second, to arouse the audience's emotions.
    (B) Both paragraphs reiterate and develop matters that the speaker discussed earlier.
    (C) Both paragraphs are meant to provoke ultra-nationalistic feelings for the new South Africa.
    (D) Each paragraph provides details meant to explain why South Africans can expect an increasingly bright future.
    (E) The first paragraph is meant to prove why the speaker is optimistic; the second to implore the people to support the government's plans.

25. All of the following describe the contribution made by the final paragraph (lines 99–104) to the speaker's rhetorical purpose EXCEPT

   (A) he is putting into words what he would like his historical legacy to be.
   (B) the speaker considers the presidency of South Africa to be the capstone of his career.
   (C) throughout his speech, he wants the audience to understand the theme that has dominated his entire career.
   (D) to win the hearts and minds of his audience, he offers to become a martyr in their behalf.
   (E) it is meant to inspire the audience to live up to the ideals he has described throughout much of his speech.

> **DIRECTIONS:** *Questions 26–32.* Carefully read the following passage and answer the accompanying questions.

The passage below comes from the draft of a book for a college course in sociology.

Passage 3

(1) Sociologists have approached the study of work from many perspectives. (2) Often the goal is to understand how to increase productivity of individual workers as well as those organized into teams, how to give them greater satisfaction, or how to accomplish both
Line these aims at once. (3) Thus, a prime research question relates to the nature of authority in
(5) work organizations and how employers cope with workers who are very traditional in their outlook to the nature of authority.

(4) In shops, factories, and offices, the relations between workers is a subject of interest to sociologists, who often study the drama that occurs when personalities clash. (5) With regard to drama, it's no accident that Lady Gaga, Jennifer Aniston, Kathy Bates, Russell
(10) Crowe, and other performers have one thing in common: they started out waiting on tables in restaurants. (6) It happens that sociologists are drawn to eating places, not by their menus, but because they are ideal settings for analyzing conflicts between workers. (7) In fact, *drama* is an appropriate key word because hundreds of young aspiring actors and actresses with big personalities have always helped turn restaurants into ideal settings for
(15) studying interpersonal drama.

(8) Because a central concern of sociologists has always been the ways that power is generated and exercised by some people over others. (9) Typically, in restaurants, the hierarchy of authority starts at the top with the owner or manager. (10) It then descends several levels to dishwashers and clean-up crews. (11) Sociologists study the dynamics of how
(20) power is generated to motivate individuals with diverse skills and personalities to achieve a singular objective, namely, pleasing customers with good food and drink served flawlessly in hospitable surroundings.

(12) On behalf of the National Restaurant Association, a team of researchers led by William Foote Whyte recently carried out interviews and participant-observation studies of
(25) twelve restaurants in the Chicago area. (13) Whyte's general goal was to understand how to maximize worker loyalty and dedication of employees to their jobs.

(14) He began by showing how restaurants of various sizes are social systems in which people playing more-or-less set roles interact in standardized ways with each other. (15) In a particular establishment, the customer gives orders to the service employees (waiters and (30) waitresses) and may also do so to the manager. (16) A service employee places orders with the kitchen staff and sometimes also to the personnel like busboys, whose job is to fill water glasses, provide bread and butter, and clear dirty dishes. (18) And the manager gives orders to all three other kinds of workers at the restaurant. (19) As orders flow in these directions, food and clean dishes flow along other paths. (20) A change in any one of these flows will (35) affect the others, and could sour the relations between any two roles to the detriment of staff morale and performance. (21) Take, for instance, the consequences of a situation in which a busboy breaks ranks by informing the head chef that a customer complained that she had been served an overcooked salmon fillet. (22) Such criticism delivered from a busboy might cause embarrassment, resentment, or worse. (23) Had the chef been told by the restaurant's (40) manager or *maître d,*' however, the news, while unwelcome, might have simply led to the chef's resolve to be more careful in the future.

(24) Whyte observed relations between wait staff and the counter people (who put together food orders from the kitchen). (25) The counter people liked to think they were superior to the waitresses, but the waitresses give the customers' orders to the countermen. (45) (26) This violation of expected status relations caused blowups unless something was done to insulate the countermen from the wait staff, for example using a high counter so they could hardly see each other, or having an impersonal system through which the counter people dealt with the order slips delivered digitally by the waiter or waitress. (27) Using electronic means to communicate orders to the cooks and counter people eliminates any (50) physical or visual contact with each other, thus avoiding potentially serious interpersonal problems, especially in very large restaurants.

26. The writer is thinking of revising sentence 3 (reproduced below) in order to describe more explicitly the interests of sociological researchers.

> *Thus, a prime research question relates to the nature of authority in work organizations and* how employers cope with workers who are very traditional in their outlook

Which of the following versions of the underscored segment best achieves that purpose?

(A) (as it is now)
(B) the consequences for workers of having more or less control over their own labor
(C) whether workers expected bosses to show paternalistic feelings of responsibility toward them
(D) how often managers take advantages of employees for the sake of expedience
(E) whether entrepreneurs believe themselves to be paragons of virtue because they provided jobs to people less well-off than they are

27. The writer is considering a revision or deletion of sentence 5 (reproduced below) in order to provide a more effective introduction to the subject of the passage. Which of the following choices best fulfills that goal?

    With regard to drama, it's no accident that Lady Gaga, Jennifer Aniston, Kathy Bates, Russell Crowe, and other performers have one thing in common: they started out waiting on tables in restaurants.

    (A) (leave it as it is)
    (B) Countless young, aspiring actors and actresses started out waiting tables, washing dishes, and helping out in restaurant kitchens.
    (C) Drama between staffers is perhaps the most difficult situation to solve.
    (D) Just as actors must work together in movies and plays, teamwork in restaurants is imperative and essential.
    (E) (delete the entire sentence)

28. To improve coherence between the second and third paragraphs of the passage, the writer plans to revise sentence 8 (reproduced below).

    Because a central concern of sociologists has always been the ways that power is generated and exercised by some people over others.

    Which of the following best achieves that goal?

    (A) (leave it as it is)
    (B) A sociologist's aim is to study the interpersonal dynamics between groups of workers, each of them carefully subject to their analysis.
    (C) The sociologists' central problem is how an organization of distinctively individualistic and diverse personalities work to achieve a common purpose.
    (D) To begin, sociologists assume that a restaurant is a social system in which people playing set roles interact in standardized ways with each other.
    (E) Sociologists focus on the dynamics going on between each group of workers, who must be carefully scrutinized.

29. The writer wants to rephrase the beginning of sentence 11 (reproduced below), adjusting the capitalization as needed, for the purpose of more fully explaining the relevance of ideas expressed in sentences 9 and 10.

    Sociologists study the dynamics of how power is generated to motivate individuals with diverse skills and personalities to achieve a singular objective, namely, pleasing customers with good food and drink served flawlessly in hospitable surroundings.

    Which of the following versions of the underlined text best helps to achieve this purpose?

    (A) (keep it as it is)
    (B) Of sociological interest to researchers is generally
    (C) This structure allows sociologists to study the dynamics of
    (D) Since power in this structure is unevenly divided, sociological researchers study
    (E) As a consequence of this configuration,

30. Keeping in mind the main purpose in the passage, which of the following versions of the underlined text of sentence 13 (reproduced below) is most supportive of the writer's main concern in the passage?

    Whyte's general goal was to understand how to maximize <u>*worker loyalty and dedication of*</u> <u>*employees to their jobs*</u>.

    (A) (as it is now)
    (B) reward dedicated workers with regular cost-of-living pay increases
    (C) whether supervisors treated employees with respect
    (D) encourage employees to participate in making decisions that improve customer satisfaction
    (E) the extent to which employees knew exactly how their job contributed to the restaurant's success

31. Which of the following best describes the primary rhetorical function of the hypothetical situation discussed in sentences 21–23?

    (A) It serves as evidence of the researcher William Whyte's (see sentence 12) expertise and understanding of interpersonal dynamics in organizations.
    (B) It dramatizes a common occurrence in the restaurant business.
    (C) It is meant to support the stereotype of hypersensitivity attributed to chefs in highly rated restaurants.
    (D) It conveys in everyday terms an abstract concept typical of human behavior and interaction.
    (E) It illustrates destructive behavior often wrought by extreme competition.

32. The writer wants to add the following idea to the sixth paragraph (sentences 24–27) to more fully explain the customary restaurant hierarchy.

    In general, Whyte hypothesizes, relations are best when higher status persons are able to originate work for lower status ones, and relations will be problematic when low status persons originate work for higher status ones.

    Where would the sentence best be located?

    (A) Before sentence 24
    (B) After sentence 24
    (C) After sentence 25
    (D) After sentence 26
    (E) After sentence 27

> **DIRECTIONS:** *Questions 33–40.* Carefully read the following passage and answer the accompanying questions.

The passage below comes from the draft of a book for a college course in business administration.

Passage 4

(1) The notion that virtue leads to long-term business success is not a new idea. In his decades-old book *Capitalism and Democracy*, political scientist Henry Kershaw traced how the relationship between ethical behavior and business success became commonplace in
Line the U.S. over a century ago. (2) According to Kershaw, a policy of ethical behavior gives
(5) companies a competitive advantage in the marketplace.

(3) Helmut Schmidt, an engineer working for a German automaker, didn't take that important principle seriously. (4) Had he done so, he wouldn't have recently found himself being led into a federal courtroom in Detroit in handcuffs and leg irons. (5) He was wearing a blood-red jumpsuit, his head was shaved, and his deep-set eyes seemed to ask, "How did
(10) I get here?" (6) As Schmidt's wife tried to suppress tears in a second-row pew, U.S. District Judge Sean Caldwell sentenced her husband to what, had it been imposed in Schmidt's native Germany, would rank among the harshest white-collar sentences ever meted out: seven years in prison. (7) Schmidt was being punished for his role in Volkswagen's "Dieselgate" scandal, one of the most audacious corporate frauds in history. (8) For nearly a
(15) decade, from 2006 to September 2015, VW anchored its U.S. sales strategy, aimed at vaulting the company past Toyota to become the world's No. 1 carmaker.

(9) But it turned out to be a huge hoax, which led to numerous lawsuits. (10) VWs were touted as "Clean Diesel" vehicles and sold in the U.S. under the company's VW, Audi and Porsche brands. (11) With great fanfare, including Super Bowl commercials, the com-
(20) pany appeared to be an environmentalist's dream: high performance cars that managed to achieve excellent fuel economy and squeaky-clean emissions.

(12) But it was all a software-conjured mirage. (13) The exhaust control equipment in the VW diesels was programmed to shut off as soon as the cars rolled off the regulators' test beds. (14) At this point the tailpipes spewed illegal levels of two types of nitrogen oxides
(25) (referred to collectively as NOx) into the atmosphere. (15) This caused smog, respiratory disease and, possibly, premature death. (16) Volkswagen insisted the fraud was pulled off by a group of rogue engineers, although the company has quietly backed away from that claim.

(17) Prior to Barnum & Bailey's founding in 1871, circuses functioned dishonestly. (18) From the moment customers entered until they returned home, they ran a high risk of being
(30) cheated. (19) Ticket takers would short-change them at ticket windows; pickpockets were paid commissions to roam the grounds and victimize visitors. (20) Circus sideshows were tacky; and games were impossible to win. (21) So-called Monday Men stole from nearby clotheslines and houses while homeowners attended the circus shows and parades. (22) Longtime columnist Jim Tully recalled about how innocent rubes were exploited:

(35)   (23) When a large group of rustics assembled, the circus's barker would
            say, "Now Ladies and Gentlemen, we aim to run an honest show—but
            as you perhaps know there are thieves in high and low places all around.
            (24) In fact, you may have a band of thieves right here in your own fair
            city. (25) Hence, I warn you: Protect your valuables." (26) Immediately
(40)   rustic hands would feel for wallets and purses. (27) The pickpockets
            would watch where the hands went and would follow soon after.

(28) Circuses that practiced deception often earned quick profits, but their success was short-lived. (29) Disappointed and suspicious, customers soon stopped attending. (30) But in 1880, Barnum & Bailey Circus set in motion a variety of changes in the circus industry, *(45)* marketing the circus as an honest entertainment for families. (31) Unlike earlier circuses, Barnum & Bailey created value for their customers.

(32) By 1910, Barnum & Bailey, as well as other "clean" circuses such as Ringling Brothers, had moved to the top of the industry and consistently profited from their honest business methods. (33) A few circuses continued to take advantage of the rubes, but the *(50)* dominant business model became Barnum & Bailey's so-called Sunday-school approach. (34) The experience of Barnum & Bailey illustrates the point that markets reward firms that try to do the right thing.

33. The writer wants to add a phrase at the beginning of sentence 3 (reproduced below) adjusting for capitalization as needed, to set up a coherent sequence of thoughts between the first and second paragraphs.

    Helmut Schmidt, an engineer working for a German automaker, didn't take that important principle seriously.

    Which of the following best serves the writer's purpose?

    (A) Irregardless,
    (B) In spite of Kershaw's widely distributed but not statistically logical hypothesis,
    (C) Moreover,
    (D) Too bad that
    (E) Admittedly,

34. The writer's primary rhetorical goal in sentences 4–6 can best be described as an effort to

    (A) illustrate the long-term consequences of being blind to ethical principles.
    (B) encourage readers to behave ethically in their everyday lives.
    (C) imply that, like crime, unethical behavior in business does not pay.
    (D) introduce a worst-case scenario resulting from an ethical lapse.
    (E) provide an emotional dimension to what is ordinarily a straightforward factual situation.

35. The writer wants to express the idea in sentence 8 (reproduced below) in standard written English.

    For nearly a decade, from 2006 to September 2015, VW anchored its U.S. <u>sales strategy, aimed at vaulting the company past Toyota to become the world's No. 1 carmaker</u>.

    Which of the following versions of the underlined text best accomplishes that purpose?

    (A) (as it is now)
    (B) reputation in a sales campaign that would be vaulting VW into the No. 1 position as the world's carmaker
    (C) sales strategy intended to vault VW into first place among the carmakers of the world
    (D) efforts to sell more cars than any company including Toyota to be the world's No. 1 carmaker
    (E) sales strategy, aimed at vaulting the company past Toyota, to become the world's No. 1 carmaker

36. In sentence 9 (reproduced below), which of the following versions of the underlined text best supports the writer's position on the main argument of the passage?

> But it turned out to be a huge hoax, _which led to numerous lawsuits_.

(A) (as it is now)
(B) which damaged the company's worldwide reputation
(C) which forced the company to pay more than $18 billion in fines and court fees
(D) which resulted in lost sales of more than 105,000 cars worth about $5.2 billion
(E) which, when combined with ancillary problems, was said to reach $30 billion

37. The writer is thinking of adding the following sentence to the third paragraph (sentences 12–16) in order to provide essential information.

> U.S. authorities have extracted $25 billion in fines, penalties, civil damages, and restitution from VW for the 580,000 tainted diesels it sold in the U.S.

Where would the sentence best be placed?

(A) (the sentence should not be added)
(B) Before sentence 14
(C) After sentence 14
(D) After sentence 15
(E) After sentence 16

38. Which, if any, of the following substitutes for sentence 16 (reproduced below) best establishes a rhetorical shift in the development of the passage?

> Volkswagen insisted the fraud was pulled off by a group of rogue engineers, although the company has quietly backed away from that claim.

(A) (as it is now)
(B) There's no doubt that Schmidt was guilty, and he paid the price.
(C) No one can say for sure, but if Schmidt had paid more attention in business school, he might have earned higher grades and learned about the ethical innovations practiced by the Barnum & Bailey Circus during the nineteenth century.
(D) Circuses more than one hundred years ago also functioned dishonestly.
(E) From the experience, the world learned that unethical businesses trying to prosper in a market where good ethics are the norm, are inevitably doomed to fail.

39. In sentence 22 (reproduced below), which of the following versions of the underlined phrases would help to validate the authenticity of Jim Tully's account of the exploitation of circus customers?

> Longtime columnist Jim _Tully recalled about_ how innocent rubes were exploited:

(A) (as it is now)
(B) Tully recalled from firsthand experience
(C) Tully, reminiscing on his younger days, wrote
(D) Tully researched
(E) Tully, a Pulitzer Prize–winning journalist, wrote about

40. In sentence 31 (reproduced below), which of the following versions of the underlined text best establishes the writer's position on the main argument of the passage?

> *Unlike earlier circuses, Barnum & Bailey* <u>*created value for their customers*</u>.

(A) meticulously monitored the behavior of workers, punishing those who lied and cheated

(B) vouched for the honesty of ticket takers and other circus personnel

(C) made their business ethical and honest because it was the right thing to do, and in the process made it profitable

(D) hired private detectives to catch and scare off the pickpockets and other lowlifes

(E) convinced the crowds that they had indeed come to "the greatest show on earth," as their publicity claimed again and again

---

DIRECTIONS: *Questions 41–45.* Carefully read the following passage and answer the accompanying questions.

The passage below is part of a recent article written for publication in a widely-read magazine. It is a draft.

Passage 5

(1) "Gaming disorder," as it is called, is defined as excessive and irrepressible preoccupation with video games, resulting in significant personal, social, academic or occupational impairment for at least twelve months. (2) The latest edition of the *Diagnostic and Statistical*
Line *Manual of Mental Disorders*, the American Psychiatric Association's clinical bible, recog-
(5) nizes "internet gaming disorder"—more or less the same thing—as a signal that a child's grades in school are in jeopardy. (3) The World Health Organization's (W.H.O.'s) decision has received substantial pushback, in part because the modern meaning of "addiction" is an uneasy amalgam of several contradictory legacies. (4) There is a religious one, which has censured excessive drinking, gambling and drug use as moral transgressions. (5) A scien-
(10) tific one, which has characterized alcoholism and drug addiction as biological diseases. (6) A colloquial one, which casually applied the term to almost any fixation. (7) People have written about behavioral addictions—to eating, sex and gambling—for centuries. (8) In recent decades, some psychiatrists and counselors have even specialized their treatment. (9) But the idea that someone can be addicted to a behavior, as opposed to a substance,
(15) remains contentious.

(10) Predictably, some of the W.H.O.'s staunchest critics are leaders in the gaming industry, who believe that having good grades and a good relationship with parents are signs that a child's video gaming is unlikely to be a problem. (11) A sizable faction of scientists also disputes the idea that video games are addictive. (12) The arguments against the validity
(20) of video-game addiction are numerous, but they generally converge on these points. (13) Furthermore, excessive game play is not a true addiction but rather a symptom of a larger underlying problem, like depression or anxiety. (14) The notion of video-game addiction emerges more from moral panic about new technologies than from scientific research and clinical data. (15) Making video-game addiction an official disorder risks pathologiz-
(25) ing a benign hobby and proliferating sham treatments. (16) Ariel Prentiss, the director of research at the Cambridge Internet Institute, agrees that it's "absolutely not an addiction."

(17) But such denials become more difficult to accept when juxtaposed with the latest research on behavioral addictions. (18) A substantial body of evidence now demonstrates that although video-game addiction is by no means an epidemic, it is a real phenomenon (30) afflicting a small percentage of gamers. (19) This evidence has emerged from many sources. (19) There are studies indicating that compulsive game play and addictive drugs alter the brain's reward circuits in similar ways. (21) Psychiatrists report being visited by young adults whose lives have been profoundly disrupted by an all-consuming fixation with gaming. (22) Yet striking parallels between video games and online gambling and the gaming (35) industry's embrace of addictive game design that contribute to differences of opinion.

41. Which of the following sentences, if placed before sentence 1, would both interest readers and provide an effective introduction to the topic of the passage?

(A) Yes, it's a great thing that lots of folks enjoy.

(B) A manual published intermittently by the American Psychiatric Association is an essential book found in every psychiatrist's office.

(C) The book, *Diagnostic and Statistical Manual of Mental Disorders*, known as the *DSM*, added a hugely popular addiction to its pages in 2019.

(D) In 2019, the World Health Organization officially added a new disorder to the section on addictive behavior in the latest version of the *Diagnostic and Statistical Manual of Mental Disorders.*

(E) Even though video games have been around for almost fifty years, people nowadays need to spend more time playing to feel good.

42. In sentence 2 (reproduced below), which of the following versions of the underlined text best establishes the writer's position on the main point of the passage?

The latest edition of the Diagnostic and Statistical Manual of Mental Disorders, *the American Psychiatric Association's clinical bible, recognizes "internet gaming disorder"—more or less the same thing—as a signal that a child's grades in school are in jeopardy*.

(A) (as it is now)

(B) as a condition warranting more research

(C) although it is far more common in boys and men than in girls and women

(D) a problem that is estimated to affect between 1% and 9% of all "gamers," as they apparently have been labeled in age-old psychiatric terminology

(E) like cell phones, social media, chocolate—what is felt when captured by addiction

43. The writer wants to add a phrase or more at the beginning of sentence 5 (reproduced below), adjusting for capitalization as needed, to develop the idea introduced in sentences 3 and 4.

A scientific one, which has characterized alcoholism and drug addiction as biological diseases.

(A) (as it is now)

(B) Then, there is

(C) In addition to that, comes

(D) Secondly,

(E) Among still others, there is

44. In sentence 10 (reproduced below), the writer wants to provide a convincing explanation for the gaming industry's opposition to the actions of the W.H.O.

    Predictably, some of the W.H.O.'s staunchest critics are leaders in the gaming industry, <u>who believe that having good grades and a good relationship with parents are signs that a child's video gaming is unlikely to be a problem</u>.

    Which version of the underlined text best accomplishes this goal?

    (A) (as it is now)
    (B) who advise gamers to participate in other activities every day, including exercise
    (C) who habitually condemn federal, state, and local restrictions on the free enterprise system
    (D) many of whom fear that the new diagnostic label will further stigmatize their products
    (E) who offer to sponsor and equip so-called "gaming clubs," for children and adults of all ages

45. The writer wants to add the following sentence to the second paragraph (sentences 10–16):

    Throughout history, technological innovations and new forms of entertainment have consistently provoked alarmism.

    Where would the sentence best be placed?

    (A) Before sentence 11
    (B) After sentence 11
    (C) After sentence 12
    (D) After sentence 13
    (E) After sentence 14

Section II

Three Essay Questions

TIME: 2 HOURS AND 15 MINUTES

Write your essays on standard 8-½" × 11" composition paper. At the exam you will be given a bound booklet containing 12 lined pages.

Essay Question 1

SUGGESTED TIME:
15 MINUTES FOR READING THE QUESTION AND SOURCES
40 MINUTES FOR WRITING AN ESSAY

The emerging science of astrobiology is a multidisciplinary approach to study the origin, evolution, distribution, and future of life on Earth and in the universe. Its central focus is directed toward questions that have intrigued humans for a long time: Where do we come from? What is life? Are we alone in the Universe? Mars is considered as a key target for the search of life beyond the Earth. But whether mankind should actually go to Mars is a controversial issue.

Carefully read the sources listed below, including the material that introduces each source. Then, in an essay that synthesizes at least three of the sources, take a position on the claim that humankind should do whatever is necessary to send people on a mission to land on Mars and return safely to Earth.

Source A (MARS ONE)
Source B (Bharmal)
Source C (The Daily Telegraph)
Source D (Carberry)
Source E (Smith and Spudis)
Source F (Graph)
Source G (Dick)

Instructions:

- Respond to the prompt with a thesis that may establish a line of reasoning.
- Provide evidence from at least three of the provided sources to support the thesis. Indicate clearly the sources used through direct quotation, paraphrase, or summary. Sources may be cited as Source A, Source B, etc., or by using the description in parentheses.
- Explain the relationship between the evidence and the thesis.
- Demonstrate an understanding of the rhetorical situation.

Source A

"Why should we go to Mars?" An online statement published in 2019 by MARS ONE.

MARS ONE is an organization that has undertaken the challenge of securing enough funding to move plans for a Mars mission ahead.

Why did Columbus travel west? Why did Marco Polo head east? Because it is that pull, that unknown, that prospect of adventure that compels humans to seek new frontiers to explore.

There are a number of reasons to travel to Mars.

The first is the realization of an amazing dream! Sending a manned mission to Mars is a fantastic adventure. Imagine living on another planet, millions of miles from the Earth; looking up into the sky with the knowledge that one of the 'stars' is actually the planet you were born on. Who can even envision the incredible feeling of being the first human in history to step out of the capsule and leave your footprint on the surface of Mars? By this we implore you to not just think of that feeling for the astronaut, but the experience for all those watching back home. Those who observed Neil Armstrong land on the Moon all those years ago still remember every detail—where they were, who they were with and how they felt. The moment the first astronauts land on Mars will be our moment to remember.

A second reason is good, old-fashioned curiosity. Where did Mars come from? Can it teach us about Earth's history? Is there life on Mars? These are just three of the hundreds of burning questions for scientists all over the world.

Thirdly: progress. You could say that sending people to Mars is 'the next giant leap for mankind.' This mission will jumpstart massive developments in all kinds of areas, a few examples being in recycling, solar energy, food production and the advancement of medical technology.

Mars is an obvious target for exploration because it is close by in our Solar System, but there are many more reasons to explore the Red Planet. The scientific reasons for going to Mars can be summarized by the search for life, understanding the surface and the planet's evolution, and preparing for future human exploration.

Searching for life on Mars

Understanding whether life existed elsewhere in the Universe beyond Earth is a fundamental question of humankind. Mars is an excellent place to investigate this question because it is the most similar planet to Earth in the Solar System. Evidence suggests that Mars was once full of water, warmer and had a thicker atmosphere, offering a potentially habitable environment.

While life arose and evolved on Earth, Mars experienced serious climate change. Planetary geologists can study rocks, sediments and soils for clues to uncover the history of the surface. Scientists are interested in the history of water on Mars to understand how life could have survived. Volcanoes, craters from meteoroid impacts, signs of atmospheric or photochemical effects and geophysical processes all carry aspects of Mars's history.

Samples of the atmosphere could reveal crucial details on its formation and evolution, and also why Mars has less atmosphere than Earth. Thus, Mars can help us to learn more about our own planet. Understanding Martian geophysical processes promises to uncover details of the evolution and history of Earth and other planets in our Solar System.

Source B

Zahaan Bharmal, "The Case Against Mars Colonization," *The Guardian*, August 29, 2018.

The Guardian is a British newspaper that claims editorial independence from political and commercial interference.

Earlier this month, a group of 60 prominent scientists and engineers met behind closed doors at the University of Colorado. Organized by Elon Musk's SpaceX and attended by members of NASA's Mars Exploration Program, the goal of this inaugural "Mars Workshop" was to begin formulating concrete plans for landing, building and sustaining a human colony on Mars within the next 40 to 100 years.

This workshop signals the growing momentum and reality behind plans to actually send humans to Mars. But while SpaceX and partners ask whether we could live there, others still ask whether we should. A Pew Research Centre survey carried out in June asked US adults to rank the relative importance of nine of NASA's current primary missions. Sending humans to Mars was ranked eighth (ahead only of returning to the Moon) with only 18% of those surveyed believing it should be a high priority.

We have known for some time that the journey to Mars for humans would be hard. It's expensive. It's dangerous. It's boring. For some time I advocated Mars exploration. I thought the sacrifices were worth it. But I've changed my mind. We should leave the red planet alone.

Humans will contaminate Mars

It is hard to forget the images six months ago of Elon Musk's midnight cherry Tesla floating through space. Launched atop the Falcon Heavy, SpaceX hoped to shoot the Tesla into orbit with Mars. A stunt, for sure—but also a marvelous demonstration of technical competence. But not everyone was happy. Unlike every previous craft sent to Mars, this car—and the mannequin called Starman sitting behind the wheel—had not been sterilized. And for this reason, some scientists described it as the "largest load of earthly bacteria to ever enter space."

As it happens, the Tesla overshot its orbit. At the time of writing, it is 88 million miles from Mars, drifting through the darkness of space with Bowie on an infinite loop. But the episode illustrates the first argument against human travel to Mars: contamination. If humans do eventually land on Mars, they would not arrive alone. They would carry with them their earthly microbes. Trillions of them. There is a real risk that some of these microbes could find their way onto the surface of Mars and, in doing so, confuse—perhaps irreversibly so—the search for Martian life. This is because we wouldn't be able to distinguish indigenous life from the microbes we'd brought with us. Our presence on Mars could jeopardize one of our main reasons for being there—the search for life. Furthermore, there is no one way of knowing how our microbes may react with the vulnerable Martian ecosystem. In *Cosmos*, the late Carl Sagan wrote, "If there is life on Mars, I believe we should do nothing with Mars. Mars then belongs to the Martians, even if the Martians are only microbes ... the preservation of that life must, I think, supersede any other possible use of Mars."

Source C

"Felix Baumgartner Says, 'Mars Is a Waste of Money,'" *The Daily Telegraph.* Copyright 2012.

The Daily Telegraph is a newspaper published in London and is known for its conservative, center-right slant. Felix Baumgartner is an Austrian stunt man known best for jumping to Earth from a helium balloon from the stratosphere in October 2012 and landing in New Mexico.

Given the way in which he achieved his fame, it is perhaps not unreasonable to assume that Felix Baumgartner would be a champion of space exploration. But the Austrian daredevil, who travelled to the edge of space before jumping back to Earth, has branded NASA's aim to discover whether there is life on Mars a waste of money.

In an interview with the *Daily Telegraph*, Mr. Baumgartner, who became the first man to break the sound barrier after leaping from 128,100 feet above the Earth almost two weeks ago, urged the US Government to divert the money it spends on Mars to environmental projects on Earth.

"A lot of guys they are talking about landing on Mars," he said. "Because [they say] it is so important to land on Mars because we would learn a lot more about our planet here on Earth. But by going to Mars actually makes no sense to me. We know a lot about Earth and, yet, we still treat our planet, which is very fragile, in a really bad way.

"So, I think we should perhaps spend all the money which is going to Mars to learn about Earth. I mean, you cannot send people there because it is just too darn far away. The little knowledge we learn from Mars—well, I don't think it makes sense."

Earlier this year NASA landed the Curiosity rover on Mars. The plutonium powered robot will explore the surface of the Red Planet for upwards of 10 years at a cost of $2.5 billion (£1.5 billion).

"That is tax money," Mr. Baumgartner, 43, adds. "People should decide 'are you willing to spend all this money to go to Mars?' I think the average person on the ground would never spend that amount of money—they have to spend it on something that makes sense, such as definitely saving our planet."

Mr. Baumgartner, whose Red Bull Stratos mission was watched by more than seven million people around the world, also took aim at Sir Richard Branson after the Virgin boss hinted that his company could attempt to break the Austrian's record.

Writing on his blog, Sir Richard said that he was approached by someone in 2005 who wanted to jump from 400,000 feet, saying: "Such a record is theoretically possible. However, the timing wasn't right."

Sir Richard, whose company Virgin Galactic is attempting to become the first to send commercial flights to space, added: "Nevertheless, the technology of space travel and exploration is moving forwards every day. Who knows, the next record leap could one day be from Virgin Galactic's Space Ship Two.

"Haven't had a challenge myself for a while. Could be fun for Virgin to give Red Bull a run for their money." But Mr. Branson's comments were dismissed by Mr. Baumgartner.

"It sounds like kind of a joke because it looks like he wants to use our positive momentum and gain publicity on his side and that is kind of lame." He said that the idea of someone leaping from 400,000 feet was "completely insane."

"You have seen on TV how hard it is to go up 129,000 feet and how hard it is to come down."

Mr. Baumgartner's jump saw him break records for the highest manned balloon flight and the highest skydive as well as becoming the first man to break the sound barrier outside of an aeroplane.

Source D

Chris Carberry, "Six Essential Reasons Why We Need to Send Humans to Mars," published in January 2017, and broadcast on Fox News.

Chris Carberry is the founder and CEO of Explore Mars, Inc., a nonprofit space advocacy organization created to advance the goal of sending humans to Mars by 2037.

Today, as America plans to lead efforts to send humans to Mars in the early 2030s, it is important to clearly articulate the rationale for undertaking such ambitious missions. This often has been a challenge, as there are dozens of compelling reasons to pursue such a goal. However, those reasons can be succinctly organized into the six categories set forth below. In addition, unlike the Cold War motivation of the 1960s that led us to the moon, the reasons for going to Mars are likely to result in a program that is far more sustainable than the Apollo lunar program, which ended in 1972 after only a handful of missions.

The reasons for sending humans to Mars fall within the following categories:

1. **Discovery and Scientific Knowledge:** Mars is the most scientifically interesting location in our solar system that humans can reach in the foreseeable future. Although robotic exploration of Mars over the past 50 plus years has provided us with a wealth of information and incredible discoveries, most experts agree that it will probably take human explorers to determine whether there ever was or even still is life on Mars and to conduct many other scientific investigations that are not possible with robots alone.

2. **Inspiration and Innovation:** Space exploration is widely recognized to be one of the most effective ways to inspire students to become interested in STEM education and it is a well-known driver of technology and innovation. Returning to the Moon after 50 years is unlikely to require major advancements in technology. In contrast, an ambitious mission to the next frontier of Mars will inspire new generations of engineers, scientists, physicians, innovators, educators, and industrialists to reach for the stars.

3. **Prosperity and National Morale:** Apart from national prestige, morale is essential for a nation's growth and prosperity. U.S. led missions to Mars would not only make a bold and unequivocal statement that we are still capable of great things—perhaps the greatest achievement in human history—but it would also dramatically improve our national outlook and economy. Building on lessons learned from the International Space Station (ISS), commercial partners are anticipated to have a major and innovative role in the exploration of Mars. This involvement will be the underpinning of new and incredibly promising industries for the next century.

4. **Security and Diplomacy:** While Mars missions will not be run by the military, many of the capabilities required to achieve these missions have potential security applications. In addition, an ambitious and strong space program can be one of our most effective diplomatic tools, as people around the world look at our space program with awe and appreciation.

5. **Advancement and Expansion of Humanity:** Can humans establish a permanent presence on another planet? Mars offers the potential for self-sufficiency that simply is not possible anywhere else in the solar system with our current levels of technology. Mars has water, an atmosphere, and other resources that should allow us to live off the land. But, we won't know if a permanent presence is possible until we try.

6. **To Understand Earth:** Mars is the planet in our solar system that is most similar to Earth. Mars used to be a warm and wet planet like Earth, when Mars had a much thicker atmosphere than it does today. What happened—and could the same thing happen on Earth? Our analysis of what could happen to the Earth cannot be based on just one data point—that of the Earth. It is imperative to understand the evolutions of other planets, particularly planets like Earth so that we can wisely take care of our home.

In addition to these overarching societal reasons, there are some immediate political and commercial reasons to keep Mars as the focus of our human spaceflight program.

Source E

O. Glenn Smith and Paul D. Spudis. "Mars for Only $1.5 Trillion," *Space News*, March 8, 2015.

Smith is former manager of shuttle systems engineering at NASA's Johnson Space Center; Spudis is a staff scientist at the Lunar and Planetary Institute in Houston.

Ever since NASA successfully accomplished the seemingly impossible task of landing humans on the moon, space leaders have set Mars as a goal. Hoping to regain the glory of Apollo, President Barack Obama in 2010 called for a human trip to Mars by 2035. Five years later, NASA is projecting success and spending nearly all its $4 billion annual budget for human space exploration on the Space Launch System and Orion capsule, supposedly built for Mars trips. Incredibly, NASA still does not have a feasible mission design or a credible overall cost estimate for the first human trip to Mars. However, there is enough known about the mission and required equipment to provide a ballpark estimate of its cost.

The most critical element needed for a trip to Mars is also the most expensive. A new vehicle must safely sustain the crew for two to three years without resupply and embody all the functions of the current ISS and be a lot better. These requirements include an environmental control and life support system that monitors and controls partial pressures of oxygen, carbon dioxide, methane, hydrogen and water vapor. This system for Mars also must provide potable water and perform habitation functions, such as food preparation and production, hygiene, collection and stabilization of metabolic waste, laundry services and trash recycling. Waste management systems safeguard crew health, controlling odors and retarding the growth of microbes.

Other critical systems include electric power generation and control, communications and navigation, attitude control (control moment gyroscopes), exercise equipment, propulsion to dodge foreign objects, puncture repair kits, fire suppression equipment, medical equipment for first aid and continuing care of potentially sick or disabled crew, airlock, spacesuits for extravehicular activity, manipulator arm and control station, and food, extra supplies of oxygen, nitrogen, fuels and other expendables. Long-term exposure to space radiation in excess of levels encountered on the ISS will require significantly enhanced protection for the crew. Finally, to underscore the difficulty and danger, there would be no possibility of crew rescue during a human mission to Mars.

This extraordinary vehicle could rightly be called a Traveling Space Station, or TSS. The most applicable cost analog for a TSS is the existing ISS, which was built in sections and assembled over a period of 20 years. Total cost of the ISS was about $100 billion in 2015 dollars, including contributions from international partners, but excluding shuttle, Soyuz and other transportation costs. It has been difficult to get reliable cost data from our main partner, Russia. The requirement for greatly improved reliability calls for extensive redundancy and lengthy and expensive testing. Thus a ballpark total cost for one TSS could be at least 30 percent greater than the ISS, bringing the cost of the first single TSS to about $130 billion.

The overall cost of the first Mars mission in 2035 would total $230 billion. Second and subsequent missions, occurring at three-year intervals, would cost an additional $142 billion.

Source F

"Mars Generation" Final Report: U.S. Support for Mars Exploration, March, 2013.

The graph below is part of a report on a survey conducted by the Boeing Company to measure public opinion about Mars exploration.

Perceived Value of U.S. Human Space Missions

Human exploration of Mars would be a multi-year deep space mission. The four missions listed in the graph are designed to increase our understanding of living and working in deep space.

Percentage of respondents indicating which mission below is the most valuable to our country. (% of all respondents)

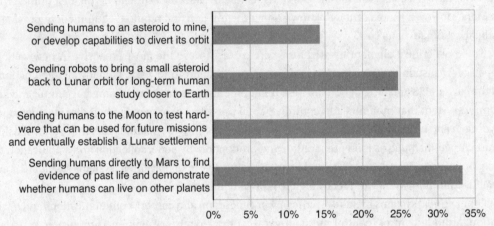

Source G

Steven J. Dick, "Why We Explore: Societal Impact of the Space Age." A NASA online publication.

The author is NASA's chief historian.

As controversies swirl about funding, resources, motives and methods for spaceflight, it is well to consider the consequences of exploring space—and of choosing not to do so.

The consequences of space exploration as already undertaken stand before us for examination. They occur on many levels: commercial applications, education and inspiration to youth, applications satellites, scientific benefits, and philosophical implications. All are open to analysis, and as we approach the fiftieth anniversary of the Age of Space, we should examine, with historical objectivity, precisely what the impact of the Age of Space has been.

One feature unlikely to be paralleled with the Age of Discovery, at least in the near future, is contact with other cultures. Shipboard observers often carefully noted exotic plants and animals seen during the course of their voyages, and the ultimate experience was contact with exotic humans.

In the Age of Space, the search for microbial life has been a main driver of space exploration, in particular with regard to Mars, but also now extended to more exotic environments like the Jovian moon Europa. With that search for life on new worlds, planetary protection protocols have been put in place, both for our own planet and others.

Contact with intelligent extraterrestrials beyond the solar system will remain a more remote possibility, and when and if it happens we should learn from the history of culture contacts on Earth.

But the immediate impact of the Space Age is far more diverse than the ultimate discovery of life in space. In her new book *Rocket Dreams: How the Space Age Shaped Our Vision of a World Beyond*, Marina Benjamin argues that space exploration has shaped our worldviews in more ways than one. "The impact of seeing the Earth from space focused our energies on the home planet in unprecedented ways, dramatically affecting our relationship to the natural world and our appreciation of the greater community of mankind, and prompting a revolution in our understanding of the Earth as a living system," she wrote.

Benjamin thinks it is no coincidence that the first Earth Day on April 22, 1970, occurred in the midst of the Apollo program; or that one of the astronauts developed a new school of spiritualism; or that people "should be drawn to an innovative model for the domestic economy sprung free from the American space program by NASA administrator James Webb." Exploration shapes world views and changes cultures in unexpected ways, and so does lack of exploration.

Space has had more tangible impacts on society. To take only one, imagine where we would be without applications satellites. We now take for granted photographs of weather and Earth resources data from space, as well as navigation and worldwide communications made possible by satellite.

Along with human and robotic missions, the late twentieth century will be remembered collectively as the time when humans not only saw the Earth as a fragile planet against the backdrop of space, but also utilized near-Earth space to study the planet's resources, to provide essential information about weather, and to provide means for navigation that was both life-saving and had enormous economic implications. Worldwide satellite communications brought the world closer together, a factor difficult to estimate from a cost-benefit analysis. Names like Landsat, GOES (Geostationary Operational Environmental Satellites), Intelsat and Global Positioning System may not be household words, but they affect humanity in significant ways not always appreciated.

Important as they are, applications satellites pale in significance to what space may represent for the future of humanity. While some argue that robotic spacecraft are cheaper and less risky than human spaceflight, it is my belief that humans will nevertheless follow robotic reconnaissance as night follows day.

Humans will not be content with a Space Odyssey carried out by robotic surrogates, any more than the other great voyages of human history. Robots extend the human senses, but will not replace the human mind in the foreseeable future, even with advances in artificial intelligence. HAL in Arthur C. Clarke's famous novel and movie was not as smart as he thought, and will not be for a long time. As President Bush said in announcing his new initiative in January 2004, humans will spread through the solar system, fulfilling the vision of what British philosopher Olaf Stapledon 55 years ago called "interplanetary man."

Eventually humans will spread into the cosmos at large. One cannot set a timeline, but by 3001 "interstellar humanity" will likely follow. We do not know what surprises and challenges we will find. But they will be there and humans will revel in them. That is the nature of humans with their inbuilt curiosity and penchant for exploration, one might say the very definition of what it is to be human.

Essay Question 2

SUGGESTED TIME: 40 MINUTES

(This question counts as one-third of the total score for Section II.)

DIRECTIONS: The following sketch, "A Fair and Happy Milkmaid," written in 1615 and credited to two possible authors—Thomas Overbury and John Webster—pays tribute to a lovely young lass.

Read the passage carefully. Then write an essay in which you analyze how the speaker uses rhetorical strategies and stylistic devices to convey his affection for the milkmaid.

A fair and happy milkmaid is a country wench, that is so far from making herself beautiful by art, that one look of hers is able to put all outsides face-physic out of countenance. She knows a fair look is but a dumb orator to commend virtue, therefore minds it not. All
Line her excellencies stand in her so silently, as if they had stolen upon her without her knowl-
(5) edge. The lining of her apparel . . . is far better than the outsides of tissue: for though she be not arrayed in the spoil of the silk-worm, she is decked in innocency, a far better wearing. She doth not, with lying long abed, spoil both her complexion and conditions; nature hath taught her, too immoderate sleep is rust to the soul: she rises therefore with chanticleer, her dame's cock, and at night makes the lamb her curfew. In milking a cow, and straining
(10) the teats through her fingers, it seems that so sweet a milk-press makes the milk the whiter or sweeter; for never came almond glove or aromatic ointment on her palm to taint it. The golden ears of corn fall and kiss her feet when she reaps them, as if they wished to be bound and led prisoners by the same hand that felled them. Her breath is her own, which scents all the year long of June, like a new made haycock. She makes her hand hard with
(15) labour, and her heart soft with pity: and when winter evenings fall early (sitting at her merry wheel), she sings a defiance to the giddy wheel of fortune. She doth all things with so sweet a grace, it seems ignorance will not suffer her to do ill, being her mind is to do well. She bestows her year's wages at next fair; and in choosing her garments, counts no bravery in the world, like decency. The garden and the bee-hive are all her physic[1] and chirurgery,[2]
(20) and she lives the longer for it. She dares go alone, and unfold sheep in the night, and fears no manner of ill, because she means none: yet to say truth, she is never alone, for she is still accompanied with old songs, honest thoughts, and prayers, but short ones; yet they have their efficacy, in that they are not palled with ensuing idle cogitations. Lastly, her dreams are so chaste, that she dare tell them; only a Friday's dream[3] is all her superstition: that she
(25) conceals for fear of anger. Thus lives she, and all her care is that she may die in the spring time, to have store of flowers stuck upon her winding sheet.

---

[1]*physic: medicine, cures*
[2]*chirurgery: surgery*
[3]*Friday's dream: Christ's passion took place on a Friday; hence, Friday's dreams are ominous*

Essay Question 3

SUGGESTED TIME: 40 MINUTES

(This question counts as one-third of the total score for Section II.)

> **DIRECTIONS:** The following lines from Edwin Arlington Robinson's poem, "Richard Cory," written in 1897, describe what people often feel when they see others who apparently lead happier, richer, more satisfying lives than they do.

> *We thought that he was everything*
> *To make us wish that we were in his place.*

The kind of envy to which Robinson refers may serve as a strong motivating force for some people to improve their condition and place in life. On the other hand, envy may be frustrating, crippling, and destructive because it compels people to strive in vain for unattainable goals.

After considering the meaning and implications of the quotation, plan and write an essay that supports, refutes, or qualifies the claim that envy is generally an unfavorable force in people's lives. Use evidence from your reading, studies, observations, or personal experience to develop your argument.

END OF PRACTICE TEST 4

ANSWER KEY
Practice Test 4

Answers to Multiple-Choice Questions

1.	**B**	13.	**B**	25.	**B**	37.	**A**
2.	**C**	14.	**C**	26.	**B**	38.	**C**
3.	**C**	15.	**A**	27.	**E**	39.	**B**
4.	**E**	16.	**E**	28.	**D**	40.	**C**
5.	**A**	17.	**A**	29.	**C**	41.	**D**
6.	**C**	18.	**D**	30.	**E**	42.	**B**
7.	**D**	19.	**B**	31.	**A**	43.	**A**
8.	**A**	20.	**B**	32.	**A**	44.	**D**
9.	**E**	21.	**A**	33.	**D**	45.	**C**
10.	**B**	22.	**C**	34.	**C**		
11.	**E**	23.	**A**	35.	**E**		
12.	**D**	24.	**D**	36.	**D**		

Summary of Answers in Section I (Multiple-Choice)

Number of correct answers _____

Use this information when you calculate your score for this exam. See page 363.

Answer Explanations to Multiple-Choice Questions

Passage 1—An excerpt adapted from Mark Twain, *Life on the Mississippi*

1. **(B)** The writer compares the Mississippi to other major rivers in the world, in part to emphasize its grand and unique characteristics. By implication, the passage touches on other choices, too, but to a far lesser extent.

2. **(C)** To support and develop the claim that the Mississippi is worth reading about, the writer compares such features as the Mississippi's length, amount of flow, and size of its drainage basin with those of other rivers and places around the world. These facts are meant to inform, generate interest in the topic, and entice the audience to read on.

3. **(C)** A quantity in numerical form makes an immediate visual and cognitive impact on the brain. Because processing spelled-out numbers requires greater concentration and thought, the figures gain in textual importance.

4. **(E)** Until this point, the writer has cited no sources to support information in the passage. The reference to the newspaper offers at least a modicum of validity.

5. **(A)** The writer's diction suggests the river's human qualities: For one, it is the "youthfulest batch of country" (lines 31–32). It also has a "disposition" (line 33) to reconfigure itself. The other choices contain elements of truth but are not necessarily germane to the passage.

6. **(C)** To illustrate one of the river's "curious effects" (lines 35–36), the writer describes a situation in which a man's life may be profoundly changed by an arbitrary change in a river's flow.

7. **(D)** The excerpt in question is meant primarily to establish a connection between writer and readers. The Mississippi River's uniqueness is stressed throughout the passage, but not in the writer's parenthetical comment, which has a more practical purpose.

8. **(A)** Even today, we view America's founding principles as innovative and fresh—a justifiable belief considering the centuries of suffering and repression that humankind has endured.

9. **(E)** De Soto's sighting of the river has virtually no meaning unless we know what transpired as a direct result of his experience.

10. **(B)** By discussing the first white man's viewing of the river in the context of momentous events and currents in the history of Western civilization, the writer elevates the importance of De Soto's experience.

11. **(E)** The writer's diction, as in "roasting, and racking," (line 74) and burning "a bishop or two" (line 76)," makes light of horrific practices. All the other choices would be hard to justify.

12. **(D)** When noteworthy events rarely take place, the immediacy of the latest one is likely to linger for long periods of time. In other words, it takes a long time for the label "new" to dissipate.

13. **(B)** The writer's hypothetical example of what might occur if a minor creek were to be found says it all: The news would set off competitive efforts to make the most of the discovery.

Passage 2—An excerpt adapted from a speech by Nelson Mandela, May 10, 1994

14. **(C)** The passage contains ideas that suggest all the choices, but (C) is the most all-encompassing one.

15. **(A)** To the speaker, the abolition of apartheid is a great triumph to be heralded by all of humanity, not only by South Africans.

16. **(E)** After years of being denied the right to vote, South Africans in great numbers swarmed to polling sites to cast their ballots.

17. **(A)** The speaker singles out various groups not to flatter them but to acknowledge and thank them for their role in transforming South Africa.

18. **(D)** The "oppression of apartheid" (line 23) is identified as the impetus for actions such as serving "as the conscience of white South Africa" (line 24) and holding "the flag of liberty high" (line 25).

19. **(B)** Much of the speech to this point acknowledges the efforts of many groups that worked to abolish apartheid, suggesting that (C) may be the best answer, but the main idea of the passage relates to the history of South Africa's governance, which ranged from a tyranny of the minority to equality for all.

20. **(B)** is the only choice that is neither mentioned nor implied by the passage.

21. **(A)** All the choices except (A) make reference to broad and diverse swaths of the country's population. The "working class," on the other hand, consists largely of a specific group defined by income, jobs, lifestyle, values, etc.

22. **(C)** To create an emotional effect, the speaker contrasts a time of despotic cruelty in South Africa with a countervailing force—the struggle for democracy.

23. **(A)** The lines in question are dominated by a chronological account of the growth of democracy in South Africa. They are meant to convince the audience that equality of all people serves as one of the country's bedrock values.

24. **(D)** Both paragraphs call for actions to assure that the people's desire for change will be met by both the work of the people themselves and a series of government programs.

25. **(B)** For the speaker, the fact that he is the new president of South Africa is important only because it provides an opportunity to put into effect transcendent ideas such as universal freedom and equality that have driven him all the days of his life.

Passage 3—An excerpt adapted from William Foote Whyte, "The Social Structure of the Restaurant," *American Journal of Sociology* 54, pp. 302–310, 1949.

26. **(B)** is the best choice because it is devoted primarily to the topic being discussed, namely the effects of authority on workers—in this case, how workers behave when they are largely in charge of how they do their jobs.

27. **(E)** Although the sentence may be of interest to trivia fans, it adds nothing of substance and slows down the development of the passage.

28. **(D)** Only choice (E) adds coherence to the text of the passage and explains in appropriate, error-free English why sociologists are drawn to study restaurant personnel.

29. **(C)** is the best answer because it provides clarity and coherence to a series of diverse ideas regarding the main subject of the passage.

30. **(E)** Because Whyte focused his research on why some restaurants are more successful than others, he studied the roles of staff members—in particular, whether employees understood how their specific jobs made a difference in determining the restaurant's success or failure.

31. **(A)** Each choice has some degree of validity, but in the context of the passage, (A) correctly identifies the need for adhering to a prescribed organizational structure in the workplace.

32. **(A)** The opening words—"In general"—provide a clue that the sentence may serve as the topic sentence of the paragraph. Indeed, the material that follows develops and supports the given sentence.

Passage 4—An excerpt adapted from Rachel Kotkin, et al., "The Virtue of Business: How Markets Encourage Ethical Behavior," Institute for Faith, Work and Economics, 2018.

33. **(D)** is the only logical choice. The others distort meaning, add irrelevance, or use nonstandard English.

34. **(C)** Each choice contains valid elements, but in the context of a passage about ethical business practices, (C) is the most applicable answer.

35. **(E)** is correct because it is the only complete, grammatically correct, and accurately punctuated version. (A) and (C) are sentence fragments; (B) uses a faulty verb tense; (D) contains an incomplete comparison.

36. **(D)** is the best answer because it is most closely related to the passage's main theme, namely losses of business attributed to unethical behavior.

37. **(A)** Although the information may be of interest, it is only marginally related to the main idea of the passage.

38. **(C)** serves as the best choice because it creates a purposeful connection between the VW story and the Barnum & Bailey experience discussed in the rest of the passage.

39. **(B)** While all the choices have some merit, (B) best authenticates Tully's qualifications to write about the topic.

40. **(C)** The idea expressed by this answer reiterates the passage's main idea, as stated in the first lines: " . . . virtue leads to long-term business success."

Passage 5—An excerpt adapted from Ferris Jabr, "Can You Really Be Addicted to Video Games," *New York Times Magazine*, October 27, 2019.

41. **(D)** The fact that authorities finally recognize the addictive—i.e., harmful—qualities of gaming is worth noting. Such recognition is bound to pique readers' interest, and, therefore, is the best answer. Choice (A) is too ambiguous. Choice (B) is hardly a riveting or appealing idea. Calling an addiction "hugely popular," as in Choice (C), seems to poke fun at a serious mental ailment. Ambiguity of meaning disqualifies choice (E) as a reasonable answer.

42. **(B)** is the best answer because it acknowledges that a new disorder requires considerable study before the disorder and its consequences can be thoroughly understood and managed. None of the other choices is logical or appropriate in the context of the passage.

43. **(A)** All the additional words and phrases are superfluous, adding verbiage but no substance to the list. As written, each of the "contradictory legacies" is stated clearly and economically.

44. **(D)** is the best answer because it suggests that the gaming industry would naturally object to an action likely to reduce sales.

45. **(C)** To follow sentence 12, which introduces the notion that numerous arguments oppose the existence of video addiction, the writer goes back in time ("Throughout history"). This conveys the idea that the argument is not merely a current fad or notion but has long been understood to be valid. Then, too, the use of the transitional word "Furthermore" in sentence 13 signals the omission of an idea between sentences 12 and 13. The added sentence fills the gap.

Answers to Essay Questions

For an overview of how essays are graded, turn to "How Essays Are Read and Evaluated," page 37.

Although answers to the essay questions will vary greatly, the following descriptions suggest a possible approach to each question and contain ideas that could be used in a response to the question. Perhaps your essay contains many of the same ideas. If not, don't be alarmed. Your ideas may be at least as insightful, or even more so, as those below.

Essay Question 1

Some Arguments In Favor of Human Voyages to Mars

- Sending humans to Mars is an adventure that would represent one of mankind's greatest achievements. (Source A)
- Mars may provide an answer to the eternal question about the existence of life in the universe outside the Earth. (Source A)
- Such space exploration serves the cause of education by inspiring interest in technology and innovation. (Source D)
- On-site study of Mars could help humans understand not only the future of the Earth but how to take care of our planet and take steps to preserve it. (Source D)

Some Arguments Against Human Voyages to Mars

- Surveys indicate that fewer than 1 in 5 people think that sending humans to Mars is worth the expense and effort. (Source B)
- That an Austrian daredevil supports a Mars journey bolsters the argument that such an adventure is foolhardy, or virtually insane. (Source C)
- Martian exploration is too expensive and dangerous. If something were to go wrong, there would be no possibility of rescuing the crew. (Source E)
- Only one out of three Americans surveyed in a national poll support the idea that sending humans to Mars to find evidence of past life and to demonstrate that humans can live on other planets is worthwhile. (Source F)

Essay Question 2, Based on "A Fair and Happy Milkmaid" by either Thomas Overbury or John Webster

The equivalent of a prose poem, this sketch idealizes the subject's appearance, behavior, and state of mind. Using the language and sentence structure of his day—the 17th century—the speaker compiles a list of the young maid's virtues, endowing her with the qualities of a saint.

The girl embodies excellence. She is innocent, beautiful, natural, and good in every way. And best of all she is unaware of these extraordinary assets: Her "excellencies stand in her so silently, as if they had stolen upon her without her knowledge" (lines 4–5). To create this portrait of near-perfection the speaker relies mainly on images taken from nature and rural life: the girl rises "with chanticleer" (rooster) and retires with the lambs. Her breath smells fresh like a "new made haycock" (lines 14–15); the "garden and the beehive" assure her good health. What's more, she is devout. Spinning at her wheel on winter evenings, she sings a "defiance to the giddy wheel of fortune," (line 16) implying her belief that God is watching over her.

Using hyperbole, the speaker gives the maid her own godlike qualities: Ears of corn, for example, "fall and kiss her feet when she reaps them" (line 13); milk that passes through her fingers becomes "whiter or sweeter." Because she "fears no manner of ill" (lines 20–21), she is immune to worry and apprehension. In spite of such qualities, however, she is still subject to human anxieties. She fears being overcome with anger (lines 24–25) toward those who crucified Jesus, and she has concerns about death. The maid even displays a touch of vanity, for she hopes to die in the springtime in order to have flowers available to decorate her "winding sheet," (line 26) the garment in which corpses are wrapped.

Essay Question 3, Based on a Quotation from "Richard Cory" by Edwin Arlington Robinson

Envy usually ranks up there with anger, vengefulness, and hate as an undesirable—even a sinful—emotion. Beginning with that assessment, you might argue that envy is always insidious and destructive, breeds despair, erodes self-confidence, incites hatred, and worse. The title character of Shakespeare's *Othello* is an example. A brave and respected warrior, he is brought to a catastrophic end by rage sprung from uncontrollable jealousy. Or consider a hypothetical high school senior—let's call her Jessie—who is over-the-top envious of her friend Astrid's success in school and in life. Jessie feels that she can't match Astrid's intellect, physical prowess, social graces, or any other of her enviable gifts. So, instead of rejoicing in Astrid's good fortune, Jessie sulks and scowls and suffers in silence.

Like a toxic weed, envy can grow almost anywhere. The owners of a small business, envying a competitor's reputation or success in controlling a certain market, can try to undermine, or even sabotage, their rival. Or how about a workplace where an employee envies the performance of certain colleagues? Over time, he may begin to perceive imaginary slights or insults, and then take action—sometimes deadly action—against them. History is rife with instances of nations coveting land, resources, seaports, or the riches of other countries and sending armies to seize them. Germany's actions in the 1930s provoked the world into war for that very reason.

In spite of its bad reputation, envy now and then has the potential to do good. Your essay, therefore, could take the position that envy has salutary effects—at least on occasion. Should you adopt this as your main idea, you could argue that in some circumstances envy can motivate people to improve themselves. Say, for instance, that an acquaintance, Nicky, is blessed with a generous and compassionate nature. She never fails to help needy people in any way she can. Others admire Nicky, or perhaps even envy her natural affability and altruism. Seeing the good that she does could spur them to emulate Nicky and begin their own efforts to help those in need.

A similar dynamic might occur among the world's downtrodden multitudes—say, the poor, the dispossessed—perhaps refugees from war-ravaged lands who crave what others enjoy: peace, opportunity, and a degree of stability in their lives. Envy may inspire them to break from their plight and strive to achieve goals that initially may have seemed way out of reach. Or consider what took place not long ago when American car manufacturers looked enviously at the safety and reliability of vehicles made by Japanese companies. After years of plummeting sales, General Motors and Chrysler struggled to restore their reputation for quality and gradually regained consumers' trust.

Countless other scenarios of envy as a force for good or ill could be incorporated into your essay. But once you have determined your main idea, build an argument using only a small number of specific situations in which envy plays a part. Aim to show AP essay readers the depth rather than the breadth of your thinking.

How to Score the Essays

The following essay-scoring guidelines apply to all three essays on the exam. The maximum score on an essay is 6; the minimum, 0.

Points are awarded in three categories:

1. Thesis (0–1 point)
2. Evidence and Commentary (0–4 points)
3. Sophistication (0–1 point)

THESIS (0–1 point)

No credit is given for an absent, erroneous, or incoherent thesis or one that merely restates or paraphrases the essay prompt.

One point is awarded for a thesis that states or strongly implies a reasonable interpretation of the issue raised by the prompt for Essay #1, the synthesis essay. Similarly, for Essay #2 one point is given for a reasonable thesis related to rhetoric in the given passage. For Essay #3 add a point for a thesis that clearly articulates a position on the issue raised by the prompt.

EVIDENCE AND COMMENTARY (0–4 points)

No points are given for restating the thesis in different words or for material irrelevant to the prompt.

One point is earned for evidence that tends to help develop the thesis.

Two points are given for evidence that clearly supports the thesis but may not add significantly to the writer's line of reasoning.*

Three points are awarded in Essay #1 for evidence that supports the thesis and also begins to show how source material supports your point of view. Give three points for evidence in Essay #2 that identifies and offers some analysis of rhetoric in the passage. Likewise, in Essay #3, give three points for specific evidence that helps to develop an argument for or against the main idea expressed by the prompt.

Four points indicate that you have consistently and effectively included compelling evidence to support all claims in a line of reasoning and also have clearly employed at least three sources to strengthen your position on the given issue (Essay #1), identified ample relevant evidence of rhetoric in the given passage (Essay #2), and cited compelling evidence to support your argument in favor of or against the given issue (Essay #3).

SOPHISTICATION (0–1 point)

No credit is given for ideas, however discerning, that you mention but don't develop.

One point is awarded for the development of ideas that broaden an interpretation of the issue (Essay #1), cite and explain significant rhetorical features of the passage (Essay #2), and discuss the opinions expressed in the given passage (Essay #3) by one or more of the following:

- (a) Identifying and discussing complexities or tensions in the text.
- (b) Illuminating an interpretation of the work by situating it within a broader context.
- (c) Suggesting alternative interpretations of the work.
- (d) Employing a consistently vivid and persuasive writing style.

Use of Standard English: No specific credit is given for the use of standard English. Readers are bound to be favorably impressed, however, by well-expressed, economical, virtually error-free prose.

---

*The term **"line of reasoning"** refers to the means by which an idea or thesis is supported. For instance, an essay may focus on the writer's choice of words, use of logic, sequence of ideas, or even the essay's title in order to validate the thesis. A poor line of reasoning exists when there is a gap between the thesis and the evidence presented.

Essay Evaluation Worksheet

In the spaces below enter the number of credits earned in each category. See pages 361–362 for detailed scoring guidelines.

Category	Essay 1 Synthesis Essay	Essay 2 Analytical Essay	Essay 3 Argumentative Essay
Thesis (0–1)			
Evidence and Commentary (0–4)			
Sophistication (0–1)			
TOTAL SCORE ON EACH ESSAY (0–6)			

Enter each essay score on the Test Score Worksheet.

Test Score Worksheet

Use this page to calculate your score on the AP English Language Practice Test 4.

SECTION 1. Multiple-Choice Questions

STEP A Enter the number of correct answers (out of 45) _____

SECTION 2. Essay Questions

STEP B Transfer your essay scores (0–6) from your Essay Evaluation Worksheet.

Essay 1 (Synthesis) ____ Essay 2 (Analysis) ____ Essay 3 (Argumentative) ____

Add the three essay scores ____ (This is your Essay Raw Score.)

STEP C Multiply Essay Raw Score by 3.055 _____

For your Final Essay Score, round to the nearest whole number. _____

SECTION 3. Composite Score

To determine your Composite Score, add the figures from STEP A and STEP C.

STEP A ____ + STEP C _____ = Composite Score _____

SECTION 4. Convert Composite Score to AP Test Score

Composite Score	AP Grade
90–100	5
68–89	4
36–67	3
13–35	2
1–12	1

_____

AP essays are ordinarily judged in relation to other essays written on the same topic at the same time. Therefore, the scores you assign yourself for these essays may not be the same as the scores you would earn on an actual exam.

Appendix

At one point several hundred thousand years ago, snow began falling over the center of the earth's largest island. The snow did not melt,
Line and in the years that followed, storms brought
(5) even more. All around Greenland, the arctic temperatures remained low enough for snow to last past spring and summer. It piled up, year after year, century after century, millennium after millennium. Eventually, the snow
(10) became the Greenland ice sheet, a blanket of ice so huge that it covered 650,000 square miles and reached the thickness of 10,000 feet in places. Meanwhile, in Antarctica, a similar process was well underway. There, as snow fell
(15) upon snow for years without end, the ice sheet spread out over a much vaster area: 5.4 million square miles, an expanse far larger than the lower 48 states. By the start of the modern era, when power plants and electric lights began
(20) illuminating the streets of Manhattan, about 75 percent of the world's fresh water had been frozen into the ice sheets that lay over these lands at the opposite ends of the earth.

The ice sheets covering Greenland and large
(25) areas of Antarctica are now losing more ice every year than they gain from snowfall. The loss is evident in the rushing meltwater rivers, blue gashes that crisscross the ice surface in warmer months and drain the sheets' mass
(30) by billions of tons annually. Another sign of imbalance is the number of immense icebergs that, with increasing regularity, cleave from the sheets and drop into the seas. In late August, for instance, a highly active glacier in Greenland
(35) named Jakobshavn calved one of the largest icebergs in history, a chunk of ice about 4,600 feet thick and about five square miles in area.

If the ice sheets on Greenland and Antarctica were to collapse and melt entirely, the result
(40) would be a sea-level rise of 200 feet or so. This number, though fearsome, is not especially

helpful to anyone but Hollywood screenwriters: No scientist believes that all that ice will slide into the oceans soon. During the last year, (45) however, a small contingent of researchers has begun to consider whether sea-level-rise projections, increased by the recent activity of collapsing glaciers on the periphery of the ice sheets, point toward a potential catastrophe. It (50) would not take 200 feet to drown New Orleans. Or New York. A mere five or ten feet worth of sea-level rise due to icebergs, and a few powerful storm surges, would probably suffice.

How soon could that happen? When it (55) comes to understanding the implications of ice-sheet collapse, the speed of that breakdown is everything. It could mean sea levels that rise slowly and steadily, perhaps a foot or two per century, which might allow coastal communi- (60) ties to adapt and adjust. Or it could mean levels that rise at an accelerating pace, perhaps five feet or more per century—forcing the evacuation of millions of refugees and almost unimaginable financial costs. The difference between (65) slowly and rapidly is a crucial distinction that one scientist described as "the trillion-dollar question."

—Excerpt from Jon Gertner, "Ice,"

New York Times Magazine,

November 15, 2015, pp. 48–57, 80–81.

Here is the same passage annotated by the author:

❶ At one point several hundred thousand years ago, snow began falling over the center of the earth's largest island. The snow did not *Line* melt, and in the years that followed, storms (5) brought even more. ❷ All around Greenland, the arctic temperatures remained low enough for snow to last past spring and summer. It piled up, year after year, century after century, millennium after millennium. Eventually, the (10) snow became the Greenland ice sheet, a blanket of ice so huge that it covered ❸ 650,000 square miles and reached the thickness of 10,000 feet in places. Meanwhile, in Antarctica, a similar process was well underway. ❹ There, as snow (15) fell upon snow for years without end, the ice sheet spread out over a much vaster area: 5.4 million square miles, an expanse far larger than the lower 48 states. By the start of the modern era, when power plants and electric lights (20) began illuminating the streets of Manhattan, about 75 percent of the world's fresh water had been frozen into ❺ the ice sheets that lay over these lands at the opposite ends of the earth.

❻ The ice sheets covering Greenland and (25) large areas of Antarctica are now losing more ice every year than they gain from snowfall. The loss is evident in the rushing meltwater rivers, blue gashes that crisscross the ice surface in warmer months and drain the sheets' mass (30) by billions of tons annually. Another sign of imbalance is the number of immense icebergs that, with increasing regularity, cleave from the sheets and drop into the seas. In late August, for instance, a highly active glacier in Greenland (35) named Jakobshavn calved one of the largest icebergs in history, a chunk of ice about 4,600 feet thick and about five square miles in area.

1. The writer refers to a "point" in prehistory, a rhetorical tactic meant to draw curious readers into the passage. After all, who can know what happened on the earth "several hundred thousand years ago"? That much of our planet got buried in snow that didn't melt for thousands of years is a startling fact.

2. By alluding to the familiar concepts of spring and summer (line 7), the writer keeps the reader interested. Then, using a series of repetitive phrases ("year after year, century after century, millennium after millennium") the writer not only emphasizes the vastness of the earth's accumulated snowfall but offers readers still another amazing bit of information.

3. Statistics tell the reader about the amount of the world's ice. Knowing that figures such as "650,000 square miles" and "10,000 feet" are not easy to grasp, the writer declares that the size of the Antarctic ice sheet is "far larger than the lower 48 states" (lines 17–18), thereby adding a straightforward and comprehensible fact to the discussion.

4. In line 15, hyperbole ("years without end") emphasizes once more how long it took for earth's ice sheets to form, in contrast—as readers will soon see—to the rapid melting to be described in the next paragraph. Indicated by the writer's diction: "rushing meltwater," "gashes that crisscross the ice," "icebergs . . . cleave from the sheets and drop into the seas." In lines 33–37 the writer cites a specific example of an immense loss.

5. The first paragraph has explained that ice formed in both the northern (Greenland) and southern (Antarctica) hemispheres. This leads to the observation that the earth's frozen fresh water covers lands "at the opposite ends of the earth" (line 23) and implies that the ice sheets have worldwide implications—a topic discussed in the next paragraph.

6. The writer now uses the present tense to discuss the status of the world's ice: It is vanishing rapidly and uncontrollably, as indicated by the writer's diction: "rushing meltwater," "gashes across the ice," "icebergs . . . cleave from the sheets and drop into the seas." In lines 33–37, the writer cites a specific example of an immense loss.

❼ If the ice sheets on Greenland and Antarctica were to collapse and melt entirely, (40) the result would be a sea-level rise of 200 feet or so. This number, though fearsome, is not especially helpful to anyone but Hollywood screenwriters: No scientist believes that all that ice will slide into the oceans soon. During (45) the last year, however, a small contingent of researchers has begun to consider whether sea-level-rise projections, increased by the recent activity of collapsing glaciers on the periphery of the ice sheets, point toward a (50) potential catastrophe. **❽** It would not take 200 feet to drown New Orleans. Or New York. A mere five or ten feet worth of sea-level rise due to icebergs, and a few powerful storm surges, would probably suffice.

(55) How soon could that happen? When it comes to understanding the implications of ice-sheet collapse, the speed of that breakdown is everything. It could mean sea levels that rise slowly and steadily, perhaps a foot or two per cen- (60) tury, which might allow coastal communities to adapt and adjust. Or it could mean levels that rise at an accelerating pace, perhaps five feet or more per century—forcing the evacuation of millions of refugees and almost unimagina- (65) ble financial costs. **❾** The difference between slowly and rapidly is a crucial distinction that one scientist described as "the trillion-dollar question."

7. In this paragraph the writer begins to speculate on the future—on the consequences of a vast disappearance of ice.

(Clearly, the passage has been organized into three sections—a narrative form that deals with the past, the present, and the future. Use of this structure helps attract a more interested audience. Storytelling, as a rhetorical device, tends to hold readers more firmly than text-book versions of the same material.)

Because the future is always uncertain, the tone in the passage is speculative: "If the ice sheets . . .," "would probably suffice," "It could mean . . .," etc.

8. The phrase "potential catastrophe" (line 50) sets the tone for the remainder of the passage, for the writer focuses on the possible consequences—none of them favorable—of sea-level rise. Using allusions to such things as forced "evacuations," "millions of refugees," and "unimaginable financial costs," the writer has created a frightening doomsday scenario. References to specific places (New Orleans, New York) vividly suggest the immediacy of the threat.

9. The conclusion serves as a kind of disclaimer for the writer. Whether sea-level rise will cause havoc throughout the world remains to be seen. At present it is still a "trillion-dollar question."

Annotation Summary

The purpose of the passage is to inform the reader about the earth's ice fields and glaciers and to sound an alert about the potential consequences of their disappearance, brought about by global warming. To achieve this goal, the writer describes first the origin, location, and dimensions of the earth's frozen water. He then focuses on the current meltdown of ice in both the northern and southern hemispheres and speculates on the effects of worldwide sea-level rise caused by steadily increasing temperatures. The writer uses factual material, especially statistics, to highlight both the dimensions of the world's ice and its rapid decline. His language choices describing mankind's potentially catastrophic future are meant to both educate and unsettle the reader, but at the very end, the writer implies that some scientists, uncertain about what lies in store, have adopted a wait-and-see attitude.

Glossary

The list that follows is made up of words and phrases used by scholars, critics, writers—in fact, all literate people—to exchange ideas and information about language. Most of the words and phrases have appeared in recent years in the multiple-choice or essay sections of AP Language and Composition exams.

abstract (*n.*) An abbreviated synopsis of a longer work of scholarship or research. (*adj.*) Dealing with or tending to deal with a subject apart from a particular or specific instance.

ad hominem Directed to or appealing to feelings or prejudices instead of to intellect or reason.

adage A saying or proverb containing a truth based on experience and often couched in metaphorical language. Example: "There is more than one way to skin a cat."

allegory A story in which a second meaning is to be read beneath the surface.

alliteration The repetition of one or more initial consonants in a group of words or lines in a poem.

allusion A reference to a person, place, or event meant to create an effect or enhance the meaning of an idea.

ambiguity A vagueness of meaning; a conscious lack of clarity meant to evoke multiple meanings or interpretations.

anachronism A person, scene, event, or other element that fails to correspond with the appropriate time or era. Example: Columbus sailing to the United States.

analogy A comparison that points out similarities between two dissimilar things; a passage that points out several similarities between two unlike things is called an *extended analogy*.

anecdote A brief narrative often used to illustrate an idea or make a point.

annotation A brief explanation, summary, or evaluation of a text or work of literature.

antagonist A character or force in a work of literature that, by opposing the *protagonist*, produces tension or conflict.

antecedent A word to which a pronoun refers.

antithesis A rhetorical opposition or contrast of ideas by means of a grammatical arrangement of words, clauses, or sentences, as in the following: "They promised freedom but provided slavery." "Ask not what your country can do for you, but what you can do for your country."

aphorism A short, pithy statement of a generally accepted truth or sentiment. Also see *adage* and *maxim*.

Apollonian In contrast to *Dionysian,* it refers to the most noble, godlike qualities of human nature and behavior.

apostrophe A locution that addresses a person or personified thing not present. Example: "Oh, you cruel streets of Manhattan, how I detest you!"

arch (*adj.*) Characterized by clever or sly humor, often saucy, playful, and somewhat irreverent.

archetype An abstract or ideal conception of a type; a perfectly typical example; an original model or form.

assonance The repetition of two or more vowel sounds in a group of words in prose or poetry.

bard A poet; in olden times, a performer who told heroic stories to musical accompaniment.

bathos Insincere or overdone sentimentality.

belle-lettres A French term for the world of books, criticism, and literature in general.

bibliography A list of works cited or otherwise relevant to a particular subject.

bombast Inflated, pretentious language.

burlesque A work of literature meant to ridicule a subject; a grotesque imitation.

cacophony Grating, inharmonious sounds.

canon The works considered most important in a national literature or period; works widely read and studied.

caricature A grotesque or exaggerated likeness of striking qualities in persons and things.

carpe diem Literally, "seize the day"; "enjoy life while you can," a common theme in life and literature.

chiasmus Using two clauses with a reversal of meaning in order to create an inverse parallel, as in this statement by Frederick Douglass: "You have seen how a man was made a slave; you shall now see how a slave was made a man."

circumlocution Literally, "talking around" a subject; i.e., discourse that avoids direct reference to a subject.

classic A highly regarded work of literature or other art form that has withstood the test of time.

classical, classicism Deriving from the orderly qualities of ancient Greek and Roman culture; implies formality, objectivity, simplicity, and restraint.

clause A structural element of a sentence, consisting of a grammatical subject and a predicate. *Independent clauses,* sometimes called *main clauses*, may stand on their own as complete sentences; *dependent clauses*, which are used as nouns or modifiers, are incomplete sentences and cannot stand alone grammatically. Dependent clauses are sometimes called *subordinate clauses*. Dependent clauses that function as adjectives, nouns, or adverbs are known, respectively, as *adjective, noun*, and *adverbial clauses*.

climax The high point, or turning point, of a story or play.

comparison and contrast A mode of discourse in which two or more things are compared and contrasted. Comparison often refers to similarities, contrast to differences.

conceit A witty or ingenious thought; a diverting or highly fanciful idea, often stated in figurative language.

concrete detail A highly specific, particular, often real, actual, or tangible detail; the opposite of abstract.

connotation The suggested or implied meaning of a word or phrase. Contrast with *denotation*.

consonance The repetition of two or more consonant sounds in a group of words or a unit of speech or writing.

critique An analysis or assessment of a thing or situation for the purpose of determining its nature, limitations, and conformity to a set of standards.

cynic One who expects and observes nothing but the worst of human conduct.

deductive reasoning A method of reasoning by which specific definitions, conclusions, and theorems are drawn from general principles. Its opposite is *inductive reasoning*.

denotation The dictionary definition of a word. Contrast with *connotation*.

dénouement The resolution that occurs at the end of a narrative or drama, real or imagined.

descriptive detail Graphic, exact, and accurate presentation of the characteristics of a person, place, or thing.

deus ex machina In literature, the use of an artificial device or gimmick to solve a problem.

diction The choice of words in oral and written discourse.

didactic Having an instructive purpose; intending to convey information or teach a lesson, usually in a dry, pompous manner.

digression That portion of discourse that wanders or departs from the main subject or topic.

Dionysian As distinguished from *Apollonian*, the word refers to sensual, pleasure-seeking impulses.

dramatic irony A circumstance in which the audience or reader knows more about a situation than a character.

elegy A poem or prose selection that laments or meditates on the passing or death of someone or something of value. The adjective describing an elegy is *elegiac*.

ellipsis Three periods (. . .) indicating the omission of words in a thought or quotation.

elliptical construction A sentence containing a deliberate omission of words. In the sentence "May was hot and June the same," the verb *was* is omitted from the second clause.

empathy A feeling of association or identification with an object or person.

epic A narrative poem that tells of the adventures and exploits of a hero.

epigram A concise but ingenious, witty, and thoughtful statement.

epithet An adjective or phrase that expresses a striking quality of a person or thing; *sun-bright topaz, sun-lit lake,* and *sun-bright lake* are examples. Can also be used to apply to vulgar or profane exclamations.

eponymous A term for the title character of a work of literature.

ethos A speaker's or author's authority to express opinions on a subject. The ethos of a professional wrestler, for instance, to speak credibly about, say, philosophy or metaphysics, is questionable.

euphemism A mild or less negative usage for a harsh or blunt term. Example: *pass away* is a euphemism for *die*.

euphony Pleasing, harmonious sounds.

exegesis A detailed analysis or interpretation of a work of prose or poetry.

explication The interpretation or analysis of a text.

exposé A factual piece of writing that reveals weaknesses, faults, frailties, or other short comings.

exposition The background and events that lead to the presentation of the main idea or purpose of an essay or other work; setting forth the meaning or purpose of a piece of writing or discourse.

extended metaphor A series of comparisons between two unlike objects.

fable A *short tale*, often with nonhuman characters, from which a useful lesson or moral may be drawn.

fallacy, fallacious reasoning An incorrect belief or supposition based on faulty data, defective evidence, false information, or flawed logic.

fantasy A story containing unreal, imaginary features.

farce A comedy that contains an extravagant and nonsensical disregard of seriousness, although it may have a serious, scornful purpose.

figure of speech, figurative language In contrast to literal language, figurative language implies meanings. Figures of speech include, among many others, *metaphor*, *simile*, and *personification*.

frame A structure that provides a premise or setting for a narrative or other discourse. Example: a group of pilgrims exchanging stories while on the road is the frame for Chaucer's *Canterbury Tales*.

genre A term used to describe literary forms, such as novel, play, and essay.

harangue A forceful sermon, lecture, or tirade.

homily A lecture or sermon on a religious or moral theme meant to guide human behavior.

hubris Excessive pride that often affects tone.

humanism A belief that emphasizes faith and optimism in human potential and creativity.

hyperbole Overstatement; gross exaggeration for rhetorical effect.

idyll A lyric poem or passage that describes a kind of ideal life or place.

image A word or phrase representing that which can be seen, touched, tasted, smelled, or felt; *imagery* is the use of images in speech and writing.

indirect quotation A rendering of a quotation in which actual words are not stated but only approximated or paraphrased.

inductive reasoning A method of reasoning in which a number of specific facts or examples are used to make a generalization. Its opposite is *deductive reasoning*.

inference A conclusion or proposition arrived at by considering facts, observations, or some other specific data.

invective A direct verbal assault; a denunciation; casting blame on someone or something.

irony A mode of expression in which the intended meaning is the opposite of what is stated, often implying ridicule or light sarcasm; a state of affairs or events that is the reverse of what might have been expected.

kenning A device employed in Anglo-Saxon poetry in which the name of a thing is replaced by one of its functions or qualities, as in "ring-giver" for king and "whale-road" for ocean.

lampoon A mocking, satirical assault on a person or situation.

litotes A form of understatement in which the negative of the contrary is used to achieve emphasis or intensity. Example: *He is not a bad dancer.*

logos The logic used by a speaker or writer to support a claim or point of view. In an argument in favor of more healthful food in the school cafeteria, for example, statistics about teenage obesity can be persuasive.

loose sentence A sentence that follows the customary word order of English sentences, i.e., subject-verb-object. The main idea of the sentence is presented first and is then followed by one or more subordinate clauses. See also *periodic sentence*.

lyrical prose Personal, reflective prose that reveals the speaker's thoughts and feelings about the subject.

malapropism A confused use of words in which the appropriate word is replaced by one with a similar sound but inappropriate meaning.

maxim A saying or proverb expressing common wisdom or truth. See also *adage* and *aphorism*.

melodrama A literary form in which events are exaggerated in order to create an extreme emotional response.

metaphor A figure of speech that compares unlike objects. When several characteristics of the same objects are compared, the device is called an *extended metaphor*. A metaphor referring to a particular person, place, or thing is called a *metaphorical allusion*; for example, referring to someone as "a Hercules."

metaphysical A term describing poetry that uses elaborate conceits, expresses the complexities of love and life, and is highly intellectual. More generally, *metaphysical* refers to ideas that are neither analytical nor subject to empirical verification; that is, ideas that express an attitude about which rational argument is impossible.

metonymy A figure of speech that uses the name of one thing to represent something else with which it is associated. Example: *"The White House says . . ."*

Middle English The language spoken in England roughly between 1150 and 1500 C.E.

mock epic A parody of traditional epic form.

mock serious Characterized by feigned or deliberately artificial seriousness, often for satirical purposes.

mode The general form, pattern, and manner of expression of a piece of discourse.

montage A quick succession of images or impressions used to express an idea.

mood The emotional tone or prevailing atmosphere in a work of literature or other discourse. In grammar, mood refers to the intent of a particular sentence. The *indicative mood* is used for statements of fact; *subjunctive mood* is used to express doubt or a conditional attitude; sentences in the *imperative mood* give commands.

moral A brief and often simplistic lesson that a reader may infer from a work of literature.

motif A phrase, an idea, or an event that through repetition serves to unify or convey a theme in an essay or other discourse.

muse (*n.*) One of the ancient Greek goddesses presiding over the arts; the imaginary source of inspiration for an artist or writer. (*v.*) To reflect deeply; to ponder.

myth An imaginary story that has become an accepted part of the cultural or religious tradition of a group or society.

narrative A form of verse or prose (both fiction *and* nonfiction) that tells a story. A storyteller may use any number of *narrative devices*, such as skipping back and forth in time, ordering events chronologically, and ordering events to lead up to a suspenseful climax. Also see *frame*.

naturalism A term often used as a synonym for *realism*; also a view of experience that is generally characterized as bleak and pessimistic.

non sequitur A statement or idea that fails to follow logically from the one before.

objective (*adj.*) Of or relating to facts and reality, as opposed to private and personal feelings and attitudes. Its opposite is *subjective*.

ode A lyric poem usually marked by serious, respectful, and exalted feelings toward the subject.

Old English The Anglo-Saxon language spoken from approximately 450 to 1150 C.E. in what is now Great Britain.

omniscient narrator A narrator with unlimited awareness, understanding, and insight of characters, setting, background, and all other elements of the story.

onomatopoeia The use of words whose sounds suggest their meaning. Example: *bubbling, murmuring brooks*.

oxymoron A term consisting of contradictory elements juxtaposed to create a paradoxical effect. Examples: *loud silence, jumbo shrimp*.

parable A story consisting of events from which a moral or spiritual truth may be derived.

paradox A statement that seems self-contradictory but is nevertheless true.

parallel structure The structure required for expressing two or more grammatical elements of equal rank. Coordinate ideas, compared and contrasted ideas, and correlative constructions call for parallel construction. For example: Colleges favor applicants with *good academic records, varied interests*, and they should earn a high score on the AP exam. The underlined section of the sentence lacks the same grammatical form as the italicized phrases. To be correct, it should read *high scores*.

paraphrase A version of a text put into simpler, everyday words or summarized for brevity.

parody An imitation of a work meant to ridicule its style and subject.

pastoral A work of literature dealing with rural life.

pathetic fallacy Faulty reasoning that inappropriately ascribes human feelings to nature or nonhuman objects.

pathos That element in literature that stimulates pity or sorrow. Also, the emotional appeal used to persuade an audience to accept a certain point of view or opinion.

pedantic Narrowly academic instead of broad and humane; excessively petty and meticulous.

periodic sentence A sentence that departs from the usual word order of English sentences by expressing its main thought only at the end. In other words, the particulars in the sentence are presented before the idea they support. See also *loose sentence*.

persona The role or facade that a character assumes or depicts to a reader or other audience.

personification A figure of speech in which objects and animals are given human characteristics.

plot The interrelationship among the events in a story; the *plot line* is the pattern of events, including exposition, rising action, climax, falling action, and resolution.

point of view The relation in which a narrator or speaker stands to a subject of discourse. A matter discussed in the first person has an *internal* point of view; an observer uses an *external* point of view.

predicate The part of a sentence that is not the grammatical subject. It often says something about the subject. A noun that provides another name for the subject is called a *predicate nominative*, as in:

Lynn (subject) is the *president* (predicate nominative) of the company.

An adjective that describes the subject is called a *predicate adjective*, as in:

Harold (subject) is *courageous* (predicate adjective).

prose Any discourse that is not poetry. A *prose poem* is a selection of prose that, because of its language or content, is poetic in nature.

proverb A short, pithy statement of a general truth that condenses common experience into memorable form. See also *adage* and *maxim*.

pseudonym A false name or alias used by writers.

pulp fiction Novels written for mass consumption, often emphasizing exciting and titillating plots.

pun A humorous play on words, using similar-sounding or identical words to suggest different meanings.

realism The depiction of people, things, and events as they really are without idealization or exaggeration for effect. See also *naturalism*.

rebuttal or **refutation** The part of discourse wherein opposing arguments are anticipated and answered.

reiteration Repetition of an idea using different words, often for emphasis or other effect.

repetition Reuse of the same words, phrases, or ideas for rhetorical effect, usually to emphasize a point.

retraction The withdrawal of a previously stated idea or opinion.

rhetoric The language of a work and its style; words, often highly emotional, used to convince or sway an audience.

rhetorical mode A general term that identifies discourse according to its chief purpose. Modes include *exposition* (to explain, analyze, or discuss an idea), *argumentation* (to prove a point or to persuade), *description* (to recreate or present with details), and *narration* (to relate an anecdote or story).

rhetorical question A question to which the audience already knows the answer; a question asked merely for effect with no answer expected.

rhetorical stance Language that conveys a speaker's attitude or opinion with regard to a particular subject.

rhyme The repetition of similar sounds at regular intervals, used mostly in poetry but not unheard of in prose.

rhythm The pattern of stressed and unstressed syllables that make up speech and writing.

romance An extended narrative about improbable events and extraordinary people in exotic places.

saga A long, historical, episodic narrative often focusing on a single hero, family, or group. A popular modern-day saga is *Game of Thrones*.

sarcasm A sharp, caustic attitude conveyed in words through jibes, taunts, or other remarks; sarcasm differs from *irony*, which is more subtle.

satire A literary style used to poke fun at, attack, or ridicule an idea, vice, or foible, often for the purpose of inducing change.

sentence structure The arrangement of the parts of a sentence. A sentence may be *simple* (one subject and one verb), *compound* (two or more independent clauses joined by a conjunction), or *complex* (an independent clause plus one or more dependent clauses). Sentences may also contain any of these structures in combination with each other. Each variation leaves a different impression on the reader, and along with other rhetorical devices, may create a countless array of effects.

sentiment A synonym for *view* or *feeling*; also a refined and tender emotion in literature.

sentimental A term that describes characters' excessive emotional response to experience; also nauseatingly nostalgic and mawkish.

setting An environment that consists of time, place, historical milieu, and social, political, and even spiritual circumstances.

simile A figurative comparison using the words *like* or *as*. Example: She sings *like a canary*.

stream of consciousness A style of writing in which the author tries to reproduce the random flow of thoughts in the human mind.

style The manner in which an author uses and arranges words, shapes ideas, forms sentences, and creates a structure to convey ideas.

stylistic devices A general term referring to diction, syntax, tone, figurative language, and all other elements that contribute to the "style" or manner of a given piece of discourse.

subject complement The name of a grammatical unit that comprises *predicate nominatives* and *predicate adjectives.*

subjective (*adj.*) Of or relating to private and personal feelings and attitudes as opposed to facts and reality. Its opposite is *objective*.

subtext The implied meaning that underlies the main meaning of an essay or other work.

syllogism A form of deductive reasoning in which given certain ideas or facts, other ideas or facts must follow, as in *All men are mortal; Mike is a man; therefore, Mike is mortal.*

symbolism The use of one object to evoke ideas and associations not literally part of the original object. Example: The American flag may symbolize freedom, the fifty states, and the American way of life, among many other things.

synecdoche A figure of speech in which a part signifies the whole (*fifty masts* for *fifty ships*) or the whole signifies the part (*days* for *life*, as in *He lived his days under African skies*). When the name of a material stands for the thing itself, as in *pigskin* for *football*, that, too, is synecdoche.

syntax The organization of language into meaningful structure; every sentence has a particular syntax, or pattern of words.

theme The main idea or meaning, often an abstract idea upon which an essay or other form of discourse is built.

thesis The main idea of a piece of discourse; the statement or proposition that a speaker or writer wishes to advance, illustrate, prove, or defend.

tone The author's attitude toward the subject being written about. The tone is the characteristic emotion that pervades a work or part of a work—the spirit or quality that is the work's emotional essence.

tragedy A form of literature in which the hero is destroyed by some character flaw or by a set of forces that cause the hero considerable anguish.

transition A stylistic device used to create a link between ideas. Transitions often endow discourse with continuity and coherence.

trope The generic name for a figure of speech such as image, symbol, simile, and metaphor.

understatement A restrained statement that departs from what could be said; a studied avoidance of emphasis or exaggeration, often to create a particular effect.

verbal irony A discrepancy between the true meaning of a situation and the literal meaning of the written or spoken words.

verisimilitude Similar to the truth; the quality of realism in a work that persuades readers that they are getting a vision of life as it is or could have been.

verse A synonym for poetry; also a group of lines in a song or poem; also a single line of poetry.

voice The real or assumed personality used by a writer or speaker. In grammar, *active voice* and *passive voice* refer to the use of verbs. A verb is in the active voice when it expresses an action performed by its subject. A verb is in the passive voice when it expresses an action performed upon its subject or when the subject is the result of the action.

ACTIVE: The crew raked the leaves.

PASSIVE: The leaves were raked by the crew.

Stylistically, the active voice leads to more economical and vigorous writing.

whimsy An object, device, or creation that is fanciful or rooted in unreality.

wit The quickness of intellect and the power and talent for saying brilliant things that surprise and delight by their unexpectedness; the power to comment subtly and pointedly on the foibles of the passing scene.

Index

A

Absence of proof, 113
Active sentences, 157–158
Active verbs, 155–156
Addresses, commas in, 185
Adjectives, 144, 175
Adverbs, 144, 175–176
Allusion, 93–94
Analogy, 94
Analytical essay
  analyzing the question, 129–130
  concluding, 147–148
  description of, 19
  developing paragraphs, 145
  main idea, 133
  outline for, 131–133
  planning, 131–133
  sample question, 34–36
  sample text, 187–195
  transitions, 146–147
  writing, 128–130
Annotation, 8
Antecedent-pronoun agreement, 182–183
AP essay writing style, 137–138
Apostrophes, 184–185
Appositives, 185
Argumentative essay
  arranging ideas, 136–137
  description of, 19
  five-paragraph essay formula, 136–137
  practice topics, 135–136
  as synthesis essay, 104
  varying sentences, 138–144
  writing, 133–134
Audience, 106–107
Author's, purpose, 107

B

"Bare Bones" of a sentence, 166–167

C

Capitalization, 102
Chiasmus, 140
Circular reasoning, 113
Citing sources, 32, 116
Clauses
  coordinate, 91
  dependent, 139, 144
  If, 173
  independent, 91, 167
  main, 91, 139, 173
  subordinate, 90, 91, 139
Collective nouns, 170
Commas, 185

Comma splices, 165, 167
Commentary, 115–116
Complex sentences, 91, 139, 173
Composing, essay, 102
Compound sentences, 91, 139, 185
Compound subjects, 169–170
Concluding paragraph, 136, 144
Conjunctions, 144
  coordinating, 91, 167
Connotation, 92–93
Contractions, 184
Coordinate clauses, 91
Coordinating conjunction, 91, 167
Counterargument, 112

D

Dangling modifiers, 149–150
Dates, comma in, 185
Declarative sentences, 89, 91, 141
Dependent clause, 139, 144, 166, 173
Determine, question type, 4
Dialogue, comma in, 185
Diction, 91–92
Direct quotes, 114–115
Discern, key words, 4

E

Editing, essay, 102, 148
Essay(s)
  analytical. *See* Analytical essay
  AP writing style, 137–138
  arranging ideas, 136–137
  editing, 102, 148
  five-paragraph essay formula, 136–137
  paragraphing, 144–145
  prewriting, 101, 102
  proofreading, 102, 148
  repetition of ideas, 141–142
  scoring of, 37–42, 82–84
  self scoring, 40–42
  sentence types, 141
  steps for writing, 102
  writing style, 137–138
Euphemisms, 138
Evidence, 111–112
Exclamatory sentences, 88–89, 141
Extremes, going to, 114

F

Faulty reasoning, 112–114
First-person pronoun, 36
Five-paragraph essay formula, 136–137
Five rules of thumb, 85
Fragments, 165–166

G

Gerunds, 178
Going to extremes, 114
Grammar, in argument, 42
Grammatical form, parallelism, 151

H

Handwriting tips, 165

I

Identify, question type, 4
If clause, 173
Imperative sentences, 141
Indefinite pronouns, 170–171, 182
Independent clauses, 91, 167
Indirect quotes, 115
Infer, question type, 4
Infinitives, 173
Interrogative sentences, 89, 141
Interrupters, 166
Introductory paragraph, 136, 144
Inversions, 144
Irrelevant testimony, 113

L

Language questions, tone, 107
Line of reasoning, 83
Long sentences, 90, 142–143

M

Main clause, 91, 139, 173
Main idea, 104, 133
Mechanics, editing for, 165
Metaphorical language, 93–95
Metaphors, 93, 95
Metonymy, 95
Mini-workout
  active verbs, 156–157
  adjectives and adverbs, 176
  modifiers, 150–151
  needless words, 161–162
  noun-verb/subject-verb agreement, 171–172
  parallel structure, 154
  passive sentences, 158
  pronoun agreement, 183–184
  pronoun case, 179
  pronoun references, 181
  punctuation, 186–187
  transitions, 147
  verb tenses, 174
  writing correct sentences, 168
  writing specifically, 164
Misplaced modifiers, 149
Modifiers, 149–150

Mood, 147
Multiple-choice questions, tone, 87–91

N
Needless words, 159–160
Nominative case, 177
None, 183
Nouns, 169–170
    possessive, 185
Noun-verb agreement, 169–170

O
Objective case, 177
Objectivity, 107
Open-ended essay questions, 133
Opposing viewpoints, 112
Order, of ideas, 34
Outline, 131–133
Oversimplification, 114

P
Paragraphing, 144–145
    developing, 145
    supporting sentences, 145
    topic sentences, 145
    transitions in, 146–147
Parallelism, 151–153
Paraphrasing, 115
Participles, 144, 173
Passive sentences, 157–158
Past perfect tense, 173
Periodic sentences, 90
Persuasive essay, 108, 134
Place names, comma in, 185
Plagiarism, 117
Plurals, punctuation, 184
Plural verb, 169–171
Point of view, 19, 32, 103
Position statement, 108–109
Possessive nouns, 185
Prepositional phrases, 91, 139–140, 144,
    166
Prewriting, essay, 101, 102
Pronouns
    antecedent agreement, 182–183
    case, 177–178
    first-person, 36
    indefinite, 170–171, 182
    references, 180
    singular, 182
Proof, absence of, 113
Proofreading, essay, 102, 148
Publication, source, 106
Punctuation, 184–186

Q
Qualifying words, 109
Question type, 4
Quotation marks, 186

R
Reading
    power, 6–7
    and rhetoric, 86–95
    techniques for, 4–6
Reasoning, 40, 112–114
Recognize, question type, 4
Repetition of ideas, 141–142
Rhetorical questions, 86–87
Rhythm, 141
Rules of thumb, 85
Run-on sentence, 165, 167

S
Sample(s)
    analytical essay questions, 34–36,
        128–133
    annotated passages, 7–18
    argumentative essay question, 36–37,
        133–138
    passage, writing question and, 96–99
    synthesis essay, 24–34
Select, question type, 4
Semicolons, 186
Sentence(s)
    active, 157–158
    "bare bones" of, 166–167
    comma splices, 165, 167
    complex, 139
    compound, 91, 139, 185
    connotation, 92–93
    declarative, 89, 91, 141
    developing paragraphs, 145
    diction, 91–92
    exclamatory, 88–89
    fragments, 165–166
    imperative, 141
    interrogative, 89, 141
    length, 90
    long, 142–143
    passive, 157–158
    repetition, 141–142
    run-on, 167
    short, 142–143
    simple, 91, 138
    structure, 90–91
    supporting, 145
    topic, 145
    types, 141
Series, comma in, 185
Short sentences, 142–143
Simple sentences, 91, 139
Singular pronouns, 182
Singular subject, 182
Snob appeal, 113
Sources, 1
    citing, 32, 116
    commentary, 115–116
    direct quotes, 114–115

indirect quotes, 115
    paraphrasing, 115
    plagiarism, 117
    publication, 106
    reading, 104–106
    validity of, 106–107
Specific writing, 163–164
Subject, compound, 169–170
Subject-verb agreement, 169–171
Subordinate clauses, 91, 139
Synecdoche, 95
Synthesis essay, 111–112
    as argumentative essay, 104
    citing sources, 116
    counterargument, 112
    description of, 19
    faulty reasoning, 112–114
    main idea, 40
    opposing viewpoints, 112
    position statement, 108–109
    qualifying words, 109
    sample question, 117–128
    sources, 107–108, 114
    supporting your position,
        111–112
    thesis statements, 109–110
    writing of, 103–106

T
Telling only half the story, 114
Tense, of verb, 172–173
Thesis statements, 109–110, 133
Tone, 107–108
Transitions, in paragraphs,
    146–147
Truisms, 173

U
Uniformity, 151

V
Validity of sources, 106–107
Verbal infinitives, 144
Verbs
    active, 155–156
    correct, 169
    multiple noun/pronoun, 169–170
    tenses, 172–173

W
Words
    diction, 91–92
    needless, 159–160
    qualifying, 109
Wordy phrases, 160
Writing questions, 95–99
Writing specifically, 163–164
Writing steps, 102
Writing style, 137–138